Revenge, Punishment and Anger in Ancient Greek Justice

Also available from Bloomsbury

Demagogues, Power, and Friendship in Classical Athens
by Robert Holschuh Simmons
Experiencing Hektor by Lynn Kozak
Future Fame in the Iliad by Yukai Li
The Spear, the Scroll, and the Pebble by Richard A. Billows

Revenge, Punishment and Anger in Ancient Greek Justice

Joe Whitchurch

BLOOMSBURY ACADEMIC
LONDON • NEW YORK • OXFORD • NEW DELHI • SYDNEY

BLOOMSBURY ACADEMIC
Bloomsbury Publishing Plc
50 Bedford Square, London, WC1B 3DP, UK
1385 Broadway, New York, NY 10018, USA
29 Earlsfort Terrace, Dublin 2, Ireland

BLOOMSBURY, BLOOMSBURY ACADEMIC and the Diana logo are trademarks of Bloomsbury Publishing Plc

First published in Great Britain 2024

Cover image: *Nemesis and Themis* (detail). Nicolai Abraham Abildgaard, 1743–1809. Purchase, Charles and Jessie Price Gift, 2011. Accession number 2011.254. Met Museum, New York

A catalogue record for this book is available from the British Library.

Library of Congress Cataloging-in-Publication Data
Names: Whitchurch, Joe, author.
Title: Revenge, punishment, and anger in Ancient Greek justice / Joe Whitchurch.
Description: London ; New York : Bloomsbury Academic, 2024. | Includes bibliographical references and index.
Identifiers: LCCN 2024017702 (print) | LCCN 2024017703 (ebook) | ISBN 9781350451544 (hardback) | ISBN 9781350451582 (paperback) | ISBN 9781350451551 (pdf) | ISBN 9781350451568 (ebook)
Subjects: LCSH: Punishment (Greek law) | Criminal law (Greek law) | Punishment—Greece. | Homer—Political and social views.
Classification: LCC KL4395 .W45 2024 (print) | LCC KL4395 (ebook) | DDC 340.5/38--dc23/eng/20240509
LC record available at https://lccn.loc.gov/2024017702
LC ebook record available at https://lccn.loc.gov/2024017703

ISBN: HB: 978-1-3504-5154-4
ePDF: 978-1-3504-5155-1
eBook: 978-1-3504-5156-8

Typeset by RefineCatch Ltd, Bungay, Suffolk

Contents

Acknowledgements

At the beginning of my undergraduate degree, one of the first classes I attended was on the Greek world. It was taught by Professor Hans van Wees and I haven't left him alone since. Hans's intellectual impact on this book is plain, but his greatest effect on me lies in *how*, not *what*, I think. My work and life are the richer for his input.

There is no way I could have reached this point without the help of my family. Sisters and brothers, by birth and by law, have all been supportive, and encouragement, money and shelter have been generously supplied when needed by my parents, Maeve and Nick, and in-laws, Sandra and Dave. To the last, who is sorely missed, go special thanks for his early belief in this endeavour; I hope he would be proud.

It takes an exceptional kind of person to hold a months-old baby in her arms and say to her husband that he should pack up his business, leave plumbing behind, and go to university after all. Twelve years later, if Jeni has since regretted expressing that sentiment to me, she hasn't let on. Rather, with truly remarkable resolve, she has accommodated close to a decade of evenings lost to study, giddying emotional variety and frequent financial precarity. She and my children have given me more than I ought to have asked for and the following pages are certainly inadequate compensation. Such as it is, however, this book is their achievement as much as mine.

Introduction

> *Ever since you walked into this room, you've been acting like a self-appointed public avenger! You want to see this boy die because you personally want it, not because of the facts!*[1]

Who today would not share Juror Eight's disdain, in the 1957 film *Twelve Angry Men*, for a juror who is looking to use his position to exact revenge? The film appears to disapprove of the idea of jury-room anger, displaying the abhorrent potential for injustice inherent in that emotion (and several other emotions besides). As one reviewer put it at the time: 'the men are jurors, and angry is the one thing they should never be.'[2] As the verdicts of the eleven jurors gradually turn, under Juror Eight's influence, from guilty to not guilty over the course of the film, 'reason and responsibility are winning over anger and prejudice', says the same critic. It never appears to strike this reviewer that the film is called *Twelve Angry Men*, not *Eleven*.

Anger and revenge are afforded no legitimate place in the modern act of punishment. But do we really think revenge is inherently unjust? Few people hear Maximus Decimus Meridius' threat in *Gladiator* and hope that he does not in fact get his vengeance, in this life or the next. Perhaps today we would prefer the case to go through the courts, for Commodus to 'face justice' in the dock and receive the punishment stipulated by the law, but that is not because there is no justice in Maximus' revenge so much as that we think the laws and the courts bring about a better kind of justice on the whole. When it comes to acts of the state, however, modern Westerners feel a strong aversion to the idea of a revenge motive. Following the assassination of Osama bin Laden by US Navy SEALs, Senator John Kerry was at pains to clarify that 'we are a nation of peace and laws, and people everywhere should understand that our 10-year manhunt was in search of justice, not revenge'.[3] One can see why it would feel like justice to kill the man seen as the chief architect of the mass casualties suffered on 11 September 2001, but why should we not call it revenge too?

Today, when the state acts against one who has broken its laws, we refer to that act as punishment and absolutely not as revenge. Indeed, it is often hard to think of the modern state as capable of anything so inherently emotional as revenge without hypothesising some rogue judge with a personal gripe. We see the state as an unfeeling entity, curbing the worst excesses of the emotions in those it governs. But, whether or not this is true of the state today, is this how states begin? This study argues that emotions were central to the institutions surrounding justice and punishment as they emerged in a world in which the settling of disputes had always depended on revenge.

State formation

According to Norbert Elias's idea of the 'civilising process', since the Medieval period and in correlation with the growth of the state, European societies have come to take greater control of their emotions and reduce their levels of violence. Anger is perhaps the most violence-prone emotion of all and, if Elias was right, then a growing state will render a society not only less violent but less vengeful in particular and less expressive of anger in general. For William Harris, applying this model to the ancient Greek world, 'the internalization of restraining doctrines' (particularly relating to his main focus, 'rage') 'can be glimpsed through the text of Homer and seen more clearly in later texts'; in this we see a 'precursor [of the civilising process] in the classical world'.[4] Kostas Kalimtzis does not refer to Elias in his survey of ancient Greek attempts to 'tame' anger, nor does he invoke the idea of the state, but he does perceive 'the power of institutions to raise their members above their passions for cooperative purposes'.[5]

The Greek world unquestionably saw a marked decline in violence, at least outside of war, between the early archaic and classical periods. As Hans van Wees's survey of arms bearing and burial practices has shown, Greeks over this period gradually abandoned carrying swords and spears in public and burying men with their weapons and armour, adopting instead less- or non-violent means of displaying status.[6] Clearly, Greek men were becoming less expectant of violent attack and less inclined to equip themselves for the violent avenging of slights.

This reduction in private acts of violence implies a change in the Greek character – an 'adjusted drive economy', as Elias puts it.[7] Were Greek men less aggressive and less inclined to feel anger in societies where their traditional outlets for violence had contracted? Gabriel Herman certainly thinks so of Athens where there occurred, he claims, 'a radical restructuring of man's psychological profile'.[8] With reference to Elias, he says 'men began to take pride in discarding "macho" behaviour and the citizens turned to embrace an entirely new form of "honour" that had nothing to do with violent retribution'.[9] However, the closing of one outlet for revenge does not mean no outlet remained. Indeed, though this period saw a fall in violence within the private sphere, it also saw an increase in violence in the public sphere in the form of punishment for public crimes. This study will consider the possibility that the state's growing monopoly of legitimate violence opened up a new opportunity for the violent expression of anger even as it closed an old one.

In one sense then, the following will add to the growing literature that highlights the persistence of anger and revenge as important values for the individual Athenian citizen. But while existing scholarship tends to focus on the individual acting in a private capacity, this study will explore the ongoing importance of those values in public service, specifically as a juror. This represents a significant departure from the traditional view of the state as the entity that stands in the way of aggressive emotional expression. The Hobbesian assumption that humanity is fundamentally aggressive underpins much of what has been written on the state. For Hobbes, when 'men live without a common power to keep them all in awe, they are in that condition which is called war... every man against every man'.[10] Elias's model makes the same assumption and the claim continues to find support today – humans are vengeful and, with it, violent unless and until Leviathan emerges and imposes order.[11] Van Wees has argued that the Hobbesian reasoning is back to front, at least with regard to Homer: 'instead of the struggle for prestige turning violent *because* of the fragmentary nature of society... it is the Homeric struggle for prestige which causes aggressive behaviour and hence fragmentation.'[12] In the former of these perspectives, anger is a problem to be solved for the good of society, while in the latter it is an obstacle to the means of solving that problem. Both may at once be right, but is that all anger is: a problem and an obstacle?

This study does not offer a comprehensive theory of how the state emerged in Greece despite the obstacle of rivalrous emotions like anger, but it will explore the possibility that the solution lay partly in anger itself, which has cohesive as well as divisive qualities. Jacob Black-Michaud showed how the practice of feuding, while obviously causing division, also constitutes a 'cohesive force' that brings people together against a foe.[13] This is different to anything that occurs in the Greek world because, above all, Black-Michaud's work deals with societies that lack an instituted authority; indeed, feud as he understands it can occur only 'in conditions of anarchy'.[14] It is clear from our earliest sources that the community has the means to ensure that this kind of behaviour is controlled. However, the principle that anger and revenge could be 'cohesive' is translatable to the Greek context. I will show how anger (an ostensibly self-interested emotion) can drive cohesion and strengthen the identification of the individual with the group.

Revenge, punishment and the state

Essential to the idea that the state is unemotional is the claim that the state imposes punishment where revenge once prevailed. To explore this principle in the Greek context, it is necessary to distinguish and define the two modes of retaliation, as well as the important and related concepts of honour and anger. And given the contentiousness of the idea that the state existed at all in the ancient Greek world, I shall also define and justify my use of this term.

Revenge and punishment

There is no consensus as to what it is that sets punishment apart from revenge, but most agree that something does.[15] This ongoing philosophical (and occasionally merely semantic) debate is this study's concern, but the definitions that modern scholars of antiquity have used in their work point to what I believe is an anachronism that has hampered previous attempts to understand Greek punitive concepts. The Greek term *τιμωρία* has forced many scholars to grapple with this particular issue of definition since it appears in every respect to mean revenge, yet it is also the most frequently used term for describing the punishments imposed by the Athenian courts.[16] A solution popular with translators of legal texts like speeches has been to use 'revenge' when the subject is a private individual and 'punishment' when the subjects are the jurors themselves. The implied assumption is that courts do not, by definition, take revenge. It is not only translators who take this stance. For Danielle Allen: 'acts of revenge are illegitimate responses to wrongdoing; acts of punishment are legitimate and therefore authoritative responses.'[17] This mutually exclusive formulation describes well the modern Western judicial ideal because legitimate authorities are never supposed to take revenge; the 'punisher' (whether judge, jury, prison guard, or any other punitive agent) ought to be impartial, dispassionate and objective. But this does not mean that acts of punishment cannot also be acts of revenge.[18]

Michel Foucault could not have been clearer on this. With reference to early modern France, he makes the point that any crime was necessarily in part an offence against the king, and so:

> in punishment there must always be a portion that belongs to the prince. . . Now, this portion belonging to the prince is not in itself simple: on the one hand, it requires redress for the injury that has been done to the kingdom. . .; but it also requires that the king take revenge for an affront to his very person.[19]

The king is surely a legitimate authority, but he is also a man with a sense of honour. Other examples might include the indisputably legitimate authorities of the Yahweh of the Old Testament, frequently credited with taking vengeance on his enemies, and the Jesus Christ of the New, expected to avenge himself on unbelievers when he returns.[20] One could imagine a Venn diagram in which the concepts of revenge and punishment overlap; the determined efforts of modern societies to ensure that no acts occupy that space should not lead us to conclude that the overlap does not exist.

The goal of this study is not to pick the best English word for a Greek behaviour, but to describe the meaning of that behaviour and particularly its emotional roots in its social context. To this end, I will follow Allen in requiring legitimacy and authority for punishment but withhold the stipulation that revenge cannot be legitimate. Thus, revenge indicates that the behaviour is motivated by anger at a slight and is directed at the reclamation of honour, while punishment indicates that the agent is a legitimate authority. The strength of these definitions (apart from their being, in my opinion, true reflections of the English terms) is that they allow us to take *τιμωρία* consistently to mean 'revenge' without denying it the potential also to mean 'punishment'. Whether the retaliations of Homeric society and Athenian courts ever occupied that area of conceptual overlap is a question that this study will attempt to answer.

Honour

A core element of revenge, the concept of honour needs also to be addressed. William Pitt-Rivers defined it as follows:

> Honour is the value of a person in his own eyes, but also in the eyes of his society. It is his estimation of his own worth, his claim to pride, but it is also the acknowledgement of that claim, his excellence recognised by society, his right to pride.[21]

The strength of this definition is its lack of specificity about what the source of one's value or worth might be, but there has been a tendency to assume that only certain kinds of attribute or behaviour can qualify. And these are invariably associated with (the potential for) aggression and violence in men, especially through revenge.[22] Pitt-Rivers thus goes on to say that 'to leave an affront unavenged is to leave one's honour in a state of desecration'.[23] And this assumption remains popular; in his study of the decline in violence, Steven Pinker contrasts 'a culture of honor – the readiness to take revenge' with 'a culture of dignity – the readiness to control one's emotions'.[24] This narrow concept certainly does not suit Greek *τιμή*. One might lose *τιμή* through a slight and regain it through revenge, but one might equally, as we shall see, lose still more *τιμή* by pursuing a petty feud or regain it by restraining angry impulses for the benefit of others.[25] And it is not only the ancient Greek concept that confounds this criterion. We recognise such things as honour killings, to be sure, but we also honour our parents, we bestow 'honours' on university graduates and philanthropists, and we claim to be 'honoured' at the opportunity to help those we esteem. Even for those who feel offended, revenge is surely not the only path to honour; people who are perceived to remain dignified in the face of provocation can, in certain contexts, be held in high 'honour' by those for whom restraint is an admirable quality. Douglas Cairns has taken to task the notion that honour is 'a scarce non-material commodity, pursued mainly by men in small-scale, face-to-face communities in more or less aggressive forms of zero-sum competition', and shown that honour is in fact far more complicated and pervasive.[26] Honour is about much more than 'self-assertive masculinity', says Cairns, and I tend to agree. This is a study of revenge and punishment and as such the attempts to protect and increase honour described here will frequently pose no problem for definitions like Pinker's. But when restraint is also placed under the microscope, we shall see that honour can be not only lost but won as well. Honour is what one appears to be worth, and its measure is at the heart of many of our emotional states. Slights and failings reduce it painfully and prestigious achievements (including, but not limited to, revenge) increase it pleasurably.

The reason for the pervasive assumption that what people in 'honour cultures' value cannot be the same as what 'we' in 'dignity cultures' value is perhaps that we go about acquiring it in such different ways. These differences are a product of the different kinds of community we live in. As J. E. Lendon has observed of the Roman world:

> The definition – the recipe – of honour, and to a lesser extent its very value, was always in contention between rival communities of opinion in the Roman world, and the aristocratic conception of honour, broadly conceived, exerted a profound influence on how the rest of society conceived of honour.[27]

The growth of Christianity brought with it a totally different source of honour. It was not that 'the Christian holy man, half-naked and stinking atop his pillar' was disinterested in honour, but he had a very different way of acquiring it to the traditional pagan aristocracy.[28] This is how honour will be understood to work in this study. It comes down to a question of what one is worth, but the standards by which that is measured are defined by the social environment(s) in which one lives.

Anger

Honour can be won in all sorts of ways, as the Christian holy man demonstrates, but it can also be lost, and, when it is, the emotion of anger generally comes into play, an especially common consequence of dishonour in the ancient Greek world. Aristotle defined *ὀργή* as 'desire, with pain, for an apparent revenge over an apparent slight towards oneself or one of one's own when that slight is undeserved', and this will define anger in what follows.[29] Compared to the scope of the English 'anger' in common usage, this is a rather narrow definition. We might use 'anger' to describe emotional states that have no particular culprit in mind, such as frustration at the vicissitudes of fate or simple irritation at the world in general. There are certainly similarities between these kinds of emotion, but anger in particular has (or at least looks for) an object of blame.

Historians of emotion have been wrestling with how best to discover and analyse the emotions of the past for several decades. The tools available to historians of emotion have grown in sophistication since Peter and Carol Stearns conceptualised the standards a given group 'maintains towards basic emotions' with the term 'emotionology'.[30] William Reddy, offering a means to explain change in a society's emotionology, conceived of individuals' emotions as shaping and being shaped by the prevailing 'emotional regime'.[31] Barbara Rosenwein has been keen to point out that complex societies are made up not of a single 'regime' but of various overlapping 'emotional communities'.[32] One who assaults a rival in the street, for instance, may receive praise from his peers, disapproval from his family and punishment from the state – three groups with three different standards of emotional expression. Treated with flexibility, both these concepts are of use here. What is important to this study is to recognise that any individual can be part of multiple emotional communities, each of which imposes its own set of standards, its own regime. In what follows the focus will be on the twin identity of the citizen as both a private individual whose emotional life is informed by his submission to the community as a whole, and a public individual whose emotional life is informed by the submission of others to him as a member of the community.

Another aspect to Rosenwein's work has been the move away from the idea of 'basic emotions' that was taken for granted by the Stearnses: 'Although scientists today think of emotions as universal, biological and invariable, this is not true at all.'[33] 'Basic emotions' is a doctrine, associated above all with psychologist Paul Ekman, that holds that there is a list of emotions that are biologically built-in and apply to all humans universally.[34] Other historians have joined the endeavour to dismantle this theory, perhaps because, as Rob Boddice has recognised, universality is generally felt to undermine the idea of change over time.[35] But the theory's most prominent critic is the psychologist Lisa Feldman Barrett who has made the case, based on a vast and growing collection of studies, that the biological foundations for basic emotions are not universal. A basic emotion is thought to have a 'fingerprint' – a set of bodily manifestations by which it can be identified. But whether the category is facial expression, blood pressure, temperature, the firing of particular circuits in the brain, or anything else, none of them appears to occur consistently.[36] The foundation on which basic emotions have always been built appears to be sand and so support grows for more relativist-friendly models based on the idea of 'construction', according to which instances of emotion are constructed by the body to serve the perceived needs of the situation.[37]

If correct, this brings a welcome freedom to historians who need not feel obliged to match the emotions they read in their sources with those they feel themselves. It also, according to Boddice, allows 'the history of emotions to work' because 'to say that emotions change over time is incompatible with claims that there is something fundamentally transcendent or "basic" about (some) emotions'.[38] But why stop here? Historians have often taken for granted that there is something inherently human to our nature, that observations about one culture have implications for another. But is this to be abandoned when it comes to the history of emotions? All humans have the capacity to construct emotions according to what they have learned, but perhaps that is where the similarities end.

It seems to me that, as far as anger is concerned, there is something to be salvaged from the idea of basic emotion. We need not accept that there is anything universal or innate about the physicality of anger in order to accept that there is some core that occurs in all cultures. Among the historical culprits that Feldman Barrett associates with the discredited 'classical view' of emotion is Aristotle who provides a list of emotions and ascribes to them certain consistent characteristics.[39] However, his qualifiers are very different to Ekman's. Aristotle's *ὀργή* requires bodily manifestations only in the vague and subjective sense of 'pain' – at the perception that one's honour has been slighted – and 'pleasure' – at the anticipated reclamation of that honour. And this sense of demeaned worth remains at the heart of many definitions used by psychologists today.[40] Without challenging the compelling evidence against basic emotions, what Aristotle describes does appear to be a feature of all cultures to a greater or lesser degree. Surveys of anthropological evidence from across the world suggest that revenge is a human universal and, since Aristotle's definition of *ὀργή* boils down largely to a desire for revenge, it seems likely that this is a universal too.[41] Anger can look and feel very different from one cultural context to another, it can differ across individuals in the same cultural context, and the same individual can manifest it in different ways in different situations. Yet, it also has a core to it that will, I think, be familiar across cultures because a sense of one's own (demeaned) worth is also ubiquitous. This is to say that the inadequacy of the traditional basic emotion model ought not to mean that the processes observed here are incompatible with other cultural contexts so long as the relevant emotional community recognises the concept of feeling pain at a slight and desiring revenge in response.

The state

The transition from revenge to punishment is an important supposed characteristic of the process of state formation, but what the state is and whether it existed in the ancient Greek world are points of contention. I use 'state' throughout with reference not only to classical Athens but also to Homer and so will offer some justification. Weber's stipulation that there must be a monopoly of legitimate force is widely accepted but often restrictively applied.[42] To take a recent example, in the introduction to their volume on violence and the community in the eastern Mediterranean world, Ioannis Xydopoulos and Kostas Vlassopoulos say that Greek communities did not 'monopolise the use of legitimate force' because:

> Greek communities usually lacked standing armies; their military forces consisted of amateur armed citizens and were ready for use only when specifically mobilised for a particular purpose. Their police forces and bureaucratic apparatuses, where they existed at all, were embryonic and generally functioned reactively, rather than proactively. This meant that self-help was an essential aspect of dealing with violence and dispute settlement. It was not the few policemen who dealt with arresting criminals; people largely relied on self-help for this. There was no public prosecution of theft, assault or homicide: such

> violent acts could be punished only if the victims, or other private citizens on their behalf, were willing and able to undertake prosecuting the culprits.[43]

This adds to a long tradition of scholars pointing out that Greek communities did not control the means of force.[44] Most responses to this line of reasoning have sought to salvage the idea of the state, at Athens in particular, with reference to institutions like the Scythian archers and the Eleven.[45] This approach, attempting to prove that the Athenian state controlled the means of force through its official agents, is both hopeless and unnecessary. Athens possessed nothing like a police force and so was highly reliant on self-help for its command of coercion. But what matters is *legitimate* force, and there is no reason to limit that to the acts of paid professionals. If, for instance, a man is authorised by the court to go to his enemy's house and forcibly reclaim his property, that is an act both of self-help and legitimate force, and its legitimacy comes from the state. Another man may kill his rival upon finding him in bed with his wife – an act that modern states are little better equipped to prevent than the classical Athenian one was – but he does so knowing that when the victim's family takes him to court, it will be the state that decides whether he acted legitimately.[46]

For some, the application of the term has become too inclusive. Andreas Osiander bemoans how 'the word "state" is nowadays employed systematically, indeed insistently, with regard to *all* historical epochs: something is always found to apply it to, as if it were not permissible for epochs to get away with not having had the state'.[47] So long as the interlocutors appreciate when debates about the existence of the state in a given setting have turned from evidence to semantics, there is perhaps no problem in continuing to disagree about the word's meaning. But the transition from family- or clan-based authority to a submission of all to the centre is, in my opinion, sufficiently momentous to warrant a place under the banner of 'state formation'.

On this basis then – that an authority with a monopoly on the legitimate use of force is a state regardless of whether that authority also controls the means of force – I am persuaded that it is reasonable to talk of classical Athens as a state; I also apply the term to the society depicted in Homer, partly on the basis of the conclusions of Chapter 3. Yet, disagreements over the appropriateness of this term need not derail the arguments presented here. If there was a state, then it was a relatively simple one; if there was not a state, then there was at least a centralised authority with institutions that exerted some influence over the settling of private and public disputes.

The community

In discussions around the existence and activities of the state, it is inevitable that the idea of the 'community' will also need to be invoked. In any society, however, there are many different communities that might be spoken of, so clarification is in order here too. Given this book's focus on legitimate judicial authority and state institutions, the communities it is interested in are primarily those that had some sort of share in the administration of justice: Homer's *λαοί* and Athens' *δικασταί*. As such, the anger and associated behaviours that are depicted and analysed here are, with few exceptions, those belonging to free, adult, native men. Much like Greek justice, then, this book largely ignores the majority of the people that made up the broader Greek community in its exploration of the relationship between anger and the formation of the state.

It is obvious that the anger and other emotions of slaves, children, foreigners, women and other disenfranchised groups was also influential. We know, for instance, that Athenian jurors were frequently motivated by considerations of what others might think of or feel towards them, such as by fear or shame at the thought of what women might think of the vote they cast (e.g. Dem. 59.111). It is reasonable to suppose that the anger (and other emotions) of the women in their lives was a strong motivating factor in the decisions made by men in their official capacity. However, a study of the essence of legitimate punishment must focus, at least at first, on the anger of the judges, even if I do think there is considerable scope for going beyond this book's boundaries to explore the state-forming impact of a broader set of emotions felt by a broader group of people.

Historiography

The study of these concepts – revenge and punishment, honour, anger and the state – often together, has a long tradition in the historiography of the ancient Greek world. The way in which the community as a whole (or the state) related to the disputants within it across the archaic and classical periods has traditionally been viewed in terms of significant change. Specifically, the marriage of two trends – the replacement of revenge with punishment, and the emergence and growth of state institutions – is an established dogma that defines many comparisons of Homeric society and classical Athens. For Mary Mackenzie, 'the external and statutory agent of punishment is entirely lacking [in Homer]... This removes a major defining mark of punishment, without which the activity must be reduced to the status of revenge', and 'in the *Iliad* there are no punishments. But in the centuries after Homer, the moral climate alters and there are crimes, there are criminals, and there are punishments'.[48] 'The lawcourt', says Richard Seaford, 'replaces… this hostile reciprocity with socially agreed punishment for crime.'[49] And as Edward Harris puts it, 'the formal justice of the law courts replaced the informal justice of the vendetta'.[50]

Within this narrative two assumptions stand out: that Homeric society knew revenge but did not know punishment, and that classical Athenian society knew forms of punishment that were not vengeful. Put differently, the justice wrought on Homeric wrongdoers did not proceed from a legitimate authority, and the justice that the Athenian state wrought on wrongdoers was not (ideally) an act of anger intended to reclaim honour. If the story of Greek justice starts with revenge, then Homer's depiction of anger is a good place to start.

Anger in Homer

Defining 'anger' is a tricky prospect in Homer simply because there are so many words for it and all appear to make their own unique contribution. Without addressing the differences across these terms, Aristotle treated epic as having an anger essentially the same as the *ὀργή* he knew, but modern scholars have tended to disagree with him. The requirement for a personal slight is not present in the *μῆνις* of Leonard Muellner's study or the third-party anger of David Konstan's, and even Cairns, who sees Aristotle's definition as applicable in the main, observes no slight in several instances.[51] If this is so, and if Aristotle is at least right about fourth-century *ὀργή*, then the emotion (or the vocabulary) of anger has undergone something of a simplification. Is it true that one word, for the most part, came to serve in the place of what were once many? And did Greeks once possess but later lose the capacity for anger in the absence of a perceived slight against their honour? This study will explore whether there was in fact a core to the emotion of anger and, if so, how Homer's several terms could differ within it.

As to the outworking of anger, much scholarship has started from the assumption that the competition for honour in the Homeric world is zero-sum; honour gained by one is honour lost by another.[52] Honour is of a fixed quantity and it can be won only at another's expense, and so any honour lost can be reclaimed only through revenge. Thus, Harris sees revenge as a strong obligation for the angry in the *Iliad*, while restraint is undesirable.[53] Donna Wilson, in her study of 'ransom' and 'revenge' in the *Iliad*, recognises that the demands of honour could be met through restraint if appropriately and sufficiently compensated. Her work is evidently informed by the zero-sum model, which she explicitly endorses, and so her reading still treats honour as an account to be settled between none other than the two parties – will the offender return to the victim (in suffering or in material goods) the disputed honour? There can be little doubt that Homeric heroes are generally short-fused, rising to anger with little apparent provocation, but is it true that victims of slights had no positive option but to avenge themselves, or were there more cooperative options available given the communal context? In fact, the role of the Homeric community in the angry and vengeful interactions that occur within it – something that the zero-sum model tends to understate – remains inadequately explored and yet has much to reveal about anger's cohesive and divisive qualities.

Homer and judicial institutions

'Punishment… as we know it', says Arthur Adkins, 'does not exist in Homeric society'.[54] Adkins does not clarify what 'we know' punishment to be, but the withholding of 'punishment' from epic is widespread and follows naturally from the belief that there was no legitimate authority beyond the household. The question of what kind of authority exists in Homer has been the subject of extensive debate. It is now widely accepted that justice is in some sense administered in Homeric society, but its precise nature remains contentious. Tradition once held that submission to court-based justice is purely voluntary in Homer.[55] In its extreme form, devoid of any kind of coercive third party, this means an absence of regulation of offenders and avengers. As Adkins put it, 'human beings have no rights *qua* human beings in Homer. They have only what, if *agathoi*, they can defend for themselves… The rest of the world is indifferent or hostile: it competes or ignores'.[56]

Among the several problems with this Hobbesian depiction two stand out. It requires that the 'justice' of Homer was totally unlike the 'justice' of classical Athens in that it represented arbitration in the form of compromise rather than retribution in the form of redistributed honour and wealth to the victim. And it lacks evidence in that intense escalating feuds such as it ought to predict are not found in Homer. Hans Julius Wolff addressed this to a degree by giving recognition, in the absence of genuine force, to the signs of a soft kind of coercion in the form of friends, family and the wider community who can exert pressure on disputants to go to the court and to accept its judgements.[57] That the wider community had such a role is clearly correct, yet this remains a rather toothless sort of justice. Wolff also afforded a role for a mysterious individual 'who protected a member of the community who was threatened with private force;... arranged for the settlement of disputes by trial; and... policed, and perhaps presided over, the assembly before which this trial took place'.[58] Here we have a coercive force that ensures the smooth running of the process, while the punishment itself is an act of self-help; a guilty verdict means that the protection would be removed from the culprit.

This is certainly a more state-like model in that it is able to withhold or bestow legitimation on private violent actors. Its retention of a reliance on self-help alongside a centralised judgement of sorts also makes it a plausible ancestor to the kind of justice that would develop in Athens – one also heavily reliant on self-help. But this still seems relatively weak. Is the community's coercive capacity really limited to the temporary prevention of harm on the accused, and how is this prevention realised? What if the accuser does not accept a verdict of innocence?

This model – like all others that deny the process a central, individual judge – must confront the awkward absence of evidence for formal decisions being made purely by the vocal crowd, and the numerous passages that assume a central judicial authority or 'king' figure. Turning away from the traditional (but increasingly unsatisfactory) gambit of dismissing such instances as artifacts of the poems' Mycenaean past, Pierre Carlier took the apparent judge-king at face value and posited that there is in Homeric society an individual who passes judgements and is able to impose those judgements on those who do not like them.[59] In principle, this kind of justice is of much the same sort as that practised in classical Athens: the accused can be compelled to face punishment, the accuser must live with defeat, and any use of force is legitimate only if the court permits (or fails to condemn) it.

It seems to me that models based on consent have been easier for scholars to accept than those based on coercion because of the assumption that a society that so emphasises the power of the individual and the heroic value of revenge cannot have had a system capable of imposing justice from above. However, with the growing acceptance of the view that the classical Athenian courts combined a centralised legitimate authority with an ethic of private vengeance among its litigants, perhaps there is room for a similar, if less sophisticated, system in Homer. With this in mind, this study will seek to reconcile the prominence of anger and revenge with the evidence for the authoritative administration of justice.

Athens and revenge

At the other end of our timeline are the classical Athenian courts and their supposedly non-vengeful punishments. Herman provides a recent and emphatic rendering of what is an old idea when he places the state, represented by the jurors, in between the person claiming victimhood and the alleged wrongdoer and attributes to them the task of judging whether wrongdoing has occurred and inflicting the appropriate punishment.[60] The Athens Herman imagines is more emotionally restrained and forgiving than most are willing to accept, but the model is, in principle, orthodox. Stephen Todd, for instance, says that 'punishment at Athens was designed neither to fit the crime nor to fit the criminal, but to reorder the relative position of the two litigants'.[61] The two might disagree on the question of crime, and Todd's version is more retributive, but they both treat punishment as the act of a third party that has little to do with the punisher's own honour.

For all that the laws and institutions of classical Athens may look familiar to us in principle, the rhetoric – so often littered with vitriol, insult, and seemingly irrelevant accusations – does not. It strikes a tone that fails to chime with the idealistic and forgiving Athenian society Herman describes. Attempting to explain the prominence of enmity, David Cohen put revenge motives back at the heart of the process, reframing private motives in terms of what he called 'litigation as feud'.[62] He showed that prosecutors could, and often did, exact vengeance by pursuing private enemies through the courts. Though others have sought to temper this view with an emphasis on the concurrent pressure to do what was right for the city, the principle that private enmity was a common and legitimate prosecutorial motive is now widely accepted.[63] And some have pointed out that it was not only lawsuits that might be driven by enmity and revenge, but also the punishments themselves; it might not be an unfamiliar agent of the state coming to reclaim property, but a personal enemy.[64] It is in view of this reliance on self-help that Allen has concluded that 'our intuitive distinction between "revenge" and "punishment" breaks down'.[65]

Self-help was indeed the primary means of enforcing judgements in private cases, but what about public cases where the jurors were deciding whether the city itself had been wronged? For Allen the emotion of anger sits at the heart of punishment, not only the anger of the litigants but that of the jurors as well. Indeed, 'anger and personal interest', she says, 'provided the only truly legitimate basis for an attempt to punish someone. Punishments inspired by anger provided a means of recalibrating status and honor in the city after a wrongdoing.'[66] This begins to sound a lot like revenge – an act of anger intended to reclaim honour – but Allen's analysis takes a peculiar turn that makes the punishments she has in mind retributive but certainly not vengeful. The punishing jurors are taken as angry at wrongdoing, but they are not seen as the victims of that wrongdoing. Their role in punishing, if they join in the anger of the prosecutor, is to strip 'a convicted wrongdoer of honor' and give 'honor back to his victim, honor that the act of wrongdoing had taken away'.[67] Thus the model remains substantially as it ever has been – punishment is inflicted by the state, on a wrongdoer, for the victim – only now the jurors are angry.

A short but significant study by Lene Rubinstein has both confirmed and problematised the prominence Allen gives to dicastic anger.[68] Her quantitative analysis of appeals to anger and punishment in the forensic speeches reveals a picture considerably more complex than Allen's model allows for. It points to a system where dicastic anger and punishment were strongly associated in the minds of litigants and jurors. But it also reveals that a great many cases did not have anything to do with the jurors' anger and nor were their outcomes referred to as punishments. Perhaps, the evidence suggests, punishment was (or at least could be) a product of anger and as such making the jurors angry was a very important goal for prosecutors, but we cannot treat punishment by the court as the goal of all prosecutors. Rubinstein's analysis calls for a different kind of model, one that recognises both the importance of dicastic anger and the nuance in the role it played.

Foucault's analysis of early modern punitive principles points us towards a different possibility:

> Besides its immediate victim, the crime attacks the sovereign: it attacks him personally, since the law represents the will of the sovereign; it attacks him physically, since the force of the law is the force of the prince.[69]

Thus, when it comes to punishment, 'in the execution of the most ordinary penalty, in the most punctilious respect of legal forms, reign the active forces of revenge'.[70] For Foucault, the early modern prince was a victim in acts of illegality just as was the person whose property had been stolen or whose body had been violated. This study will situate this idea of a vengeful sovereign in the Athenian context. Were the Athenian state's punishments, as the traditional model goes, inflicted purely (if at all) on behalf of offended plaintiffs, or on behalf of the punishers – the jurors – for slights that they perceived themselves to have suffered?

The possibility that Athenian punishment was essentially an act of revenge is not, on the face of it, a comfortable companion to the idea that Athenian society was based on the rule of law. For Harris, 'the ideal of the "rule of law"' was 'prominent among [the] values' not only of Athens but of all Greek *poleis*.[71] Those who are sceptical about this claim tend still to see the law as highly valued, only not as supreme: Matthew Christ says simply that 'jurors valued legality and held the laws in high esteem', but that they did not feel 'bound to apply individual laws to the letter'.[72] This study will view this issue through the lens of anger. Did jurors punish according to the law when they were not angry, and did they acquit in line with the law despite their anger?

The kind of punitive system hypothesised here, one based on a principle of vengeful punishment, is not absent in the existing literature, nor is it especially new. In 1875, Jean Joseph Thonissen wrote:

> Another moral and legal phenomenon, also dating back to the heroic age and surprising to find amidst the noble splendours of the city of Minerva, is the vivid and profound sense of the legitimacy of individual or collective vengeance. This vengeance, associated with religious ideas, as it were, has never ceased to be one of the main motives for the exercise of the right to punish.
>
> The accuser proudly displays the hatred inspired by the accused; he glories in it and demands, like the payment of a sacred debt, the satisfaction of a brutal passion. The plaintiff seeks revenge by demanding the punishment of the guilty. The state seeks revenge by punishing those who disturb public order, conspirators, embezzlers, and traitors. Even the gods themselves are avenged when malefactors who have profaned their altars or violated their precepts are delivered to the executioner.[73]

More recently, Evangélos Karabélias has said: 'The configuration of penalty in classical Athens is shaped by the concept of vengeance, not only as a moral compensation for the victim and their family but also as a punishment for the offender.'[74] Fiona McHardy has said of Athenian trials that 'the attitudes of the participants, their emotions and their motivations frequently indicate that their prosecutions are vengeful in spirit and therefore not proper civic punishment'.[75] And Rubinstein has taken her work on *τιμωρία* further with a paper that takes seriously the fact that jurors were, in certain contexts, being asked to take 'communal revenge'.[76] The idea that Athenian punishments were (sometimes) acts of revenge is not new, but a model that explains how that worked as legitimate practice in a society with courts, procedures and laws is wanting.

Sources and outline

The first half of this book deals with 'Homeric society'; the second with classical Athens. Chapters 1 and 2 will explore the concepts of anger and revenge in Homer, using Aristotle's definitions as a means of comparison with the classical Athenian world. The focus will be on the emotional nature of the act of revenge and the ways in which it affected and was affected by the community. Chapter 3 will consider institutions and the constraints that the community placed on the anger of its members. Chapter 4 will turn to the Athenian courts and investigate, through quantitative and qualitative analyses of anger and punishment appeals in the forensic speeches, whether the significant institutional changes that had occurred since the seventh century brought with them a new kind of punishment or continued to accommodate the old principle of revenge. Chapters 5, 6 and 7 will look at particular speeches from public, private and homicide trials respectively, speeches that appear at first glance to undermine the conclusions of chapter four in their use of anger and punishment appeals.

Homer

The principle that epic reveals the society of the time in which it took its final form, which I take to be early seventh century, remains a subject of discussion.[77] There is no need to reiterate this debate here, but there are some logical arguments to be made in favour of the approach taken. First, while we might question the representativeness of Homeric material culture, it is considerably less problematic to suppose that the emotional and behavioural values that underpin Homeric society were, in their fundamentals, familiar to his audience. While there is sure to be some 'epic distance' between the anger of Achilles and that of a young early-archaic Greek man, the differences are likely to be of degree rather than kind so that the 'real' individual would recognise and relate to the emotion of the 'fictional'.

Second, the findings here emphasise continuity. For the reader who is sceptical as to the historicity of Homeric values, emotions and institutions, findings of difference between Homer and the classical world might understandably be treated as meaningless. Why, after all, should we expect to see similarities between a society of pure invention and one of reality? But indications of continuity between Homer and classical sources – several of which are to be found in this study – offer support of their own for the claim that the societies of Homer's audience were in important and fundamental ways similar to those of his heroes. If the emotion of anger and its ways of relating to the community are demonstrably similar in epic and in the classical courts, surely the same is likely to be true of the original Homeric audience.

Finally, the presence of judicial institutions in Homeric society, as demonstrated in Chapter 3, points to a feature of society that the poet has observed rather than invented or inherited from some distant past without understanding its implications.

I treat Homer's poems as evidence of reality and of various social realities. No two early archaic Greek *poleis* were identical, but, in view of the reach of the poems across the Greek world, there is bound to have been some emotional and societal commonality alongside the cultural variety. And we can, I think, speak in general and tentative terms about commonly felt 'Greek' emotions and the ways that those emotions contributed to division and cohesion within their communities.

The law-court speeches

The corpus of classical Athenian forensic speeches is remarkably large and varied, offering a wealth of information on, amongst other things, the norms and values surrounding justice and punishment. The challenge lies in knowing how to interpret them. First, it is worth noting who their primary audience was. The current consensus holds that, besides being male citizens, jurors were typically considerably older than the minimum permitted age of thirty and were relatively poor.[78] This ought to inform how we understand the speeches' rhetorical aims. It also suggests that the motives behind Athenian punishment will reflect the values of, on average, older and poorer male citizens, rather than of 'Athenians' in general. But does this matter? The aim here is to understand what motivated punishment and the speeches are useful for that, even if it happens that the Athenian state tended to punish in line with the judgement of poor old men.

The principal means of reading the motivations of jurors is theoretically simple and has been long used: we can infer jurors' values from the assumptions that lie behind the speakers' arguments, appeals and self-presentation.[79] A problem that often surfaces in attempts to discern values from law-court speeches is the tendency to assume that any qualities attributed to the speaker are morally positive while any attributed to the opponent are negative. In fact, the portrayal of an admirable persona to the jurors was only one of several possible aims. Another was to convince the jurors of one's version of events. Thus, when one defendant portrays himself as having fled the city in order to avoid a confrontation, it is not because the average Athenian respects someone who runs from a fight but because the jurors will think him unlikely to have initiated the fight that is the subject of the present trial. Forensic rhetoric will always leave space for different interpretations, but one must seek to understand the aims of the orator before reaching any conclusions as to his or his audience's values.

Assuming we accurately distil from a speech what the speaker believes his jurors' values to have been, we are then left with more questions. How well did the speaker know his audience? It cannot be taken for granted, as is often done, that the very fact that these speeches have been preserved since antiquity suggests that contemporaries thought they were among the best of the genre. And are we to suppose that all jurors were homogenous? Presumably the same argument that won over one juror might have alienated another because in Athens, as in any society of this size and complexity, there was not a single universally agreed upon set of values, even among a single demographic. Often, the best an ancient historian can do with the meagre evidence available is to take a single line or paragraph and carefully speculate as to its implications, always remembering that what we have may be a poor reflection of reality. But when it comes to the forensic corpus the quantity of data can be used to mitigate these risks.

Quantitative analysis has been put to use by scholars of rhetoric for a long time, though typically it tended to be limited to lists in footnotes that serve to emphasise a point. Rubinstein has pioneered a more systematic approach, particularly in her studies on negative emotion among jurors.[80] The great strength of this approach is that it sheds light on how typical a given example is and helps prevent one from reading norms into outliers. Rather than cherry-picking a favourable example, through quantitative data one can be led by a general picture of the evidence. There are, of course, problems with this approach. Quantitative analysis is inherently reductive, which can be a major challenge with something so complicated and varied as emotion: by attributing the same numerical value to all appeals for *ὀργή*, I conceal the fact that they may represent very different kinds of *ὀργή* in terms of intensity, rationale, outcome and other dimensions. But the weaknesses of the quantitative are the strengths of the qualitative and so by using the two together – as I attempt to do here – the best of both worlds can hopefully be enjoyed.

Omitting tragedy

Any reader with at least a passing familiarity with the literature on ancient Greek revenge will note the absence of tragedy here. Indeed, in many of the major works on the subject, tragedy is not only addressed but is the primary focus of attention.

The tendency for studies of revenge to be drawn to tragedy is to be expected – the genre is laden with it. And there is certainly a great deal to be taken from tragedy (not to mention comedy, historiography, philosophy, inscriptions and so on) for any study of anger and vengeance in this period, particularly as a means of revealing contemporary values on the subject. However, I do not attempt to add to the discussion around this genre specifically here. Rather, given the extent of the work already done by others, the aim of comparing the values surrounding punishment in the classical courts with their early archaic antecedents is best served by focusing on the Homeric poems and the Athenian legal corpus.[81]

While I am not investigating tragedy myself in what follows, I have nevertheless been informed by the existing literature on it and consider the scheme laid out here to disagree little with the conceptions (particularly in terms of definition and social function) of Athenian revenge gleaned from tragedy. Mary Blundell's work, which remains essential, embraces the Aristotelian conception of anger and revenge and builds its thesis around the contention that Greeks held their honour in high regard and would be inclined to restore it where they perceived it to have been diminished.[82] Anne Burnett's survey deftly explores the extensive variety that the emotion of anger can encompass in Attic tragedy, even while the bounds of its definition remain broadly Aristotelian, and the limits of its social acceptance reflect those seen in Homer and the forensic corpus.[83] Allen, as she does in her work on the law-court speeches, observes the central role played by anger in the Athenian view of revenge and punishment. Her understanding of how and why anger manifests in the wider community remains, at times, a problem in her treatment of tragedy, but my objections to this model are outlined in Chapter 4 in the context of the Athenian courtroom.[84] The great strength of Allen's work, however, lies in its highlighting of how invested the community was in resolving the angry disputes that arose between its members, a central pillar of this study as well. And McHardy's work uses tragedy, among other genres, to support her primary thesis that 'men calculate the risks they are taking and do not fly to take revenge without consideration' – an assertion that is perhaps too categorical but is a welcome correction to a tradition too often dismissive of the reasoning capacity of the angry.[85] Moreover, while what follows here does not engage specifically with tragedy, it has benefitted from McHardy's use of that genre to demonstrate that Greek revenge was a morally complicated category, a behaviour that could be acceptable or unacceptable depending largely on its social context. I have not attempted here to provide a complete list of the major works on tragic revenge, but merely to highlight those tragedy-related works that have had the most significant influence on this study. Insofar as there is any consensus among scholars on the definition of tragic anger and the role it plays in the community, this study has no quarrel with it.

On genre comparison

There is an obvious methodological objection to what I am doing here: how can we compare societies through sources of such different genres? To what extent, if any, can the emotions and behaviours of the fictional Achilles as portrayed in an epic poem really be compared to those of the real classical Athenian jurors as inferred from the speeches they heard? Certainly, mine would be a simpler task if the early archaic world had left us a set of forensic speeches that we might hold up to the corpus of classical Athens. However, such comparisons have a long pedigree. Aristotle saw no reason not to use Homeric illustrations in his definitions of emotions, anger in particular, and the practice of tracing continuity or change between the two periods has become something of a commonplace today. Frequently, as already mentioned, it is change that is observed, especially when the classical sources in question are law-court speeches.[86]

Others, however, have observed continuity. Lendon has traced a likeness between the motives, including revenge, that drove the individual warriors of Homer's *Iliad* and those that underpinned the Peloponnesian War as depicted in Thucydides: '"Always to be the best and preeminent above others" was the aim of the heroes of the *Iliad*, and that aim was passed down the generations into later Greece, with only the respects in which an individual sought to excel changing over time.'[87] McHardy, highlighting the role of Athenian revenge in protecting one's access to material and reproductive wealth, also draws heavily on Homeric evidence to support her interpretation of various classical sources.[88] And though the methodological concerns cannot be entirely put to bed, they do fade somewhat in these latter examples that emphasise similarity over difference. For while the former are open to the charge that the differences they observe are functions of genre, the latter (like this study) offer reassurance in the fact that the similarities they observe shine through despite the differences of genre.

The sources being what they are, I do believe that it is possible to observe a given aspect of human nature from different perspectives. One can place oneself in the shoes of the archaic bards' audiences just as one can those of the classical Athenian juror and note the points of similarity.

1

Anger and the Community in Homeric Society

Introduction

Whether it boils on Achilles' surface, or simmers at Odysseus' core, anger is fundamental to both Homeric plots. Even if we set these two characters aside, the fingerprints of anger are everywhere – the pain of its experience and the fear of its arousal, the desire for its satisfaction and the regretting of its consequences – so that barely a human experience is portrayed that has not been significantly shaped by anger.

What exactly we are speaking of when we refer to the 'anger' of the *Iliad* and *Odyssey* has been a matter of debate. Aristotle appears to have thought that his definition, intended to suit the emotion felt by the audiences of Athenian public life, applied equally to the feeling that keeps Achilles from battle. This chapter will show that Aristotle's definition does indeed correspond neatly to the anger felt by Homeric heroes.

The three centuries between Homer and Aristotle are characterised by profound political, institutional and cultural change. If, in such a context, the essence of anger does indeed remain constant and prominent, this presents challenges to our assumptions about changes in the way disputes begin and are settled. Certainly, the institutions surrounding dispute in fourth-century Athens – laws, courts, officials, procedures and so on – would have been unrecognisable to Homer's seventh-century audiences, but the emotional heart of the matter would have been decidedly familiar.

One notable feature of anger in Homer is that it frequently becomes a communal affair, being felt by and towards those whose personal link to the actual offence can be quite tenuous. From epic's detailed accounts of the emotional experience, and the extensive lexicon of anger terms available to Homer, it is possible to put together an account of how the anger that defined a relationship between two individuals could reach out to draw in others. This occurs in two main ways. Homer's numerous third-party avengers demonstrate how the honour of family, friends and wider community was bound up with that of the victim so that a slight against one could become, by degrees, a slight against all. Equally, the offence of one might also tarnish others who, in the victim's eyes, fail to condemn an offence that transgresses established norms. These points again introduce continuity between Homer and Aristotle, whose definition recognised the potential for anger to be felt at insults to 'one's own' as well as to oneself, and was partly intended to help public speakers evoke or quell anger in representatives of the wider community over the actions of its individual members.

Anger, as the primary emotion in defining disputes between individuals within a community and between the community and its members, holds important keys to our understanding of what drives centralisation. How does the anger of one individual towards another grow to become a threat to the wider community? What leads the community as a whole to perceive slights from offenders without and within? And by what qualities does anger create an appetite for greater centralisation and a willingness to lend one's strength to the community?

Concepts of anger

Aristotle characterised anger (*ὀργή*) as 'desire, with pain, for an apparent revenge over an apparent slight towards oneself or one of one's own when that slight is undeserved'.[1] His word for the emotion, *ὀργή*, dominated the classical concept, but was not part of the rich Homeric vocabulary. However, he illustrated this definition with no fewer than five Iliadic examples that employ two different terms, *χόλος* and *κότος*, or do not use explicit terms for anger at all.[2] Clearly, he thought that his definition of anger applied as much to Homer's heroes as to fourth-century Athenians. This definition carries several important implications. First, a slight is necessarily a matter of honour so that whatever other harm is inflicted, word or deed, the anger that results requires the perception that one's worth has been undervalued or diminished. Second, the requirement of a slight means that one must be angry with someone in particular.[3] Third, the angry person must wish to retaliate.

Aristotle's is not the only fourth-century Greek perspective on what characterised the emotion of *ὀργή*. In the *Rhetoric to Alexander*, a work of unknown authorship, *ὀργή* is said to be achieved by demonstrating that 'either we or those for whom we happen to have concern have been undeservedly slighted or wronged by them (the speaker's opponents) or their loved ones' (34.14). These two perspectives diverge in two main ways: Aristotle treats all anger as caused by 'slights' exclusively, while our other author allows also for 'wrongs' as a possible cause; the former sees anger as felt only by victims and their loved ones, while the latter appears to see it as felt by those who have witnessed offences but have not themselves suffered them.

Modern scholars have generally found Aristotle's definition to be in some way inadequate for the Homeric context and some of their reasons find crossover with the principles espoused in the *Rhetoric to Alexander*.[4] For Cairns its requirement for a slight sometimes goes unmet, and for Konstan it fails to account for the motives behind angry third parties whose honour, he asserts, has not been harmed.[5] Muellner departs from Aristotle without engaging with him, in finding *μῆνις* to be felt at taboo behaviour without requiring personal offence.[6] I hope to demonstrate that Aristotle's characterisation of *ὀργή* is an accurate description of interpersonal anger in Homer. Seven Homeric anger terms function consistently within the Aristotelian paradigm.[7] And what follows uses these terms to examine the emotional dynamics behind the experience of anger and the social implications that follow from it.

It is worth noting that Aristotle's definition of *ὀργὴ* comes at the head of a list of emotional definitions, some of which overlap in ways that make them relevant to the Homeric concept of anger as well. His discussion of *ἔχθρα* (enmity) and *μῖσος* (hatred), for example, is particularly relevant. The point of overlap for Aristotle is that *ὀργὴ* is one of the possible causes of *ἔχθρα* and *μῖσος* (*Rh.* 2.4.30). We shall see that in Homeric language the term *κότος* bears the hallmarks of enmity and hatred, but also consistently appears to follow on from a slight, a quality so characteristic of *ὀργὴ*. In this way, *κότος* may indicate *μῖσος* even as it reveals *ὀργὴ*. Here I show how the classical concept of *ὀργὴ* can consistently be seen in Homer, but in so doing I do not intend necessarily to exclude other emotions.

Anger, it is generally thought, has a fraught relationship with society. Within the Hobbesian tradition, anger contributes to the naturally violent nature of the individual and, consequently, the 'brutish and short' nature of life in general.[8] It is a self-interested impulse that the centralised coercive apparatus of the state must control. Van Wees has contended that it is not enough simply to assume that aggression will naturally occur in the absence of restraint; humanity's innate capacity for aggression needs stimulation and in Homer that comes from 'status rivalry'.[9] Within this model, anger serves alongside other aggressive impulses as part of a system of competitive values that set individuals against each other, resisting central cohesion. This view of anger finds much support in what follows; community division clearly is a function of anger in Homer and, surely, in all social contexts. But we shall also see that there is another, more cohesive, side to the coin because anger also has the power to unite people against a common offender.

The slight

The offence that has brought anger about is not always immediately obvious. In one such example, the Thebans are so angry following their defeat at the hands of Tydeus in a series of contests to which he has challenged them that they attempt an ambush as he leaves (*Il.* 4.385–92). Cairns has questioned whether Aristotle's condition that anger requires an undeserved slight is met in this instance.[10] They cannot have expected, argues Cairns, that Tydeus would throw the contests and so it does not make sense for them to feel slighted by him when he wins.[11] However, the slight here may lie in the challenge more than in the victory. Perhaps one would not be expected to spare an opponent's honour in a contest (though this is not unthinkable either), but to enter into a contest is to risk causing offence.[12] This is not the only time in Homer that violent anger is provoked by competitive challenges (*Od.* 8.226–8) and invidious boasts (*Il.* 2.594–600), which imply an unfavourable estimation of another's ability. Agamemnon appears to view the challenge as provocative when he says that, though Tydeus was a stranger and alone among many, he did not fear but challenged the locals to contests (4.387–9). In a similar situation, Odysseus avoids these social pitfalls, saying that he will accept a contest with anyone except his host, Laodamas: 'who would contend with one who hosts him? That man is senseless and worthless who offers rivalry in games with his host in a foreign land and cuts off all that is his' (*Od.* 8.207–11).[13] Tydeus does not cause offence simply by winning, but rather by entering a foreign land, challenging its occupants, *and then* winning. When they are unapparent to the modern reader, slights may nevertheless have been contextually evident to contemporary audiences. Even in this more obscure instance, however, it seems clear that a slight has been perceived and was probably intended.

At the heart of the issue for the slighted is the perception that their honour has been diminished or undervalued. Whatever the harm they suffer – physical, verbal or otherwise – it is around this non-material commodity that the cycle of offence, anger and revenge revolves. Achilles, for example, asserts that he loves

Briseis like a wife (*Il.* 9.340–3) and yet rejects the offer of her return along with many gifts saying, 'let [Agamemnon] lie beside her and be happy' (336–7). Having heard the embassy's arguments and pleas for him to return to battle, Achilles appraises his anger's hold over him as follows:

> *πάντά τί μοι κατὰ θυμὸν ἐείσαο μυθήσασθαι·*
> *ἀλλά μοι οἰδάνεται κραδίη χόλῳ ὁππότε κείνων*
> *μνήσομαι ὥς μ' ἀσύφηλον ἐν Ἀργείοισιν ἔρεξεν*
> *Ἀτρεΐδης ὡς εἴ τιν' ἀτίμητον μετανάστην.*
>
> (*Il.* 9.645–8)

> All this you appear to say in accordance with my spirit.
> But my heart becomes swollen with anger when
> I remember that he wrought indignity on me among the Argives,
> the son of Atreus, as if I were some dishonoured wanderer.

Achilles' anger is rooted in a memory of profound dishonour and alienation.[14] The loss of Briseis is less of an issue than the taking of her, an act that belittled Achilles in the extreme because he has a reputation as one of the best of the Achaeans and yet Agamemnon treated him as though he were an outsider with no honour at all.

The affective result of this apparent dishonour is a feeling of pain (*ἄχος*) in the victim. The establishment of Achilles' anger is announced with the phrase, 'and pain came upon the son of Peleus' (*Πηλεΐωνι δ' ἄχος γένετ'*; *Il.* 1.188), and that pain returns on remembrance of the offence (16.52–63). Pain also marks the beginning of anger for Zeus towards Ate for her thwarting of his plans for Heracles (19.125–7), for Telemachus towards the suitors for their mockery (*Od.* 16.87–9), and for the heroes who mutilate the centaur Eurytion for his evil deeds (21.297–301). Athena even ensures that Odysseus continues to suffer outrages from the suitors so that he will feel greater pain (18.346–8, 20.284–6). Homeric anger is rooted in pain felt at the perception that one has been dishonoured.

Anger at oneself

The verb *χώομαι* indicates Aristotelian anger unproblematically for the most part, but six instances present a challenge. It is said on four occasions to be felt by warriors when their spears miss their mark (*Il.* 13.165, 14.406, 16.616, 22.291) and once by Diomedes, having just dropped his whip, at seeing Eumelus pull away from him in the chariot race (23.385).[15] Seemingly, these five examples entail no offence or blamed agent and cannot, therefore, be equated with the kind of anger Aristotle has in mind.[16] As I see it, there are two possible reasons for this feature. If it is correct that no one is to blame in these instances, it may be that *χώομαι* refers to something that takes place before the attribution of blame required for Aristotelian anger – the pain that comes with the loss of honour.[17] Aristotle qualifies his 'slight' with the adjective 'apparent' (*φαινομένην*), steering the experience through the filter of appraisal.[18] For Aristotle, emotions depend on perception so that to experience proper anger one must have time to recognise an offence. Perhaps then, *χώομαι* refers to the first painful step in the process that triggers the occasionally unsuccessful search for a culprit.

However, the sixth example offers a different and, I think, preferable explanation. Achilles prophesies that Agamemnon will 'tear at the spirit within him in anger (*χωόμενος*) that he did not honour the best of the Achaeans' (*Il.* 1.243–4). Achilles conceives of Agamemnon's anger falling not on himself, Agamemnon, as a whole but on his spirit (*θυμὸν*) as if he is expected to become angry with a part of himself which he blames for what has happened to him, or, perhaps, at the person he remembers being.[19] It may be that, by turning Agamemnon's ire on himself, Achilles is using a word outside of its usual context for rhetorical effect. On the other hand, if this is indicative of a possible function of *χώομαι*, then it might also apply to our five other instances. The loss of face felt by Agamemnon over his foolish treatment of Achilles can be likened to that of those whose spears miss their target and of Diomedes who has dropped the whip, allowing his horses to slow.[20] The desire to retaliate is a prototypical quality of anger according to Aristotle and even in this instance, where the taking of revenge is not truly possible, the all-important desire to do so is suggested by Achilles who expects Agamemnon to tear at his own spirit. Aristotle does not discuss whether the angry individual might be a legitimate target of their own anger (given that he is attempting to demonstrate to orators how best to persuade public audiences, it is unlikely to be a relevant concern). But in Homer at least, the usage of the term *χώομαι* suggests that when the pain of dishonour fails to find an external agent on whom to fixate, it can turn inwards.

Though anger does not always land on external offenders, forty-six of the fifty-two instances of *χώομαι* suggest that it tends to. Anger's reliance on the subjective perception of offence means that it need not have an especially strong relationship with reality. This, combined with the impulse felt by the frustrated individual to find someone they can plausibly blame (and from whom they can reclaim lost honour), creates an easy path to anger. In Achilles' recollection, it was because he was the first to urge the appeasement of Apollo through Chryseis' return that Agamemnon's anger was directed at him (*Il.* 1.386–7). He represents Agamemnon's anger as searching for a target on whom to land and, while Achilles cannot be said to have insulted Agamemnon (yet), he has conveyed the message that will result in Agamemnon's shameful returning of his prize. If Achilles' later assessment of the situation is accurate, then by speaking up, albeit respectfully, he provides Agamemnon's fury with the target it seeks. The harming of one's honour is painful and sparks the search for someone to blame; in Homer, that search is usually fruitful.

The desire for revenge

Aristotle's definition encompasses not only the cause of anger but the goal as well: revenge. Simply put, one who suffers dishonour will want that honour back. In Homer too, the pain suffered on losing honour is often depicted alongside the desire to retaliate in some way. Many battlefield killings are vengeful. For instance, not until his companion Leucus is killed does Odysseus walk in 'great anger' through the 'front-fighters' and pick out a target for his javelin (*Il.* 4.490–503). Theft is avenged in escalatory measure (11.671–706), insults beget insults and head towards violence (23.473–91), and a lack of deference towards superiors is punished (2.244–69). Achilles' withdrawal from battle demonstrates that even the subordinate's weaker position is not without opportunities for retaliation.[21] Perhaps Agamemnon has learnt the importance of respecting subordinates by Book Four when Odysseus appears to take umbrage, looking from beneath his brows (*ὑπόδρα ἰδών*), at the greater man's questioning of his courage (4.349). Agamemnon swiftly apologises (356–63). This is not to say that every instance of anger results in an attempt at revenge – indeed, it is often restrained – but that anger needs restraining also indicates its propensity towards retaliation.[22]

Homeric vocabulary reveals that there are different layers to the principle that anger will desire retaliation, and those layers relate to the immediate availability of revenge. One of the main conclusions of Thomas Walsh's comparison of *χόλος* and *κότος* is that *χόλος* can be stirred up in a moment, while *κότος* is a long-lasting resentment.[23] This conclusion originates with Calchas' fearful plea for Achilles' protection against Agamemnon.

ἦ γὰρ ὀΐομαι ἄνδρα χολωσέμεν, ὃς μέγα πάντων
Ἀργείων κρατέει καί οἱ πείθονται Ἀχαιοί·
κρείσσων γὰρ βασιλεὺς ὅτε χώσεται ἀνδρὶ χέρηϊ·

εἴ περ γάρ τε χόλον γε καὶ αὐτῆμαρ καταπέψῃ,
ἀλλά τε καὶ μετόπισθεν ἔχει κότον, ὄφρα τελέσσῃ,
ἐν στήθεσσιν ἑοῖσι·

(*Il.* 1.78–83)

For I believe I will anger a man who rules mightily over all
Argives and whom the Achaeans obey.
For a ruler is stronger when he is angry with a lesser man.
For even if he swallows his anger for that day,
nevertheless, he holds on to anger that remains in his chest,
that he may complete it.

For Walsh, this passage is a definition; however, the qualities Calchas ascribes to these emotions in this instance, far from being constant, are contingent on the exceptional character of the person who experiences them. When felt by a ruler towards an inferior, *χόλος* will be especially dangerous and *κότος* will be held on to until it is completed. Sensibly though, Walsh tests this 'definition' against the terms' usages throughout epic.

Though *χόλος* can last a relatively long time – Achilles' anger towards Agamemnon continues to take that name for twenty days – it often subsides soon after its emergence. This is typically because the slight is avenged, the angry individual restrains themselves, or the offender apologises. On seeing a friend killed in battle, for example, it is almost always *χόλος* that is mentioned while the motives that lie behind *κότος* are typically more remote.[24] This is not, however, purely in terms of time.[25] Achilles' anger at Agamemnon is referred to as *μῆνις* sixteen times, *χόλος* twenty-four, and *κότος* only once. In this one instance, Agamemnon is anticipating *κότος* in the event that Achilles returns, as threatened, to Phthia (*Il.* 1.181). That this word is not used again suggests that Achilles' anger never actually comes to be seen as *κότος* despite its long duration, and yet it might have become such on day one had he left. Similarly, Odysseus' anger (*κεκοτηότι*) is not old (Polyphemus' destruction of his friends having occurred less than two days prior) when it leads him to insult the Cyclops from his escaping ship (*Od.* 9.501). But it is, and looks to remain, unsatisfied in that he had wanted to kill Polyphemus but had to settle for blinding him (299–306, 316–17). Like Achilles, Odysseus still feels there is a debt to be paid and so remains angry; yet, unlike Achilles, he is no longer going to be in a position to act on that desire and so it has become appropriate to refer to his anger as *κότος*. Cairns' summation bears repeating: *κότος* is 'what remains when the occurrent emotion of anger becomes dispositional'.[26]

Despite its relative remoteness, *κότος* remains as focused on revenge as *χόλος*. Calchas' fear demonstrates that from his perspective the ruler's *κότος* represents a lasting threat and Agamemnon's assertion that he will not take notice of Achilles' *κότος* if he leaves (*Il.* 1.181) suggests that it is something of which most would be wary. Odysseus' *κότος* so longs for vengeance that he risks everything to vaunt over Polyphemus, and Deiphobus seeks out Idomeneus with his javelin throw since he holds unceasing *κότος* towards him (13.516–17).

These two terms, then, both indicate a desire to retaliate, but they point to differing experiences. At the onset of *χόλος*, it is the emotion rather than the individual that has the agency. *Χόλος* 'falls upon the spirit' (*ἔμπεσε θυμῷ*), 'enters' (*δύω*) a person, or 'takes hold' (*λαμβάνω*) of them.[27] Furthermore, *χόλος* and not *κότος* is described as 'heart-grieving' (*χόλον θυμαλγέα*).[28] Those who feel *χόλος* are sometimes said to be in pain, but the same association is never made with *κότος*.[29] The state of *κότος* is something over which the individual has more control. The noun, which never appears in the nominative, is something that the individual 'holds' (*ἔχω*) until it is fulfilled, 'sets' (*τίθημι*) against others, or 'puts in' (*ἐντίθημι*) their own spirit.[30] The passive suffering of pain, particularly in the chest, is a central feature of *χόλος*, while it is the active adoption of a grudge that characterises *κότος*, and in both these modes do the angry pursue vengeance.

The strictly passive role that the victim takes at the onset of *χόλος* is demonstrated in Hector's attempt to stir it up in himself as he awaits Achilles:

ἀλλ' ὅ γε μίμν' Ἀχιλῆα πελώριον ἇσσον ἰόντα.
ὡς δὲ δράκων ἐπὶ χειῇ ὀρέστερος ἄνδρα μένῃσι
βεβρωκὼς κακὰ φάρμακ', ἔδυ δέ τέ μιν χόλος αἰνός,
σμερδαλέον δὲ δέδορκεν ἑλισσόμενος περὶ χειῇ·
ὣς Ἕκτωρ ἄσβεστον ἔχων μένος οὐχ ὑπεχώρει
πύργῳ ἔπι προὔχοντι φαεινὴν ἀσπίδ' ἐρείσας·

(*Il.* 22.92–7)

but he awaited mighty Achilles as he came nearer.
Just as a mountain-snake awaits a man at his hole
having eaten evil herbs, and dread anger has entered him,
and he stares terribly, coiled about the hole,
so did Hector, holding unquenched his fury, not give ground,
leaning his shining shield against the jutting wall.

The theme of digestion is introduced by Calchas who talks of swallowing *χόλος* to restrain it.[31] In this instance though, the snake has devoured something intended to help maintain its anger. Anger enhances the power of Homeric combatants as Zeus understands when Achilles threatens in his anger to storm the wall before destiny has determined (20.28–30). However, sufficient fear can also overcome anger, resulting in fleeing rather than fighting, and everything about Hector's situation ought to result in his feeling afraid. His parents have told him he has no chance, he will inevitably become food for dogs, and the city will fall without him (22.38–89). He also has available to him the option of simply entering the city and remaining behind the walls (56–7) rather than face an opponent who, in his rage, will be even more dangerous and merciless than normal.[32] Hector needs anger to banish his fear and help him compete, but the notion of having to eat 'evil herbs' highlights the fact that *χόλος* is not something that one can decide to feel; it is a product of one's experiences and sometimes, as Achilles demonstrates, one's memories of them (9.646).[33] Hector's mind, though, is not on the past; it is on a future that, whichever way he looks at it, will result in his death or a shame he cannot live with (22.98–130). In the end, he fails to generate *χόλος* in the face of fear and flees (136–7).[34]

Communicating anger

The painful onset of *χόλος* often reveals itself to others through facial expression. For James Holoka, the phrase *ὑπόδρα ἰδών*, 'looking from beneath the brows', demonstrates that someone considers themselves to have been treated in a way unbefitting of their status.[35] This is true, but not only of *ὑπόδρα ἰδών*; it is the essence of anger in general. The phrase marks an initial physiological indicator that offence has been taken and is always publicly displayed. If Homer supposes his characters ever to glower unnoticed, he never uses this phrase to say so because, it seems, an important function of it is to indicate to us not only that the subject feels angry, but also that they have communicated as much to all who are looking, including the offender – the object of their glare. By virtue of its association with the initial onset of anger, *ὑπόδρα ἰδών* has, as Walsh says, a 'special relationship' with *χόλος*.[36]

The meaning of this expression is no doubt informed by the reputation of its bearer and the context of its occurrence. Jon Hesk notes that this phrase tends to introduce violence or the threat thereof and suggests that the prospect of violence may be present even when not mentioned.[37] It seems to me though that the onset of anger always creates a situation of potential violence, and no more clearly when described with this phrase than with any other, particularly in view of certain instances where violence is surely not expected. Odysseus, for instance, is said to do it twice towards Agamemnon (*Il.* 4.349, 14.82), someone he would not presume to attack, and in the first of these the latter responds with a smile (356) before attempting to repair the damage of his words. Here the expression is most easily understood not as a signal that he is on the verge of violence but simply as a sign that he feels anger, an emotion that often does lead to violence but may also be expressed in words or non-violent actions such as Odysseus' rude dismissal of Agamemnon's criticism as 'wind' (355). When this expression is performed by a careful person like Odysseus towards his superior, it may be that violence is not expected, whereas when it appears on the face of Achilles, the implications are different. Even Achilles' first thought after *ὑπόδρα ἰδών* is not of violence but of abandoning the expedition (1.169–71), but murder soon becomes his preferred option (194).[38] The implications of another's anger for those who see it written on their face are always context-dependent.

The term *σκύζομαι* is also closely linked to *χόλος*. When Odysseus admits to his fear that Alcinous might *ἐπισκύσσαιτο* were he to arrive with Nausicaa's handmaids (*Od.* 7.306), the Phaeacian states that his heart is not the sort to *κεχολῶσθαι* without reason (310).[39] As Cairns has stated, the main difference is that *σκύζομαι*, being cognate with *σκυθρός* and *σκυθρωπός*, relates to anger's facial expression and so, metonymously, to the emotion in general.[40] There is more to their distinction than this though. They are presented as complementary aspects of Athena's emotional state towards her father when it is said that she remained silent, '*σκυζομένη* at her father Zeus, and savage *χόλος* took hold of her' (*Il.* 8.460). The anger is written in her face but its savagery bears clarification; and agency is again at issue: the scowl belongs to Athena, but Athena belongs to her anger.[41]

There is also a symbolic aspect to *σκύζομαι*, a term less bound to physicality than *ὑπόδρα ἰδών*. Achilles receives his friends, saying that he needs those who, even in his angry state (*σκυζομένῳ*), are 'dearest of all' (*Il.* 9.198), a reference to his ongoing anger that has nothing to do with his current facial expression. On seeing his friends arrive he leaps to his feet in astonishment (193–4); the anger he feels is not currently at the surface. The term seems to function as a pure metaphor, an invocation of the angry visage as an indication of the angry heart. Zeus also resorts to this image in the message he sends to Achilles, instructing him to hand Hector's body over to Priam: 'Tell him that the gods *σκύζεσθαί* at him', he instructs Thetis, 'that I beyond all the immortals am angered (*κεχολῶσθαι*)' (24.113, 134). Zeus seeks to persuade Achilles not only by telling him the gods are angry, but by giving that anger a visual quality in the image of the gods' sullen faces that ought to illustrate their readiness to act if he refuses them. For Achilles himself, apprehensive over the response of his dead friend, it is not simply the thought of Patroclus' anger that concerns him but the image: 'Do not *σκυδμαινέμεν* at me, Patroclus, if you learn, even in the house of Hades, that I released Hector to his dear father' (592–4). Even within Aristotle's restrictive definition, there is scope for a great deal of complexity; the impact of someone's anger depends on how it is communicated and the image of an angry face, even if purely imaginary, can be especially evocative.

Third-party anger

In many instances, anger is felt by those who do not themselves appear to have been directly offended. Konstan has argued that the anger felt by Achilles towards Hector cannot be Aristotelian because the killing of Patroclus was not 'a sign of contempt for Achilles'.[42] This does not in fact conflict with Aristotle who defines as angry those who desire revenge for a 'slight towards themselves or their own' (*Rh.* 2.2.1). Aristotle goes on to define slights with reference to the sufferer specifically, but he clearly considered such offences capable of evoking the same kind of emotional response in both victims and those who count them as 'their own'. Let us ask, then, not whether the angers of both victims and third parties are Aristotelian, but whether these two Aristotelian angers are nevertheless significantly different.

Much research has recently been done on the difference between the anger of victims and that of third parties.[43] That these are two distinct categories of anger is not controversial, but psychologists are yet to demonstrate a substantial difference in the affective experience of the subject and the distinction is certainly not apparent in Homer.[44]

Konstan, focusing on Achilles' anger towards Hector, points to the lion metaphor (*Il.* 18.318–23) as an indication that his is an exceptional anger, a 'violent fury'.[45] Even without the metaphor, there can be no doubt that Achilles' anger is presented as exceptional. It is fearless: while other third-party avengers might succumb to terror at witnessing a comrade's slaying (e.g. 14.506–7), Achilles chases his quarry all over the battlefield and kills any who resist him. It is focused: while others settle for a proxy victim (e.g. 13.402–14, 14.459–505), Achilles' anger does not diminish with the mass slaughter of others but remains set on Hector.[46] And it is insatiable: while others may feel satisfied that they have done enough to account for the deceased (e.g. 470–4, 13.446–7), Achilles remains unsatisfied even after he has killed Hector, cut the throats of twelve

Trojan youths and dragged his enemy's corpse behind his chariot daily for twelve days. Certainly, Achilles' anger towards Hector is exceptional, but this, for two reasons, does not mean that third-party anger is categorically different to the anger of victims. First, exceptional as it is, Achilles' anger may not be indicative of typical third-party anger in Homer. Second, the extremes to which his anger takes him, even the severe nature of his internal experience, do not require that his emotion is in a whole new category. Perhaps no two emotional experiences are ever identical but some can be said to be similar. Thus, in Homer, just as today, a son's bad actions (*Od.* 18.227), a husband's infidelity (1.433), the blinding of a son (67) and the killing of a friend (*Il.* 16.585) all lead to emotional experiences that, though surely different, are similar enough to be described as anger or, as in these instances, *χόλος*.

Konstan has asserted that Homer does not have a term suited to Achilles' experience.[47] If so, he makes liberal use of the unsuitable terms available. Achilles' anger towards Hector is described by Zeus, Menelaus, the narrator and Achilles himself with the same vocabulary as that applied to the anger of victims – *χόλος* (*Il.* 15.68, 17.710, 18.337, 19.16, 23.23), *χώομαι* (20.29, 23.37) and *ὑπόδρα ἰδών* (20.284, 22.260, 344). Moreover, these and other anger terms are employed twenty-five more times across the two poems with reference to the emotional experiences of third parties.[48] The likeness also extends to the emotion's association with pain (*ἄχος*), which features in the anger of third parties just as in that of victims. In the stand-out example, Achilles becomes angry towards Hector, pouring dust and ashes over himself, lying in the dirt and pulling at his hair as he cries and wails (18.22–35).[49] Particularly striking is a series of battlefield revenge-killings (14.458–507) in which a pattern emerges: someone is killed, initially Prothoenor at the hands of Polydamas, and the victim's side feels pain (458, 475, 486); then a comrade seeks vengeance, missing their target but killing another foe, and vaunts about their successful act of revenge causing pain in their enemy (460–74, 476–85); finally, Peneleos brings the cycle to an end when he skewers Ilioneus' head on his spear, hacks it from his body and holds it aloft while he vaunts (487–505); instead of pain, the Trojans now feel fear, their limbs trembling, and they take flight (506–7). On the other side of vengeance, Automedon's pain at the death of Patroclus reduces with the killing of Aretus (17.538–9) while Priam expects that the pain he feels at the death or enslavement of many of his sons would leave him if Achilles were to die and be eaten by dogs and vultures (22.42–5). The anger of both victims and third parties, then, begins painfully and ends with pain's retreat.

Dishonour underpins the anger of not only direct victims but third parties too, who measure their revenge against the victim's perceived worth. For Lendon, the avenger's goal is to extract honour from enemies on behalf of their comrade so that they may be compensated for what they have lost.[50] Ajax suggests as much when, on killing Archelochus in revenge for Prothoenor, he vauntingly asks Polydamas if his victim's slaying was 'worth' Prothoenor's – a calculation he makes on the basis of the Trojan's esteemed family (*Il.* 14.470–4). Similarly, Idomeneus provocatively boasts that the three men he and Antilochus have killed make a fair exchange for Deiphobus' one victim (13.446–7). A more sincere consideration of comparative worth comes from Automedon who, while despoiling his victim, says 'a little have I relieved my heart of pain for the death of Menoetius' son, though I have killed an inferior' (17.538–9). The product of anger – revenge – appears to find its measure in the victim's perceived worth.

We have seen that the impugned worth of one individual can evoke anger in those who care about them. But it is not only the offended or killed individual whose honour is at stake for angry third parties. Achilles is clearly angry for the sake of Patroclus whom he considers to have been of great worth, but are we to conclude that the difference between Automedon (who killed a man for Patroclus and felt his pain lessen) and Achilles (who slaughtered many, Hector included, without apparently feeling any better for it) is purely in their differing appraisals of Patroclus' value? For Graham Zanker, there are two impulses at work in Achilles: his 'competitive' desire for honour over shame, and his 'affective' reaction to a lost friend.[51] The second is not dissimilar to what I have outlined above, though the implication that such a motive is not honour-driven is misleading since Achilles and other third parties do have the victim's honour in mind. And while Zanker is right to recognise the concurrent importance of the avenger's own honour, Achilles' defence of his own honour in his pursuit of Hector is surely no less 'affective' than his concern for Patroclus' honour; the emotion of anger is at work in both.

Achilles makes it clear to Hector that, though he grieves for Patroclus, he takes the Trojan's actions as a personal affront.

Ἕκτορ ἀτάρ που ἔφης Πατροκλῆ' ἐξεναρίζων
σῶς ἔσσεσθ', ἐμὲ δ' οὐδὲν ὀπίζεο νόσφιν ἐόντα
νήπιε· τοῖο δ' ἄνευθεν ἀοσσητὴρ μέγ' ἀμείνων
νηυσὶν ἔπι γλαφυρῇσιν ἐγὼ μετόπισθε λελείμμην,
ὅς τοι γούνατ' ἔλυσα· σὲ μὲν κύνες ἠδ' οἰωνοὶ
ἑλκήσουσ' ἀϊκῶς, τὸν δὲ κτεριοῦσιν Ἀχαιοί.

(*Il.* 22.331–6)

Hector, you supposed, while spoiling Patroclus,
that you would be safe; for me, who was far off, you had no regard,

you fool. Far from him a helper, far greater,
was left behind by the ships, I myself,
who have loosed your knees. You will the dogs and vultures
shamefully tear apart; him will the Achaeans bury.

According to Konstan: 'we can hardly conclude from this that Hector's act was a sign of contempt for Achilles. Warriors slaughter whom they can.'[52] Warriors may not pick victims according to whose loved ones they wish to offend, but the practice of vaunting demonstrates that killings were often treated as opportunities to show contempt, and even when boasts do not follow it is in the very nature of killing that it shows contempt for would-be avengers by communicating doubt in their ability to kill in turn. Hector himself, as he stands over his dying foe, boasts that 'Achilles, though great, did not defend you' (16.837), and, when Patroclus predicts his enemy's demise at the hands of his companion, Hector questions the prophecy, asking, 'who knows whether Achilles, lovely-haired Thetis' son, will beforehand be struck by my spear, and his spirit perish' (860–1). If contempt is the demonstration of a belief that someone is of less value, and if Achilles considers himself to be indisputably the greatest warrior, then Hector's confidence – implicit in his killing of Patroclus and now explicit in his words – shows contempt.

Achilles cares a great deal about Patroclus' honour and memory but he also sees the extent of his vengeance as a measure of his own achievement, his own worth as an avenger. Achilles says to his dead friend:

μή μοι Πάτροκλε σκυδμαινέμεν, αἴ κε πύθηαι
εἰν Ἄϊδός περ ἐὼν ὅτι Ἕκτορα δῖον ἔλυσα
πατρὶ φίλῳ, ἐπεὶ οὔ μοι ἀεικέα δῶκεν ἄποινα.
σοὶ δ' αὖ ἐγὼ καὶ τῶνδ' ἀποδάσσομαι ὅσσ' ἐπέοικεν.

(*Il.* 24.592–5)

Do not be angry with me Patroclus, if you learn,
though you are in Hades, that I have released heavenly Hector
to his dear father, for the ransom he gave me is not shameful.
And from it I will give to you what is fitting.

Through his rampage and eventual killing of Hector, Achilles aims to reclaim the honour of Patroclus, but he also seeks and receives glory and fame for himself.[53] If Achilles' revenge is partly to reclaim his friend's honour, partly his own, then this division of spoils represents that dual-purpose in material terms.

This can also be seen from another perspective. Apollo, appearing as Hector's companion, Asius, says:

Ἕκτορ τίς κέ σ' ἔτ' ἄλλος Ἀχαιῶν ταρβήσειεν;
οἷον δὴ Μενέλαον ὑπέτρεσας, ὃς τὸ πάρος γε
μαλθακὸς αἰχμητής· νῦν δ' οἴχεται οἷος ἀείρας
νεκρὸν ὑπ' ἐκ Τρώων, σὸν δ' ἔκτανε πιστὸν ἑταῖρον
ἐσθλὸν ἐνὶ προμάχοισι Ποδῆν υἱὸν Ἠετίωνος.

(*Il.* 17.586–90)

Hector, what other of the Achaeans will be frightened of you now?
You having shrunk back so before Menelaus, who formerly was a
soft spearman. Now he goes single-handedly having taken
a body away from among the Trojans; he has killed your trusted companion,
brave among the front-fighters, Podes son of Eetion.

Homer magnifies Hector's failing by introducing Podes as Hector's companion whom he values above all others and with whom he shares his table (576–7). The man has been killed, his body dragged away by his enemy whose intention is no doubt to leave him out as carrion, and yet Apollo does not appeal to Hector on the basis of pity for his friend. Rather, Hector is encouraged to consider whether his enemies will still see him as a threat. The dishonour suffered by Podes is highlighted only as a mark against Hector's name: he is supposedly Troy's best, but one of those closest to him has been killed and dishonoured by an unexceptional, unassisted Achaean and no vengeance has followed.[54] The harming or killing of one's own can be a slight because it impugns one's strength, and until that doubt is banished the damage to reputation remains.

None of this is to say that there is no difference between the experience of anger for victims and third parties. Even if experientially similar, they are doubtless felt in contexts of differing social expectation. Failure to avenge oneself is perhaps less shameful than failure to avenge a loved one. What is crucial here though is the conclusion that third-party avengers are motivated by an emotion that is rooted in pain at an offence against oneself or those for whom one cares, and that aims at the reclamation of honour.

The bond between victim and avenger does not need to be especially close. The harming of a brother (*Il.* 16.319–21), child (24.584), or parent (*Od.* 17.489–91) is sure to evoke anger, and the tie of kinship reaches further to draw in avengers from among maternal brothers-in-law (*Il.* 13.464; cf.468–69), and agnatic second cousins (*Od.* 16.115–20). Beyond blood and marriage, the harming of companions (*Il.* 4.494, 501), retainers (15.436–41) and guest-friends (13.660–1) also stirs up the desire for revenge. Often, however, those who fall in battle are not surrounded by family and friends and the responsibility for revenge falls to others. Polydamas, having killed and vaunted over Prothoenor, is said to have caused pain to come upon the Argives 'and stirred most the spirit in wise-hearted Ajax, son of Telamon, because he had fallen closest to him' (14.458–60). The Argives in general feel pain simply because they are on the same side as Prothoenor, and Ajax (who has no formal connection to Prothoenor and appears not even to be of the same contingent; 2.494–5, 557) is most moved purely because he is closest by. Again, the Myrmidons, Glaucus assumes, are seeking to mutilate Sarpedon's corpse in their anger over the Lycians' killing of 'the Danaans'. (16.544–7). Friends and family play an important role in seeking justice on behalf of their loved ones, but the reach of anger can also extend to the wider community, stirring the group to avenge the wrongs suffered by its members.

It is not just external enemies that unite the community in vengeful anger. Away from the battlefield, the Ithacans, 'extremely angry' (*κεχολώατο λίην*) with Eupeithes for his part in the raiding of the Thesprotians with whom the Ithacans were in league, would have destroyed him but for Odysseus' intervention (*Od.* 16.425–9). Eupeithes' offence has not harmed any particular individuals within his own community; rather, his actions are offensive to the city he has attacked and all those that count themselves among its allies. The community itself (*δῆμος*) is the angry victim here, and those seeking Eupeithes' death are united by their membership of that community. In the Homeric community's capacity to take offence as a group, feel anger and seek revenge, we see the presence of a key ingredient to the emergence of the state.[55]

Moral outrage

Until recently, psychologists understood moral outrage to be at issue when third parties felt angry, but evidence has begun to accrue demonstrating that the anger a third party feels at wrongdoing increases according to the degree to which they care for the victim.[56] This has led some to question how much moral outrage is a product of the perception that someone has crossed a shared 'moral' line and how much it is simply a product of personal offence. Could it simply be that the outraged individual perceives an offence against a third party to whom they consider themselves linked, however remotely? Indeed, whether moral outrage exists at all or is simply a rhetorical construct has become a matter of debate.[57] We shall see that while Homeric society certainly recognises something akin to moral outrage, the offence must nevertheless be a slight against the angry individual or a person for whom they care in order for anger to follow.

The most discussed Homeric term for anger is *μῆνις*, and a feature of its usage that invites explanation is its unequal distribution between mortals and immortals. For many, this term's pattern of usage suggests a divine or religious quality.[58] Across the two epics there are thirty-five occurrences of the terms: *μῆνις*, *μηνίω*, *μηνιθμός* and *μήνιμα*. As a group, the distribution is fairly even – twenty instances describe the anger of mortals, fifteen that of gods. The verb, however, is used of mortals thirteen times and of the gods only once, while the simple noun *μῆνις* is used of mortals only four times, the gods, twelve.[59] This suggests a preference of some sort but the four uses of the noun for mortals undermine the notion that this is a kind of anger peculiar to the gods. The wrinkle, though, is that in each of these four cases the mortal in question is Achilles. By claiming Achilles' anger as exceptional, some scholars have made the case for seeing *μῆνις* as a special kind of anger felt only by gods. These arguments do not hold up. Johannes Irmscher has linked Achilles' supposedly divine anger to his semi-divine parentage.[60] But Achilles is far from the only child of a deity, and the children of gods, though they sometimes receive special treatment, do not have entirely different emotions. Patrick Considine presents one argument that emphasises Zeus' 'identification of himself with Achilles' cause' based on the god's likening of their two destructive goals (*Il.* 15.68–73), and another that highlights Achilles' indifference towards death as a point of similarity with the immortals.[61] The first can be dismissed because Achilles' anger towards Hector (to which Zeus refers) is never described as *μῆνις*, and the second because Achilles' actual *μῆνις*, towards Agamemnon, does not put him in danger at all but ensures his safety at great risk to all others. There is no reason to suppose that Achilles' anger is peculiarly divine.[62]

Jenny Strauss Clay has reasoned that *ὀδύσσομαι*, the rarest of our seven terms, corresponds to *μῆνις* because it too is mostly limited to immortals.[63] This conclusion stands on a weak footing for several reasons. Assuming, for argument's sake, that these two terms do indeed both relate exclusively to gods, it does not follow that their meanings correlate any more than, for example, *χόλος* and *κότος*. In fact, though there are several instances where *ὀδύσσομαι* appears to describe an experience that is also denoted by one of the more common anger terms, never is that term *μῆνις*.[64] Even the link they are both thought to share with the divine is undermined not only by Achilles in the case of *μῆνις* but also by Autolycus (*Od.* 19.407) in that of *ὀδύσσομαι*. Ultimately, there being only nine occurrences in Homer and Hesiod, the precise meaning of this term is obscure, and there is certainly no reason to suppose it correlates entirely with *μῆνις*, but the examples available do not suggest any conflict with Aristotle's definition.

Alongside the notion that *μῆνις* belongs to the gods is the associated idea that it has unique negative qualities. For Calvert Watkins, the absence of individuals referring to their own *μῆνις* indicates a taboo around the term, while for James Redfield this suggests merely that it is dangerous to its subject.[65] It is far from clear, however, that Achilles' anger was viewed negatively by others. Achilles' anger is understood to be *μῆνις* not only by Homer but by Achilles' comrades as well (*Il.* 9.517, 19.74–5). If he is behaving like a god rather than a mortal, then it is surprising to see no criticism, or even mention, of this. For all that he is accused of being too proud or told that he should accept payment, these criticisms come only after he has turned down Agamemnon's gifts; indeed, Phoenix affirms that in the absence of a sincere offer Achilles' continued *μῆνις* would be appropriate (9.523).

We must also account for the fact that the verb is not exclusive to Achilles among mortals. A particular emotion's noun and verb may, by virtue of their differing grammatical functions, highlight different parts of an emotional experience, but we would nevertheless say that those who 'rage' have or feel 'rage' and those who 'fear' have or feel 'fear'.[66] In the case of Achilles, as with several gods, all would presumably accept that when he *μηνίει,* he has or feels *μῆνις*, and yet are we to conclude that the four other mortals to whom the verb is attributed are experiencing something different?[67] Intriguing though the peculiar distribution of nouns and verbs is, it does not prove that they refer to different kinds of anger; the evidence is better explained by treating the concept as consistent. We shall see that, though there are sometimes significant differences between the contexts surrounding *μῆνις* among mortals and immortals, it is personal insult that leads both groups to anger.[68]

As Muellner has said, *μῆνις* 'is incurred by the breaking of basic religious and social tabus'.[69] All instances of *μῆνις* can be attributed to one of the following categories:[70] disobeying established authority, disrespecting subordinates by taking away gifts they have been given or failing to bestow proper honours on them, breaking a vow, desecrating a sacrifice, dishonouring a priest, mistreating a host or guest, failing to provide burial rites to one's own and attempted murder.[71] Unlike the common notion that *μῆνις* stands out on the grounds of severity or intensity, the link to taboo offers an explanation for certain instances that are conspicuous for never being called *μῆνις*.[72] Two that stand out are those of Achilles, who, despite his anger towards Agamemnon being described as *μῆνις* sixteen times, is never said to feel it towards Hector, and Poseidon towards Odysseus for the blinding of Polyphemus. The need for the provocation to be taboo would explain why the killing of an enemy in war and the blinding of the killer and devourer of one's companions, though severe, would not qualify. However, if *μῆνις* indicates the flouting of social norms, then it becomes necessary to explore whether this represents an anger beyond Aristotle's definition, a 'moral outrage' that anyone might feel regardless of their personal connection.

That *μῆνις* also requires a personal offence is implied by the fact that it is typically felt not by groups of people over a particular wrongdoing but by slighted individuals. One context in which we see *μῆνις* arise similarly in mortals and immortals is in disobedience to authority. Agamemnon's anger (*ἐμήνιε*; *Il.* 1.247) follows Achilles' swearing on oath that he will no longer fight for him (225–44), while it is for fear of Zeus' *μῆνις* that Athena on one occasion leaves the battle with Ares (5.34) and on another holds him back from returning to it (15.122).[73] Disobeying a ruler both breaks a social norm and offends that ruler.[74]

Similarly, gods in general can feel *μῆνις* at mortals who show disregard for their power. Diomedes and Patroclus both attempt three times to overcome Apollo despite it being clear whom they are up against. Diomedes attempts to kill Aeneas though he sees Apollo's hands over him (*Il.* 5.432–8) and Patroclus tries to mount the wall of Troy though Apollo forces him back (16.698–705). Both are warned verbally on the fourth attempt and retreat to avoid the god's *μῆνις* (5.444, 16.711). Notably, Agamemnon's anger at Achilles (1.247) is the only example of a mortal experiencing *μῆνις* over disobedience, though others can be frustrated or angered by those who stand in their way. Likewise, Zeus is the only god who feels it towards other gods. It seems that disobedience evokes *μῆνις* only in those who ought to have been obeyed.[75]

But *μῆνις* can also be felt towards a superior, and Achilles is not our only example. Aeneas' experience with *μῆνις* serves as something of a potted version of Achilles'. He stands at the edge of battle in anger (*ἐπεμήνιε*) at Priam's failure to honour him (*Il.* 13.459–61). Then, informed that his brother-in-law has been killed, his spirit is stirred (468) and he enters the battle in order to defend the body of, and seek to avenge, the deceased. Aeneas' anger is rooted in Priam's failure to honour him properly and Achilles' is rooted in Agamemnon's forceful appropriation of a gift with which he had been honoured. Achilles asserts that such an act is 'unbecoming' even before he has been singled out (1.126) and Agamemnon accepts that it will result in someone's anger (139). Again, these are acts that flout social norms but the only ones to become angry are those whom the acts offend.

Within Homeric society, certain social norms are believed to be protected by the gods so that to flout them is to show contempt for the gods' power. Sometimes gods can be angered by acts that directly affect them such as the breaking of a vow (*Il.* 1.93), desecrating of a sacrifice (5.178), or insulting of their priest (1.75). That all these acts produce *μῆνις* suggests that they do not simply offend the god but they do so through the breaking of a social norm. Apollo feels *μῆνις* towards the Achaeans while Poseidon does not towards Odysseus and his men because Chryses is a priest and Polyphemus is not. Just as offences against a priest of Apollo imply an insult against the god himself, so offences against guests and hosts imply an insult towards Zeus, who feels *μῆνις* when the Trojans steal from their host (13.624) and would feel the same were the king of the Egyptians not to protect his suppliant (*Od.* 14.283). Of all the gods, only one is angered by such acts and he, Zeus *ξείνιος*, is known to watch over such interactions. These acts offend Zeus personally because they are implicit demonstrations of contempt for his capacity to enforce the standards associated with guest-host relationships.[76]

Another norm under divine protection is the obligation to ensure burial rites for one's people. Elpenor urges Odysseus to return to his corpse and provide burial rites 'lest I become a *μήνιμα* of the gods for you' (*Od.* 11.72–8). This apparent obligation to ensure the burial of one's friends and comrades rests also on Achilles' shoulders and, while Patroclus employs pity to motivate Achilles to bury him (*Il.* 23.69–92), Elpenor opts for fear with Odysseus. Burial obligations, then, were enforced by fear of the gods' anger and the attendant community pressure.

For many, the similar example relating to Hector's body demonstrates that the obligation, at least to respect the dead, stretched to foe as well as friend.[77] Hector warns Achilles, who has just refused to return his expiring body for burial, to 'take care lest I become a *μήνιμα* of the gods upon you on the day when Paris and Phoebus Apollo destroy you, though you are brave, in the Scaean gates' (*Il.* 22.358–60). But the notion that the gods were offended by attempts to prevent an enemy's burial is refuted by several other examples. We are told in the *Iliad*'s proem that the Achaeans becoming the food for dogs and birds is part of the fulfilment of Zeus' plan (1.4–5). This is not merely symbolic of their destruction; the threat to bring an opponent's body back to the ships or the city as carrion for dogs or birds is made and carried out many times.[78] The theme of mutilation runs throughout and, lest we suppose that the disfigured bodies might nevertheless be afforded proper burial rites, that is clearly not what Hector plans for Patroclus (17.126–7) nor Euphorbus for Menelaus (38–40). The *μῆνις* that Achilles may incur is not to do with the mistreatment simply of *a* body but of *Hector*'s body.[79] Zeus makes this clear when he intervenes for the sake of Hector whom the gods loved, who was the greatest in Troy and who never failed in his sacrifices (24.66–70).[80]

According to Naoko Yamagata, Hector's prophecy that he will become a *μήνιμα* of the gods for Achilles 'soon comes true', but if it does (and it may not) it is not especially soon.[81] Some of the gods certainly care about Hector, but they are not said to feel anger towards Achilles until he has been desecrating Hector's corpse for twelve days already. Zeus at least appears unlikely to have been angry at first, given that it was for the working of shame (*ἀεικίσσασθαι*) upon Hector that he gave him to his enemies (*Il.* 22.403–4). Moreover, when at last their anger is mentioned, the gods are not said to feel *μῆνις* towards Achilles but to *σκύζεσθαί* at him and *κεχολῶσθαι* that he holds Hector by the ships and does not release him (24.114-15; cf. 134–5). It may not be the case, therefore, that we have here a fulfilment of Hector's prophecy; *μῆνις* may not be felt at all. Rather, Apollo's proposed warning to Achilles that he should take care not to become an object of blame (*νεμεσσηθῶμεν*) for the gods (53) implies that, though some of them are angry at him now, things could be worse for him. I would suggest that the *μῆνις* Hector warned of will be roused if Achilles persists in his mutilation ritual despite the gods' warning. The provocation at issue here is one of disobedience rather than the mutilation of an enemy's body. Achilles' actions bear similarities to those, already mentioned, of Diomedes and Patroclus in that his goal of destroying Hector's body and giving it to the dogs as food is conspicuously thwarted by Apollo and, in this instance, Aphrodite (23.182–91). Between them they drive the dogs away day and night and protect the corpse from harm.[82] For twelve days, despite obvious supernatural interference, which his mother surely observes (24.72–3), and no deterioration to the body, Achilles persists in his routine. The *μῆνις* Hector anticipates is rooted in the contempt Achilles shows for the gods' implicit, and soon to be explicit, wishes.

Blaming the community

A thread linking several instances of *μῆνις* is the tendency for the punishment to engulf more than those responsible for the wrongdoing. For Muellner, 'offenses that incur [*μῆνις*] are by nature group offenses'.[83] Menelaus, while despoiling Peisander's corpse, talks to his victim in plurals, stating that they ('you', plural) maltreated him, did not fear the hard *μῆνις* of Zeus and left, leading away his wife and possessions, despite having been hosted by Helen (*Il.* 13.623–7). At face value, Menelaus suggests that Zeus is angry with the Trojans in general for the actions of Paris, and this is not merely the hyperbole of an aggrieved man. Athena fears that should Ares return to battle at the death of his son, the *μῆνις* of

Zeus would fall on all the immortals, 'both those guilty and those not.' (15.122–37). It is considered possible that the whole Achaean army might suffer from Apollo's *μῆνις* over a broken vow or failed offering (1.93, cf. 5.178) and the real cause – the dishonouring of Chryses – is performed by Agamemnon alone in direct opposition to the desires of the rest of the Achaeans (1.22–3) through whom the plague will spread. The culprit's community can, despite having no involvement in, or even awareness of, the wrongdoing, become an object of anger nonetheless.

Aside from the *Iliad*'s proem, Achilles' anger is first given the name of *μῆνις* by Thetis who advises him 'to be angry at the Achaeans, staying away from all war' (*μήνί Ἀχαιοῖσιν, πολέμου δ' ἀποπαύεο πάμπαν*; *Il.* 1.422).[84] However, there remains a difference between Agamemnon's status and that of the wider community with respect to Achilles. While his relationship with Agamemnon is no longer one of friendship (16.282), he welcomes the embassy calling them '*φίλοι*. . . who even in my anger are dearest of the Achaeans' (9.197–8).[85] Moreover, the reconciliations proposed in Book Nine and carried out in Book Nineteen are transactions between the two men only with the wider community observing, helping to guide the process and assisting with the gifts.[86] The proem outlines the way that these three parties relate:

> *μῆνιν ἄειδε θεὰ Πηληϊάδεω Ἀχιλῆος*
> *οὐλομένην, ἣ μυρί' Ἀχαιοῖς ἄλγε' ἔθηκε,*
> *πολλὰς δ' ἰφθίμους ψυχὰς Ἄϊδι προΐαψεν*
> *ἡρώων, αὐτοὺς δὲ ἑλώρια τεῦχε κύνεσσιν*
> *οἰωνοῖσί τε πᾶσι, Διὸς δ' ἐτελείετο βουλή,*
> *ἐξ οὗ δὴ τὰ πρῶτα διαστήτην ἐρίσαντε*
> *Ἀτρεΐδης τε ἄναξ ἀνδρῶν καὶ δῖος Ἀχιλλεύς.*
>
> *Il.* 1.1–7

> Sing, goddess, the destructive anger of Achilles, son of Peleus
> which put pains on countless Achaeans,
> and sent to Hades many strong souls
> of heroes, and made them spoil for dogs
> and all birds, and the plan of Zeus was fulfilled,
> from when first they parted in conflict
> the son of Atreus, lord of men, and brilliant Achilles.

The conflict belongs to the two men while the consequent suffering belongs to the Achaeans, a common *μῆνις* theme. The incongruence between Thetis' instruction to her son to *μήνί Ἀχαιοῖσιν*, and the apparent absence of enmity between him and anyone but Agamemnon, is compounded by the fact that while anger terms are employed to describe Achilles' disposition towards Agamemnon forty-five times, Thetis's instruction is the only instance in which the Achaeans appear as an object. Seemingly, though Agamemnon is the target of Achilles' anger, both Thetis and her son recognise that his actions will affect the whole community.[87]

It will not do simply to group the entire community with the perpetrator as similar objects of *μῆνις* in every instance. Sometimes it appears indiscriminate, sometimes focused on the offender and sometimes, as with Achilles, somewhere in between.[88] To break a social norm is to ask the community if it will stand for such behaviour. Achilles certainly seems to think such a discourse is active as he, reacting to Agamemnon's threat, asks how any of the Achaeans can be expected to obey him now, whether going on a journey or entering battle (*Il.* 1.150–1).[89] Realising from the lack of support that their decision has gone against him (or at least has failed to go *for* him), Achilles tells Agamemnon that if the people he ruled were not 'nobodies', he would have committed his last outrage (231–2). The other Achaeans do not join in insulting Achilles – indeed their wish was for Agamemnon to accept Chryses' original gift (22–3) – but neither do they condemn one who broke their norms in offending him.

Similarly, the Ithacans fail to act against the suitors when called upon in the assembly and instead simply leave for home (*Od.* 2.257–8), thus they ought all to fear the *μῆνις* of the gods for the suitors' evil deeds (91). In such instances, the person who feels *μῆνις* is at odds not only with their offender, but with the community that fails to condemn that offender.[90] I suggest that it is the taboo nature of the provocation that creates the potential for anger's wide expression, and it is the nature of the community's response that determines whether that potential will be realised.

We have seen that the wider community can become the subject of anger, feeling offended at slights that dishonour the group; we see now that it can also become anger's object. The community is supposed to take action to condemn and resist certain kinds of norm-breaking behaviour. The potential for victims to become angry at a community that fails in this, along with the belief that the gods who watch over those norms will be angered too, point to an expectation that the community will perform some of the functions of what we would call a state. It should manifest anger and inflict punishment for offences against itself, whilst condemning and forcefully restraining those who offend others in the community in ways that contravene social norms. To do otherwise is to fail in its duty and endorse the slight.

Conclusion

Aristotle's definition of anger is as well suited to Homer as he implied. Homer's characters become angry in a variety of social contexts and for many different reasons, but beneath them all is a perception that they have been dishonoured and a desire for redress. In both these areas, however, Homer reveals details that this succinct definition leaves unclarified. Those who perceive that they have suffered dishonour seek, and usually find, a blameworthy agent on whom they can look to take vengeance, but there are also rare occasions when they realise that they have none to blame but themselves and, like Agamemnon, they 'tear at the spirit within'. And Homer's vocabulary affords him the ability to clarify whether the angry individual is driven towards vengeance by a painful compulsion (*χόλος*) or has since adopted the disposition of a grudge and is awaiting the opportunity to strike (*κότος*).

The anger of third parties also conforms to Aristotle in that the dishonouring of a loved one evokes anger, just as the dishonouring of the self does. However, we again find extra nuance in that the anger of the loved one is rooted in dishonour suffered not only by the victim, but also by the angry individual at their failure to protect or, as yet, avenge. Indeed, third-party anger and victim anger are frequently beyond disentanglement in Homer's avengers. This capacity to feel anger at the suffering of one's own, as Aristotle puts it, can have very broad reach. The close ties of family and friends result invariably in third-party anger, but the bond of identity shared by members of the same group can also be strong, especially in the absence of the more closely bound. In this way anger can at times spread to incorporate the wider community.

The term *μῆνις* enables Homer to unite the concepts of 'moral outrage' and personal anger. This emotion is triggered by the perception that a social norm has been broken but is only felt by those whom that behaviour personally offends. Here, however, the members of the community again have a role, not as those who feel anger, but as those towards whom it can be felt. The breaking of a social norm obliges the rest of that community to decide whether or not to condemn the act. In Achilles' case, they fail to do so and therefore come to share with Agamemnon in suffering Achilles' wrath.

It is no surprise that Aristotle looked to Homer to illustrate his definition of anger; epic is as detailed an exploration of the nature of anger as any in Greek literature. But it is also a warning against overstating the differences between the Homeric world and that of Aristotle. The cultural changes that occurred between the early archaic period and late-classical Athens were significant, particularly in the area of dispute settlement. But beneath those cultural changes lay continuity in terms of the essential features of the emotion of anger. Aristotle was attempting to educate public speakers in how best to inspire or assuage anger in the assembly or courtroom – decidedly different settings from the Trojan beach or the house of Odysseus – and yet he made Homeric heroes his reference point because, just as Achilles' desire for revenge was rooted in the perception that he or his own had been personally slighted, so would the Athenian juror be persuaded to punish if he believed he or the *polis* with which he identified had been slighted.

2

Revenge and the Community in Homeric Society

Introduction

We have seen that the community looms large over the emotion of anger in Homer. In terms of causation, the presence of a wider audience and the manner of their response influence the victim's perception of a slight. And the community is no less relevant with regard to the way in which that emotion is expressed. Anger's interest is in the restoration of honour but what that means in practice is a many-layered picture because, in the Homeric community, honour could be won and lost in a great many ways and simply inflicting harm in response to harm was but one of several options that lay before the slighted.

Like all kinds of reciprocity, revenge is under the influence of time, and while it is fundamentally interested in retribution for the remembered slight(s) of the past, it can also have interest in the deterrence of potential slights of the future. The complementary nature of these two punitive goals has been recognised for a long time, but Homer offers an insight into why this primarily backward-looking behaviour had consequences that reached into the future and affected the avenger's relationship with the community as a whole.

For all that anger desires it, though, we cannot assume that revenge is the only path out of wrath. If anger drives the coercive reclamation of honour from the unapologetic offender, how does it respond to the contrite? Homeric examples of apology and compensation offer a window into how, for those who longed to retaliate, prosocial values can offer a different way forward. Revenge often affects more than the two parties involved, and, with the wider community looking on, can a cooperative approach offer reputational rewards that outweigh the honour to be reclaimed through revenge?

A final option that presents itself to the slighted is to forgo satisfaction altogether. Do Homeric heroes deserve their reputation for uncompromising vengefulness? Various emotions and priorities compete to influence decisions and, however strong the drive of anger, there is no reason to assume that it was always dominant. In the context of a community with its own interests and expectations, rather than risking further reputational damage, is it not sometimes best to cut one's losses?

Retribution and deterrence

Anger's primary aim is to reclaim honour. Whether over a slight towards self, friend, relative, or fellow group-member, anger drives acts of retribution that reassert the victim's worth. The measure of revenge that retribution demands depends partly on the precise substance of the offence – be it physical harm, theft, verbal insult or something else – but that is only the surface of a far deeper issue. Notably, Achilles does not want merely to receive Briseis back, nor even is he satisfied by the prospect of seven more women and a great many other gifts besides. Rather, the wealth and lives that have been taken, the injuries and insults inflicted, are only the starting point for a calculation that must also account for three important factors: the relative status of the two parties; intent; and the presence of an audience.[1]

When the gods take revenge on mortals, proportion is almost irrelevant. Helios goes to Zeus, the god who guarantees straight justice among mortals (e.g. *Il.* 16.384–8), in search of help dealing with Odysseus' companions who have killed and eaten his cattle, and Zeus' response is not to see that the men replace the cattle but to step in himself and strike their ship with bolts of lightning, killing them all in an act of *τίσις* ('revenge'; *Od.* 12.374–419).[2] There is, of course, nothing surprising about the gods carrying out harsh reprisals on mortals who cross them, but this is merely an extreme example of a principle that impacts on acts of vengeance throughout epic. The anger of gods towards mortals is somewhat analogous to the anger of rulers towards lesser men, as described by Calchas (*Il.* 1.80–3): it is felt more easily, held on to for longer and expressed more harshly according to the offender's perceived inferiority. Odysseus finds cause to scowl at the very best (Agamemnon; 4.349) and the very worst (Thersites; 2.249) of the Achaeans, but with the former he merely trades insults (4.350–5) while the latter he savagely beats (2.245–68). Status differential affects how much dishonour a slight conveys and how much revenge it demands in return.

Some have questioned the importance of intent in the Homeric world. Most notably, Adkins claims that in Homer one is judged according to one's actions and inherited status, whereas 'intentions are almost irrelevant'.[3] However, while intent may not be the most significant factor of all, there can be no doubt that it is relevant to how people's actions are judged, and to the emotional responses they evoke. The verb *φρονέω* is frequently employed to communicate the spirit in which deeds are performed. Calchus, for example, addresses the assembly with 'good intent' (*ἐῢ φρονέων*; *Il.* 1.73), a phrase that describes the mindset of public speakers on fifteen occasions.[4] The adjective *ἑκών* and the verb *ἐθέλω* are used several times to describe the volition behind a given action and impact on the degree of offence taken. Menelaus demands Antilochus swear that he did not 'willingly' (*ἑκών*) use guile to cut off his chariot in the race (*Il.* 23.585).[5] Likewise, as Anthony Long has highlighted, Odysseus' contrasting opinions of the Phaeacians and the Phoenicians, two groups of sailors who failed to take him where they promised, depend on his belief that the former have been deceitful (*Od.* 13.209–12), while the latter were led off course unwillingly (*οὐδ' ἤθελον*) by the weather (276–7).[6] It is therefore against the former only that he hopes for revenge, saying 'let Zeus, the god of suppliants, have revenge (*τίσαιτο*) on them' (213–14).[7]

Offence can also result from a lack of intent. Though ignorance might excuse the actions of some, for those who offend the gods it offers little insulation against reprisals. During the plague, Achilles gathers the people to consult a seer 'who can say why Phoebus Apollo is so angry, whether for the sake of some vow he blames us or for a hecatomb' (*Il.* 1.62–5). It is likely, according to Achilles, that they have caused offence without knowing it, let alone intending it. Similarly, Aeneas fears that a god may be fighting against the Trojans, angry over an offering, but evidently neither he nor perhaps any of the other sufferers knows what they have done wrong (5.177–8).[8] Artemis' destruction of Oeneus' orchard, regardless of whether his failure to sacrifice to her was knowingly or forgetfully done, points to the reasoning behind the gods' disinterest in intent (9.537). In a relationship as unequal as this one, the failure to meet one's deferential obligations is as insulting as an intentional slight. We might infer a similar category of offence from mortals who fail to show appropriate deference towards their superiors.

The minds of the angry are primarily focused on the relationship between themselves and their offenders, but this interaction occurs in a broader social context. Whatever the status of the offender and the intention behind the act, the response will be informed by considerations of how the interaction is perceived by the wider community because the victim is aware not only that the perpetrator thought too little of them, but also that this appraisal was communicated to all who witnessed the slight or will come to hear of it. Achilles, in whose recollection Agamemnon's original insult is defined by the presence of the Argives (*Il.* 9.646–7), wants to reassert his worth not only to Agamemnon, but to everyone.

Reputations can be left hanging in the balance in the interim between offence and revenge. As Achilles says of his desire to kill Hector:

> *οὐδ' ἐμὲ θυμὸς ἄνωγε*
> *ζώειν οὐδ' ἄνδρεσσι μετέμμεναι, αἴ κε μὴ Ἕκτωρ*
> *πρῶτος ἐμῷ ὑπὸ δουρὶ τυπεὶς ἀπὸ θυμὸν ὀλέσσῃ,*
> *Πατρόκλοιο δ' ἕλωρα Μενοιτιάδεω ἀποτίσῃ.*
>
> (*Il.* 18.90–3)

> My spirit leads me neither
> to live nor abide among men, unless Hector
> first, beaten down by my spear, loses his life,
> and pays for spoiling Patroclus, Menoetius' son.

For Achilles, living in community with others is unthinkable while Patroclus' killer lives. Similarly, Eupeithes anticipates that he and the other suitors' relatives will need to cast their eyes downward forever if they do not take revenge on Odysseus and Telemachus (*Od.* 24.432–6). As he expires, Sarpedon tells his companion, Glaucus, to defend his corpse from despoliation and that his failure to do so will be a source of shame and reproach for the rest of his life (*Il.* 16.498–501). Glaucus, in the presence of other Trojan leaders, shares the burden of shame with Hector (531–47) who, in anger, leads the Trojans against those who have killed and would now despoil and mutilate Sarpedon. It is not only anger that drives those who would avenge the dead, but also the pressure of the community's expectation.

The social expectation that accompanies revenge also offers the positive opportunity of winning prestige. Orestes is said to have won 'fame among all people' for his slaying of Aegisthus in revenge for Agamemnon's murder (*Od.* 1.298–300), and Telemachus is urged to plot the deaths of the suitors, by guile or in public, for their attempts at marrying his mother and their devouring of his property, in order that even those not yet born would speak well of him (294–302). The community expects the slighted to avenge themselves and their loved-ones, and the fulfilment of that expectation can greatly enhance one's standing within the group. The desire for revenge is fundamentally rooted in anger and its goal is retribution, but within that context other emotions can also become involved: the shame of failure on the one hand, and the hope of glory on the other.

While revenge seeks retribution above all, it also has a deterrent function, an idea first theorised in evolutionary terms by Herbert Spencer:

> the practice, alike of immediate revenge and of postponed revenge, establishes itself as in some measure a check upon aggression; since the motive to aggress is checked by the consciousness that a counter-aggression will come: if not at once then after a time.[9]

This function is now widely recognised as an important check on potential (re)aggressors, be they the initial offender or others who witness or hear of the revenge, particularly in societies where self-help is the main avenue to justice.[10] In Homer too, the deterrence of future offence is clearly present alongside retribution for past wrongs in the goals of avengers.[11] And, like retribution, deterrence is a goal rooted in anger and aware of the community.

Homer's characters appreciate revenge's deterrent effect. Calchas has felt, or observed others feeling, the brunt of a ruler's anger and consequently perceives rulers as men whom one ought to avoid offending (*Il.* 1.74–83). He appears even to have suffered Agamemnon's anger before as the latter indicates when he rails against him for his record of bad news (106–8). It is not only Calchas but, as Odysseus warns, all the Achaeans who need to be careful of Agamemnon's anger.

> *μή τι χολωσάμενος ῥέξῃ κακὸν υἷας Ἀχαιῶν·*
> *θυμὸς δὲ μέγας ἐστὶ διοτρεφέων βασιλήων,*
> *τιμὴ δ' ἐκ Διός ἐστι, φιλεῖ δέ ἑ μητίετα Ζεύς.*
>
> (*Il.* 2.195–7)

> Let him not in anger do evil to the sons of the Achaeans.
> Great is the spirit of god-supported rulers,
> and their honour is from Zeus, and Zeus the counsellor loves them.

Everyone is assumed to know, or is at least being told, that the anger of Agamemnon is greatly to be feared. Past performance in the expression of one's anger could bear fruit as a deterrent to future would-be offenders.

The deterrent potential of punishment is well understood by Zeus who reminds Hera of how he once avenged himself on her for her treatment of Heracles.

> *ἦ οὐ μέμνῃ ὅτε τ' ἐκρέμω ὑψόθεν, ἐκ δὲ ποδοῖιν*
> *ἄκμονας ἧκα δύω, περὶ χερσὶ δὲ δεσμὸν ἴηλα*
> *χρύσεον ἄρρηκτον; σὺ δ' ἐν αἰθέρι καὶ νεφέλῃσιν*
> *ἐκρέμω· ἠλάστεον δὲ θεοὶ κατὰ μακρὸν Ὄλυμπον,*
> *λῦσαι δ' οὐκ ἐδύναντο παρασταδόν· ὃν δὲ λάβοιμι*
> *ῥίπτασκον τεταγὼν ἀπὸ βηλοῦ ὄφρ' ἂν ἵκηται*

γῆν ὀλιγηπελέων·
...
τῶν σ' αὖτις μνήσω ἵν' ἀπολλήξῃς ἀπατάων.

(*Il.* 15.18–24, 31)

Do you not remember when you were hung aloft, from your feet
I suspended two anvils, and about your hands I threw an unbreakable chain
of gold? And in the sky and the clouds
you hung, while the gods about tall Olympus were indignant,
but standing by they were not able to release you, for whoever I caught
I threw from the threshold until he landed
on the earth, powerless.
...
Of these things I will remind you again that you should desist from deceptions.

Zeus knows that by reminding others of how comprehensively and irresistibly he has avenged himself in the past, he can inspire compliance in the present. His incredulity at Hera's recent disobedience also demonstrates that he takes for granted that the gods will consider his record as a punisher before they act against him. Zeus is evidently aware of the deterrent function of revenge – he even exploits it in retrospect – but this does not necessarily mean that Homer's audience might punish primarily with such an aim in mind. Indeed, Zeus' original motivation was the pain he felt at Heracles' suffering (24–5); evidently the primary goal of his punishment was to extract payment for the past harm. Whether he had the future in mind at all is unclear, but he appears to view the power of deterrence as resting in Hera's appreciation of how ruthlessly he pursues retribution.[12] In other words, if a punisher wants to deter slights in the future, they had better effect an intimidating degree of anger about slights in the past.

It may be that in most instances the minds of punishers are not on the future and that the deterrent quality of their actions is only appreciated later, but there are also occasions where deterrence is foreseen, hoped for and sought. The beggar Odysseus advises the swineherd Eumaeus that if it is discovered that he, Odysseus, has lied then he should throw him from a great rock 'so that another beggar would avoid cheating you' (*Od.* 14.398–400). In order to deter would-be exploiters from seeking hospitality in exchange for invented stories about Odysseus' whereabouts, the swineherd ought to take this opportunity to make an example of such a person.

It is perhaps easier to focus on deterrence when the offence is as yet hypothetical, but when anger is roused it is desert and retribution that become prominent. However, even in the heat of battle, and when preparing to throw a spear at his hated enemy, Menelaus is able to pray,

> *Ζεῦ ἄνα δὸς τίσασθαι ὅ με πρότερος κάκ' ἔοργε*
> *δῖον Ἀλέξανδρον, καὶ ἐμῆς ὑπὸ χερσὶ δάμασσον,*
> *ὄφρα τις ἐρρίγῃσι καὶ ὀψιγόνων ἀνθρώπων*
> *ξεινοδόκον κακὰ ῥέξαι, ὅ κεν φιλότητα παράσχῃ.*
>
> (*Il.* 3.351–4)

> Lord Zeus, grant that I may avenge myself on him who first wronged me,
> brilliant Alexander, and overpower him beneath my hands,
> that any of those men yet to come might shudder
> to do evil to his host, who has granted him friendship.

Menelaus' goal is to right a wrong, but he sees this as going hand in hand with deterrence because both he and, he hopes, Zeus (who is responsible for enforcing the norms of guest–host relations) would benefit from the example that their revenge on Paris would set. Deterrence is not an aim available to the dispassionate alone.

A quality that links deterrent acts is the broad effect that the avenger has in mind. Odysseus recommends murder, not only to negate the original threat but also to send a message to all. Menelaus has in mind the deterrence of far more than Paris alone, more even than all the Trojans. He means to put off all who might consider mistreating their hosts – a point intended to appeal to Zeus' interests. And Odysseus' warning that the Achaeans ought not to incur Agamemnon's anger demonstrates how revenge's deterrent effect can travel with the avenger's reputation throughout the community to those who may never have incurred the individual's anger themselves. Indeed, even if these men know nothing of Agamemnon's anger in particular, the office he inhabits – that of 'god-supported ruler' (*Il.* 2.196) – signifies him as one whose fury is something to be avoided. Just as the retributive aspect of revenge tells the community what the avenger considers themselves to be worth, so does its deterrent aspect tell them what fate awaits those whose behaviour fails to conform to that valuation.

Agamemnon confirms the compatibility of the two goals, retribution and deterrence.

> *ἐγὼ δέ κ' ἄγω Βρισηΐδα καλλιπάρῃον*
> *αὐτὸς ἰὼν κλισίην δὲ τὸ σὸν γέρας ὄφρ' ἐῢ εἰδῇς*
> *ὅσσον φέρτερός εἰμι σέθεν, στυγέῃ δὲ καὶ ἄλλος*
> *ἶσον ἐμοὶ φάσθαι καὶ ὁμοιωθήμεναι ἄντην.*
>
> (*Il.* 1.184–7)

> But I myself, coming to your tent
> will take fair-cheeked Briseis, your prize, in order that you might know
> how much greater I am than you, and that another might fear
> to speak as my equal and oppose me as a peer.

Agamemnon's original threat, to take from one of the best of the Achaeans beneath him (137–9), was not to be an act of vengeance but merely the kind of unprovoked *hybris* that he thinks a ruler can get away with. However, now that Achilles has stood up to him and showered him with insults, Agamemnon has become angry and intends to put him back in his place; we are now in the realm of revenge. We see here how fundamentally inseparable retribution and deterrence often are for avengers because Achilles' implicit belief that he has the right to abuse Agamemnon in this way is not simply a potential threat, but also a slight in itself. Agamemnon aims to avenge himself by placing Achilles back where he belongs, a place from which he would not dream of openly insulting him again. He also expects that Achilles' example will serve the added purpose of deterring others.[13]

Delayed revenge

The reasoning capacity of the angry, often demonstrated in the thought they give to the goal of deterrence, can also be seen in the care they take in achieving revenge. As Pierre Bourdieu has said, there is an obligation on the offended to settle their scores swiftly; he who does not do so 'sees his capital diminished from day to day by passing time'.[14] This sense of urgency is certainly present in Homeric anger. Achilles' decision in Book One as to whether or not he should immediately draw his sword and kill Agamemnon and all who stand in the way (*Il.* 1.188–92) is a decision about whether or not he should obey his anger. Later, Odysseus must work hard to persuade him to postpone avenging Patroclus until after he has received Agamemnon's gifts and all have eaten (19.155–83); Achilles feels unable to eat until they have 'avenged outrage' (208). Anger is always a compelling force, driving its host to conflict.

However, Bourdieu also sees potential strategic advantages in waiting: delay keeps the offender guessing, watching for the moment of retaliation; 'after a certain point. . .lack of response ceases to be an oversight and becomes disdainful refusal'; by waiting the victim can extract 'deferential conduct' from the offender.[15] And, importantly for Homer, we might add that time spent planning and preparing can maximise the revenge. Vengeance has its value, but so do the planning and the threat of vengeance, and both can be leveraged to the victim's advantage.

The poems depict everything from immediate impulsive responses to carefully plotted and choreographed scenes. A look at Homer's primary example of the latter extreme reveals a feature of his use of anger vocabulary that has important methodological implications worth outlining. Between his arrival back on Ithaca and his final retaliation, Odysseus can be said to suffer as many as ten separate episodes of offence (as well as the suitors' ongoing presence in his house, courting of his wife and exploitation of his property and the maidservants' fraternisation), that either escape his vengeance or suffer it less than he would like.[16] This is part of Athena's strategy, according to which Odyssesus must 'suffer many pains in silence, accepting the violence of men' (*Od.* 13.310). In service of the greater plan, Odysseus endures provocations without showing anger and carefully limits any anger he does express. Despite the continual effrontery, Odysseus is almost never said, with the use of the standard vocabulary, to be angry until he has already begun to kill the suitors.[17] With Antinous dead, Eurymachus promises Odysseus' doom and the latter responds by 'looking from beneath the brows' (*ὑπόδρα ἰδών*; *Od.* 22.34), a clear indication of anger. An explicit anger term (*κεχολῶσθαι*) follows soon after, but in a way that merely highlights the peculiarity of the theme's absence up to this point because Eurymachus states that no blame could be attached to Odysseus' anger (22.55–9). It may be that Homeric terms for anger necessarily indicate the emotion's outward manifestation so that to mention it is to imply its display. Thus, using the standard terminology, Odysseus could not be said simultaneously to feel and conceal anger.[18] A purely lexicographical approach to Homeric anger will therefore under-represent instances of restraint since the emotional experiences of those who take offence but refrain from display are never labelled with anger terms.

In the absence of words like *χόλος* and *κότος*, metaphor and metonymy do the work of conveying Odysseus' internal experience. He 'broods over evils' (*Od.* 17.465, 20.184, cf. 17.491), 'anxiously ponders (*μερμηρίζων*) the suitors' deaths' (19.2, 51, 20.29–30), 'lies awake intending evils' (20.5–6), admits to Eumaeus that he wishes the gods would avenge the suitors' outrage (169–71), and, when his moment of vengeance is near, 'smiles bitterly in his heart' (301–2). Thus, Odysseus appears to feel what we would call anger and desperately desires revenge, but he restrains that emotion so completely as to conceal that he feels it at all. It is not that he is without what we would call emotion – indeed, Athena stirs the suitors to hostility so that 'pain' (*ἄχος*) would enter Odysseus' heart all the more (18.346–8, 20.284–6) – rather, he is employing his wits in order to ensure that his rage finds maximal fulfilment.

His plot against the suitors is Odysseus' supreme example of both restraint and revenge, and of both reason and anger, but it is not his only one. In the cave, having watched Polyphemus brutally kill and devour his companions before lying down to sleep, Odysseus plans to move in and kill the cyclops by stabbing him in the chest (*Od.* 9.299–302). But another thought restrains him (*θυμὸς ἔρυκεν*): the realisation that Polyphemus' destruction would result in theirs, he alone being capable of opening the cave (302–5). The following day, while Polyphemus is with his sheep in the mountains, Odysseus is left 'contemplating evil, whether somehow I might take revenge' (316–17). Odysseus has not thought better of revenge but, restraining himself, has sought a means of achieving both revenge and escape.

Odysseus himself likens these two vengeances in terms of the emotional discipline they require (*Od.* 20.18–21). But there is a distinction to be made in terms of the completeness of the revenge. While he accomplishes what must be considered the most total vengeance he could have hoped for against the suitors, maidservants and Melanthius, he has to settle for less satisfaction than he had originally desired and would subsequently long for from Polyphemus, saying, 'would that I were able, having rendered you bereft of soul and life, to send you to the house of Hades' (9.523–4).[19] There is a complexity to considerations of revenge and restraint whereby, depending on circumstances, one's anger may be forced to accept compromise, or be afforded greater fulfilment than it would have enjoyed had its demands been met at once.

Homer's other great instance of restraint, that of Achilles towards Agamemnon, has been likened to Odysseus'.[20] The two men, in the face of severe provocation, restrain themselves from the immediate violent response they desire and instead adopt long-term strategies. But this is where the similarities end. According to Erwin Cook, the Odyssey contrasts two opposing strategies of vengeance, those of *μῆτις* and *βίη*, his preference for the former being the cause of Odysseus' victory.[21] Wilson has claimed that this strategic decision can be extended to include the approach chosen by Achilles in the *Iliad* but this is far harder to see. The term *μῆτις* is never used in relation to Achilles or his dealings with Agamemnon, and while he does opt against violent retaliation, it is only in obedience to Athena and not because he foresees a greater or more secure victory in that direction. A significant difference is found in the extent of the restraint shown by the two heroes. When he first feels angry, Achilles considers two options: to force his way through the crowd and kill Agamemnon at once, or 'to stop his anger and restrain his spirit' (*Il.* 1.188–92). Checked by Athena in the moment of choosing the former option, he agrees not to kill but that does not mean he has chosen to stop his anger.[22] Indeed, he goes on to rail against Agamemnon verbally in this scene, and his sulk for much of the rest of the poem is repeatedly referred to as an act of anger. The absence of anger terms in descriptions of Odysseus' restrained disposition contrasts with the forty-two mentions of Achilles' towards Agamemnon.[23] These represent two extremes of anger restraint in pursuit of vengeance. One holds back from killing his provoker, but is otherwise so unrestrained in his intransigent refusal to fight that his anger is renowned throughout the army, even among the Trojans, and is afforded the first word of the poem.[24] The other suppresses his anger so far beneath the surface that even the audience might wonder whether it is being felt at all.[25] Neither of them lashes out at the first opportunity but beyond that they diverge, representing perhaps the shallowest and the deepest extents to which one might suppress one's anger. Intriguingly, the most restrained anger leads to supreme satisfaction, while the least leads ultimately to no satisfaction at all.

Anger puts a positive time-pressure on revenge, pushing the victim to settle the score sooner rather than later. But other concerns can resist that pressure, recommending delay, and Odysseus and Achilles demonstrate how restraint can pay off in such ways as those Bourdieu has outlined. Functioning in a vacuum, anger would have seen Melanthius dead on the road but it would also have exposed Odysseus, putting all the rest of his angry desires in doubt of fulfilment. Instead, by managing his anger and embracing delay, he eventually finds complete satisfaction. In a different way, Achilles' example demonstrates that the dragging out of vengeance by prolonging anger and postponing satisfaction can prompt the offering of generous gifts.

The crucial difference between the situations in which these two angers occur is the way they relate to the wider community. Odysseus' anonymity affords him the practical advantage of surprise, but it also protects him from social pressure: those who fail to retaliate to a slight suffer the loss of face. For all the insult and injury Odysseus suffers on his return, his honour remains insulated by his lowly fake identity. As a beggar, the abuse he receives imposes no obligation on him to act, because no one will think any less of a beggar who does not return harm for harm. Moreover, in the eyes of any onlookers, any reputational harm he endures is suffered by 'the beggar' rather than 'Odysseus'. For Achilles, on the other hand, a large audience bears witness to his degrading treatment; they know it is Achilles who has suffered it, that he is in a state of *χόλος and* that he is in a position to act. His next steps will communicate, to Agamemnon and everyone else, what he considers himself to be worth and where he sees himself in relation to his offender. Achilles cannot wear this abuse as Odysseus does without losing face and opts instead for the compromise of a non-violent, passive retaliation. The community's perceived understanding of the situation defines the pressure that the angry individual is under and the reputational cost of restraint.

Compensation

Revenge could be postponed, but it could also be abandoned altogether. Sometimes the offender can take the initiative in search of reconciliation. If they are quick, they may get away with nothing more than an apology. Agamemnon makes a clumsy attempt at such when, realising he has overstepped the mark in shaming Odysseus for holding back from the battle, he laughs and 'takes back his speech' (*Il.* 4.357), saying 'I do not quarrel with you nor order you' (359). Agamemnon's desire appears to be that the cause of dishonour would be withdrawn but, as with any meaningful apology, he leaves it up to Odysseus to determine whether any offence remains, saying 'I will make it good later if an evil has been spoken; all these things let the gods bring to naught' (362–3). He hopes he has taken back his words but offers what we might presume to be a gift if necessary, albeit the power dynamic might deter the lesser man from taking up such an offer. For those to whom regret comes too late, a material gift may be required.

Gifts can be offered, then, but they must also be accepted. This presents the victim with a decision: should they accept compensation or hold out for revenge? According to van Wees, the two most important considerations are the amount of compensation and the status of the giver, and the first of these is clearly crucial.[26] That gifts are not simply symbolic tokens of apology is clear from their frequent characterisation as 'worthy' (*ἄξιος*), implying that not simply any gift would suffice.[27] Indeed, quantity and quality are emphasised by Agamemnon who refers to his offering as 'past counting' and 'renowned' (*Il.* 9.120–1).[28] Achilles claims not to have a price, asserting that it would make no difference if Agamemnon's gifts were as numerous as the sand and dust (385), but this only serves to emphasise that typically quantity does matter and that he, as ever, is exceptional. Furthermore, Achilles knows, unusually, that he will soon die if he returns to battle and therefore has a unique reason not to care for material gifts and other acquisitions, like rule over cities, that he will never get to enjoy

(408–16). In other words, anyone else may well be swayed by such a great quantity of gifts.

The largely personal goal of lucrative reconciliation can be a justifiable and admirable aspiration. Phoenix tells the tale of Meleager (*Il.* 9.524–99) whose story closely mirrors Achilles' in that he, out of anger towards his mother who has cursed him, withholds himself from battle despite repeated appeals from friends and family and the offer of a substantial gift. Ultimately, at the last moment when the city has almost fallen, he dons his armour and repels the invaders, but the gifts are now no longer on offer. Maximising the compensation one can leverage from one's anger is an important principle in Phoenix's mind. Homer is aware of the obstacle that anger can pose to decision-making – Achilles himself will ultimately come to regret how it has blinded him – but he also believes it possible for the angry to be reasonable. Indeed, though the offended tend to desire a violent outcome, the hope for material compensation is not incompatible with anger. Athena apparently assumes this to be so when she stays Achilles' hand and promises that he will receive, on account of Agamemnon's *hybris*, three times what he has lost (*Il.* 1.213–14). Achilles appears to have different interests, reasoning that the gods listen to those who obey them (218), but Athena's rationale shows that material compensation was something for which the offended might hope and so be persuaded to restrain their anger.

We can see from Achilles' response to Phoenix that his objection to the deal is about more than his mortality and the consequentially diminished value of material gifts. Achilles' great concern is the harm done to his honour. This is made most clear when, despite agreeing with Ajax's assertion that he ought to show pity and accept the gift as even a grieving man would do with the killer of his brother or son, he states that he cannot forget the 'disgrace' of being treated like a 'dishonoured wanderer' (*Il.* 9.645–8). And yet honour is precisely what is now on offer. Phoenix urges acceptance because the recipient of such gifts would 'be honoured like a god' whereas he who receives no gifts, though he prevails in battle, will be honoured less (603–5).[29] There is, it seems, more than one kind of outcome that lost honour might lead one to desire, more than one kind of honour that can be reclaimed. As Achilles has already said, he does not want the honour of compensatory gifts but that his enemy should pay for all his 'heartrending insolence' (387). Similarly, Odysseus refuses Eurymachus' offer of compensation, asserting that he would not hold back from killing even for the younger man's entire patrimony and more, preferring to see all the suitors pay for their transgressions (*Od.* 22.61–4). The victim must decide whether they are willing to forego the honour of profoundly shaming or destroying their enemy and accept instead the honour that comes with the acquisition of great wealth.[30] They must also weigh the risk of declining this assured offer for the uncertain, but perhaps more desirable, reward of successful vengeance.

In a battlefield example, Agamemnon intervenes before his brother can accept the ransom being offered by the suppliant Adrastus and says:

ὦ πέπον ὦ Μενέλαε, τί ἢ δὲ σὺ κήδεαι οὕτως
ἀνδρῶν; ἦ σοὶ ἄριστα πεποίηται κατὰ οἶκον
πρὸς Τρώων; τῶν μή τις ὑπεκφύγοι αἰπὺν ὄλεθρον
χεῖράς θ' ἡμετέρας, μηδ' ὅν τινα γαστέρι μήτηρ
κοῦρον ἐόντα φέροι, μηδ' ὃς φύγοι, ἀλλ' ἅμα πάντες
Ἰλίου ἐξαπολοίατ' ἀκήδεστοι καὶ ἄφαντοι.

(*Il.* 6.55–60)

Gentle Menelaus, why do you care so for
these men? Have you been treated in the best ways in your house
by the Trojans? Let not one of them escape sheer destruction
at our hands, not even the one in his mother's womb,
the male child she carries, let not even he escape but at once all those
of Ilion perish unmourned and unseen.

Zanker has recognised that this is a decision between different kinds of honour but sees the distinction as lying between the honour of 'vengeance and death' and that of 'sparing a suppliant', the second of which just happens to come with gifts in this instance.[31] While it is clear that the former would be a source of honour, it is not clear that Menelaus stands to gain honour for showing mercy to an enemy in battle.[32] Indeed, it may be that Agamemnon is intentionally missing the point. Adrastus himself has made no explicit attempt to appeal to Menelaus' mercy, but has instead promised a ransom, citing his father's substantial wealth (46–50). We can reason from the goals of these two men that the motive more likely to lead Menelaus towards greater honour is Adrastus' – the promise of gifts – whereas Agamemnon's argument, intended to shame him into rejecting the offer, reveals mercy to be a motive that would surely not bring him honour. In order to compete with the honour of vengeance, compensation must offer honour of its own, and that honour is measured primarily in the quantity and quality of the gifts.[33]

Part of what deters Achilles from reconciling is the requirement that he resubordinate himself to Agamemnon.[34] From the moment of Agamemnon's first threat, Achilles challenges his rule, asking how any of the Achaeans will now obey him (*Il.* 1.150–1), and he confirms his desire for revolt as he asserts that were the rest of the people there not 'nobodies', Agamemnon would have performed his last outrage (231–2). Agamemnon sees this as insubordination, accusing Achilles of opposing him as a peer (187). When it comes to reconciliation, Agamemnon instructs Odysseus to follow his promise of gifts with a demand:

ταῦτά κέ οἱ τελέσαιμι μεταλλήξαντι χόλοιο.
δμηθήτω· Ἀΐδης τοι ἀμείλιχος ἠδ' ἀδάμαστος,
τοὔνεκα καί τε βροτοῖσι θεῶν ἔχθιστος ἁπάντων·
καί μοι ὑποστήτω ὅσσον βασιλεύτερός εἰμι
ἠδ' ὅσσον γενεῇ προγενέστερος εὔχομαι εἶναι.

(*Il.* 9.161–5)

All this shall I bring to pass if he changes from his anger.
Let him be subdued. For Hades is implacable and inflexible,
and therefore he, among all the gods, is most hateful to mortals.
And let him submit to me, since I am the kinglier
and since I claim to be the elder born.

Recognition of Agamemnon's superiority (in other words, a return to the previous state of their relationship) is the price Achilles will have to pay, but, as many have noted, it is not a part of the message Odysseus deems it wise to convey. Odysseus apparently anticipates this being a sticking point. Achilles appears to confirm his fear when he responds, revealing first that he can read the subtext: 'for hateful to me as the doors of Hades is that man who conceals one thing in his mind and speaks another' (312–13). He then goes on to outline the workings of his and Agamemnon's relationship as it was before and as he would not have it become again: Achilles taking great risks and acquiring great wealth on the ungrateful ruler's behalf while even the little that was redistributed to him was, as the Briseis incident revealed, insecure (314–45).[35] Achilles cannot and does not attempt to overthrow Agamemnon's rule, but neither does he want to place himself back beneath it. In response to Phoenix's reminder of the honour he has to gain by accepting Agamemnon's gifts, Achilles answers that he has no need of such honour because he is honoured by Zeus (607–8). He has removed himself from the honorific hierarchy that Agamemnon sits atop and his honour forbids him from returning to it.

The other factor van Wees sees as influencing the victim's decision to accept a gift is the status of the giver.[36] This is based on the above conclusion of Agamemnon's speech of instruction to the embassy. For van Wees, this reference to his superiority is intended as a means of persuasion – Agamemnon is superior, so Achilles should yield. However, considering that he has just outlined all that he means to give to Achilles, it seems as though his superiority of rank and age is something he is asking Achilles to recognise in return. Thus, the phrase 'let him submit to me' (*μοι ὑποστήτω*) is a condition attached to the gift representing the state he wants Achilles to be in from now on; it is not the act of acceptance itself. This passage does not, therefore, imply that authoritative status increases the likelihood that one's gift will be accepted.

Unlike Agamemnon's status, the statuses of the three ambassadors are expected to have an effect.[37] Achilles welcomes them as his 'friends', the 'dearest' to him of the Achaeans (*Il.* 9.197–8; cf. 204, 521–2, 642), a relationship that Odysseus puts to persuasive work in each of the two arguments he presents to Achilles. Primarily, Odysseus invites him to accept Agamemnon's gifts and make things right (260–99), a case for which Phoenix puts forward the strongest argument. He addresses the younger man as 'child' (*τέκος*; 437, 444), while highlighting his own advanced age (446), and recalls how Peleus sent him to Agamemnon with his ignorant child (*νήπιον*) who knew nothing of battle or the *agora*, entrusted with the task of teaching him (438–43). On the basis of this authority, Achilles' long-time tutor presents the lesson of Meleager – that one must accept gifts before the opportunity is lost. Alternatively, if Achilles' offender is too hateful to him, Odysseus urges him to pity those who are suffering in the army and take the opportunity to win glory among them by killing the overconfident Hector (300–6). While each of the men speaks of pity as it relates to the Achaeans in general, it is Ajax who personalises it. He is demonstrably hurt by Achilles' unwillingness to help him and the rest of the Achaeans who, he says, showed him such affection (624–31). And he concludes with an almost pathetic appeal for him to be gracious to those who have come under his roof and who 'desire, beyond all the other Achaeans, to be those he most loves and cares for' (641–2). Achilles remains intransigent, but the leveraging of personal ties in this way is evidently seen as a potent means of reasoning with the angry.

There appears to be an experiential difference between these two paths that anger follows – revenge and gift-acceptance. Pain is characteristic of anger; lessened pain, of revenge. However, on receiving compensation, the pain of anger is neither explicitly said to remain nor to be assuaged.[38] The pain that Athena has the suitors heap on Odysseus through their insults is intended to strengthen his resolve in the moment of vengeance (*Od.* 18.346–8, 20.284–6); indeed, he dismisses out of hand Eurymachus' offer of restitution, determined that they should 'pay for their transgressions' (22.61–4). Achilles remains in pain, lamenting and grieving (*Il.* 24.128) over Patroclus, and Thetis, keen that this should end, recommends that he eat, sleep or have sex (129–31). But even though she has also come to instruct him that, on Zeus' orders, he must accept ransom for Hector's body (133–7), there is no suggestion that this resolution will do anything to relieve her son's pain; it will merely allow him to avoid the anger of the gods. It may be that the acceptance of this gift leads only to more grief for the recipient who, wailing, assures his deceased friend that he will get his share of the ransom but fears that the dead man might be angry at the surrender of his killer's corpse (592–5).

Those who choose to reconcile for a price do not appear to experience the relief of pain enjoyed by successful avengers; rather, they must take action themselves with regard to their anger. The embassy know that more is required of Achilles than acceptance, urging him to 'change' (*μεταλλάσσω*; *Il.* 9.157, 261, 299) from, 'concede' (*ἐάω*; 260), 'throw away' (*ἀπορρίπτω*; 517) or 'quench' (*σβέννυμι*; 678) his anger. In the end, he 'unsays' (*ἀπεῖπον*; 19.35, 75) and 'stops' (*παύω*; 19.67) it.[39] We have seen that the choice to reconcile with one's offender can be an easy one for those who value the kind of honour that comes with cooperation and are not so furious that the pain they feel has no material price. However, the foregoing of revenge entails a sacrifice, a great one for those so angry as Achilles, and that sacrifice lies in the abandonment of the pursuit of a satisfactory end to one's pain.

The dangers of anger

A major theme of the appeals that are made to Achilles is the idea that to carry on now in his anger would be the wrong decision and the opinion of the community is central to that. Up to this point, he has been seen as the clear victim; after this point, he comes increasingly to be viewed as unreasonable, and for this his anger is to blame.[40] Too late, when Patroclus has died, Achilles comes to realise the folly into which his anger has led him:

ὡς ἔρις ἔκ τε θεῶν ἔκ τ' ἀνθρώπων ἀπόλοιτο
καὶ χόλος, ὅς τ' ἐφέηκε πολύφρονά περ χαλεπῆναι,
ὅς τε πολὺ γλυκίων μέλιτος καταλειβομένοιο
ἀνδρῶν ἐν στήθεσσιν ἀέξεται ἠΰτε καπνός·
ὡς ἐμὲ νῦν ἐχόλωσεν ἄναξ ἀνδρῶν Ἀγαμέμνων.

(*Il.* 18.107–11)

Would that strife perish from among gods and men,
and anger which sets one, though great-minded, to hardness,

and far sweeter than trickling honey
in the breast of men it rises like smoke;
so now did the lord of men, Agamemnon, anger me.[41]

Scholarship on this pair of metaphors has tended to highlight the contrasts. It is widely accepted that the sweet, trickling honey represents a pleasant feeling associated with anger.[42] But as to the meaning of smoke, there is no consensus. Most agree that its implications are negative but is that because it is painful to the individual or because its consequences are destructive?[43] The former is the more natural contrast (between pleasure and pain) and yet we might anticipate that regret at his anger's destructive if unintended consequences would currently be at the forefront of Achilles' mind. The answer lies in the wider context of this speech (78–126) which is a lament on how both sides of his anger's bitter-sweet nature have led him to disaster. In view of the preceding line, in which he says that it leads even the *πολύφρονά* (literally, 'person of many thoughts') to hardness, the similes appear to be describing how anger inhibits reason. From this perspective, I would suggest that he has in mind two intoxicating qualities: the honey-sweetness of cherished victimhood and anticipated revenge, and the smoke that rises from the original destructive offence. These contrasted qualities are thus united in their effect, a marriage of hoped-for future and bitterly recalled past that together can impede the judgement of their subject.

Unsurprisingly, the painful experience of *χόλος*, with its compelling drive towards vengeance, is presented as an emotion that can lead people to make bad decisions. But *κότος*, though an emotion over which people appear to have more control, can also make people do things they regret. This is most clear in Odysseus' refusal, being angry of heart (*κεκοτηότι θυμῷ*; *Od.* 9.501), to listen to the warnings of his men, instead insulting Polyphemus for a second time and divulging his name. As a result, Polyphemus appeals to Poseidon and Odysseus' troubles begin in earnest. The warnings of his men imply in this act a foolishness that its repercussions will eventually confirm. His anger ought to be governed by fear of the danger that he invites not only on himself but also the group of which he is a part and for whose safety he bears some responsibility.

Achilles has a reputation for being not only exceptionally ruthless in his anger, but also potentially misguided. Patroclus dare not take a seat in Nestor's shelter, saying he must instead return directly to Achilles because he 'might swiftly accuse even the guiltless' (*τάχα κεν καὶ ἀναίτιον αἰτιόῳτο*; *Il.* 11.654).[44] Patroclus is concerned about Achilles' tendency to assume, as van Wees puts it, 'that an act of disrespect is deliberate, until proven otherwise'.[45] As Patroclus says, Achilles' hastiness makes him a 'dangerous man' (654) and this presents a threat to those around him, including his friends, but it also endangers even himself. Antilochus, having brought the news of Patroclus' death, holds on to the grieving man's hands in case he tries to kill himself in his sorrow (18.32–4). Achilles reacts swiftly to the signals he receives, quickly perceiving disrespect and acting without a thought beyond his anger.

The capacity for restraint

The criticism that reckless anger can invite suggests that some mastery of one's anger is an important trait for even the most powerful and 'heroic' members of Homeric communities. However, while Harris acknowledges that anger sometimes comes under 'careful reflection', he seems to consider it unlikely that such reflection would lead to restraint:

> As for revenge in the Homeric world, no one feels embarrassment about exacting it, and since Greek revenge is normally a result of anger, this implies that in principle the archaic Greeks saw nothing wrong with anger. Exacting revenge on an appropriate scale was not only entirely proper but often more or less obligatory.[46]

Similarly, Herman says that 'far from being subjected to rational control, Homeric emotions were allowed (and indeed encouraged) to gush forth uninhibitedly from the psyche in all their naked glory'.[47] In fact, as we shall see, Homeric characters are ideally supposed to be able to regulate or even suppress the manifestations of not only anger but also the full range of emotional drives.

The disguised Odysseus pities Penelope, groaning over the news she has heard about her husband, 'but his eyes, as if horn or iron, stood motionless in his eyelids, and with guile he concealed his tears' (*Od.* 19.211). He must also restrain the emotions of others, such as Eurycleia whom he rebukes for displaying her joy through the holding of his face, and Eumaeus and Philoetius from whom he permits a joyful embrace because they are alone outside, but whose exclamations he interrupts for fear of discovery (21.223–9). Odysseus' plot obviously demands an act of considerable restraint from himself and others, but there are more reasons than the preserving of a disguise to hold back one's emotions. For propriety's sake, the disguised Odysseus refuses to talk of home and risk 'groaning and crying' in another's house, mourning for too long and inviting the resentment of Penelope and her slaves for appearing so drunk that he is left 'swimming in tears' (19.188–22).[48] And Idomeneus details the myriad manifestations of fear over which a man waiting in ambush will, for the sake of his reputation as a courageous warrior, exert control, including: changing skin colour, shifting of weight from side to side, accelerated heart-beat and chattering teeth (*Il.* 13.276–86).[49]

The consideration of how best to express one's emotions verbally, if at all, is implied by the common metaphor: 'What speech has escaped the fence of your teeth?' (*ποῖόν σε ἔπος φύγεν ἕρκος ὀδόντων;*).[50] In this short phrase, the poet points to a private conflict within the Homeric individual in which one must regulate (perhaps by physically keeping the mouth shut) one's speech, which appears to have a life of its own, a desire to escape and be heard. In two instances, it is misplaced anger that is so condemned: that of Agamemnon in his scathing rebuke of Odysseus for failing to advance (*Il.* 4.350), and that of Odysseus for threatening to kill Eurycleia along with the other maidservants (*Od.* 19.492). Expressions of hopelessness are challenged in the remaining six instances.

Evidently expressions of anger and hopelessness could invite opprobrium, but is judgement also ever passed on the internal affective experience itself? Are these individuals being told, in other words, that they should restrain themselves, or that there ought to be no need for restraint? The phrase itself objects to the individual's speech only, but the chastiser generally goes on to challenge the justification for the emotion too. In one instance though, Odysseus appears to mean that Agamemnon ought to have held his tongue regardless of what he felt. Odysseus outlines the standards that Agamemnon, in his defeatism, has failed to meet:

οὕτω δὴ μέμονας Τρώων πόλιν εὐρυάγυιαν
καλλείψειν, ἧς εἵνεκ' ὀϊζύομεν κακὰ πολλά;
σίγα, μή τίς τ' ἄλλος Ἀχαιῶν τοῦτον ἀκούσῃ
μῦθον, ὃν οὔ κεν ἀνήρ γε διὰ στόμα πάμπαν ἄγοιτο
ὅς τις ἐπίσταιτο ᾗσι φρεσὶν ἄρτια βάζειν
σκηπτοῦχός τ' εἴη, καί οἱ πειθοίατο λαοὶ
τοσσοίδ' ὅσσοισιν σὺ μετ' Ἀργείοισιν ἀνάσσεις.

(*Il.* 14.88–94)

Do you really intend to leave behind the broad-wayed city of Troy,
on account of which we suffer many evils?
Be silent, lest some other Achaean should hear this
speech, which no man should in any way permit to pass through his mouth,
who knows in his heart how to speak correctly
and who is a sceptre-bearer, and whom so many people
as the Argives, over whom you are lord, obey.

Odysseus' incredulous question demonstrates his disappointment with how Agamemnon feels and even challenges the sense of such an emotion in view of what they have all sacrificed. However, he does not stop there but goes on to demand silence 'lest some other Achaean should hear this speech'. It is one thing to feel a certain way or to prefer a particular course of action, but it is another actually to express those sentiments and sometimes they must be restrained, prevented from passing through the mouth. Furthermore, as this passage suggests, an understanding of which impulses ought to be followed and which suppressed is all the more important for leaders, especially a sceptre-bearing prince like Agamemnon, whom many follow.

Anger is the emotion in focus in this study, but it is important to recognise that it is experienced in an emotional community that is well acquainted with the principle that emotional expression is the uncertain product of a complicated reasoning process. Behavioural outputs are not the inevitable consequences of experiential inputs but the products of an often complex set of reasonings about how best to manage various goals. The angry in Homer are not inevitable avengers but are very capable of restraining their anger to varying degrees and for various reasons, typically informed by anticipated social consequences.

Dialogue with other emotions

Decisions about how best, if at all, to express one's anger are heavily influenced by social emotions. For Adkins, it is up to Achilles alone to decide whether or not he should accept Agamemnon's offer, but true as this is in a 'hard' sense – there are no formal obligations – it is a personal decision powerfully informed by its social context.[51] In his appeal to Achilles, Ajax rebukes his friend as *νηλεές*, 'pitiless' (*Il.* 9.632). Achilles is described several times with this adjective, a term most typically used to describe things, rather than people, like bronze (3.292), the day (11.484), a knot (10.443), or sleep (*Od.* 12.372). It seems to be a term reserved for describing things that cannot possibly feel sorry for someone, regardless of how pitiable they may be. Patroclus emphasises his friend's inhumanity as he states that his parents must have been the 'grey sea and steep rocks' rather than Peleus and Thetis, so hard is his heart (*Il.* 16.33–5). Similarly, the Myrmidons have been heard calling him pitiless for holding his companions by the ships against their will and saying that his mother nursed him on *χόλος* (203–6). He is not just very angry but peculiarly and unnaturally lacking in pity. This sense of inhumanity, associated with the inability to pity, is confirmed in consideration of the only other *νηλεές* individual in epic, Polyphemus (*Od.* 9.272, 287, 368), so described for his vicious responses to Odysseus' pleas.[52] It is an indication of the moral line that Achilles crosses in refusing the embassy that this is the point when pitilessness is first ascribed to him (*Il.* 9.497, 632). Pity for one's loved-ones and community is an emotion that can, and eventually should, take precedence over anger when the two goals are incompatible.

Against the broad and varied approach to honour observed in Homer generally, Achilles' perspective can appear relatively narrow. Odysseus reminds him of his father Peleus' instruction:

> *σὺ δὲ μεγαλήτορα θυμὸν*
> *ἴσχειν ἐν στήθεσσι· φιλοφροσύνη γὰρ ἀμείνων·*
> *ληγέμεναι δ' ἔριδος κακομηχάνου, ὄφρά σε μᾶλλον*
> *τίωσ' Ἀργείων ἠμὲν νέοι ἠδὲ γέροντες.*
>
> (*Il.* 9.255–8)

> Check your great spirit
> in your chest. For friendliness is better.
> Keep from mischievous strife, that
> the Argives, both young and old, might honour you more.

As we have seen, insults are compounded by audience. The presence of the Argives is a key component of Achilles' memory of Agamemnon's slight (647). Yet according to Peleus, an effective means of ensuring one's good reputation among that group is to pursue not vengeance but reconciliation. Indeed, the pity behind such an act would ensure that the desperate Achaeans would honour Achilles like a god (301–3), and he would gain the added opportunity of winning glory by killing Hector (303–4). Enmities within a community can be harmful to all, so the sacrificial, prosocial act of swallowing one's anger, even if compensated for it, wins the recognition of the group.

Shame can also be a powerful force against the fulfilment of anger. Angry verbal exchanges can reflect poorly on those involved, as Aeneas recognises when he tells Achilles that they should not be squabbling like women who insult and accuse each other, but fighting with their spears (*Il.* 20.251–8).[53] Similarly, Idomeneus and the Oilean Ajax trade insults over who can better judge which chariot is winning the race and are on the verge of violence when Achilles interrupts them:

> μηκέτι νῦν χαλεποῖσιν ἀμείβεσθον ἐπέεσσιν
> Αἶαν Ἰδομενεῦ τε κακοῖς, ἐπεὶ οὐδὲ ἔοικε.
> καὶ δ' ἄλλῳ νεμεσᾶτον ὅτις τοιαῦτά γε ῥέζοι.
>
> (*Il.* 23.492–4)

> No longer now exchange hard and evil words
> Ajax and Idomeneus, since it is not becoming.
> And you would be indignant towards another who did such things.

These are not enemy combatants like Aeneas and Achilles and the implication is that in this context, to follow one's anger down a path of escalating insults, perhaps even to violence, would be deemed petty by observers. A face-saving solution is not provided and it seems to be assumed that, to avoid embarrassment, anger is simply suppressed, at least temporarily. Whether verbal or physical, expressions of anger can result in the losing rather than the saving of face.

Phoenix, angry with his father for cursing him to childlessness, decided to kill him but had his anger checked by an immortal who reminded him of 'rumour of the people and many reproaches of men, lest he be called a parricide among the Achaeans' (*Il.* 9.459–61). However, he cannot restrain himself altogether and, despite many citizens (*ἔται*) and cousins intervening to hold him in the house, on the tenth night he escapes and flees to Phthia.[54] The thought of the rumours that would spread and the blame he would receive (that is, the anticipation of shame if not a stronger sanction) stays Phoenix's hand, but, like those who have not yet avenged dead loved ones, his anger will not permit him to remain in his community. The only path both these emotions can accept is exile. Even the beggar, Arnaeus, feels ashamed at the prospect of having to be violent towards the aged beggar Odysseus (*Od.* 18.10–13).

Achilles does not perform a shameful act of vengeance but his honour is certainly at risk, and perhaps harmed, by his intransigence. Phoenix makes clear that, having received a generous offer from a contrite offender, Achilles' position with regard to the wider community now hangs in the balance: 'before, none could blame you for your anger' (*πρὶν δ' οὔ τι νεμεσσητὸν κεχολῶσθαι*; *Il.* 9.523).[55] Evidently, by refusing the gifts, Achilles is now opening himself up to public criticism.[56] This manifests almost immediately as Ajax, losing patience with his friend, calls him 'cruel' (*σχέτλιος*) and forgetful of the love and honour his companions have shown him (630–1). Here we find echoes of the accusations Achilles levelled at Agamemnon who he claimed had forgotten that they had followed him to Troy for the sake of his and his brother's honour (1.158–60). Ajax urges Achilles to be gracious and 'respect your own house, for we are under your roof' (9.640), suggesting that Achilles is not only being unusually hard-hearted but is even breaking a rule of some kind. Ajax appears to think (perhaps for rhetorical effect) that the offering of generous compensation has not only afforded Achilles an opportunity but has placed him under an obligation; custom would have him accept or cause offence.[57] Criticism soon comes even from those closest to him. Patroclus expresses the desire never to experience such anger (16.30) and the Myrmidons whisper that it is evil (200–6).[58] Achilles might be harming his enemy in his refusal to fight, but he appears also to be harming his own reputation; he certainly is not enhancing it.[59]

Perhaps the most common emotional battleground in Homer is that between anger and fear. Anger leads men to face dangers they would otherwise shy away from, such as when men avoid engaging in battle until they witness a friend's death and feel compelled to avenge it.[60] This can go both ways, however, with fear of danger sometimes overcoming anger. Arnaeus' anger at the disguised Odysseus (*Od.* 18.25), which led him to agree to fight, is replaced by fear when he sees his rival's intimidating muscular form (66–72). His spirit, we are told, 'was evilly troubled and yet the manservants girded and led him by force, him being afraid, and his flesh was trembling on his limbs' (75–7). The suitors observe that his heart is no longer in the fight and, anger having abandoned the beggar, Antinous attempts to trump fear of Odysseus with terror of Echetus, the brutal and sadistic ruler on the mainland to whom Arnaeus will be sent if he loses (79–87). Unfortunately, this results only in greater trembling (88) because fear, it seems, is not as useful an emotion to the combatant as anger. Similarly, the suitors, angry at the death of Antinous, swiftly promise Odysseus' destruction (22.26–30). But upon their comprehending the killer's true identity and intent, 'pale terror seized them all and each glanced about for a way by which he might flee sheer destruction' (42–3).[61]

As these and other examples demonstrate, fear often resists the concerns of status. Arnaeus' anger at Odysseus' presence is born of his jealous protectiveness of what the suitors will supply, but he is also interested in how he will look to the men, who are urging him on with their winking (*Od.* 18.10–11) and expressing a desire that all should watch the fight (30–1). Soon though, when he has perceived Odysseus' strength and concluded that he will suffer in the fight, Arnaeus' fearful reaction invites scorn from Antinous (18.78). Fear for his wellbeing displaces any hopes he had entertained of impressing his lordly observers.

This addresses the potential for one's anger to be replaced or even pre-empted by fear of the culprit, but anger can also be intruded on by fear of third parties. In a 'soft' sense, we have already explored this: the expectation that others will think less of one for expressing anger might also be termed a fear of shame. But there are also 'harder' repercussions to be afraid of. When Zeus decides that Achilles must relent in his anger and release Hector's body, he instructs Thetis to speak to her son:

σκύζεσθαί οἱ εἰπὲ θεούς, ἐμὲ δ' ἔξοχα πάντων
ἀθανάτων κεχολῶσθαι, ὅτι φρεσὶ μαινομένῃσιν
Ἕκτορ' ἔχει παρὰ νηυσὶ κορωνίσιν οὐδ' ἀπέλυσεν,
αἴ κέν πως ἐμέ τε δείσῃ ἀπό θ' Ἕκτορα λύσῃ.

(*Il.* 24.113–16)

Tell him that the gods frown on him, and I beyond all
immortals am angry, that raging in heart
he holds Hector by the curved ships and has not returned him,
perhaps he will fear me and release Hector.

At no point until now has Achilles' anger shown any signs of lessening – even his anger towards Agamemnon is merely replaced by his greater anger towards Hector – but fear of Zeus, it is thought, might have an impact. This proves to have the desired effect as Achilles, having respect for Zeus as he had for Athena in Book One (216–18), is moved to obey. Later, his fear of Zeus even leads him to take pre-emptive measures in order to avoid circumstances that might raise his ire. He has the body of Hector covered so that Priam will not become angry on seeing it and, through his actions, provoke anger and deadly retaliation from Achilles in transgression of Zeus' commands (583–6).[62] This kind of authority extends also to mortals such as Odysseus, who is said to have 'held back and checked' the Ithacans in their bloodthirsty anger at Eupeithes for his involvement in piracy against their allies, the Thesprotians (*Od.* 16.424–30).

Finally, even anger itself can restrain anger when a new offence proves both incompatible with and more demanding of revenge than the existing grievance. Achilles' anger towards Agamemnon, which has remained resolute in the face of petitions, gifts and disapproval, is swiftly set aside when a greater offence occurs. On hearing the news of Patroclus' death, Achilles' first emotion is sorrow, dramatically displayed (*Il.* 18.22–36), but he soon expresses regret over his anger towards Agamemnon (107–11) and on seeing Patroclus' body his anger turns to his new foe, Hector, whom he intends to kill (along with twelve Trojan youths) and whose head and armour he plans to bring back for his friend (334–7). Thus far there is no explicit mention of a change in his state of anger towards Agamemnon, but then he also has no means of avenging Patroclus until his armour is replaced (17.709–11), suggesting that, so long as his anger at the lesser offence is not obstructing his vengeance for the greater one, Achilles can burden the two simultaneously.[63] However, no sooner has his new armour arrived, intensifying his anger (19.15–17), than Thetis instructs him to renounce his original anger and prepare for battle (35). This Achilles immediately does, meeting Agamemnon in the *agora* and saying,

ἀλλὰ τὰ μὲν προτετύχθαι ἐάσομεν ἀχνύμενοί περ
θυμὸν ἐνὶ στήθεσσι φίλον δαμάσαντες ἀνάγκῃ·
νῦν δ' ἤτοι μὲν ἐγὼ παύω χόλον, οὐδέ τί με χρὴ
ἀσκελέως αἰεὶ μενεαινέμεν.

(*Il.* 19.65–8)

but we will permit these things to be left in the past, however much we suffer,
subduing the dear spirit in my chest as necessary.
Now surely, I am stopping my anger, it is not necessary for me
stubbornly always to be angry.

Achilles' anger at Agamemnon has not ceased, as if naturally superseded by his fury towards Hector. Rather, he needs actively to 'permit' Agamemnon's offence to be left in the past, 'subdue' his spirit and 'stop' his anger. This is surely why the elaborate ceremony of reconciliation that Odysseus insists on is so important – the receipt of gifts does not itself assuage anger so it is necessary formally to display, through gift acceptance and a shared meal, that one has abandoned it.[64]

Conclusion

Revenge in Homer is rarely, if ever, truly 'private'. It may be carried out by a private individual rather than the state, but the decisions that surround it are informed to a considerable extent by the effect they will have on the individual's relationship with the community. Revenge is a product of anger, rooted in perceived slights to one's honour, and as such it is fundamentally retributive. But it is also functionally, and often intentionally, deterrent in the warning that it places against any such future offences. And in both these goals the avenger aims at the improvement of their situation within the community. They seek the reclamation of honour in the eyes of the offender and of all; they hope for the glory and fame that come with a great act of requital; and, when their minds are on the future as well, it is more than the offender alone that they wish to put off.

Anger does not have to end in revenge, however. Through the offer of compensation offenders can hope to escape the vengeance of those they have angered, an outcome on which the pressure of the group can come to bear. The tendency for the anger of its members to impact negatively on the wider community means that both the offering and the accepting of reconciliatory gifts can come under significant social pressure. A generous gift can confer a great deal of prestige on its recipient, enhancing their standing in its own right.

However, in cases such as that of Achilles where the community is suffering as a result of the dispute, there is also honour to be won by those who would forgo satisfaction and the relief of pain for the sake of the group. In this we see different kinds of honour at stake – that of the powerful avenger and that of the self-sacrificing forgiver – each offering enhanced social standing in its own way.

To the slighted individual, anger is an unavoidable necessity in Homer, but it is also inherently problematic. This is not because it is conflictual – those who have been wronged are deserving of redress – but because it is an imperfect judge of offence. Anger's desire for revenge undermines its subject's judgement and leads them to make poor decisions over what is the best course of action, to perceive insult where there is none, and to lash out even at those they know to be innocent. As such, the community, which casts a long shadow over the emotional pressures that resist anger's desires, can place great value on restraint. If anger is to bring about revenge, it must win out against pity for family, friends and community, shame attached to petty or taboo acts, fear of the resistance that might come not only from the target of the vengeance but also from others in the community, and even the sometimes conflicting demands of other angers.

3

Punishment and the State in Homeric Society

Introduction

Anger is fundamental to the perpetually renegotiated relationships within a Homeric community. When one perceives their worth to have been undervalued, they become angry and seek to restore their honour. Within the angry individual burns a painful desire for revenge, an emotional state that can follow any of a number of different paths and may never achieve its goal. Anger may be repressed by its subject, it may be restrained from anything beyond words or facial expression by shame, apology, or some other priority, but when anger remains set on its goal and the offender is unwilling to meet its demands, the conflict is primed for an escalation of the stakes and an expansion of its participants. The early-archaic communities of Homer's audiences had a problem that it was in their interests to solve. How well equipped these communities were for this task is the subject of the present chapter.

Late seventh-century Athens, viewed through Draco's homicide law, provides a useful near-contemporary comparison. This was a community with the authority and means to permit or thwart self-help, even in response to homicide. Legal standards were upheld, through punishments, by an official judicial authority. As for the Homeric world, we have seen that the community has informal means of incentivising restraint. The feeling of shame at being deemed petty or excessive in one's vengeance is a deterrent of a 'soft' nature, a threat of damage to one's reputation rather than one's body or property. But can we speak also of formal, institutional means at the community's disposal? When the threat of shame is ineffective, can the community turn to action of a 'harder' sort?

Debate surrounding the administration of justice in Homeric society has moved on from discussing whether it existed to what form it took. Justice is an important value in Homer and much is thought to hang on its proper upholding, but is the 'justice' of Homeric communities characterised by a system of laws and coercively enforced judgements such as we see in Athens or does it hinge on consensus and the pursuit of an outcome that both sides can accept? The backdrop to this question is the wider community because elite power is contingent on the obedience of the common people. This search for the Homeric community's solution to the problem of anger will lead us back to emotions, those of the wider group, and the motivations at the heart of the monopolisation of legitimate force.

Draco's Athens

One problem with the search for institutions in Homer is that he is far less interested in institutions than in values, rarely offering any more detail in that regard than his stories demand. Another is that there was no single panhellenic means by which early Greek communities administered justice – laws, customs and procedures were not universal. The emergence of written laws testifies to differences of opinion even within *poleis*, a demand for greater clarity about rights and obligations.[1] But these laws also offer a point of comparison with the institutions and customs found in Homer. The best surviving example of a Greek *polis*, relatively contemporaneous to Homer, taking measures to intervene in the anger-driven interactions of its citizens is Draco's law.[2] A large portion is preserved in a 409/8 reinscription:

> And if someone kills someone without premeditation, he shall be exiled. The *basileis* are to δικάζεν as responsible for homicide either [he who killed with his own hand or] he who planned the killing. The ephetai are to διαγνο̃ναι. Pardon is to be granted, if there is a father or brother or sons, by all, or the one who opposes it shall prevail. And if these do not exist, pardon is to be granted by those as far as the degree of cousin's son and cousin, if all are willing to grant it; the one who opposes it shall prevail. And if there is not even one of these alive, and the killer did it unintentionally, and the fifty-one, the ephetai, decide that he did it unintentionally, then let ten members of the phratry admit him to the country, if they are willing. Let the fifty-one choose these men according to their rank. And let also those who killed previously be bound by this ordinance. A proclamation is to be made against the killer in the agora by relatives as far as the degree of cousin's son and cousin. The prosecution is to be shared by cousins, sons of cousins, sons-in-law, fathers-in-law, and members of the phratry... responsible for homicide... the fifty-one.... If someone kills the slayer or is responsible for his being killed while he is avoiding a frontier market, games, and Amphiktyonic rites, he shall be treated on the same basis as one who kills an

> Athenian. The ephetai shall bring in the verdict. . . . one who is the aggressor. . . slays the aggressor. . . the ephetai bring in the verdict. . . he is a free man. . . . And if a man immediately defends himself against someone who is unjustly and forcibly carrying away his property and kills him, the dead man shall receive no recompense. . . .[3]
>
> *IG* I^3 104

This law carries significant implications about late seventh-century Athens. There was a public sphere that administered justice in private disputes (at least those over homicide) with sophisticated means and considerable authority. The means included judges, procedures and laws; and the authority was sufficient to intervene in the kind of dispute most resistant to external interference: homicide, an offence that provokes much anger and puts relatives under exceptional pressure to avenge.

According to one scholarly tradition, such qualities are more or less absent from Homeric society. Finley writes that the poet was 'writing at a time. . . of some limited administration of justice. But he was singing about a time when that was not the case, except for the intangible power of public opinion.' And the principle was one of 'strictly private rights privately protected'.[4] While few now question whether there is any administration of justice, debate persists over what kind of justice it is and how it is administered, and the issue of the relationship between the public and private spheres remains fundamental. For some, attending court and accepting judgements were voluntary acts, such that the 'justice' on offer was simply whatever decision both parties could accept (or be persuaded to accept by the soft pressure of public opinion).[5] For others, the court's judgements were backed by meaningful coercive authority and the threat of force, allowing for the imposition of a 'justice' that conforms to some kind of legal standard.[6]

This debate has implications for change and continuity. If, as many now agree, Homeric society is to be dated to the early or mid-seventh century, then major differences between it and near-contemporary Greek societies demand explanation.[7] If the world of Homer's audience lacked authoritative justice, if it did not formally distinguish between those in the right and those in the wrong, if it did not allow for intent as a legal category, and if it did not possess coercive means of enforcing judgements, then either the Athenian tradition represents a cultural division among Greek communities, or (as is widely held to one degree or another) Draco's law introduced such a system at the end of the seventh century in a striking departure from the norm.[8] While neither of these views is impossible, it seems to me that the writing-down of existing custom for the first time is a remarkable enough innovation without including the invention of radical new legal standards and the implementation of a new system for the execution of justice. It should surprise, in other words, were we to find that Homeric society was very unlike that implied by Draco's homicide law.

On the surface, Homeric society is light on public institutions, but with good reason. Institutions are unlikely to have been at the forefront of the worldview held by those for whom epic poetry was performed. The Homeric world is one of heroes, individuals who effect change by dint of their own strength and cunning, not a place of officeholders and procedure. And yet Homer cannot entirely hide the institutional features of these heroes' environment. There are public officials: heralds call people to assembly, hold the elders' sceptres and police the crowd's behaviour; and special umpires are instructed to serve at the games in Phaeacia.[9] There are also symbols of institutional authority: sceptres indicate not only status but the inherited office of the elder as do the special stones on which they sit in court.[10] For all Homer's emphasis on the private sphere, his is a world of substantial cooperative endeavour with a vocabulary of public institutions.[11] Archaic elites either believed or hoped that the world revolved around them and their achievements, but they acted in a context of formal public organisation.

A careful look at Homer reveals the ideology and judicial system necessary to administer justice to a degree not unlike Draco's Athens. Injustice is seen as a threat to all and a problem for the community as a whole to solve. The community has at its disposal the officials, procedures and customary standards necessary to judge private disputes, but it also has the authority to impose limits on private self-help.

Centralised justice and the ruler-judge

In Homeric society, the ruler is the community's judicial authority.[12] As Nestor says of Agamemnon:

οὕνεκα πολλῶν
λαῶν ἐσσι ἄναξ καί τοι Ζεὺς ἐγγυάλιξε
σκῆπτρόν τ' ἠδὲ θέμιστας, ἵνά σφισι βουλεύησθα.

(*Il.* 9.97–9)

over many
people are you master, and Zeus has put into your hand
sceptre and trials, in order that you may take counsel for them.[13]

Agamemnon is *the* man responsible for judgements on account of his position (cf. 2.203–6). In Pylos, Nestor 'knows judgements (*δίκας*) and wisdom beyond others' not simply because he is old, but because he has ruled for three generations (Od. 3.244–5);[14] it is the experience not of long life but of long rule that makes for a good judge because judgement is the domain of rulers alone.

These qualities are confirmed in the one instance where a ruler (albeit a dead one) clearly is said to be acting as a judge:

ἔνθ' ἦ τοι Μίνωα ἴδον, Διὸς ἀγλαὸν υἱόν,
χρύσεον σκῆπτρον ἔχοντα, θεμιστεύοντα νέκυσσιν,
ἥμενον, οἱ δέ μιν ἀμφὶ δίκας εἴροντο ἄνακτα,
ἥμενοι ἑσταότες τε κατ' εὐρυπυλὲς Ἄϊδος δῶ.

(*Od.* 11.568–71)

Then I saw Minos, Zeus' splendid son,
holding a golden sceptre, sitting and presiding over trials for the dead.
They were asking their lord for judgements,
sitting and standing about him throughout the wide-gated house of Hades.

Here we see in action the link between the ruler's sceptre and his judgements.[15] His role is to ensure not that the society is a just one in some abstract sense, but that the quarrels his people bring to him are fairly judged.[16] The community of the dead at least is portrayed as being judged by its ruler, but is this indicative of the judicial practice of early archaic societies, or would the scene have been as alien as its setting to Homer's audiences?[17] Elsewhere in Homer, rulers tend to make decisions on the basis of advice, but Minos appears not to. Either he is the uniquely excellent sort of ruler to whom the advice of others contributes nothing, or Homer is showing us only that part of the process that depends exclusively on the ruler. Either way, this is an idealised vision of what a great ruler does – judge.[18]

The social function of this judicial role is suggested in Sarpedon's obituary: he 'who defended Lycia with his judgements and his might' (*ὃς Λυκίην εἴρυτο δίκῃσί τε καὶ σθένεϊ ᾧ*; *Il.* 16.542). From the narrator's perspective, the judgements of rulers are not simply a service to the disputants but acts that protect the community from a threat similar to that posed by an external enemy.[19] Similarly, the disguised Odysseus likens the fame of Penelope to that of a god-fearing noble *basileus* who rules over many strong men and upholds righteous dealings (*εὐδικίας ἀνέχῃσι*; *Od.* 19.109–11). Under such rule the land produces plenty, the sheep reproduce, the sea provides fish and the people prosper (111–14). Conversely, crooked judgements lead to hurricanes and furious downpours at harvest time that flood rivers and ruin men's works (*Il.* 16.384–92). The community's fortunes rest on the justness of its ruler's judgements.

But if Homer's audience was demographically similar to the elites to whom the rhapsode sings in the *Odyssey* (8.471–521), then should we think of Homer's glorified representation of Sarpedon as no more than wishful thinking?[20] An alternative seventh-century assessment comes from Hesiod, who depicts the ruling elite as unworthy even of being witnessed let alone celebrated when he recommends that his brother spend his time working rather than observing the court in action (*WD* 29–30). This disinterest appears more like cynicism in view of his repeated warnings of the potential for crooked judgements (219, 221, 262, 264). Such judgements are harmful not only to those on the receiving end, but to the community (*δῆμος*) whom Zeus will make pay for 'the wickedness of lords who, in conscious mischief, bend judgements, speaking crookedly' (260–2). Hesiod's view of the judicial system has presumably been coloured by his own experience of court where he has suffered an unfavourable judgement in his inheritance dispute (37–9). He critically characterises those who judged his case, and the *basileis* in general, as 'gift-devouring lords' (*βασιλῆας δωροφάγους*; cf. 221, 238).[21] Evidently, the court could be seen as an acquisitive institution that did little to benefit the community at all, let alone defend it from danger.

However, Hesiod also saw fairly administered centralised justice as an essential feature of a prosperous community. He compares those who, judging unjustly, lead their people to suffer evil (*WD* 220–4) with the alternative, those who 'give straight judgements both to foreigner and countryman and never step aside from righteousness' (225–6). And the list of blessings associated with such men is extensive: a thriving city, prosperous people, peace, freedom from natural disaster, bountiful harvests, generous wool yields, pregnancies that last to full term and produce children who resemble their fathers, and freedom from needing to go to sea (230–7). For Hesiod, as for Odysseus, a land governed by a good judge prospers.

In the *Theogony* (79–92), Hesiod attributes the success of a good *basileus* to his muse-given ability to speak gracious words: 'having spoken assuredly in the *agora*, in a short while and with understanding he puts an end even to a great quarrel' (86–7). Here the just ruler's role is more clearly stated – he ends disputes – but again this is seen as positive for all because his judgement and his words in the *agora* result in him being greeted like a god by those he passes and treated with respect (91–2). Rather than the scorn that Hesiod's own experience engenders, we see here a witnessing (or at least an imagining) of the sort of respect that Homer's elite audiences believed themselves to deserve and an acknowledgement that if they were good at their job, as Sarpedon is said to have been, then such respect would be appropriate. Homer presents the acquisitive behaviour of *basileis* as an unproblematic feature of life – lords take from their subjects and provide protection from external and internal threats in return. Hesiod's perspective on this institution differs as he emphasises the potential for resentment among those who perceive the result as unjust. Sarpedon's Lycia is a plausible ideal; it is not a fantasy.[22] Homer and Hesiod are products of societies that recognise, like Draco's Athens, a central judicial authority.

The judicial procedure

Homer and Hesiod appear to attribute responsibility for judgements differently. The latter blames multiple *basileis* for the bad judgement he received (*WD* 38) and refers to the *basileis* whose judgements determine the fortune of the (single) city (225–7), whereas the former attributes special responsibility to a single ruler in particular. This relates to how the Homeric hierarchy functions. The question of whether we can call the prominent member among the Homeric *basileis* a king has been much discussed.[23] In an attempt to avoid the areas of this debate least relevant to the present study while retaining the sense of authority necessary for a judge with coercive power, I will refer to the lead-*basileus* as 'ruler'.[24] More important here is the question of how this individual relates to the many other *basileis* and how they administer justice.

For some scholars, the exceptional individual *basileus* and the group of *basileis* are irreconcilable. Kurt Raaflaub has argued that the singular figure is an artifact of an earlier, monarchic time;[25] Luraghi agrees, concluding that 'there is no methodology that makes it possible to distil a history of political institutions out of' the Homeric poems.[26] Others have, however, successfully outlined how the Homeric polity may function. As van Wees has shown, Homer's *basileis* are hierarchically organised into two groups with one of their number at their head.[27] The category in general is an inherited position held by an adult male belonging to one of the families that have power over the community. Within this group there are 'elders', the heads of the noble families who carry a sceptre as a symbol of their status. And finally, at the head of this group of elders, there is a single dominant man – a 'ruler' – with the power to make unilateral decisions. However, important decisions are typically made following advice from the elders and sometimes informed by public opinion. Though the ruler can ignore these if he wishes, disaster tends to follow when he does.[28] We can see this model of decision-making at work in the trial depicted on Achilles' shield.

Hephaestus' depiction is described as follows:

λαοὶ δ' εἰν ἀγορῇ ἔσαν ἀθρόοι· ἔνθα δὲ νεῖκος
ὠρώρει, δύο δ' ἄνδρες ἐνείκεον εἵνεκα ποινῆς
ἀνδρὸς ἀποφθιμένου· ὃ μὲν εὔχετο πάντ' ἀποδοῦναι
δήμῳ πιφαύσκων, ὃ δ' ἀναίνετο μηδὲν ἑλέσθαι·
ἄμφω δ' ἱέσθην ἐπὶ ἴστορι πεῖραρ ἑλέσθαι.
λαοὶ δ' ἀμφοτέροισιν ἐπήπυον ἀμφὶς ἀρωγοί·
κήρυκες δ' ἄρα λαὸν ἐρήτυον· οἳ δὲ γέροντες
εἵατ' ἐπὶ ξεστοῖσι λίθοις ἱερῷ ἐνὶ κύκλῳ,
σκῆπτρα δὲ κηρύκων ἐν χέρσ' ἔχον ἠεροφώνων·
τοῖσιν ἔπειτ' ἤϊσσον, ἀμοιβηδὶς δὲ δίκαζον.
κεῖτο δ' ἄρ' ἐν μέσσοισι δύω χρυσοῖο τάλαντα,
τῷ δόμεν ὃς μετὰ τοῖσι δίκην ἰθύντατα εἴποι.

(*Il.* 18.497–508)

The people were assembled in the *agora*. There a quarrel
had arisen. Two men were striving over the requital
for a man who had been slain. One claimed the right to pay in full,
declaring his case to the people, while the other refused to take it.
Both were willing to take the verdict of a *ἴστωρ*,
and the people were shouting for both, showing support for each side.
The heralds were restraining the people, and the elders
sat on hewn stones in a sacred circle
holding in their hands the sceptres from the loud-voiced heralds.
They then shot up and, one after another, gave judgements.
Sat in the middle of them were two gold talents
to give to him among them who should most straightly speak justice.[29]

The long scholarly debate over how best to interpret this passage has consequences for the kind of 'justice' that the Homeric judicial system is able to bring about: are its judgements authoritative demands enforced by a coercive authority, or are they merely recommended compromises backed up by the soft pressure of social expectation? There are two main areas of disagreement: the substance of the case, and the means by which the decision is made. Let us consider the process first.

The crux of this question is the identity of the *ἴστωρ*. Interpretations can mostly be divided into those that see the *ἴστωρ* as the elder whose judgement is ultimately preferred, and those that see him as a separate individual who chooses the 'straightest judgement' from those offered by the elders.[30] In the former reading, the passage offers no clear answer to the question of how the straightest judgement is chosen. Typically, scholars infer that the assembled crowd, who are very vocal participants, somehow make the decision. According to Michael Gagarin, they 'probably indicate their response to the proposals vocally by shouts of approval or disapproval, thereby providing feedback to the elders and helping them find an acceptable settlement'.[31] The fact that they are mentioned at all, and four times at that, suggests that the people do have a meaningful role to play here, but for a number of reasons this is unlikely to be it. First, decisiveness is no more attributed to them than to any other individual or group. Second, this model of decision-making is not typical in Homer.[32] And finally, there are presumably several judgements proposed, some of them very similar to each other, and yet these elders, who are all apparently very eager to stand and offer the solution that will win them the prize, are supposed to agree on who has received the loudest cheer. These objections, while not rendering the idea of verdict by popular support inconceivable, do recommend that we look elsewhere for an explanation.[33]

If this passage tells us who decides which judgement is straightest then that person is the *ἴστωρ*. Understood in this way, the elders offer judgements in competition for the prize and the *ἴστωρ*, from whom the disputants are willing to accept a verdict (*πεῖραρ*), decides which judgement is 'straightest'. In the only other occurrence of the term in Homer, Idomeneus, while watching the chariot race, challenges Ajax to a wager over who has correctly recognised which chariot's horses are leading, and proposes Agamemnon as *ἴστωρ*, meaning that he should act as umpire (*Il.* 23.486). It is natural to assume that just as a *ἴστωρ* judges between two competing gamblers, so might he judge between two rival disputants in court, but this does not follow. At the chariot race, Agamemnon's proposed role is to decide which competitor shall win the prize so it does not correlate to see the *ἴστωρ* at the trial as the elder who claims the prize himself by having his judgement accepted.[34] There are in fact two contests taking place: the legal dispute and the competition between the elders – the main focus of the passage. The job of the *ἴστωρ* is evidently to make a judgement, but not primarily between the disputants, rather he must determine which elder has won the prize of two gold talents, and in so doing decide which judgement the disputants must accept.[35]

Another dispute related to the chariot race is conspicuous for its failure to involve a *ἴστωρ*. Having accused Antilochus of overtaking him unfairly, Menelaus calls on the leaders and councillors (*ἡγήτορες ἠδὲ μέδοντες*) of the Argives to judge (*δικάσσατε*) between them (*Il.* 23.573–4). It is of course possible that he had a *ἴστωρ* in mind even if he did not use the term, but if the role of the *ἴστωρ* is to find a mutually amenable solution then this is just the sort of situation in which one ought to be invoked. Instead, the suggested job of the leaders here is the same as that of the elders on the shield – to *δικάζειν*. The verb recurs moments later when Menelaus suggests instead that he himself will *δικάσω*, which is to say that he will instruct Antilochus to swear that he did not obstruct Menelaus' chariot by guile. This is not a compromise – the goal is to place one man firmly in the wrong – but neither is it a judgement so much as an apparently fair means of reaching one. Here Menelaus' solution negates the need for third-party judgements, or for a *ἵστωρ* to decide which is best. This is not an authoritative decision; it is merely a suggested path forward that Menelaus is confident will be deemed straight (*ἰθεῖα*). Based on the few examples we have available, the community's elders are associated with offering judgements while the *ἵστωρ* determines the winner of a contest, and on the shield that contest is not the homicide dispute but the judging competition.

The term *ἤϊσσον* highlights the importance of the elders' competition. For Eric Havelock, *ἤϊσσον* is a term the urgency of which requires that it must be the disputants rather than the elders who 'rush up' to 'argue the justice' of their case.[36] But this would mean that the subject of the passage is the disputants for four lines (*Il.* 18.498–501), then the people (502), the heralds (503) and finally the elders (503–8), but with a brief and confusing reversion to the disputants again in the middle (506). We must also explain why the verb *δίκαζον* is attributed to them when this is an action typically performed by judges, not the judged.[37] Instead, let us take the more obvious translation – that it is the elders who 'shoot up' and 'give judgements' – and seek to understand their haste. The explanation is in the prize on offer – both material and symbolic – which inspires the competitive struggle for the *ἵστωρ*'s approval.[38]

This is a more formalised version of the kind of group interaction we see on other decision-making occasions. As Nestor tells Agamemnon: 'when many are assembled, you will be persuaded by him who devises the best advice' (*Il.* 9.74–5).[39] The *agora*, like the battlefield, is a place where glory can be won (1.489–91). Diomedes is apparently worse than his father was in battle but better in the *agora* (*Il.* 4.400) and, much as we might expect of the hypothetical winning elder on the shield, Agamemnon tells Nestor that he is victorious (*νικᾷς*) in the *agora* for the advice he has given (2.370). Competitive tension is on display in Nestor's response to Diomedes in the assembly. Following Agamemnon's proposal that they should all admit defeat and flee (*Il.* 9.17–28), Diomedes chides the greater man, stating that even if all the other Achaeans were to leave he and Sthenelus would fight on (32–49). This wins him great and vocal approval from all the sons of the Achaeans (the crowd's input being as important here as on the shield) before Nestor stands and speaks (50–2).[40] He commends Diomedes for his wisdom, which he says is the 'best of all men his age' (54), a backhanded compliment. Speaking up first is a risky strategy for a young man like Diomedes (cf. 14.111) and Nestor sticks with the age theme to dislodge him from his current place of public approval, pointing out that because he is so young, young enough to be Nestor's youngest son (9.56–8), he has failed to bring his words to a conclusion. Indeed, Nestor claims that he, being older, should be allowed to speak, and he promises to 'declare and penetrate the whole matter, and no man shall dishonour my words, not even ruler Agamemnon' (60–2).[41] Both these men are clearly interested in guiding the army towards success, but there are also personal victories to be won. To offer advice in the assembly is to hazard one's honour for potential greater acclaim; the 'winners' come away with their honour augmented, the 'losers' with theirs diminished.[42]

Agamemnon has the power to make decisions contrary to advice and crowd support but his leash is, in practice, short. The *Iliad* is to a large extent an exploration of the dreadful consequences of a decision made in contradiction to the wishes of the crowd and adhered to in rejection of the advice of elders. Having been criticised for recommending flight, Agamemnon acknowledges his error and says: 'now let one who has better wisdom than this speak, whether young or old in years, and what he says shall please me' (*Il.* 14.107–8). Agamemnon is not what we might call 'an ideas man', but that does not mean he is not a decision-maker. As he says here, the aim for the next speaker will be to think of a plan that pleases him. Agamemnon's approval (or at least the absence of his disapproval) is crucial for the making of important decisions. This model is at work throughout Homer and its application to judicial as well as political decisions is to be expected.

Though it is clear that rulers are associated with the passing of judgements, beyond the trial on the shield, judicial decision-making is never described in detail. In other words, Homer tells us there are judges but never depicts them judging. I believe the best explanation for this lies in the nature of the Homeric plots. The *Iliad* has only one dispute that is clearly in need of resolution by a court, that between Achilles and Agamemnon, and this is complicated by the fact that one of the disputants is the community's judge. We do, in fact, see features of the traditional mode of dispute settlement attempting to work. Right at the outset, Nestor steps in and attempts to resolve the issue by urging Agamemnon not to take Briseis, and Achilles not to compete with Agamemnon (*Il.* 1.275–84), but the ruler-judge simply decides in his own favour and scorns reconciliation (285–91). Perhaps he would have had his own way had his victim been at all coercible, but Achilles is too proud to accept this treatment; he is also strong and cosmically well-connected enough that his absence from battle wins him leverage. The *Iliad* follows the kind of exceptional quarrel that confounds the community's normal means of dispute settlement.[43]

As regards the *Odyssey*, Ithaca's ruler is, for the entire tale, either absent or only secretly present. According to Alexander Loney, 'unlike historical legal texts, the *Odyssey* has no impartial arbiters or procedures that can determine what constitutes a just exchange of harm for harm'.[44] This is certainly true of Ithaca without Odysseus but there is enough in the text to demonstrate that the third-party system is merely failing, rather than altogether absent. The social problems faced by a rulerless community are an important theme and the poem's moments of societal dysfunction reveal the shape of the hole that Odysseus' absence has created. His decision-making role is so crucial that his absence means twenty years without assemblies (*Od.* 2.26), despite the judging of disputes in the *agora* being such a regular occurrence that there was a particular time of day associated with it (12.439–40).[45] The first assembly after this period depicts a scene that, up to a point, follows the format of trials and non-judicial assemblies.[46] Heralds call the Achaeans to the assembly (2.6–8), Telemachus presents his case (40–79), Antinous responds (85–128) and the elders Halitherses (161–75) and Mentor (230–41) offer their judgements.[47] At this point, however, the procedure breaks down in the absence of a decisive figure and no 'straightest judgement' is chosen.[48] For Sally Humphreys, the community here is 'reduced to silent acquiescence in a questionable victory of the stronger party', and indeed the suitors, remaining unchecked, have succeeded.[49] But neither side is truly victorious because, in the ruler's absence, no decision is made.[50]

There is nothing in Homer to undermine the coherence of this picture of trial procedure: the senior *basileis* (the heads of the noble families) hear the disputants' claims and then competitively present judgements from which the ruler will choose the one he deems 'straightest'. But Hesiod's failure to distinguish between the exceptional *basileus* and the rest of the elders remains an issue. From the perspective of the *basileis* this distinction would surely matter greatly, but I submit that this difference, though apparent, would not be especially important to an outsider like Hesiod who is wealthy but not a noble. He sees formal judgement as the work of others, observing and experiencing justice from without and with a critical eye. The case on the shield is fraught, the crowd is divided and it feels to the reader as though both sides are likely to find support among the elders leaving the ἵστωρ with a tricky decision to make, but that is probably not typical. Presumably, in other instances the case is deemed straightforward, one *basileus* stands and offers an argument to which none objects or, perhaps, a different voice offers a different argument for the same decision. In such an instance the ruler may seem almost irrelevant from the perspective of the losing party. To see the group of *basileis* as responsible for the judgement is simply to emphasise the whole without distinguishing its parts.[51]

It remains to consider the role of the common people. Homer gives no explicit indication that they influence the outcome of any decisions. Indeed, the heroic elites occupy the centre of every stage that epic depicts, and yet occasionally it seems that the people play a part that the poet cannot ignore. When Agamemnon rudely dismisses Chryses, he does so against the unanimous will of the people (*Il.* 1.22–5), which, though not authoritative, is a voice he ought to have listened to.[52] There are few whose anger Agamemnon fears – even Achilles' threats bounce off him – but the prospect of the Achaeans in general being angry with him and refusing, like Achilles, to go on fighting does worry him (14.490–51). Similarly, Hector considers Paris fortunate not to have been stoned by the Trojans already (3.56–7), the suitors fear that the Achaeans might hear of their attempt on Telemachus' life (*Od.* 16.376–82), and the people attempt to kill Eupeithes for his involvement in piracy against Ithaca's allies (16.424–9).[53] The nameless 'people' influence decisions by their displays of approval and the threat of their anger.[54]

In the case of the shield, the people are referred to four times and by two names. The *λαοὶ* are the people ruled by the *basileis*;[55] the *δῆμος* is the entire political community, which usually, though not always (e.g. *Il.* 2.188–206), includes the *basileis*. When Mentor chides the Ithacan *δῆμος* for sitting in silence instead of speaking up against the suitors (*Od.* 2.239–41), he surely does not mean to spare those most equipped to act.[56] By telling us that the *λαοὶ* rather than the *δῆμος* are assembled in the *agora*, the poet implies that this is the only part of the community whose presence is worthy of note; that the *basileis* would be there is a given. These *λαοὶ* are not only present but animated too: they are shouting, divided, in need of restraint. In adding this detail, Hephaestus conveys the seriousness of the occasion and highlights a significant informal pressure on the decision that is being made. It is safe to assume that many or most cases that came to court in archaic communities, including boundary disputes or quarrels over inheritance, did not draw such a crowd nor cause such excitement in it; but this is a grave matter with serious implications and there is no better way to impart that message visually than through an animated crowd.[57]

Given that the *λαοὶ* are mentioned three times, the identification of the *δῆμος* as those to whom the killer makes his case confirms that it is not simply the common people who will make this decision. On the other hand, if this is the work merely of the elders and the *ἵστωρ,* then the term *δῆμος* seems unnecessarily broad. This indicates how Homeric audiences conceived of the decisions of their courts: a judgement bestowed by the community even if the active roles were the preserve of a few. Not being part of the elite, Hesiod offers a more pragmatic view of popular involvement at trial, urging his brother not to spend time at court and away from work until he has stored up plenty of supplies (*WD.* 28–35).[58] Of course, for all outside the leisure class there will have been a variable practical tension between the demands of work and the desire to attend court. But Hesiod's advice implies an appetite for attending court and we can suppose that on the occasion of a trial as important as the homicide dispute on Achilles' shield, people would have made a special effort. Perhaps most cases that came before early Greek courts did not have an especially animating effect on the crowd, but in some instances, judges needed to take account not only of fact and custom but also of the political temperature. The division within the crowd is not merely a dramatic detail but an indication that this is the kind of case that demands the most of a community's elders. Though they had no formal power, the common folk could not be ignored and in a situation such as this, the judgement that the *ἵστωρ* approved needed to take the threat of the people's anger into account.[59] The early archaic world of Homer and Hesiod was made up of societies that not only followed the abstract principle that a central authority was responsible for justice, but also, again like Draco's Athens, had concrete procedural means of achieving that end.

Blood-vengeance and the state

The ultimate test of a state's capacity to constrain private anger is homicide, an offence that causes great anger and puts relatives under exceptional pressure to avenge. Draco's law implies a state able to enforce significant limitations on private action towards homicides. On the one hand, it limits revenge by protecting unintentional killers from retaliation so long as they abide by the terms of exile. On the other, it appears to afford the right to pardon only to relatives of the unintentionally killed, requiring the death of those intentional killers who cannot first escape into exile. A broadly similar level of authority can be seen in Homeric society.

The authority to act as gatekeeper, determining who is entitled to exact vengeance and how, is displayed in the second much-debated feature of the trial on Achilles' shield – the substance of the case.[60] The first disputant's claim is either that he should be allowed to pay the blood-price, which the other party refuses to accept (as in the translation adopted above), or else that he has already paid, which the other party denies. The two sides of the argument have tended to be characterised as viewing the matter in dispute as either 'legal' or 'factual'.[61] In other words, is the court about to state what kind of requital (blood or blood-price) the relative is permitted to extract or whether or not payment is owed and how much?

For a long time, the study of this passage remained bogged down in the details, aiming to establish the most natural interpretation of particular words and phrases. This is a debate worth addressing because the arguments in it continue to influence scholarship, but the more compelling and decisive evidence is, as we shall see, to be found in how the passage relates to the poem as a whole.[62]

Gagarin has highlighted what he deems to be the three main arguments in support of the 'factual' interpretation. First, *εὔχομαι*, when used with the aorist infinitive to mean 'claim' rather than 'vow', refers to past actions and so the 'claim' here must pertain to something that has happened – the debt has been paid.[63] However, there are only three such examples and in each one aspect justifies the use of the aorist. While it is possible to read the phrase as a claim that the *ποινή* has already been paid, two other interpretations are available. Muellner has demonstrated parallels with Linear B texts which indicate that *εὔχομαι*, in a legal context, may represent an assertion of a right.[64] Or, even if the act of 'giving' (*ἀποδοῦναι*) is taken to be in the past, it is possible that the situation may be the same as that in Book Nine when Agamemnon's gifts to Achilles are referred to as having been 'given' (*διδούς*) even after they have been rejected and despite never actually having been presented at all (*Il.* 9.699). Ultimately, the strongest indication as to the meaning of *εὔχομαι* is to be found in the avenger's response to it.

In order to accommodate the idea that the dispute is over a factual claim, the phrase *ὃ δ' ἀναίνετο μηδὲν ἑλέσθαι* has tended to be rendered along the following lines: 'the other claimed that he had received nothing.'[65] The first problem here is that 'to receive' fails to convey the intent that *ἑλέσθαι* implies.[66] Taken more naturally, *ἑλέσθαι* tells us simply that the avenger has not actively taken payment. More tellingly, *ἀναίνετο* has, as David Elmer has demonstrated, appeared in this context before with the meaning of 'refused' or 'rejected' rather than 'denied'.[67]

Phoenix twice uses it to indicate the response Achilles must avoid regarding Agamemnon's gifts (*Il.* 9.510, 585), and Odysseus is forced to sum up Achilles' rejection as *σὲ δ' ἀναίνεται ἠδὲ σὰ δῶρα* ('he rejects you and your gifts'; 679). In view of these parallels, it is to be expected that *ἀναίνετο* in the trial scene also refers to a refusal to accept *ποινή* rather than a denial that compensation has been received.[68]

Gagarin's second point is that *πάντα* 'implies that the dispute concerns a specific sum of money already determined'.[69] However, as Loney has shown, it mirrors Achilles' statement to Hector that the latter will now pay back all (*πάντ' ἀποτίσεις*; *Il.* 22.271) and thus *πάντα* refers not to a fixed or decided sum but to the total satisfaction which Achilles expects from Hector's destruction and which the killer in the trial promises his victim's avenger in the form of a blood-price.[70]

Finally, Gagarin argues that the phrase *δήμῳ πιφαύσκων*, 'showing to the people', refers to 'demonstrating' that one has already paid. Alternatively, as Derek Roebuck has suggested, it may mean that the killer is literally displaying the proffered but rejected items in court.[71] However, the verb *πιφαύσκω* surely means what it does at the assembly session in *Odyssey* Book Two, where it is said that one might *τι δήμιον . . . πιφαύσκεται* ('present some public matter'; 32). This killer is 'presenting to the people' his case that he should be permitted to pay the blood-price rather than face exile or death.

Though the legal interpretation seems to me preferable, the language of the passage is ambiguous enough to leave certainty unachievable. But the scene's poetic context renders the legal view considerably more secure. There is no other evidence of ambiguity over compensation payment and significant evidence that this was probably implausible. As Eva Cantarella has acknowledged, the paying of a *ποινή* was not a discreet private interaction but a highly public one.[72] Thetis tells Achilles, who intends to return to battle the moment he receives his armour, that he must call the Achaeans to the *agora* and there renounce his anger against Agamemnon (*Il.* 19.29–36). The statement of renunciation made, Achilles again seeks immediately to rouse the army to battle and Agamemnon invites him either to prepare himself and his people right away or to remain while the gifts are brought to the gathering 'in order that you may see that what I give is satisfactory' (138–44). Odysseus' intervention clarifies which option is appropriate.

Ἀγαμέμνων
οἰσέτω ἐς μέσσην ἀγορήν, ἵνα πάντες Ἀχαιοὶ
ὀφθαλμοῖσιν ἴδωσι, σὺ δὲ φρεσὶ σῇσιν ἰανθῇς.
ὀμνυέτω δέ τοι ὅρκον ἐν Ἀργείοισιν ἀναστὰς

μή ποτε τῆς εὐνῆς ἐπιβήμεναι ἠδὲ μιγῆναι·
ἣ θέμις ἐστὶν ἄναξ ἤ τ' ἀνδρῶν ἤ τε γυναικῶν·
καὶ δὲ σοὶ αὐτῷ θυμὸς ἐνὶ φρεσὶν ἵλαος ἔστω.

(*Il.* 19.172–8)

Agamemnon
must bring them into the middle of the agora in order that all the Achaeans
may see them with their eyes and that you may be cheered.
And he must, standing in the midst of the Argives, swear an oath
that he has never gone upon her bed to have intercourse.
Such is the custom, master, of men and women.
And let the spirit in your chest be gracious to him.

Obviously, the dispute between Agamemnon and Achilles is of unique importance so it may be that elements of its resolution (its scale, certainly) are unusual. Yet the public setting seems essential to the function of compensation payments in view of Odysseus' following exhortation. Achilles has already said that he (along with Agamemnon) will overpower the spirit (*θυμὸν*) in his chest and stop his anger (67) and yet now Odysseus urges him here to go further: to let his spirit be gracious (*ἵλαος*) towards Agamemnon. Evidently, there are degrees of reconciliation and Odysseus is not willing to settle for one that goes no deeper than words but demands that through the ritual of publicly giving and receiving gifts before sharing a meal the two men should altogether let go of their animosity. The giving of material wealth to cover a debt of honour was a public transaction and the claim that the community could be unsure as to whether or not it had occurred is most unlikely. The notion that such a peculiar dispute would be chosen for depiction on Achilles' shield is unlikelier still.

Furthermore, while the factual interpretation fails to stand up in comparison with the Homeric paradigm for the material repayment of *ποινή*, the legal one fits suspiciously well with the story as a whole.[73] The central plot of the *Iliad* up until this moment in Book Eighteen could be summed up with a line taken directly from the passage: 'two men were striving over a *ποινή*.' Agamemnon offers material compensation for an offence for which Achilles desired blood. Just as the shield's disputants, having heard various possible judgements, stand awaiting their verdict, so do the poem's two main protagonists, having heard many proposed solutions, finally find themselves in a moment pregnant with resolution. But here the analogy breaks down. The trial process, the elders, the *ἵστωρ* and so on that are poised to resolve the dispute on the shield are not afforded to Agamemnon and Achilles.[74] As has been shown, this may be for a number of practical reasons, but it seems to me that it serves a plot concerned in large part with the wider societal harm associated with disputes that transcend the bounds of the community's judicial institutions. Of the cities depicted on the shield, the trial scene appears in the one at peace and is a demonstration of what is unavailable to Agamemnon and Achilles – the capacity of a functioning *polis* to resolve a dispute over the rights to pay or refuse a compensatory material *ποινή*.

Legal customs: intentionality

Part of the problem in understanding this passage lies in the frequently made assumption that *ποινή* means a material payment.[75] It actually refers to a debt whose repayment can be given or extracted in various forms.[76] The quarrel is not over whether or not the *ποινή* has been paid, nor indeed whether it will be paid, but over the currency: will it be paid in material goods or blood? The killer's claim that he has the right to pay (*εὔχετο πάντ' ἀποδοῦναι*), reveals that some Homeric killers have this right and some do not, hinting intriguingly at the possibility of categories of homicide.

Scholars divide the repercussions facing Homeric killers into three categories: blood-vengeance, blood-price and exile. Of the non-battlefield killers, eight are exiled and one is killed in revenge, while the paying of a blood-price is referred to twice fictionally.[77] The absence of 'real' examples of killers paying a blood-price has led some to dismiss the practice as a Homeric custom.[78] However, Ajax's reference to the willingness of some to accept a blood-price from a killer (*Il.* 6.632–4; see below) surely assumes an audience familiar with such a custom. Furthermore, drawing conclusions from the frequency at which different fates befall killers is complicated by the poet's agenda. He does not highlight exile status in order to furnish the reader with statistical data, but to communicate something about the individual and their journey to this point, particularly as an explanation of their status in their adopted community.[79] Regardless of their frequency, Homer's audience was evidently familiar with all three kinds of outcome.[80]

It is widely held that homicide in Homer is an undifferentiated category that is consistently responded to in the same way: blood-vengeance is sought and the killer attempts to flee.[81] Adkins, in view of the different kinds of scenario that all lead to exile, says: 'hence, as regards punishment no distinction is drawn between deliberate homicide, homicide with provocation or without premeditation, accidental homicide, and (possibly) attempted homicide.'[82] This assumes that the same consequence – exile – cannot result from more than one category of homicide, but Athenian tradition proves otherwise. According to Draco's law, the judgement in a case of homicide can precipitate any of three possible outcomes for those found to have killed. Some killers are deemed unpardonable and, unless they can escape into exile, are put to death. Others are deemed pardonable at the family's discretion and may be either pardoned or sent into exile. Thus, those who are not killed or pardoned either flee into exile in anticipation of an unfavourable judgement or are sent into exile as a consequence of judgement.[83] If the world to which Homer sang dealt with homicide according to similar principles, then a preponderance of exiles rather than indiscriminately slain killers is to be expected.[84]

There are faint indications that Homer's exiles may differ in kind. Some are in genuine flight. Theoclymenus is being pursued abroad by the relatives of a man he has killed (*Od.* 15.271–82, cf. 224). In one of his tales Odysseus tells of how, having ambushed and killed a man on Crete, he went at once to a ship and bought passage off the island (13.259–75). Again, urgency is evident in Eupeithes' demand that the Ithacans waste no time in avenging the dead suitors lest Odysseus should escape to Pylos or Elis (24.430–7). It is no wonder that Odysseus, in anticipation of this, tells Telemachus:

> *καὶ γάρ τίς θ' ἕνα φῶτα κατακτείνας ἐνὶ δήμῳ,*
> *ᾧ μὴ πολλοὶ ἔωσιν ἀοσσητῆρες ὀπίσσω,*
> *φεύγει πηούς τε προλιπὼν καὶ πατρίδα γαῖαν·*
> *ἡμεῖς δ' ἕρμα πόληος ἀπέκταμεν, οἳ μέγ' ἄριστοι*
> *κούρων εἰν Ἰθάκῃ· τὰ δέ σε φράζεσθαι ἄνωγα.*
>
> (*Od.* 23.118–22)

> For anyone, having killed one man in a land,
> who might not have many avengers,
> flees, forsaking his kinsmen and the land of his fathers.
> We have killed the foundation of the city, the very best
> young men in Ithaca. I ask you to think on this.

Odysseus is not stating a rule requiring killers to flee but outlining to Telemachus how much worse is their situation than that of a typical killer: men flee the avenging relatives of even one man, so what are they to do when all the strongest families in Ithaca are out for their blood?[85] More importantly, his observation is not necessarily supposed to include all killers but only those who expect to be killed in return. Having planned and carried out the mass slaughter of many young men, Odysseus and Telemachus are surely in the category of killers who could expect a violent response. Swift flight under genuine threat of violent reprisal was certainly a possible outcome in homicide cases but it was not the only one.[86]

According to Draco's law, the victim's kin will never have the option of choosing between death and pardon. Either the killer's death is required by the state, or the relatives can decide between pardoning the killer or demanding exile. Ajax's reference to a hypothetical pardoner hints at a similar principle.

> *καὶ μέν τίς τε κασιγνήτοιο φονῆος*
> *ποινὴν ἢ οὗ παιδὸς ἐδέξατο τεθνηῶτος·*
> *καί ῥ' ὃ μὲν ἐν δήμῳ μένει αὐτοῦ πόλλ' ἀποτίσας.*
>
> (*Il.* 9.632–4)

> And a man, from his brother's killer,
> or his dead son's, accepts requital.
> And the man remains in the country having paid much compensation.

Ajax, hoping to point out how exceptionally stubborn Achilles is being, is presumably invoking the most trying circumstances under which someone will accept material compensation. Why then does he not speak of one choosing between payment and blood-vengeance, which is surely the most desirable outcome? Perhaps Ajax cannot conceive of such a choice because the option to pardon is available only alongside the option to demand exile, just as in Draco's law.

If there is a legal distinction between those homicides that can be avenged in blood and those that cannot, it is most likely intent. According to classical sources, Draco's law deals with intentional and unintentional homicide and yet the inscription we have addresses unintentional only. This, combined with the fact that the missing section of the inscription sat below the extant portion, has caused confusion for those who expect the more severe offence of intentional homicide to precede.[87] But it may be that Draco prioritised the law that would be most useful and, while it was clear what was to happen to intentional killers, the question of who among the victim's agnatic kin had what rights and obligations in the case of unintentional homicide was more likely to require reference.[88] Gagarin's suggestion that intentional homicide is implicitly included in this inscription by virtue of the inclusive 'even if' translation must be dismissed for requiring that all homicides must then have received the same punishment; classical Athenians certainly did not interpret the law this way (e.g. Antiph. 5.10,

Dem. 21.43).[89] In late seventh-century Athens the consequences faced by killers depended on intent, but if the same is true in Homer then it is less clearly stated. For some, intent is not even a recognised distinction in Homeric homicide.[90] If so, then either the Athenian tradition represents a division among Greek communities between those that allowed for intent and those that did not, or Draco's law introduces this feature in a striking departure from the recently familiar. It would be odd if intent, though so relevant to how people judged others' actions in other contexts, were ignored with regard to homicide.[91] But this is not what the evidence suggests.

The possibility of 'unintentional' (*οὐκ ἐθέλων*) homicide is clearly acknowledged. In response to Odysseus' killing of Antinous the remaining suitors say:

> *'ξεῖνε, κακῶς ἀνδρῶν τοξάζεαι· οὐκέτ' ἀέθλων*
> *ἄλλων ἀντιάσεις· νῦν τοι σῶς αἰπὺς ὄλεθρος.*
> *καὶ γὰρ δὴ νῦν φῶτα κατέκτανες ὃς μέγ' ἄριστος*
> *κούρων εἰν Ἰθάκῃ· τῷ σ' ἐνθάδε γῦπες ἔδονται.'*
> *ἴσκεν ἕκαστος ἀνήρ, ἐπεὶ ἦ φάσαν οὐκ ἐθέλοντα*
> *ἄνδρα κατακτεῖναι· τὸ δὲ νήπιοι οὐκ ἐνόησαν,*
> *ὡς δή σφιν καὶ πᾶσιν ὀλέθρου πείρατ' ἐφῆπτο.*
>
> (*Od.* 22.27–33)

> 'Stranger, wrongly do you shoot at men. Never again will you compete
> in other contests. Now your utter destruction is sure.
> For just now you killed the man who was the very best
> of the young men in Ithaca. For that, here will vultures devour you.'
> So spoke each man, since they surely supposed that it was unwillingly
> that he had killed the man. And in their folly they did not perceive
> that over them all the end of destruction had taken hold.

So far as the suitors can tell, Odysseus has not killed Antinous on purpose and yet they threaten blood-vengeance. This is not, however, evidence that intention was immaterial to guilt and punishment.[92] The poet's purpose in telling us that the act was presumed unintentional is to postpone the suitors' fear until Odysseus reveals himself; unaware of the stranger's malicious intent, they do not appreciate their danger.[93] That they are explicitly planning to kill Odysseus for this apparent accident tells us only that in Homeric society, as in those of the modern world, hot-blooded retaliatory murder was possible, but it says nothing about whether that was socially acceptable. Indeed, the suitors (of all people) cannot be taken as a paradigm for normal, acceptable or legal behaviour. Throughout the poem, their deeds have been characterised by deviancy and we might as readily wonder whether their actions point us not towards but away from the legitimate.[94]

Odysseus has already been warned by Antinous that the centaur Eurytion's inebriated condition did not win him pardon from reprisals for his 'evil acts', and neither will that excuse save Odysseus if he strings the bow (*Od.* 21.288–310).[95] This does not tell us about any hard rules around drunkenness and mitigated responsibility, but it does tell us there was such a thing as mitigated responsibility and that intoxication might sometimes support one's claim to it.[96] Antinous believes that more or less valid claims to mitigated responsibility do exist, even for those whose role in the causing of harm was beyond doubt.[97]

Patroclus recalls our other example of unintentional homicide:

εὖτέ με τυτθὸν ἐόντα Μενοίτιος ἐξ Ὀπόεντος
ἤγαγεν ὑμέτερόνδ᾽ ἀνδροκτασίης ὕπο λυγρῆς,
ἤματι τῷ ὅτε παῖδα κατέκτανον Ἀμφιδάμαντος
νήπιος οὐκ ἐθέλων ἀμφ᾽ ἀστραγάλοισι χολωθείς.

(*Il.* 23.87–8)

when Menoetius brought me, being young, from Opus
to your house by reason of a baneful manslaying,
the day I killed the son of Amphidamus
foolishly, not willingly, in anger over a game of dice.

This statement confirms that the killer's intent meant something, but was that meaning merely reputational or did it have legal relevance? It is possible that Patroclus aims to excuse his actions by reminding Achilles that they were the product of hot passion rather than cold calculation, but Homer gives no indication that such a killing would be viewed disapprovingly.[98] As to legal relevance, it is frequently assumed that the fact that Patroclus needed to go into exile despite having killed without intent demonstrates that no allowance was made for unintentionality.[99] However, we might as easily say that he was spared death because allowance *was* made for unintentionality. His claims to have acted 'not willingly' and 'in anger' appear consistently throughout our sources as mitigating factors. Demosthenes, for example, considers *ὀργή* to be a 'decent and moderate excuse' (*ἀνθρωπίνη καὶ μετρία σκῆψις*) for insulting someone and seeks to make it clear to the jurors that Meidias has acted not in anger but by design (*βεβουλευμένως*; Dem. 21.41), a juxtaposition that echoes in reverse Patroclus's argument that he acted out of anger rather than intent.[100] In following on from the recollection of his having been exiled for homicide, this justification appears causally linked.[101] In other words, he may well be stating not only that he had to leave because he had killed someone, but also that he was *permitted* to leave because he had done so unintentionally.[102] There are certainly indications, but not proofs, that the right to blood-vengeance was withheld from the relatives of those unintentionally killed and there are no compelling reasons to dismiss such a conclusion.

Νέμεσις and the coercive community

There is a central authority in the Homeric community that judges private offences, but we must consider whether that authority has the inclination and the power to intervene in any practical sense. Inclination can best be observed in the emotion of *νέμεσις* (indignation). Konstan speaks for the prevailing scholarly opinion in saying that Homeric *νέμεσις* 'is generally aroused at behaviour that runs contrary to socially accepted norms'.[103] As this implies, *νέμεσις* does not require a perceived offence against another, and even when there is one the emotion focuses not on the victim's experience but on the contravening of the community's standards.

Cairns provides a list of instances where, he claims, *νέμεσις* is felt at personal slights in a way similar to anger.[104] I contend, however, that perceived slights evoke anger, not *νέμεσις*. In two of Cairns' examples, *νέμεσις* and anger terms occur together not for emphasis but as references to distinct emotions. When Hector rebukes his brother for his absence from battle, Paris assures him that neither anger nor indignation (*χόλῳ οὐδὲ νεμέσσι*) is the cause (*Il.* 6.335–6).[105] Similarly, when Zeus witnesses Athena and Hera disobediently leaving for the battle, he sends Iris to call them back, promising harsh treatment if he should see them. This is nothing new from Hera, however, so he is not so indignant or angry with her (*νεμεσίζομαι οὐδὲ χολοῦμαι*; 8.407, 421). This pairing suggests some similarity in that when hostility is perceived, both emotions are to be considered possible causes. But it also suggests difference in that to deny anger apparently says nothing about whether or not one is indignant and vice versa. In both instances, the speaker is clarifying that they are neither angry at a personal slight nor indignant at norm-breaking behaviour.[106]

Anger and indignation also co-occur when Zeus sends Iris with the threat of violence should Poseidon not withdraw from battle. In high dudgeon Poseidon invokes both *νέμεσις* (*Il.* 15.211, 227) and *χόλος* (217) in a way that implies synonymity. In fact, only the latter describes the emotion evoked by Iris' message, which betrays Zeus' lack of respect for his brother and equal (186). In agreeing to give way despite his *νέμεσις*, he refers to the emotion that has been driving his involvement in the conflict since the Trojans reached the ships. Witnessing Zeus' support for the Trojans, Poseidon had felt pity for the suffering Achaeans and *νέμεσις* towards Zeus (*Il.* 13.15–16, cf. 353), an emotion he now accepts he must restrain.[107]

In another case, Hera, having been rebuked and threatened by the awakened Zeus, returns to the other gods and 'in indignation (*νεμεσσηθεῖσα*) spoke among them all: "Fools are we who thoughtlessly rage against Zeus"' (*Il.* 15.103–4). The object of her *νέμεσις* here is surely Zeus whom she calls 'arrogant and hard' (*ὑπερφίαλος καὶ ἀπηνής*; 94), and his victims are those to whom she now speaks for they have no choice but to suffer his 'evil works' (97, 109). Indeed, she informs Ares that he has already suffered a tragedy in the form of his son's death (110–12). Any potential Hera had for anger was banished by fear (34) following Zeus' threats (13–33). She cannot compete with him, but she can retain her indignation at his overly authoritarian rule.[108]

Though *νέμεσις* cannot be felt over personal offence, it can certainly be felt over perceived offences towards others such as: someone who casts aspersions on a commander's work ethic (*Il.* 10.115), those who abuse another's hospitality (*Od.* 1.228–9, 2.64, 22.40) and a woman who shames her parents by mixing with men unmarried (6.286–8). However, there is more to the emotion than simply the perception that someone has wronged someone else. Anger, as we have seen, is felt at slights against oneself, one's own, even one's community because the honour of the individual is bound up with the honour of those close to them and that of the group to which they belong. But when the community's norms are broken without seriously slighting those one cares about, it is *νέμεσις* that is roused. It is born of a sense of protectiveness about the standards by which everyone is supposed to live, but not a pain at personal dishonour.

Some other examples demonstrate the centrality of norm breaking over dishonour. A common trigger is the perception that people are not pulling their weight. Poseidon (as Calchas) tells the strong that his heart is indignant with them for holding back from battle (*Il.* 13.119), fear of others' indignation deters Idomeneus from talking too long with Meriones when they could be in battle (293), and Glaucon expects the same to motivate the Trojans to protect Sarpedon's body (16.544).[109] In such instances, the relevant expectation is that everyone will give their all for the communal endeavour. The failure to do so is not necessarily an insult to anyone or to the community as a whole, but it does fall short of expectation.

Having been woken in the night by Nestor, Odysseus responds rudely by failing to address the older man and simply asking why he is roaming about at night (*Il.* 10.141–2). Presumably, this kind of behaviour is associated with nefarious nocturnal activity such as thievery or spying. Nestor, who evidently understands the context, responds politely with a full list of epithets – 'son of Laertes, sprung from Zeus, resourceful Odysseus' – and urges him not to be indignant (*μὴ νεμέσα*; 144–5). There is no slight here and Odysseus' response is not a truly angry one, but it does carry an implied accusation that he has transgressed a standard that everyone else values and upholds – that one does not wander around alone outside at night.[110]

Athena (as Mentes) sums up the way *νέμεσις* works when she says of the suitors' behaviour that 'a man would feel indignation (*νεμεσσήσαιτό*) on seeing these many disgraceful acts, should one who is prudent come' (*Od.* 1.228–9). Unlike anger, which requires personal offence, *νέμεσις* can be felt by a stranger. They need only be prudent, someone who knows good from bad, because it is simply the nature of the behaviour that triggers the emotion, not their part in it.[111]

Though those who feel *νέμεσις* tend to desire the individual's harm, the absence of personal offence appears to lessen that drive compared to anger.[112] When a powerful third party feels *νέμεσις* the result can be merely an agreement not to stand in the way of revenge. Hera, angry at Ares for his excessive destruction of the Achaeans, asks Zeus if he is not indignant with him (*Il.* 5.757). Her desire is not that Zeus would intervene, perhaps because she does not expect him to feel anger as she does, but she hopes that *νέμεσις* towards Ares for his excess might lead him to grant her licence to strike Ares and drive him from the battle (762–3). Indeed, Zeus grants permission and recommends Athena as punisher (765–6).

The main deterrent to wrongdoing is the anger and vengeance of the victim. But on top of that, would-be malefactors have to consider how the community might augment the victim's capacity to retaliate. They may take no personal offence at what has been done, but *νέμεσις* can still lead them to intervene by permitting or even assisting in revenge. Sometimes the unfavourable judgement inherent in this emotion is deterrent enough, regardless of whether it manifests forcefully, as when Telemachus claims that the *νέμεσις* of the people keeps him from sending Penelope back to her father (*Od.* 2.136–7). But often *νέμεσις* and the words that give it expression serve as a warning of a more serious and violent threat. Apollo considers that the prospect of the gods' *νέμεσις* ought to be enough to put an end to Achilles' maltreatment of Hector (*Il.* 24.53). Again, no physical force is required but here threat is implied and Achilles' acquiescence demonstrates the coercive potential of the *νέμεσις* of third parties.

It is not only gods whose *νέμεσις* can coerce. The role that the *νέμεσις* of the community is supposed to play in its members' private disputes comes across clearly in the case of Telemachus and the suitors. There are two means by which someone in Telemachus' position might resolve their dispute. If he were powerful like his father he could help himself to vengeance (*Od.* 1.265–9), but his only realistic option is to call an assembly and state his case to the people (269–74). In making this speech, he acknowledges that, for those who are able, the first line of defence ought to be a man's own strength, but for him and his household this will not suffice (2.58–64). Thus, he asserts to the people:

> *'νεμεσσήθητε καὶ αὐτοί,*
> *ἄλλους τ' αἰδέσθητε περικτίονας ἀνθρώπους,*
> *οἳ περιναιετάουσι· θεῶν δ' ὑποδείσατε μῆνιν,*
> *μή τι μεταστρέψωσιν ἀγασσάμενοι κακὰ ἔργα.'*
>
> (Od. 2.64–7)

> 'You yourselves be indignant too,
> and feel shame before other nearby men,
> those who live about you. And cower before the anger of the gods,
> lest they somehow turn around and begrudge evil deeds.'

Telemachus is not alone in deeming the suitors' behaviour worthy of *νέμεσις*. Mentes has already told Telemachus any prudent man would feel it at the suitors' actions (1.228); Odysseus tells Eurymachus before killing him that fear of the gods and of the *νέμεσις* of men ought to have restrained the suitors from their outrages (22.40); it is even hoped that Antinous will feel it at his own behaviour (2.138–9).[113] Telemachus' hope is that the Ithacans will be indignant at the outrageous behaviour of their own (the suitors) towards their own (Telemachus, his father and his household) and will intervene.

The Ithacans' failure to intervene is supposed to shock us. Nestor can think of only two reasons why such a state of affairs might be permitted to continue: either Telemachus is allowing the suitors' behaviour, or the people hate him (*Od.* 3.214–15). In proper circumstances, it seems, Telemachus ought to be able to rely on the rest of the community to help him at least get rid of the men. Telemachus highlights the pressures surrounding the community's role: the threat of ill-repute among neighbours and the punishments of the gods, both of which fall indiscriminately on the community as a whole for the outrages it fails to police among its number (2.65–7). And Mentor soon confirms the shame that the Ithacans' passivity invites; their lack of *νέμεσις* evokes *νέμεσις* in him:

'νῦν δ' ἄλλῳ δήμῳ νεμεσίζομαι, οἷον ἅπαντες
ἧσθ' ἄνεῳ, ἀτὰρ οὔ τι καθαπτόμενοι ἐπέεσσι
παύρους μνηστῆρας καταπαύετε πολλοὶ ἐόντες.'

(*Od.* 2.239–41)

'Now I am indignant with the rest of the community, that you all
sit silently, and do not in any way, speaking words of rebuke,
restrain the few suitors, you being many.'

The suitors are free to take whatever risks they like (235–8), but the rest of the community is obligated to respond. This is not a request or recommendation but a reminder of responsibility. And the crowd's silence reveal's the weight of this obligation. Both sides have their say and two community voices speak in support of Telemachus, but in the end it is one of the accused that breaks up the assembly without Telemachus having received an answer. The people evidently cannot justify their inaction. The indignation and intervention of the community is precisely what would typically happen in such an instance as this; the Ithacans' failure in this regard is an important pillar of the Odyssean plot.

Mentor expects *νέμεσις* expressed in 'words of rebuke' to be sufficient to restrain the suitors but only if supported by the threat of superior force, the people being many and the suitors few. The responding suitor, Leocritus, does not dispute the principle that the community have a responsibility to restrain the suitors and even accepts that it would be difficult for the suitors to fight against greater numbers, but implies that for the sake of a meal it is not worth their interfering (*Od.* 2.244–5). This illuminates the moral position of the Ithacan people: they have the responsibility and the power to act, but they lack the will.[114]

This issue hangs in the balance throughout the poem and we see later, when the suitors' confidence in the tolerance of the community wanes, that the *δῆμος* does represent a meaningful threat to those who abuse its members. On discovering that Telemachus has evaded the suitors' ambush, Antinous considers what might result.

ἀλλ' ἄγετε, πρὶν κεῖνον ὁμηγυρίσασθαι Ἀχαιοὺς
εἰς ἀγορήν—οὐ γάρ τι μεθησέμεναί μιν ὀΐω,
ἀλλ' ἀπομηνίσει, ἐρέει δ' ἐν πᾶσιν ἀναστὰς
οὕνεκά οἱ φόνον αἰπὺν ἐράπτομεν οὐδ' ἐκίχημεν·
οἱ δ' οὐκ αἰνήσουσιν ἀκούοντες κακὰ ἔργα·
μή τι κακὸν ῥέξωσι καὶ ἡμέας ἐξελάσωσι
γαίης ἡμετέρης, ἄλλων δ' ἀφικώμεθα δῆμον·

ἀλλὰ φθέωμεν ἑλόντες ἐπ' ἀγροῦ νόσφι πόληος
ἢ ἐν ὁδῷ·

(*Od.* 16.376–84)

But come, before that one calls the Achaeans
to assembly, for I think he will not let it go
but will be angry, and standing he will declare among them all
that we contrived sheer murder for him but did not hit the mark.
And they will not praise us, hearing our evil deeds.
They might do some evil and drive us out
of our land, and we will arrive at the land of others.
But let us act first, seizing him in the country, away from the city,
or on the road.

Telemachus is weak but not defenceless; the Achaeans of Ithaca can be expected to assist him. And this is not only if he finds relatives or friends to help him, but if he calls an assembly and makes his allegations before the *δῆμος*.[115] The solution is to act fast and keep Telemachus away from the city, whose institutions can help those victims of offence who are too weak to defend and avenge themselves.

Public offence, public anger

Close to a century ago, Robert Bonner and Gertrude Smith claimed that 'the Solonian Heliaea is itself the direct descendent of the Homeric *agora*, which on occasion meted out justice to public offenders'.[116] But the debate over administered justice has since tended not to explore the question of public offence and punishment.[117] In terms of evidence, if trials for private offences are barely noticeable in Homer, trials for offences against the community are more or less invisible and neither does Draco's law indicate whether they occurred in late seventh-century Athens.[118] Again, however, despite the poet's interests lying away from the institutional aspects of Homeric life, the ingredients for public offence, procedure and punishment are observable even if we never see them fully combined.

Penelope recounts to Antinous the time when his father, Eupeithes, had fallen foul of public ire.

ἦ οὐκ οἶσθ' ὅτε δεῦρο πατὴρ τεὸς ἵκετο φεύγων,
δῆμον ὑποδείσας; δὴ γὰρ κεχολώατο λίην,

οὕνεκα ληϊστῆρσιν ἐπισπόμενος Ταφίοισιν
ἤκαχε Θεσπρωτούς· οἱ δ' ἡμῖν ἄρθμιοι ἦσαν·
τόν ῥ' ἔθελον φθῖσαι καὶ ἀπορραῖσαι φίλον ἦτορ
ἠδὲ κατὰ ζωὴν φαγέειν μενοεικέα πολλήν·
ἀλλ' Ὀδυσεὺς κατέρυκε καὶ ἔσχεθεν ἱεμένους περ.

(*Od.* 16.424–30)

Do you not know of the time when your father came here fleeing,
terrified of the people? For indeed they were exceedingly angry,
on account of the fact that he had joined with Taphian raiders
inflicting pain on the Thesprotians who were united with us.
Thus were they willing to kill him and bereave him of his dear life
and devour his means of living, great and desirable.
But Odysseus restrained them and this though they were eager.

This offence has not personally harmed any of those now angry with him and there is nothing wrong in principle with raiding, but Eupeithes has attacked an ally of Ithaca, an act presumably all the more infuriating to the Ithacans for the culprit being one of their own.[119] The offended and angry victim here is the *δῆμος*, individuals united by their membership of the Ithacan community. Alongside its tendency towards division and social fragmentation, anger in Homer carries the potential for unification and centralisation.

This demonstrates public vengefulness but in the form of a lynch mob, not formal processes. There is though a general distinction between public and private matters being brought before the *agora*. At the Ithacan assembly, the elder Aegyptius asks if the purpose of the meeting is to bring news of the army's return or to 'declare some other public matter', *τι δήμιον ἄλλο πιφαύσκεται* (*Od.* 2.30–2), and Telemachus answers that it is neither, but 'business of his own', (42–5). The same distinction applies in foreign dealings so that Telemachus, on arriving before Nestor, must clarify that he has come to 'speak on private business, not public' (3.82; cf. 4.314).[120] Clearly there were issues of a public nature that concerned the whole community and demanded a communal response.

Aegyptius asks about the predominant public matter in Ithaca – the long-absent army – but there were evidently several kinds of *δήμιος* issue. In classical Athens, the crime of Eupeithes is the sort of offence that would have been the subject of a public suit and potentially a public punishment. While it appears that in this instance he is fleeing vigilantes, it seems to me likely that in other circumstances, where public opinion is yet to be won or the facts or legality of the act are in dispute, this is the kind of accusation that might be brought up as a public matter at the *agora* and be punished accordingly.

The private and public are blurred in the allegations Eupeithes later brings against Odysseus after the suitors' massacre.

ὦ φίλοι, ἦ μέγα ἔργον ἀνὴρ ὅδ' ἐμήσατ' Ἀχαιούς·
τοὺς μὲν σὺν νήεσσιν ἄγων πολέας τε καὶ ἐσθλοὺς
ὤλεσε μὲν νῆας γλαφυράς, ἀπὸ δ' ὤλεσε λαούς·
τοὺς δ' ἐλθὼν ἔκτεινε Κεφαλλήνων ὄχ' ἀρίστους,
ἀλλ' ἄγετε, πρὶν τοῦτον ἢ ἐς Πύλον ὦκα ἱκέσθαι
ἢ καὶ ἐς Ἦλιδα δῖαν, ὅθι κρατέουσιν Ἐπειοί,
ἴομεν·

(*Od.* 24.426–32)

Friends, a great deed has this man devised against the Achaeans.
Some, many and good, he led with ships,
but he lost the hollow ships and completely lost the men.
Others, the best of the Cephallenians, he killed on returning.
But come, before that one goes quickly to Pylos
or divine Elis, where the Epeans hold power,
let us go.

The identity of Eupeithes' audience here is ambiguous. We can assume the relatives of the dead are present, as are Medon, the singer (439–40) and Halitherses (451–2). Beyond this, we are told that Rumour has gone throughout all the city with news of the massacre and that 'they gathered' (*οἱ. . . ἐφοίτων*) at Odysseus' house (415). 'They' then collect the dead, bury their own and send home those from other cities before assembling at the *agora*. Given that 'all the city' has been told the tale and that the respondents have not been identified as kin, we might suppose that those involved are to be thought of as all the Ithacans. Furthermore, the need to arrange for the transportation of the non-Ithacan dead is a burden for the community as a whole so it would make sense for more than the relatives of victims alone to be involved.[121]

Speaking to the whole Ithacan community, then, Eupeithes does not simply call on the rest of the bereaved to avenge their kin, but also (and principally) addresses the public matter of Odysseus' record in the Trojan expedition. He uses the same verb, *ὄλλυμι*, to describe what has happened to the army as he does for the ships, and even if we translate this as 'destroy' it is clear that he places this in a different category to the fate of the suitors – Odysseus has not 'killed' his comrades, but he is as responsible for their demise as he is for the loss of the ships. The mention of the ships alongside the men as marks against him frames this matter in terms affecting the entire community: a city's ships and fighting men are a source of security and power, and their mishandling ought to be a cause of public ire.[122] Even the private matter of homicide carries an element of public interest. The burden to avenge them is a private one – Eupeithes speaks in the following lines of the shame that will haunt the fathers and brothers of the unavenged (*Od.* 24.432–6) – but many of those killed do not have relatives present, their families not having had time to receive the news and travel there. Whether or not the suitors' value to the community might cause the unbereaved to take offence at their murder, Eupeithes appears to aim at evoking a sense of responsibility for the loved ones of others. It may be that the political implications of such a massive slaughter of important men are bound to be a cause for public as well as private concern. Homicide is a private matter, but Odysseus' actions include offences of a public nature and demand, in Eupeithes' view, the entire community's retaliation.

Eupeithes now seeks to direct the public anger from which he once fled in fear; his refuge before is his target now. But, unlike Eupeithes' own offence, Odysseus' actions do not yet appear to have evoked the anger of the entire *δῆμος*; it is a matter for public debate. Eupeithes wins the pity of all (*Od.* 24.438) and, we might infer, the anger of the more than half of those present who follow him (463–4). But the rest remain behind in fear of the gods, who Medon testifies are supporting Odysseus (450), and perhaps in acceptance of Halitherses' accusation that they are to blame for the consequences of what they have failed to police (455–62). Odysseus cannot be tried and punished for his actions in the way that others might (he is the judge and many of the elders are related to the victims), but Eupeithes does present a case intended to win the violent support of his audience in punishing someone who has offended the whole community.

Conclusion

Early Greek communities had a central judicial authority. In Homer, this is a set of elders, the male heads of elite families, who made judicial decisions with one of their number serving as the recognised ruler and judge. In Draco, the body of elders is formalised as the Areopagus Council and its panel of *ephetai*, while the judge is replaced by a majority vote, but aside from this move towards republican institutions the fundamental principles of the administration of justice were essentially the same. There is more at stake than bad blood in the act of judging;

a righteous judge can mean the difference between natural disasters and fruitful harvests. Such drastic consequences indicate the burden the decision-maker carried. His role was not to find the happy medium between the two parties, but to impose a 'just' verdict, to state who owed what to whom. The degree of authority that the centre wielded over how private quarrels were to be settled is demonstrated on Achilles' shield where even the kin of a homicide victim cannot act without the judge's say-so, a decision that may well be guided, as in Draco's law, by an assessment of intent. This then is a world of legal standards, those in the right, those in the wrong and a judge to tell them apart.

It is not only the elite but the *δῆμος* as a whole that, despite the common people having no formal say, is conceived of as sharing responsibility for the judgements of the court. Whether or not decisions were always representative of majority opinion, the common people's numerical superiority gave them two important functions. The prospect of their approval and the threat of their discontent afforded the people influence over decisions, meaning the elites, charged with judging between those divided by offence and anger, were kept somewhat in check by the anger of those they ruled. But the power of the people was also a crucial ingredient in the recipe of coercion: its indignation towards those who broke with its norms and its anger at those who caused it offence could provoke the community to respond with anything from verbal warnings to homicidal violence. In this way the basic building blocks of the state emerge from the pages of Homer and Hesiod, born of the emotions of the communities they depict. This coming together of the group in the effort to manage the anger of its individuals creates a new conduit for that same emotion: a community with honour that can be slighted, anger that can be roused and a capacity for vengeance that can be turned to the punishment of its offending parts.

4

Punishment and Anger in the Athenian Courts

Introduction

The preceding chapters have removed one of the two legs on which stands the traditional narrative surrounding the administration of justice in Greece from Homer to classical Athens. The notion that, in Homeric society, responses to offences were exclusively private acts of revenge with little or no regulation from the community is untenable. Homer depicts something like a 'state' that exercises control over private anger and retaliation and is able to mobilise the anger of the community in avenging slights against its collective honour.

The other leg on which the traditional narrative of change stands will be considered in the remaining chapters. The focus of this study will now turn to the concept of punishment in classical Athens, asking whether the norm of revenge over slighted honour found in Homer has given any ground to the idea of punishment for the dispassionate upholding of justice.

Central to this distinction is the punisher's state of mind. In the Homeric world, punishment is defined by anger, the emotion that identifies offence and drives retaliation. But for many, the punishments of classical Athens were in a new category. For some scholars, anger had become at best problematic, straddling the boundary of legitimacy as a motive that jurors knew to be wrong but frequently refused to restrain. For others, anger had lost its role in punishment altogether, serving only to obstruct rather than facilitate justice. According to its most pointed rendering, this model is one in which state institutions stepped in when called upon to punish wrongdoers on behalf of their victims.[1] So was there really no legitimate role for anger among jurors in the classical Athenian law court? Or was there an emotional resemblance between the Homeric hero taking out his wrath on those who had slighted him and the Athenian juror voting for the infliction of penalties on law breakers?

We have seen already that centralised, authoritative institutions able to manage and even exploit private anger were not post-Homeric inventions. We will now see that the concept of punishment in fifth- and fourth-century Athens had by no means been divorced from angry self-interest. The principle remained unchanged that punishment would be an expression of anger. By voting for punishment, jurors took revenge for perceived slights against themselves and their community. In many ways, jurors in classical Athens administered justice on the same principles as the Homeric *basileis*.

Punishment terminology

If we are to understand the emotional quality of classical Athenian punishments, we ought to begin with a survey of the core vocabulary. The Athenian forensic corpus uses four main terms for punishment: *τιμωρία, κόλασις, δίκην λαμβάνω/δίδωμι, ζημία*.[2] What follows is a limited appraisal of their meanings in the context of the Athenian courts. Aristotle is an important source for this analysis, though what these terms actually meant in the trial context is truly revealed only by the law-court speeches themselves. The defining of these terms is a task addressed throughout the following chapters in service of the deeper goal of understanding the nature of Athenian punishment.

Τιμωρία

The tradition that law and punishment at Athens had, by the fourth century, evolved away from the personal and emotional and towards the detached and rational has had to confront the fact that by far the most common term for punishment used in the Athenian forensic corpus is *τιμωρία* (and *τιμωρέω/-ομαι*), a term whose component parts strongly imply revenge: 'the guarding of one's honour.'[3] But etymology is the least of this tradition's problems. Fifth- and fourth-century playwrights and historians routinely used *τιμωρία* to describe indisputably vengeful acts. And the court context was no exception, *τιμωρία* being used there to denote violent retaliation against private offenders.[4] The question is not whether *τιμωρία*'s range of meaning in the classical law-court setting included revenge, but whether it included anything else besides.

According to Herman, 'in Athens the word *τιμωρία* was used to mean something more like 'punishment'' where 'punishment is an expression of the communal will and is applied impartially to all members of the citizen body irrespective of status, power or prestige'.[5] Recognising the earlier meaning, he goes on to say that 'the remarkable stability of the Athenian democracy may in part be attributable to the success of the *dikast* system in preventing the meaning of *τιμωρία* from regressing from "punishment" to "vengeance"'.[6] Herman's reasons for withholding the term 'revenge' from the acts of the court boil down to the assumptions, addressed in the introduction, that revenge is private and violent.[7] This argument hinges more on the meanings of the English terms than on the Greek. If one accepts, as I do, that revenge need not be violent and can be performed by states, then there is no reason to withhold that translation from *τιμωρία*.

If there were multiple recognised meanings in the Athenian court context, Aristotle makes no note of them. According to him,

> *διὰ θυμὸν δὲ καὶ ὀργὴν τὰ τιμωρητικά. διαφέρει δὲ τιμωρία καὶ κόλασις· ἡ μὲν γὰρ κόλασις τοῦ πάσχοντος ἕνεκά ἐστιν, ἡ δὲ τιμωρία τοῦ ποιοῦντος, ἵνα πληρωθῇ.*
> (*Rh.* 1.10.16–17)

> Passion and anger are the causes of acts of revenge. But there is a difference between τιμωρία and κόλασις; the latter has in mind him who suffers it, the former him who inflicts it, that he may obtain satisfaction.

Aristotle, then, considers anger to be the only driver of *τιμωρητικά*. He also considers *τιμωρία* to be the only goal of anger, as his definition of *ὀργή* reveals:

> *ἔστω δὴ ὀργὴ ὄρεξις μετὰ λύπης τιμωρίας φαινομένης διὰ φαινομένην ὀλιγωρίαν εἰς αὐτὸν ἤ τι τῶν αὐτοῦ, τοῦ ὀλιγωρεῖν μὴ προσήκοντος.*
> (*Rh.* 2.2.1)[8]

> desire, with pain, for an apparent revenge over an apparent slight towards oneself or one of one's own when that slight is undeserved.

Given that this appears in his list of seven causes of all human action, it is equally significant where he chooses not to place *τιμωρητικά*. The previous category of 'calculation' (*λογισμός*; 1.10.16), acts that are expedient, is surely the cause that we would expect to lead to non-angry, non-vengeful punishments, and yet only anger can inspire acts of *τιμωρία*. Of course, Aristotle is separating out the component parts of what he thinks motivates people, and any number of the seven may be at work simultaneously. In practice one person may harm another out of habit, the calculation that it will benefit them, and anger at an apparent slight, but if we are to call that act *τιμωρία* then only the last of these is essential.

Aristotle's definition of *τιμωρία* chimes with our 'revenge' in that it is performed by those who are angry at having been slighted and who are in search of satisfaction. And the speeches, as we shall see, provide ample confirmation for Aristotle's definition in that context.[9] An act of *τιμωρία* is one that reclaims one's honour and, insofar as the English term shares this meaning, I consider 'revenge' to be the best translation.[10] However, reflecting my stance outlined in the introduction that acts of revenge may also be punishments, I will also refer to the acts of *τιμωρία* taken by the court as 'punishments'.

κόλασις

The meaning of *κόλασις* has been a source of disagreement, not least in the law-court context. For many, the distinction from *τιμωρία* is of great significance in terms both of the punishment's implied goals and of historical cultural change. As Allen puts it:

> The word *kolazein* shifts the focus away from the idea of exchange between parties, away from the idea of reciprocity and victim-driven punishment, and to the idea of how the nature of the wrongdoer is affected by punishment. The switch of focus from the victim to the wrongdoer entails a switch in understandings of the social relations involved in justice.[11]

In this view, scholars have generally taken their lead from Aristotle and the distinction cited above, but applying that definition to the forensic corpus is problematic. Robert Nichols agrees that 'Aristotle rigidly distinguishes τιμωρία and κόλασις: one inflicts τιμωρία in the interests of the victim, while one inflicts κόλασις in the interests of the attacker'. However, for him this distinction was absent in court where the two terms were 'equally retributive and directed towards the victim of wrongdoing'.[12] In this, Nichols has hit upon the problems that the forensic speeches pose for the traditional rendering of Aristotle's distinction, but has come, I think, to the wrong conclusion. Aristotle did not disagree with convention on the meaning of *κόλασις*; we have misunderstood Aristotle.

Κόλασις, like *τιμωρία*, is motivated by anger, whether in Aristotle or in the speeches. This is clearly Aristotle's understanding – both *τιμωρία* and *κόλασις* are *τιμωρητικά* and, as such, products of passion and anger (*Rh*. 1.10.16–17) – and it holds throughout his works. Violent and abusive men retaliate with *κόλασις* out of anger (*EE*. 1221b), some lose their temper and refuse to be reconciled without obtaining *τιμωρία* or *κόλασις* (*NE*. 1126a) and the severity of *κόλασις* will depend on the degree of offence taken (*Rh.* 2.3.5). In the orators, Demosthenes encourages jurors to respond angrily (*ὀργίλως*) by *κολάζοντας* a defendant (Dem. 24.211; cf. 218, 21.36–7, 45.67, Lyc. 1.111), and in another speech implies that the failure to *κολάζειν* with death is due to a shortage of *ὀργή* (*Dem.* 21.70). In a more general sense, speeches in which *κόλασις* is called for tend also to include calls for *ὀργή* (26 of 29) and the remaining three contain only one reference to *κόλασις* each; orators apparently thought angry jurors would be more inclined towards *κόλασις*. The jurors in Aristophanes' *Wasps* come to court with three days' worth of anger in order to inflict *κόλασις* on Laches (244; cf. 407). The primary emotional driver of *κόλασις* was anger both in Aristotle's model and in court.

As with punishment more generally, there is also evidence that appears to support the view that *κόλασις* did not need and perhaps ought not to be a product of anger. Xenophon recommends, in view of the catastrophic consequences of a military commander's rash decision, that *κόλασις* should never be done in anger, even towards slaves (*Hell.* 5.3.7). First, he clearly accepts that *κόλασις* can in principle be done in anger – that is what led to the disaster – but he seems also to be allowing for *κόλασις* in the absence of anger. Xenophon assumes a situation where one is already angry just as the commander in the narrative was made angry (*ὀργισθεὶς*) by the destruction of a portion of his army (5.3.5). What one must not do is to *κολάζειν* in the moment of anger first being felt 'for anger does not look ahead (*ἀπρονόητον*), while judgement (*γνώμη*) considers the avoidance of harm no less than the infliction of it on the enemy'. This is a useful example of what we shall see is a broader theme in our sources, particularly the forensic corpus, regarding the role of anger in punishment; for now, it is sufficient to say that *κόλασις*, like all punishment, requires anger, even if the pain felt at its onset may have simmered down by the time the victim acts.

Both *τιμωρία* and *κόλασις* are responses to anger, but they are not identical. The preference for a calculated approach to *κόλασις* makes sense in view of its purpose. According to Aristotle, its cognate, *ἀκολασία* (along with *ἀκόλαστος* and *ἀκολασταίνω*) is the vice for which *σωφροσύνη* is the related virtue (*EE.* 1221a).[13] The central theme is self-control with *σωφροσύνη* the quality possessed by those who can resist their desires and even take pleasure in doing so (*NE.* 1104a) while *ἀκολασία* belongs to those who pursue whatever will bring them pleasure at any moment regardless of negative long-term consequences (*EE.* 1231a; *NE.* 1104b; *Vir.* 1250a). Thus, common translation options for *ἀκολασία* include licentiousness, intemperance, profligacy and indiscipline. Aristotle confirms the connection between these words saying that the *ἀκόλαστος* person is one who has not been *κεκολασμένος* (*EE.* 1230a–b). *Κόλασις* is evidently concerned with its sufferer's correction and in a more precise way than the term 'punishment' conveys. A punished person does not necessarily change their ways and an undisciplined person may well have been punished but to no lasting effect. This interest in behavioural outcomes over means of creating them is reflected in the use of *κόλασις* to describe a master's treatment of his slave in the hopes of discouraging his vices (*Econ.* 1344a) and particularly in the fact that this may be a purely verbal chastisement (*λόγῳ προκολάζειν*; *Rh.* 2.3.15).[14] We would tend not to refer to a warning or reprimand as a kind of punishment so much as a precursor to one but *κόλασις* is concerned more with changing than harming its target.

Two idiosyncratic instances illuminate the nature of the behavioural change that *κόλασις* seeks. Aristotle describes sick and insane people as needing one of two types of *κόλασις* – medical (*ἰατρικῆς*) or official (*πολιτικῆς*) – and adds that treatment with drugs is *κόλασις* just as much as flogging is (*EE.* 1214b). Equally peculiar is Theophrastus' anecdote that some describe as *κόλασις* a certain horticultural practice intended to straighten almond trees which are out of order (*ὑβρίζον*) whereby an oak peg is driven into it and covered with soil (*Enquiry into Plants* 2.7.6). These acts aim at correction. The only common ground between medication and flogging is the endeavour to correct the person's behaviour while the goal of the oak peg is to correct the tree's shape. Perhaps as striking as the use of *κόλασις* here is the use of *hybris* to describe a tree which is taking the wrong shape. *Hybris* is characteristic of someone who has forgotten their place and is behaving in a way which their position does not justify, and *κόλασις* is often associated with putting such people back in their place.[15] As such, *κόλασις* is an act overwhelmingly inflicted by superiors on inferiors, be they hegemonic *poleis* on their allies (Th. 1.40.5, 43.1, 3.40.7, 46.4–6), higher-ranked officers on lower (Xen. *An.* 3.2.31; *Cy.* 1.6.20; Arist. *NE.* 1132b), or masters on their slaves (Ar. *Cl.* 7; Arist. *Econ.* 1344a). Central to *κόλασις* then is the attempt to return the offender to their correct hierarchical place.

Given Aristotle's categorisation of it as a *τιμωρητικός* (act of revenge), it is perhaps surprising to see that Aristotle also refers to the disciplining of a child as *κόλασις* (*NE.* 1119b6).[16] Even allowing for a context where anger and violence were normal and acceptable features of parenting, this apparent association of revenge concepts with the disciplining of children seems unnatural. However, while acceptable parenting practice and revenge as it is typically conceived today are unlikely to be reconciled, they can at least be brought closer together. Responding out of anger over a perceived slight could just as easily describe the punitive actions (whether a violent beating or banishment to a bedroom) of a disobeyed parent as the retaliatory murder of a spouse's lover; questions of honour and respect pertain to both. The values of honouring parents and respecting elders remain familiar today, even if the phrases are somewhat old-fashioned. A parent, perceiving dishonour or disrespect, may discipline in an attempt to restore the appropriate sense of hierarchy and deference. The broad moral range of *κόλασις* is confirmed by the suggestion that one might punish (*κολάσεις*) 'paternally' or with contempt (*Pol.* 1315a).

Clearly, *κόλασις* includes acts that are not revenge, specifically the punishing of those who have made one angry but are not one's enemy, those towards whom the primary feeling is one of goodwill. But that quality is not essential; the term can refer to the vengeful acts of those who desire the suffering of the punished, and this is the overwhelming sense behind the acts of *κόλασις* spoken of in court (albeit predominantly by prosecutors). Many scholars have been led by the second part of Aristotle's definition to see *κόλασις* and *τιμωρία* as profoundly different, perhaps even mutually exclusive. The definition treats *τιμωρία* as inflicted *ἕνεκα* the punisher, *κόλασις ἕνεκα* the punished. Typically, *ἕνεκα* has been translated here as 'in the interests of' which implies, I think wrongly, that acts of *κόλασις* always intend the wrongdoer's benefit.[17] The disciplining of a child fits with this interpretation, but the majority of examples, certainly those in the court setting, do not. It is incompatible (or only imaginatively compatible) with the recommendation that jurors execute the defendant.[18] *Κόλασις* is focused on the punished in a way that *τιμωρία* is not, but it is not inherently generous in the sense that the disciplining of one's child could be. If we render *ἕνεκά ἐστιν* as 'has in mind', we can avoid these notions of care and allow for a punitive goal that remains oriented around helping the punisher.

Let us look at Aristotle another way. He feels the need to clarify the difference between *τιμωρία* and *κόλασις* not because they are so different, but because they are so similar. Both are products of anger and, therefore, of perceived slights to oneself or one's own. But more particularly, both are *τιμωρητικά*, a choice of term that indicates strongly where Aristotle considers the common ground to lie. I would suggest that he means by this term 'acts of *τιμωρία*', meaning he can be summarised as saying some acts of *τιμωρία* are also acts of *κόλασις* but others are not. This accounts for the fact that appeals for both terms appear alongside each other without contradiction, often near-synonymously, throughout the orators.

Both *τιμωρία* and *κόλασις* are born of anger and both seek to redress the honour imbalance, but while the former focuses purely on reclaiming what was lost, the latter aims to put the offender back in their place. We have seen that this was a common function of revenge in early Greece and so it remains in classical Athenian law courts. Just as Agamemnon's treatment of Achilles is both a vengeful reaction to a perceived slight and a calculated attempt to remind Achilles and others that they are beneath challenging him, so could Athenian jurors be persuaded that in expressing their anger against a defendant through vengeance they could at the same time deter future offences by putting the punished individual back in their place.

Δίκην λαμβάνω/δίδωμι

Δίκη refers to the debt of honour, often represented materially, owed to a victim by the person who has wronged them and is what the victim hopes to acquire through an act of *τιμωρία*. *Δίκην λαμβάνω* and *τιμωρέομαι* are more or less synonyms in this sense. The important point here, particularly in contrast to *κόλασις*, is that these terms are interested primarily in reclaiming something lost in the past. Their focus is on the dishonour that the culprit has inflicted on the victim – the money lost, the pain suffered – as opposed to a chastening of the culprit.[19]

Δίκην λαμβάνω is used to denote the action of the victim, *δίκην δίδωμι* that of the punished. These phrases do not have obvious English equivalents. In each, *δίκη* is the object and this creates at least a superficial problem for constructions involving the word 'punish', which naturally treats the wrongdoer as its object. This problem becomes most meaningful when the wrongdoer gives a *δίκη* to the plaintiff rather than the state. Demosthenes tells the jurors 'I have found this man… more worthy to *δοῦναι δίκην* than the other' (30.1) and goes on to acknowledge his intention to '*δίκην με λήψεσθαι*' (6), confirming that if the defendant does give a *δίκη* it will be to him rather than the state. If punishment in the law-court context is an act of the state, then to render *δοῦναι δίκην* as 'to be punished' here implies that the *δίκη* is being given to the state when it is in fact being given directly to the plaintiff.

The phrase 'to give/take justice' is at least syntactically similar to the Greek but is not ideal.[20] It conveys the notion that the *δίκη* is essentially a repayment of a debt, but 'justice' must be understood in strictly relative terms. To the person taking *δίκη* the act may seem just, but it probably will not to the person giving it (e.g. Lys. 25.32) and perhaps not to observers either.[21] Demosthenes, for example, asks his audience to 'estimate what Meidias must have suffered before he could plan such *δίκη* against a fellow citizen' (21.88). Meidias, having been found guilty by default for failing to attend an arbitration, took *δίκη* from the arbitrator by contriving to have him disenfranchised and Demosthenes evidently expects the jurors to agree that this *δίκη* exceeded 'justice'. I therefore prefer 'to give/take satisfaction', which retains the Greek terms' subjective quality.

Ζημία

Unlike the other terms, *ζημία* does not mean punishment at all, though it frequently refers to punishments. It is loss, damage or harm of some kind. In legal contexts, this can take the form of either disgrace (*ὄνειδος*) or something material such as a fine or exile (*Rh.* 1.12.10). However, unlike *τιμωρία* and *κόλασις*, *ζημία* is not inherently legitimate in the subject's eyes. It does not presume that the object owes a debt of honour and may in fact be entirely unprovoked. Though the forensic orators mostly use it with reference to the 'legitimate' acts of the state, it can also describe unambiguously 'wrong' acts like the taking of bribes which damage (*ζημιοῦσι*) the city (Lys. 30.25; cf. Pl. *L.* 846a). And it can describe a loss with no moral baggage at all. In those many instances, however, where it is inflicted in response to a perceived slight, *ζημία* denotes the loss, damage or harm imposed in order to redress an imbalance of honour.

The measure of honour that *ζημία* restores can be very large, such as that owed by those guilty of betraying the city as one of the Thirty Tyrants (Lys. 12.34) or reckless generalship (Aeschin. 3.131). It can also be very small, such as the fulfilling of the agreed consequences of defaulting on a contract (Dem. 56.44). It is worth noting that our speakers do not tend to use *τιμωρία* to describe more trivial cases such as this, but that does not necessarily mean honour is not involved.

Punishment, anger and ambivalence

According to Herman, anger was losing currency as a punishment motive by the fourth century in Athens.[22] For Harris, on the other hand, 'it was appropriate for jurors to feel anger when punishing a defendant for an offense.'[23] The numbers bear out the latter view. Rubinstein's analysis has shown a clear relationship between anger and punishment, particularly in prosecutorial rhetoric.[24] Thirty-nine (of ninety-nine) speeches – all but one for the prosecution – ask jurors to impose punishment (a total of 441 times), and thirty of these speeches (76.9 per cent) also ask the jurors to show anger (Figure 4.1). Likewise, thirty-six speeches ask jurors to show anger (a total of ninety-three times) and thirty of these speeches (83.3 per cent) also ask the jurors to impose punishment. Moreover, the number of appeals to anger is much higher in speeches that also call for punishment and the number of calls for punishment is much higher in speeches that also appeal to anger (Figure 4.2). Twelve speeches tell the jurors not to be angry and thirteen tell them not to punish; eight of these appeal against both anger and punishment and all but one of them is made for the defence.[25]

The pattern in which these appeals occur suggests a relationship between anger and punishment, but the places in which they do not occur is equally telling. The fifty-four speeches that contain no appeals to anger or punishment are made up of all nine *διαδικασίαι*, twenty-six of the twenty-nine defences (private and public), eighteen of the thirty-two private prosecutions, and one of the twenty-nine public prosecutions.[26] That punishment appeals are rare in the defences and *διαδικασίαι* is unsurprising given that the jurors had no formal recourse to punishment, but the low number of anger appeals in these speeches suggests that anger, when called for explicitly, related more to punishment than persuasion. The absence of punishment appeals in most private prosecutions means not that no adverse consequences were available for the defendants in these cases, but merely that the state was not being treated as a victim. Among these cases the only potential for state punishment lies in two prosecutions for false testimony (Is. 3 and 6), an act that could, after three offences, be sanctioned with disenfranchisement.[27] The strong implications are that punishment was an act of a victim (sometimes the state and sometimes the private individual to whom compensation was paid) and that anger was generally or always associated with it.

These quantitative data demonstrate a clear correlation between anger and punishment, but they do not on their own prove causation. Given that anger is a motive and revenge a behaviour, it may be reasonable to infer a causal link of the kind Aristotle tells us to expect, but we can do better by analysing the qualitative evidence. First, however, I will address the numerous critiques of anger in the forensic corpus that appear to challenge the notion that this emotion, as felt by the jurors, had a legitimate part to play in court.

For all the explicit appeals to anger, there are several instances in which orators (mostly defendants) warn against the threat that this emotion poses to justice. Rubinstein represents the conclusions most scholars have taken from these two apparently opposed points of view in saying that 'the Athenians clearly were ambivalent when it came to the issue of dicastic emotions and the extent to which they should inform the response of the court'.[28] In a limited sense, this is indisputable. There are two seemingly contrasting datasets: a great number of

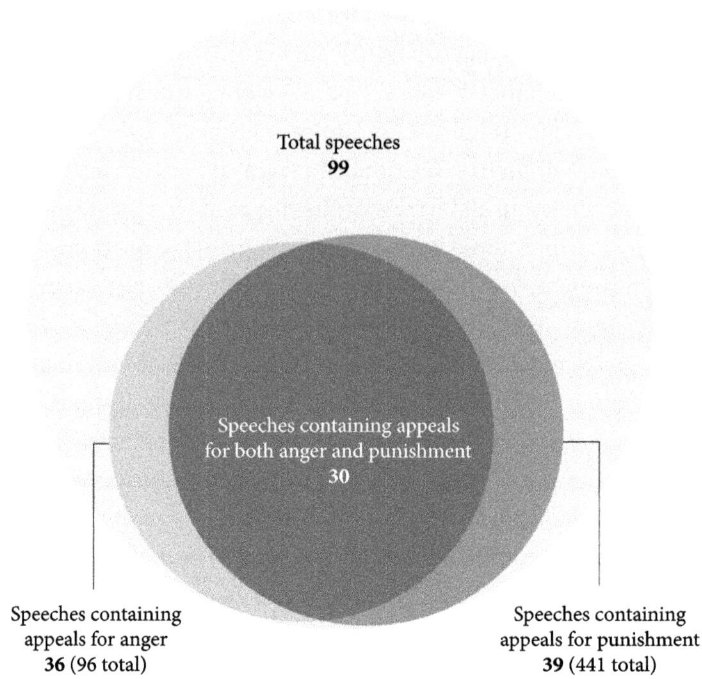

Figure 4.1

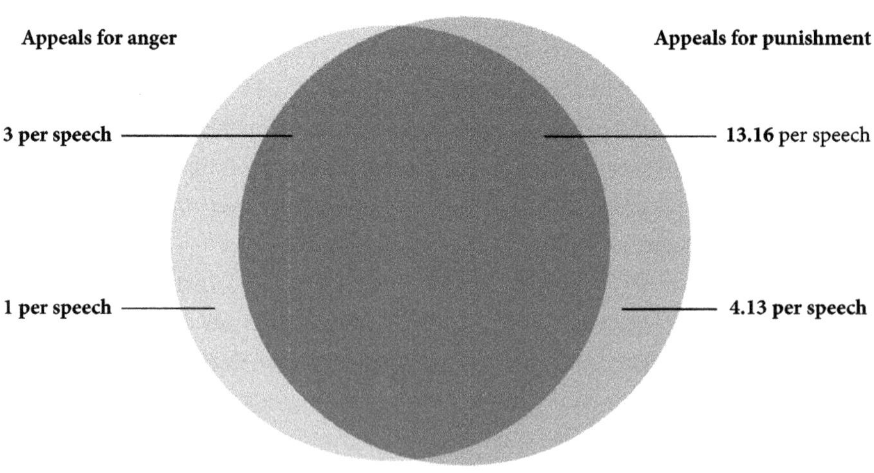

Figure 4.2

explicit appeals for dicastic anger, and a smaller but also substantial collection of warnings against it. Yet, never does a speaker clearly acknowledge that there is significant disagreement about the acceptable standards. Indeed, if dicastic anger did exist in a moral grey area, then some speechwriters appear rather careless about where the line may be drawn. Lycurgus extols truth over anger as the reason for the passing of a proposal and yet calls his audience to anger five times in the same speech.[29] Aeschines decries those who circumvent the courts and win decisions in the assembly instead by appealing to anger, before making three such appeals of his own.[30] And Demosthenes, in a speech containing three anger appeals, lists anger among those bad motives that can lead people astray and contribute to undermining the *polis*.[31] The orators and their audiences do not appear ambivalent in the sense of having contradictory ideas about anger; they seem to assume two areas of more or less agreed-upon certainty.

As regards anger's undesirable aspect, most of the warnings play on a similar theme. Anger ought not to be allowed to destroy 'reason' (*γνώμη*) and bring about bad decisions (Antiph. 5.69–72, cf. 91),[32] nor should it be preferred over 'truth' (*ἀλήθεια*) as a motive for court decisions (Lyc. 1.116) or used instead of 'just arguments' (*δικαίοις λόγοις*) as a method of persuasion (Aesch. 2.3; cf. 3.4). Along the same lines, anger is said to lead jurors astray (Dem. 19.228), bring about decisions contrary to the public interest (26.17) and provoke misplaced punishment (Lys. 25.5, Dem. 57.3). These examples make explicit the concern that the truth of the allegations may be missed if the jurors allow anger to influence their interpretation of the facts. The Athenians feared what Achilles regretted – anger's potential to harm one's judgement.

As well as impairing the jurors' decision-making, anger could also make them hasty, refusing even to hear the defendant's side of the story. One of many kinds of audience–speaker interaction that took place in court involved the jurors audibly expressing their anger at the accusations that they had apparently already accepted as true, sometimes forcing the defendant and his supporters to abandon their speeches.[33] Thus, it is quite common for defendants, who always spoke second, to request that they get a fair hearing, reminding the jurors of their obligation to give an impartial hearing to all. Both Demosthenes and Aeschines point to the other's manipulation of the jurors' anger as their means of repressing the defence's speech.[34] As Aeschines says (2.1–3), Demosthenes urges the jurors to 'first refuse to listen to the defenders of treachery... and then punish before the eyes of the world the man who has traitorously sold himself' (Dem. 19.301). He follows this swiftly with a reminder of why they have good reason to be angry (302). In another instance, jurors are told that because the facts are so well known, there is no need to listen to the defendants and even that their punishment will only be sufficient if it includes a refusal to hear them (Lys. 27.8–9).[35] Evidently, the potential for dicastic anger to bring about wrongful convictions, even through preventing the hearing of the defendant at all, was a real and recognised problem.

While some orators warned against allowing anger to obstruct reason and fair hearing, others chose to attack the reason for the anger rather than the anger itself. Andocides (1.8) and Hyperides (4.31) are both apparently forced to respond to scattergun prosecution strategies that make multiple accusations in the hope that not all of them can be disproven and that all the jurors will find something to be angry about. They respond not by challenging the fundamental appropriateness of anger, but by disproving the accusations. Other defendants opt for redirecting the jurors' anger towards the 'actual' culprits.[36] In these instances it is the false accusations which are being condemned, not the anger that results; had the accusations been true, it seems, the jurors' anger would have been appropriate.

The implication in these statements – that anger is not wrong per se – confirms the general impression created by the large number of explicitly made appeals. Anger had a legitimate role in public trials and we can see in places what that role was. Anger and punishment are often treated as meaning close to the same thing. *Ὀργή* can be the opposite of acquittal (Dem. 21.222), akin to condemnation (Lys. 12.90) and synonymous with punishment (*τιμωροῖσθε*; Lys. 29.9), while the failure to punish is seen as analogous to the abatement of *ὀργή* (Dem. 21.186). Dinarchus says that *τιμωρία* happens when *ὀργή* is felt (Din. 3.8) and Lysias so blurs the lines between *ὀργή* and punishment that he tells the jurors 'it is [their] work (*ἔργον*)... to show *ὀργή* at' the defendant's actions (Lys. 28.2–3). Orators also see the severity of the punishment as a reflection of the amount of *ὀργή* felt. Demosthenes asks whose *ὀργή* falls short of demanding death (Dem. 21.70) and equates greater or lesser punishment with more or less *ὀργή* (183, cf. 42), the laws are said to permit adjustment of a punishment according to the *ὀργή* that a particular wrongdoing requires (Dem. 24.118), and Lycurgus states that a failure to give the death penalty would demonstrate a lack of *ὀργή* (Lyc. 1.27). Aeschines sums this up when he says that 'the third water is poured in for the question of the penalty and the extent of your *ὀργή*' (Aesch. 3.197).[37] Anger was not only a particularly potent motivator of legitimate punishment; it was *the* motivator.[38]

There are several things that I am not saying here. My point is not that jurors never voted to convict out of hatred, envy, fear, shame or any other emotion besides anger. Nor do I think prosecutors appealed only to anger and not to other negative emotions. Explicit appeals to other emotions, especially to *μῖσος*, *ἔχθρα* and *φθόνος*, exist, albeit in significantly lower numbers than those made to anger, and one need not search for long to find reasonably indisputable examples of implicit appeals such as to hatred of those who have not obviously caused offence but are – as outsiders like women, foreigners, or slaves – objects of prejudice.[39] In any given conviction, the motivations at work were surely varied. One can imagine a panel where many jurors doubt the accusation of, say, treason but convict anyway, some because they hate the man for his licentious lifestyle, others because they envy him as an ex-slave become rich, and others because everyone around them seems to favour conviction and they fear being thought of as sympathetic. Others on the same panel may well believe the accusation that they and their city have been betrayed by the defendant, feel anger at the offence, and vote to convict in order to reclaim their honour. In practical terms these men all perform the same act – they vote to convict and execute the defendant – and this act may look like legitimate punishment because it takes place in court, but whether it is such in a moral sense is not an empty philosophical question. While for the angry in this hypothetical panel this is an act of *τιμωρία*, a reclaiming of the honour they have lost to the offence, those who convict out of hatred, envy, fear and so on are doing something else and it seems to me that the legitimacy of such motives was at best dubious by comparison to anger. We might say that what jurors chose to do with their votes in court was by definition legitimate, but the rarity of appeals to emotions other than anger suggests far less confidence among prosecutors that such tactics would be well received. Jurors were willing at times to bend or break the rules and conventions of their system when they felt strongly enough, but anger, unlike other motives, did not require any such bending or breaking. Anger as a means of persuading jurors of defendant guilt was unambiguously wrong; anger as a consequence of the reasonable belief in a defendant's guilt was unambiguously right and necessary. But for all that the Athenians aimed at a justice system that shunned the former and embraced the latter, these are not two separate emotions but two morally opposed sides of the same coin.

We can see in places how anger's dark side could show its face in court. Andocides, outlining the emotional discipline required of a juror, says:

> *ἔτι δὲ καὶ τόδε ἐνθυμητέον, ὅτι πολλοὶ ἤδη πολλὰ καὶ δεινὰ κατηγορήσαντες παραχρῆμα ἐξηλέγχθησαν ψευδόμενοι οὕτω φανερῶς, ὥστε ὑμᾶς πολὺ ἂν ἥδιον δίκην λαβεῖν παρὰ τῶν κατηγόρων ἢ παρὰ τῶν κατηγορουμένων· οἱ δὲ αὖ, μαρτυρήσαντες τὰ ψευδῆ ἀδίκως ἀνθρώπους ἀπολέσαντες, ἑάλωσαν παρ' ὑμῖν ψευδομαρτυρίων, ἡνίκ' οὐδὲν ἦν ἔτι πλέον τοῖς πεπονθόσιν. ὁπότ' οὖν ἤδη πολλὰ*

> *τοιαῦτα γεγένηται, εἰκὸς ὑμᾶς ἐστι μήπω τοὺς τῶν κατηγόρων λόγους πιστοὺς ἡγεῖσθαι. εἰ μὲν γὰρ δεινὰ κατηγόρηται ἢ μή, οἷόν τε γνῶναι ἐκ τῶν τοῦ κατηγόρου λόγων· εἰ δὲ ἀληθῆ ταῦτά ἐστιν ἢ ψευδῆ, οὐχ οἷόν τε ὑμᾶς πρότερον εἰδέναι πρὶν ἂν καὶ ἐμοῦ ἀκούσητε ἀπολογουμένου.*
>
> (And. 1.7)

> And still another thing to be kept in mind: that many times before now liars have brought terrible accusations and been immediately disproved with such clarity that you would have found much more pleasure in taking satisfaction from the accusers than the accused. Others again, having destroyed people unjustly by giving false evidence, have been convicted by you of false testimony when it was no longer of any use to their victims. Since this sort of thing has already occurred many times, it is appropriate for you not yet to deem the statements of the prosecutors trustworthy. For though you can judge whether the accusations are serious or not from the statements of the prosecutor, you cannot know whether they are true or false until you have also heard my defence.

Accusations could, and surely would, evoke anger before their veracity had been established, with the jurors thinking 'if this is true, this person needs to be punished'. Until a juror could be convinced, he had to keep his emotion in check and would ideally wait until he had made a dispassionate judgement at the end of the speeches before allowing expression to his anger.[40] But anger would naturally come to the surface as the juror felt increasingly persuaded of the truth of the charges and that moment might come before the defence had finished speaking, sometimes before he began, and perhaps, if the case was well known, before the juror had even arrived at court.[41]

Dinarchus, having urged his jurors to punish Philocles without hearing his defence (Din. 3.7), says:

> *ἆρ' ἴσθ' ὅτι ἐπὶ μὲν τῶν ἄλλων ἀδικημάτων σκεψαμένους ἀκριβῶς δεῖ μεθ' ἡσυχίας καὶ τἀληθὲς ἐξετάσαντας, οὕτως ἐπιτιθέναι τοῖς ἠδικηκόσι τὴν τιμωρίαν, ἐπὶ δὲ ταῖς φανεραῖς καὶ παρὰ πάντων ὡμολογημέναις προδοσίαις πρώτην τετάχθαι τὴν ὀργὴν καὶ τὴν μετ' αὐτῆς γιγνομένην τιμωρίαν;*
>
> (Din. 3.8)

> Do you understand that, although when it comes to other offences it is necessary to consider carefully and quietly so as to discover the truth, and then to take revenge on the wrongdoers, yet in cases of clear treason, recognised by all, anger should come first and the revenge that goes with it?

Dinarchus admits that the job of a juror is to consider the facts before expressing his anger in punishment. In this case, though, he claims, the facts are so indisputable that there is no need to hear the defendant, before giving their anger its head. It is true that the jurors were probably considerably more confident of where they stood with regard to this case than was typical, the Areopagus Council having already investigated the case under an *ἀπόφασις* and presented a preliminary verdict to the assembly. But that did not mean that it would have been proper to deny Demosthenes the opportunity to respond. We can assume that it was the hope of many prosecutors that they might persuade the jurors to convict without allowing themselves the opportunity to be dissuaded, and yet Dinarchus' exhortation is unusual for its brazenness. Prosecutors rarely urged jurors to refuse to hear a defendant for fear that they might offend the jurors. The ambiguity of the role of anger in public trials surrounds the moment when anger is engaged, not whether anger is appropriate or not. Anger was supposed to be a consequence, not a cause, of the juror's belief in the defendant's guilt.[42] But the challenge for the conscientious juror was to check the prejudicial tendencies of the anger that had been roused during the prosecutor's speech until the end of the defendant's.

This dynamic has some interesting implications. For one thing, it explains the remarkably high number of explicit anger appeals. The lexicographical approach can reveal only a small portion of the attempts speakers made at evoking dicastic emotion; envy, for instance, is roused much more easily by pointing out what someone else owns than by instructing someone to be envious, and to invoke the word itself may well have backfired by flagging up the attempted manipulation. The idea that emotional appeals were a suspect means of persuasion will have deterred orators from signposting them. We should not then expect the names of the emotions we are looking for to crop up at a high frequency. The fact that *ὀργή* is such an emphatic outlier in this regard identifies it as an emotion in need of a special explanation, and that is that it alone of the emotions had an essential and legitimate role in the trial process. Indeed, it may be said that the emotion of anger, specifically its justification and satisfaction, is what Athenian trials and punishments were for.[43]

This does not mean, however, that the decision to appeal to *ὀργή* could be made without concern for how it would be received. Anger, unlike other emotions, could be called for with at least plausible legitimacy but any given appeal could also be presented by the defence, and interpreted by the jurors, as an illegitimate attempt to persuade. Indeed, prosecutors could hide behind ostensible legitimacy as they invoked the theme of anger, while hoping that the result of that anger would be the suppression of the defendant's speech by the irate crowd. Public prosecutors were supposed to walk the line of earning the jurors' anger without exploiting it (of course, whether they did this or not was less important than whether they appeared to).

Athenians as a whole were indeed ambivalent towards the exploitation of dicastic emotion as a means of persuasion, and anger could fall into that category like any other emotion. In principle the emotional manipulation of jurors was seen as detrimental to sound decision-making and was therefore to be avoided, and yet emotions of all kinds clearly were, as numerous studies have now shown, played on by speakers.[44] And the explicit nature of some appeals demonstrates that jurors were, up to a point, willing not only to tolerate but also potentially to be led by them. But, unlike other emotions, anger also had an unambiguously legitimate role to play in the prosecuting of public offenders and on this point there was no ambivalence: anger was the mechanism that linked proven offence to punishment.

It is worth taking a moment to consider the practicalities of this reliance on jurors' emotions for the application of justice. How long could a juror be expected to continue being angered and, given that many of the men who made up the panel one day would be there again the next, for how many days could they keep up this emotional effort? First, we ought to remember that not every prosecutor asked for or even wanted their jurors to be angry. In particular, most private prosecutors were making no accusations of public offence and so were not seeking anger so much as legitimisation of their own anger. Second, even in cases where accusations of public offence were made, those accusations had to be believed in order for anger actually to be felt; public prosecutors sought anger but did not always achieve it and perhaps even left their audiences feeling something entirely different. And yet, we also know that stamina could be an issue.

> *μάλιστα δὲ τοῦτο ἔχοι ἄν τις ἰδεῖν, ὅταν πολλοὶ ἐπὶ τῇ αὐτῇ αἰτίᾳ εἰς ἀγῶνα καταστῶσιν. ὡς γὰρ ἐπὶ τὸ πολὺ οἱ τελευταῖοι κρινόμενοι σῴζονται: πεπαυμένοι γὰρ τῆς ὀργῆς αὐτῶν ἀκροᾶσθε, καὶ τοὺς ἐλέγχους ἤδη ἐθέλοντες ἀποδέχεσθε.*
> (Lys. 19.6)
>
> This is most clearly to be seen when several people face trial on the same charge, because most of the time the last ones to be judged are spared. For, hearing their cases once your anger has ceased, you willingly accept their counterarguments.

It seems that anger could wane and that this was seen as a weakness in the system. We have already seen that jurors who were too hasty in their anger could undermine justice by failing to give defendants a full and fair hearing. Conversely, jurors could also sometimes expend their anger at a particular offence before all those responsible had suffered punishment. Anger was a problematic, imprecise and entirely essential tool for the directing and inflicting of punishment.

The rhetoric of offence

If anger was fundamental to punishment in classical Athenian courts, let us also consider what provoked that anger. We have seen that Aristotle's requirement that anger be a product of a slight is met consistently by Homer, writing some three centuries before Aristotle, who uses several different words to describe the emotion in various contexts, not including Aristotle's term. We could reasonably suppose that the definition is no less accurate in describing the precise word it defines in the very context to which it was tailored – *ὀργή* in the fourth-century law court. A closer look at the evidence will confirm this, but it will also reveal new ways in which the Athenian community perceived slights that had not been present in the early archaic societies of Homer's original audience.

Allen understands the Athenian trial as a struggle where both the prosecutor and the defendant stood to lose or gain honour depending on the outcome, and where the role of the state was to assess and determine how honour ought to be distributed.[45] This explanation works for simple private disputes, but struggles with public trials. In view of the fact that it was to the city, not the prosecutor, that the fine in a public procedure was payable, Allen says that 'a penalty that was a diminishment of honor and an injury to the punished was a benefit or profit to the prosecutor… Punishment thus provided for a redistribution of the honor relations left imbalanced by an act of violence'.[46] This again is not wrong, some public prosecutors do assert that the state's punishment of their enemy is all the revenge they need, but it fails to account for the honour represented by the fine. More importantly, it misrepresents what the jurors are said to do in a public trial. Though prosecutors often think of their public legal action as a private act of *τιμωρία*, the formal *τιμωρία* that the court inflicts is an act of the jurors, born of their anger at their own dishonour. Their primary role at a public procedure was not to redistribute the honour of private individuals; they reclaimed honour for themselves.

The quantitative data allow us to narrow down the context in which dicastic anger and punishment related in the Athenian courts. Appeals for both are overwhelmingly features of prosecution rather than defence speeches, but not all prosecutors made such appeals, and procedure proves to be a strong predictor of prosecutor strategy. In the twenty-nine public prosecutions, seventy-five and 389 positive appeals are made to anger and punishment respectively, whereas in thirty-one private prosecutions those numbers are seventeen and forty-three. Moreover, twenty-eight of the twenty-nine public prosecutions appeal to either anger or punishment, compared to only twelve of the thirty-one private prosecutions, which also do so less frequently on average. As Rubinstein's study has already shown, such rhetoric clearly did not belong in public trials exclusively.[47] And yet, there was evidently something about public procedures that made them, and not private procedures, highly likely to contain explicit instructions for the jurors to be angry and punish. The key difference lies in the identity of the victim and, whereas in a private suit it was the plaintiff who was supposed to perceive dishonour, feel angry and seek revenge, in a public suit it was the jurors.

Rubinstein has observed the greater frequency at which appeals to dicastic revenge (*τιμωρία*) were made over certain accusations.[48] That offences such as treason, desertion, embezzlement and theft of public funds, and the giving or receiving of bribes should cause anger and provoke vengeance requires little explanation.[49] Acts such as these that directly harm, betray or take from the community demonstrate a clear slight: the opinion that the community is less dangerous than the enemy or that the self is of greater value. We saw something of this sort in Homer when Eupeithes incurred public anger by taking part in a raid on Ithaca's allies. Any community, however simple its institutions, is likely to take offence at such direct and blatant attacks on its interests. But at classical Athens we see greater potential for public anger at acts that do not, at first glance, appear to slight the jurors, such as maltreatment of an orphan or adultery. That Athenians would disapprove of such behaviour and that it would incur shame is unsurprising, but that citizens with no connection to the parties involved might take personal offence and become angry is less expected and not apparent in Homer. One procedure in particular, the *γραφή ὕβρεως*, offers insight into this apparent expansion of the reach of public anger. In this, an ideal place to start is Demosthenes' speech in prosecution of Meidias. This speech has by far the largest number of explicit anger appeals and yet the nature of its complaint, a single punch, is not obviously likely to cause the jurors offence. If anger and its manifestation in punishment is about anything other than feeling personally dishonoured, this speech will show it.

It is worth first addressing the debate around the procedure for which this speech was written.[50] The case clearly began as something called a *προβολή*, which entailed bringing the accusation at an assembly gathered to deal with religious matters concerning the Dionysia festival and to hear any complaints related to the procession or the contests (Dem. 21.8); at this assembly there was a non-binding vote that went against Meidias (216). For some scholars, this is where the *προβολή* concluded while the judicial procedure that followed was, in this instance, a *γραφή ὕβρεως*.[51] For others, the *προβολή* continued into a judicial phase for which this speech was written.[52] The speech does not, to my mind, conclusively answer this problem, but this debate has tended to misunderstand Demosthenes in a couple of important respects. It is commonly stated that by citing *hybris* among the procedures he might have used against Meidias (25), he is revealing that he has not used that procedure here.[53] Perhaps so, but his point is that he might have brought a 'private' (*ἰδίας*) *γραφή ὕβρεως*, whereas the procedure he has used (whether a *προβολή* or *γραφή ὕβρεως*) is 'public' (*δημοσίᾳ*). It is also sometimes assumed that by calling this action 'public', Demosthenes reveals that it is a *γραφή*.[54] Again, this does not follow; indeed, the following chapter (26) shows that *δημοσίᾳ* refers simply to his decision to initiate proceedings through a *προβολή*. If we set aside the *δίκη-γραφή* binary (we will see below why it is unhelpful), we can at least be sure that this speech is 'public' rather than 'private' in the sense that it treats the *δῆμος* and not Demosthenes as the victim. It is also clear that the allegation of *hybris* is not simply a rhetorical attempt to turn the jurors against the defendant but an essential part of the argument; in other words, whatever the procedure, the 'wrongdoing at the festival' of which Meidias stands accused is *hybris*. We can also see that Demosthenes uses the original meeting and vote to serve as evidence of a public slight. Without the vote of condemnation at the assembly, he argues, the jurors could simply dismiss the accusations as false or as failing to amount to wrongdoing towards the festival. But the vote proves that the offence occurred and was perceived as *hybristic* at an assembly of citizens shortly after the event (214).

According to Fisher, an act of *hybris* was inherently offensive to all regardless of who the victim happened to be and the terms of the law on *hybris* certainly support this in theory, there being no indication of a legal distinction between criminal and non-criminal *hybris*.[55] The law reads as follows:

> *ἐάν τις ὑβρίζῃ εἴς τινα, ἢ παῖδα ἢ γυναῖκα ἢ ἄνδρα, τῶν ἐλευθέρων ἢ τῶν δούλων, ἢ παράνομόν τι ποιήσῃ εἰς τούτων τινά, γραφέσθω πρὸς τοὺς θεσμοθέτας ὁ βουλόμενος Ἀθηναίων οἷς ἔξεστιν, οἱ δὲ θεσμοθέται εἰσαγόντων εἰς τὴν ἡλιαίαν τριάκοντα ἡμερῶν ἀφ' ἧς ἂν γραφῇ, ἐὰν μή τι δημόσιον κωλύῃ, εἰ δὲ μή, ὅταν ᾖ πρῶτον οἷόν τε. ὅτου δ' ἂν καταγνῷ ἡ ἡλιαία, τιμάτω περὶ αὐτοῦ παραχρῆμα, ὅτου ἂν δοκῇ ἄξιος εἶναι παθεῖν ἢ ἀποτεῖσαι. ὅσοι δ' ἂν γράφωνται γραφὰς ἰδίας κατὰ τὸν νόμον, ἐάν τις μὴ ἐπεξέλθῃ ἢ ἐπεξιὼν μὴ μεταλάβῃ τὸ πέμπτον μέρος τῶν ψήφων, ἀποτεισάτω χιλίας δραχμὰς τῷ δημοσίῳ. ἐὰν δὲ ἀργυρίου τιμηθῇ τῆς ὕβρεως, δεδέσθω, ἐὰν ἐλεύθερον ὑβρίσῃ, μέχρι ἂν ἐκτείσῃ.*
>
> (Dem. 21.47)

> If anyone should commit *hybris* against anyone else, whether a child, a woman, or a man, free or slave, or should do anything illegal to one of these, whoever wishes, of the permitted Athenians, is to bring a written allegation to the *thesmothetai*, and the *thesmothetai* are to bring the matter to the *heliaia* within thirty days of the *γραφή*, unless some public matter should prevent it, and if it does, at the first opportunity. Whomever the *heliaia* condemns, his penalty must be set at once, whatever he seems to deserve to suffer or pay. Of those who write a private allegation under this law, if anyone should fail to take it to trial or, having taken it to trial, fail to win a fifth share of the votes, he will pay 1,000 drachmas to the public treasury. If he should be charged for his *hybris*, he will be bound, if it was a free person whom he treated with *hybris*, until he has paid in full.

The reliability of this text is contentious. Harris has concluded that this law is a forgery for several reasons.[56] I will address only the first two of these, since they present the greatest challenge to authenticity and are the only ones with serious implications for our understanding of the law. First, Harris claims that the phrase *γραφὰς ἰδίας κατὰ τὸν νόμον* 'makes no sense' because 'a γραφή was a public charge, and the word ἰδίας is used to apply to private charges.'[57] Harris cites Chapter 25 of *Against Meidias* as evidence of the distinction between private charges (*δίκας ἰδίας*) and public ones (*δημοσίᾳ κρίνειν*). Demosthenes expects Meidias to argue that

> *ὡς εἴπερ ἀληθῶς ἐπεπόνθειν ταῦθ' ἃ λέγω, δίκας ἰδίας μοι προσῆκεν αὐτῷ λαχεῖν, τῶν μὲν ἱματίων καὶ τῶν χρυσῶν στεφάνων τῆς διαφθορᾶς καὶ τῆς περὶ τὸν χορὸν πάσης ἐπηρείας, βλάβης, ὧς δ' εἰς τὸ σῶμ' ὑβρίσθαι φημί, ὕβρεως, οὐ μὰ Δί' οὐχὶ δημοσίᾳ κρίνειν αὐτὸν καὶ τίμημ' ἐπάγειν ὅ τι χρὴ παθεῖν ἢ ἀποτεῖσαι.*
> (Dem. 21.25)

> If I had truly suffered the things I am alleging, I ought to have brought private suits: for damages on the grounds of the destruction of the cloaks and the golden crowns and all the abuse of the chorus, and for hybris on the grounds of the hybris I claim to have been committed on my body, but not, by Zeus, to have brought him to a public trial and proposed the penalty that he must suffer or pay.

Demosthenes distinguishes between private (*ἰδίας*) and public (*δημοσίᾳ*) suits here, and within the former category he includes the charges of damages and *hybris*. This can mean one of two things: there was something known as a *δίκη ὕβρεως* procedure which he ought to have opted for instead of a *γραφή ὕβρεως*, or there were *γραφαί ὕβρεως* that were private in some way and others that were public.[58] For the former, there is no reliable evidence. The *γραφή ὕβρεως* is cited frequently, but just occasionally is a suit for *hybris* referred to as a *δίκη* and even then only in the general sense that indicates a legal action, whether a 'private' *δίκη* or a *γραφή*.[59] On the other hand, why does Ariston, who feels that a *γραφή ὕβρεως* is beyond him (Dem. 54.1), have to resort to a charge of assault in order to bring a private *δίκη*? Rather, while the terms *δίκη* and *γραφή* distinguish between who is going to punish the culprit, *ἰδίας* and *δημοσίᾳ* must refer to the representative capacity of the prosecutor: are they speaking for themselves or someone else (including other individuals or the people in general)?[60] In *Against Meidias*, the anticipated defence is very clearly that Demosthenes, not the festival, is the victim (25–35). Even if this law is a forgery (and I find the evidence uncompelling), Demosthenes himself refers here to *γραφὰς ἰδίας* to distinguish those *γραφαί ὕβρεως* where the victim speaks for himself from those where the victim is spoken for by another.[61]

Second, the initial conditional clause – 'If anyone should commit *hybris* against anyone else' – is followed by the clause: 'or should do anything illegal to one of these.'[62] Such a remarkably broad law invites suspicion, particularly from modern readers. Harris's objection, that 'several passages make it clear that the charge of *hybris* could not be brought for any offence', solves the problem it poses: since the charge of *hybris* does not cover all offences, the second clause is necessary to clarify that, although *hybris* is the most serious charge, anyone who wishes can bring any accusation of illegality before the people, even those that are not *hybristic*.[63] As Harris understandably says in view of this implication: 'surely no lawgiver would frame a law covering every imaginable crime.'[64] Odd as this intuitively sounds to us, it apparently did not sound unreasonable to the putative Hellenistic editor. Alternatively, we might note that the point of this law is not to sanction anything in particular but to subordinate all existing laws to a new procedure, the *γραφή*, whose unique contribution to the code was that it enabled anyone who wished to prosecute anyone else for anything illegal against anyone.[65] There seems to me little reason to doubt this rendering of the law, but, more crucially, there surely was such a thing as a 'private' *γραφή ὕβρεως* and the law was intended to cover all illegalities.

The law implies that an act of *hybris* against anyone (even a slave) in the community could be offensive to the jurors and subject to public judgement and punishment. Isocrates confirms this view when he writes, in *Against Lochites*, that 'in the case of other charges, only by the victim himself can the culprit be brought to trial; but in the case of *hybris*, this being a communal matter (*ὡς κοινοῦ τοῦ πράγματος ὄντος*), any citizen who wishes is allowed to bring a *γραφή*' (Isoc. 20.2). Demosthenes however, in his *Against Meidias*, appears directly to contradict this. He claims to have a list of grievances, acts of *hybris*, he says, that have provoked anger (*ὀργὴν*) in him but do not seem to call for a trial since the jurors are not involved in the matter (*ἔξω τοῦ πράγματος οὖσιν*; Dem. 21.15). So, is all *hybris* publicly offensive or not?

There are two possible explanations. Either Demosthenes refers to the acts as *hybristic* but suspects the jurors would not agree and so does not attempt to defend that claim, or he and his jurors recognised two categories of *hybris* and the lesser complaints were, he judged, in the category that was not likely to be deemed punishable. In other words, is *hybris* by definition offensive to all who perceive it as *hybris* or can one perceive *hybris* towards another but not necessarily take personal offence and feel anger? In Homer, it is the latter: third parties who perceive *hybris* become not angry but indignant (they feel *νέμεσις*), seeking not to avenge the victim but to rebuke the offender on their behalf and, if possible, to ensure that the *hybristic* behaviour stops.

From Louis Gernet's perspective, Athenian society had relatively little interest in the offences suffered by particular individuals, and so 'the notion of individual and subjective injury' cannot be the basis of 'the notion of social and objective injury'.[66] Fisher, pointing to the 'public, easily observable' nature of dishonour which was 'a blow that hit deeply into one's whole personality', objects that he sees

> simply no difficulty, above all in a 'Mediterranean society', in supposing that the social and political significance of the offence of seriously and gratuitously damaging another's honour was firmly based precisely on the real emotional and practical damage that such humiliation did do to the individual, and on the seriousness of the counter-measures that he might be impelled to take, if not given protection by the legal forces of the society.[67]

This reasoning is not un-Athenian. The principle of helping victims attain retribution safely and legitimately before things escalate to the detriment of all was well established.[68] But, while it is necessary to correct Gernet's denial of community indignation at the abuse of its members, what Fisher describes here is the emotional dynamic at work in private offences: jurors observed dishonour and the justified anger of the victim and supported him in gaining redress from the culprit. Whereas, in a public trial, jurors perceived dishonour against themselves, felt anger over it and took revenge. The *γραφή ὕβρεως* was a public procedure at which the emotional mechanism at work was (and was supposed to be) one of dicastic offendedness, anger and revenge.

The natural emotional response of third parties on perceiving that another has suffered *hybris* often was as Fisher describes, with their focus on the dishonour suffered by the individual and the need, perhaps, to step in to prevent escalation. But this left an emotional gap between what jurors may often have felt in such a trial and what they needed to feel in order to punish. The task of an orator was to bridge that gap, something Demosthenes sees as a significant challenge for his case. *Against Meidias* appeals to anger and punishment with unusual frequency.[69] While other speeches of this length are preoccupied with proving the charge, Meidias' punch was witnessed by many and is not in dispute. Instead, the biggest challenge in this speech is to prove that the events are something to be angry and vengeful about. His assertions that there is nothing more deserving of the jurors' anger than *hybris*, regardless of whom it is against (Dem. 21.46), and that anyone who fails to feel angry enough for the death penalty is 'not right' (70), betray concern as to whether these are opinions that the jurors are likely to share.

Against Meidias is a speech preoccupied with proving public offence. In large part this is because, as Fisher has said, Demosthenes is highlighting offences, not against the community, but against the festival as his particular procedure requires.[70] But this fails to explain Demosthenes' choice of offences to present to the jurors.

> *ὅσα μὲν οὖν τοὺς χορευτὰς ἐναντιούμενος ἡμῖν ἀφεθῆναι τῆς στρατείας ἠνώχλησεν, ἢ προβαλλόμενος καὶ κελεύων ἑαυτὸν εἰς Διονύσια χειροτονεῖν ἐπιμελητήν, ἢ τἄλλα πάνθ' ὅσα τοιαῦτα, ἐάσω· οὐ γὰρ ἀγνοῶ τοῦθ' ὅτι τῷ μὲν ἐπηρεαζομένῳ τότ' ἐμοὶ καὶ ὑβριζομένῳ τὴν αὐτὴν ὀργὴν ἕκαστον τούτων ἥνπερ ἄλλ' ὁτιοῦν τῶν δεινοτάτων παρίστη, ὑμῖν δὲ τοῖς ἄλλοις, ἔξω τοῦ πράγματος οὖσιν, οὐκ ἂν ἴσως ἄξια ταῦτα καθ' αὑτ' ἀγῶνος φανείη· ἀλλ' ἃ πάντες ὁμοίως ἀγανακτήσετε, ταῦτ' ἐρῶ.*
>
> (Dem. 21.15)
>
> As for all the times he annoyed me by opposing the exemption of my chorus from the army, or by putting himself forward as supervisor at the Dionysia and demanding that he be elected, these and other such things I will concede. For I am not unaware that though each of these acts caused as much anger to myself, the one treated with abuse and hybris, as would something really terrible, to the rest of you, who were not involved in the matter, these things may not seem equally deserving of such a trial. I will therefore mention only those things that will aggravate all of you alike.

Here we have two accusations that are surely related to the festival and yet Demosthenes thinks them unlikely to help his case. For him, the question is one not of relevance but of offensiveness. From his point of view, Meidias' opposing of his chorus's exemption from the army and his attempt to force his way into the office of festival supervisor are acts of *hybris* that have angered him as much as the punch, but he does not expect them to anger the jurors. The difference between publicly and only privately relevant *hybris* is bound to be vague – the law makes no such distinction – but Demosthenes suggests that in practice the two are distinguished by whether or not they make the jurors angry.[71]

The example of Euaeon gives us a further indication of how a private act of *hybris* affected different third parties in different ways. Demosthenes attempts to convey the essence of what was so provocative about Meidias' punch, saying it was not the punch itself that was so insulting but such things as the gesture, look or tone of voice (Dem. 21.72). Because of these factors, victims such as Euthynus and Euaeon (71) can become angry enough to kill the culprit in retaliation.[72] Third parties include those who hear of the *hybris* later and those who see it first-hand, and of these only the latter can truly appreciate how terrible the insult was. Euaeon was apparently fortunate for having been insulted in the company of men he knew, but we are not told whether they themselves would be angry or inclined to revenge, only that they would take his side and rebuke (*κακιεῖν*) the offender (73). Demosthenes, on the other hand, suffered *hybris* in front of an audience of foreigners and citizens (74), two groups who can apparently be less relied upon to side with the clear victim. Demosthenes does claim that the citizens assembled for his *προβολή* procedure following the festival were angry at Meidias (2, 6), angry enough to hiss and boo when he entered and before they had even heard Demosthenes' allegations (226). But he does not claim that they were angered on first seeing the incident, and given his aim of communicating that the act was offensive not only to him but to all, especially those at the festival, we should expect him to mention any sense of initial public ire. *Hybris* could cause indignation in observers and the intensity of feeling could increase depending on the closeness of one's ties to the victim, but for indignation to turn to anger one had to perceive oneself or someone one cared for as a victim.

The slippery notion of *hybris* was always potentially offensive to the community, but only potentially. One who brought such an allegation had first to persuade the jurors that *hybris* had occurred while allowing for the fact that it is profoundly subjective – the perception of dishonour depended on the value one attributed to the honour of each party. On top of this, though, the jurors needed also to be emotionally recruited; they had to feel personally slighted. In the case against Meidias, the charge is that of 'wrongdoing at the festival' and is of an explicitly public nature. Indeed, it is the people (*δημοσίᾳ*) rather than the individual who are presented as the direct victim (Dem. 21.25). But the *γραφή ὕβρεως* did not, as we have seen, require that the people or their institutions be envisioned as the direct victim; it could be a private individual, even the prosecutor himself. Had Demosthenes brought a *γραφὴ ὕβρεως* in a private capacity, the difference would have been that he, not the festival, would be the victim. This certainly does not indicate that the court would have been expected to punish the culprit on behalf of the victim to settle a private score, even if defendants would typically accuse their opponents of such motives.[73] But we can see from the theme of *hybris* in a number of speeches that even when seemingly only one individual was offended, there were rhetorical strategies for positioning this insult to touch on the honour of the jurors.[74]

Given that anger could be felt not only by the direct victim of a slight but also by those who counted that victim as their own, it is no surprise to see prosecutors in trials related to *hybris* seeking dicastic anger over what has been done to a member of their community. In one of our two prosecutions for assault (*αἰκία*), both of which emphasise the *hybris* of the assailant even though that is not the main charge, Demosthenes' client Ariston tells the jurors:

> *ὥσπερ ἂν αὐτὸς ἕκαστος παθὼν τὸν πεποιηκότ' ἐμίσει, οὕτως ὑπὲρ ἐμοῦ πρὸς Κόνωνα τουτονὶ τὴν ὀργὴν ἔχειν, καὶ μὴ νομίζειν ἴδιον τῶν τοιούτων μηδὲν ὃ κἂν ἄλλῳ τυχὸν συμβαίη, ἀλλ' ἐφ' ὅτου ποτ' ἂν συμβῇ, βοηθεῖν καὶ τὰ δίκαι' ἀποδιδόναι.*
>
> (Dem. 54.42)
>
> just as each of you, having suffered, would hate the one responsible, so should you bear anger towards Conon on my behalf, and you should not think of an affair such as this as a private matter that might befall anyone; rather, whoever should be the victim, help him and give him justice.

The notion of being angry on behalf of the prosecutor sits a little awkwardly with the principle that jurors should not allow public punishments to be exploited for the settling of private scores. Although many public prosecutors explicitly acknowledge their own private revenge motive, it is nevertheless crucial that the punishment they seek be shown to be justified by an offence against the community. Conversely, in *Against Meidias*, Demosthenes urges the jurors not to let their anger be checked and their punishment be limited by considering it to be on his behalf (*ὑπὲρ ἐμοῦ*) only (Dem. 21.127). Together, these passages point to dicastic anger at a private *γραφὴ ὕβρεως* being primarily of a third-party nature in that they could become angry at the assaulting of others in their wider community, whom they counted among 'their own'. But both examples also suggest that this was a relatively weak emotion: Meidias will suffer greater anger and harsher punishment if the jurors accept that not only Demosthenes but 'the laws, the god and the city have all been similarly wronged'; and Conon will suffer greater hatred and anger if the jurors recognise the assault as something that not only has happened to Ariston but also could happen to them, especially if they fail to punish (Dem. 54.43).

Third-party anger and punishment on behalf of the victim are also features of our other prosecution speech for assault. In his speech against Lochites, Isocrates' client also uses *ὑπὲρ*, asking the jurors how severely they ought to punish on behalf of those who have suffered physical abuse when, as evidenced by the fine they impose, they show themselves so angry on behalf of those who have suffered merely verbal abuse (Isoc. 20.3). Later, he asserts that it would be good if men like Lochites bore a distinguishing mark so that they might be punished before they wronged one of the citizens (14). Again, this roots the jurors' punishment in the dishonouring of the individual victim, but here, unlike in the Demosthenic examples, the group is invoked.[75] The speaker is a citizen like the jurors and he appears to exploit this link to help his victimisation touch the jurors' honour.

The spectre of violence and its implications for the community loom large in *Against Lochites*, where the potential for dangerous escalation is highlighted.[76] Ariston brings this up too but only Isocrates' client takes the escalation theme to the point of claiming that small offences can provoke great evils including 'wounds, death, exile and the greatest disasters' (Isoc. 20.8).[77] By 'disasters', the speaker means the two recent overthrows of the democracy (in 411 and 403) and it is the memory of this that he hopes will evoke the anger that the offence deserves (*ἀξίως ὀργισθῆναι*; 9–10). He goes on to liken Lochites to those who took part in the oligarchy and its crimes, all on the basis of what clearly was not a severe assault. Evidently threats to democracy could, particularly in the years after the oligarchies, be expected to evoke dicastic anger, even if this speech pushes such reasoning to the limits of plausibility.[78]

Much has been made of the link between *hybris* and democracy, particularly the capacity for citizens to take insults towards citizens personally.[79] But, as many have recognised, this cannot be a comprehensive explanation for the public nature of *hybristic* offending since it was not *hybris* against citizens alone that was illegal; women, children and slaves were also protected.[80] Some have resisted the implication that, as Fisher's definition requires, slaves have some degree of honour that an act of *hybris* might offend.[81] Mirko Canevaro has argued that Cairns' definition, which does not require a victim but merely the sense that the *hybristēs* has overestimated their own honour, better explains the inclusion of slaves because in the absence of a victim with honour to lose what must matter is the act of the offender alone.[82] The place of slaves in this law was remarkable even to contemporary Athenians, other Greeks and barbarians according to Demosthenes (21.48). Aeschines reasons:

> *οὐ γὰρ ὑπὲρ τῶν οἰκετῶν ἐσπούδασεν ὁ νομοθέτης, ἀλλὰ βουλόμενος ὑμᾶς ἐθίσαι πολὺ ἀπέχειν τῆς τῶν ἐλευθέρων ὕβρεως, προσέγραψε μηδ' εἰς τοὺς δούλους ὑβρίζειν. ὅλως δὲ ἐν δημοκρατίᾳ τὸν εἰς ὁντινοῦν ὑβριστήν, τοῦτον οὐκ ἐπιτήδειον ἡγήσατο εἶναι συμπολιτεύεσθαι.*
>
> (Aeschin. 1.17)

> For the lawgiver was not concerned on behalf of slaves; but, wishing to accustom you to keep far away from committing hybris towards free people, he wrote also not to commit hybris even against slaves. Overall, he held that in a democracy he who is a hybristēs towards anyone else is not suitable to share in the citizenship.

Canevaro has taken this interest in the offender over the offended as confirmation of Cairns' view.[83] Yet, we cannot deny that the *hybristai* Aeschines has in mind are all victimisers. Though the lawgiver is not concerned with the experience of slaves (and we need not necessarily believe that) he is presumed to recognise that they have suffered something and that one might act on their behalf.[84] His actual concern is apparently for the free, but why did he need to include *τῶν ἐλευθέρων* at all if *hybris* needs no victim? Again, it is not simply those who commit *hybris* but those who do so *εἰς ὁντινοῦν* who are unfit for citizenship.[85] In court there is always a victim and, in a *γραφὴ ὕβρεως*, that victim could be a slave.[86]

But Aeschines' emphasis ought to lead us away from focusing too much on the individual victim. His summary reveals that whoever the direct victim is, the interest of the jurors lies in the harm that the *hybris* will do to them (the jurors) and their community. A *hybristēs* is to be punished not simply on behalf of the victim (although sympathy for an individual's plight may play a role) but on behalf of the jurors themselves, and the victimising of even a slave is relevant because of what it communicates about how the *hybristēs* sees himself relative to the community. Without dropping the need for a victim (at least in court), the emphasis on the offender needs to be embraced. In the case against Meidias, the jurors themselves, as representatives of the *δῆμος*, are presented as the victims, but when the victim was a private individual it was not the direct dishonour but the implied disrespect for the community that made an act of *hybris* liable to draw the jurors' wrath and punishment. Someone who thinks they can disregard the honour of another, even the modest honour of a slave, is someone who does not think themselves beneath disregarding the honour of anyone, even a citizen.

In a more fundamental sense, however, violence always had the potential to cause public anger in classical Athens. The capacity to be violent without repercussions was a marker of high status in the Greek world and those whom one could assault with impunity were implicitly of less honour. Demosthenes refers to every act of violence (*βιαζόμενος*) as an offence to the community (*κοίν' ἀδικήματα*; Dem. 21.45). He has just observed that the state takes an interest in violent offence in that the laws impose no public penalty on those who steal by fraud but a fine on those who do so by force (44). He is attempting to set the bar low for the degree of violence that the jurors will deem offensive, suggesting that the *δῆμος*, whom they represent, is personally slighted whenever people are illegitimately violent. They ought, then, to be angry at Meidias since his assault represents a challenge to the supremacy of the *δῆμος* and communicates disdain for the people's supposed monopoly of force.

Ultimately, this sense of acting above one's station is what makes *hybris* offensive – valuing oneself too highly relative to the community. Whether we accept Fisher's requirement for a victim or not, it was the perception that someone was 'thinking too big' that got under others' skin and, potentially, made them angry. Members of the community with no special connection to the victim would not necessarily become angry at an insult directed by one member to another; but if they could be persuaded that the insulter's actions revealed someone who considers himself above the rules, invulnerable to repercussions and disrespectful of the community's institutions, then anger and punishment were very much on the cards. This sense of anger over the breaking of the community's norms is a departure from Homer, where such behaviour only ever invites *νέμεσις*, and leads us to the question of the role of the laws in bringing about punishment.[87]

Rule of law or rule of anger

Given the apparently fundamental nature of anger as a punishment motive, we might wonder what role the law has to play. The importance of the law in the decisions of the jurors is indisputable. Laws are cited, paraphrased or referred to throughout the forensic corpus, the finer points of their meaning are sometimes of crucial importance, and those who recommend laws that contravene existing legislation are subject to punishment. But if the jurors were supposed to punish on account of feeling offended and angry, why did they need laws to tell them whether the defendant has done wrong? Somehow, the breaking of the law and the dishonouring of the jurors worked together in the judicial machinery of classical Athens to determine who should be punished and how.

The role of the law in Athenian society has received considerable attention in recent decades with much focus on the drive behind a case being brought to court.[88] Cohen's emphasis on revenge as the driving prosecutorial motive has been rejected by Herman in particular, who asserts that 'feuding, violence and vengeance were behavioural patterns of which the dikasts... strongly disapproved'. For Asako Kurihara, while enmity was appropriate in private cases, it was deemed unacceptable in public ones, but the number of exceptions to this claim render it untenable.[89] As is now widely recognised, the purpose of claiming personal enmity in public cases was often to avoid appearing to have sycophantic motives, while the (often concurrent) emphasising of civic concern was intended to evade accusations of bringing ungrounded public suits in pursuance of private quarrels.[90] There was no 'right' stance to take on enmity, but the balancing of these demands was often an important strategic consideration.

However, it seems to me that the question of whether Athens was under the 'rule of law' is not answered by comparing it with 'feuding'.[91] The prosecutorial motive was of some relevance in public trials given that it was private initiative that brought alleged public offenders to court, but there is no reason why that individual should not have a personal axe to grind. Indeed, this was normal, unproblematic and in many cases essential for motivating the prosecution of public offenders. The more important issue is whether or not the law determined the trial's outcome, and this means looking at the motives not of the litigants but of the jurors.

Of course, the court is frequently told to punish those who have broken the law.[92] They are also often reminded that their oath requires this of them.[93] However, though prosecutors do attempt to prove illegality, their endeavours rarely end there. Rather, they tend to go on to offer justifications for the given law and attempt to prove that the defendant's behaviour has caused the city and its citizens offence. The young Alcibiades stands charged with absenting himself from the land army and the judgement is likely to hinge on whether the jurors accept that he served in the cavalry when he ought to have served as a hoplite.[94] We get an unreliable glimpse of the defence's strategy from a co-prosecutor who claims to have heard that Alcibiades will deny having wronged the city (*οὐδὲν ἠδίκει τὴν πόλιν*) when he served in the cavalry (Lys. 14.8). This points to the crux of the matter: not whether he has broken the law, but whether he has offended the *polis*.[95] This speaker has an answer for this:

> *ἐγὼ δ' ἡγοῦμαι διὰ τοῦθ' ὑμᾶς δικαίως ἂν αὐτῷ ὀργίζεσθαι, ὅτι τοῦ νόμου κελεύοντος, ἐάν τις ἀδοκίμαστος ἱππεύῃ, ἄτιμον εἶναι, ἐτόλμησεν ἀδοκίμαστος ἱππεύειν. καί μοι ἀνάγνωθι τὸν νόμον.*
>
> (Lys. 14.8)
>
> But I think you would be justly angry (ὀργίζεσθαι) with him for this, that though the law orders disenfranchisement should one serve in the cavalry without having passed scrutiny, he dared to serve in the cavalry.

And then, after the law has been read out:

> *οὗτος τοίνυν εἰς τοῦτ' ἦλθε πονηρίας, καὶ οὕτως ὑμῶν κατεφρόνησε καὶ τοὺς πολεμίους ἔδεισε καὶ ἱππεύειν ἐπεθύμησε καὶ τῶν νόμων οὐκ ἐφρόντισεν, ὥστε οὐδὲν αὐτῷ τούτων τῶν κινδύνων ἐμέλησεν, ἀλλ' ἐβουλήθη καὶ ἄτιμος εἶναι καὶ τὰ χρήματ' αὐτοῦ δημευθῆναι καὶ πάσαις ταῖς κειμέναις ζημίαις ἔνοχος γενέσθαι μᾶλλον ἢ μετὰ τῶν πολιτῶν εἶναι καὶ ὁπλίτης γενέσθαι.*
>
> (Lys. 14.9)
>
> This man carried wickedness so far and was so disdainful (κατεφρόνησε) of you and fearful of the enemy, so set on serving in the cavalry and disregarding the laws, that these dangers were nothing to him, and he desired to be disenfranchised, to have his property confiscated and to become bound by all the statutory penalties rather than to be with the citizens and serve as a hoplite.

Proving illegality is not the aim of these statements. Rather, the speaker is attempting to give the technical transgression emotional meaning by demonstrating how Alcibiades' actions slighted the jurors. In fear of the enemy, he abandoned his responsibility to serve in the more dangerous infantry and in so doing avoided serving alongside the citizens, the jurors themselves or men like them. But the speaker has also drawn in another kind of slight: the implied contempt that this wrongdoing shows for the laws and the jurors. Alcibiades, by breaking a law that carries the penalty of disenfranchisement, has shown that he neither values his citizenship nor respects the jurors' power to execute that sanction.

This setting aside of the substantive wrongdoing in order to focus on the contempt inherent in the illegal behaviour is a common rhetorical means of turning the transgression into a personal slight against the jurors. This relies on a relationship between the jurors and the laws that is profoundly personal in nature. The laws are not simply a line in the sand distinguishing right from wrong but an entity bound to the Athenians' honour. The laws are frequently presented as victims of dishonour. Defendants are accused of behaving with disdain (*καταφρονέω*), contempt (*ὑπεροράω*) and even *hybris* towards the laws.[96]

Sometimes the laws are perceived as victims of something more forceful. According to Euchares, his opponent Theocrines, thinking of himself as 'stronger' (*κρείττω*) than the laws, has 'done violence' (*βιαζόμενος*) to (Dem. 58.15) and 'betrayed' (*προϊεμένοις*) them (24), probably a reference to Theocrines' alleged sycophancy, behaviour that claims to defend the law but in fact does the opposite.[97]

On a similar note, the jurors themselves are, on two occasions, urged not to betray the laws (Dem. 19.283, 25.98). This introduces another indication of the laws' victimhood: the representation of the jurors as watching over them. On a number of occasions the jurors are referred to as 'guardians' (*φύλακες*) of the laws, and are occasionally urged to avenge their laws.[98] Antiphon's use of the active voice (*τιμωρῆσαι*) indicates punishment on behalf of those whose honour the jurors ought to reclaim, typically the dead and the gods.[99] Here it is the laws that are presented thus, having honour of their own but relying on their guardians for vengeance. Demosthenes appeals to a similar sentiment when he, apparently deeming it insufficient to prove that Meidias has broken the law on *hybris*, feels the need to highlight the 'humanity' of this law that protects even slaves from insult (21.48), and the great reputation it affords them among both Greeks and barbarians (49–50). It is in view of these reputational stakes that he says: 'consider what satisfaction he who transgresses [this law] ought to give to have given enough.' Offensive as the fundamental wrongdoing may have been to the jurors, their personal connection to the laws could evoke third-party anger too. Just as Achilles takes offence at the killing of Patroclus by virtue of Hector's implicit disregard for the threat posed by his victim's great ally, so did Athenian citizens take offence at the breaking of the laws they were proud of and had sworn to uphold.

Clearly, the laws and anger could complement each other in leading the jurors towards a conviction. Indeed, they usually went hand in hand partly because the existence of a given law was generally predicated on the fact that the offence had made citizens angry in the past, and partly because the breaking of a law had the potential to draw dicastic ire regardless of whether that particular panel in that particular context felt slighted by the alleged act. But there was no guarantee that dicastic anger and law-breaking would coincide. Demosthenes betrays a concern that this may be the case in a speech written for Diodorus' prosecution of Timocrates.

> *ὡς εἰ νῦν πράως οἴσετ' ἐφ' οἷς τότ' ἠγανακτεῖτε, δόξετ' ὀργιζόμενοι κατεγνωκέναι τὰ χρήματα τούτων, οὐκ ἀδικούμενοι. τῶν μὲν γὰρ ὀργιζομένων ἐστὶν ὀξέως τι κακὸν τὸν λελυπηκότ' ἐργάσασθαι, τῶν δ' ἀδικουμένων, ὅταν ποθ' ὑφ' αὑτοῖς λάβωσι τὸν ἠδικηκότα, τότε τιμωρήσασθαι. οὔκουν δεῖ δοκεῖν, νῦν μαλακισθέντας,*

> *τότε τῶν ὀμωμοσμένων ὅρκων ἀμελήσαντας ὑμῖν αὐτοῖς χαρίσασθαι παρὰ τὸ δίκαιον, ἀλλὰ μισεῖν καὶ μηδ' ἀνέχεσθαι φωνὴν μήτε τούτου μήτ' ἐκείνου, τοιαῦτα πεπολιτευμένων.*
>
> (Dem. 24.175; cf. Lyc. 1.116)
>
> If you are gentle today on that which annoyed (ἠγανακτεῖτε) you then, you will appear to have sentenced them to repay the money because you were angry (ὀργιζόμενοι) rather than because you had been wronged. For to do harm swiftly to one who has vexed you is a symptom of anger, whereas to take vengeance (τιμωρήσασθαι) on him when you have caught him is a symptom of having been wronged. You must not be soft now and appear to have neglected your sworn oath, favouring yourselves contrary to justice, but hate (μισεῖν) them and do not bear to hear their voices, neither of this one nor that, those whose public conduct has been of this sort.

The strategy here is to raise the spectre of shame: if the jurors show inconsistency in their sentencing, it will look as though they have punished people for the wrong reasons in the past. And the implication here is that the wrong reason would be anger while the right reason would be that they have been wronged. But Demosthenes cannot mean to distinguish angriness from wrongedness in black-and-white terms. His instruction to *τιμωρήσασθαι* implies anger; there are seven explicit anger appeals elsewhere in this speech, and he ends this passage with an exhortation to hate.[100] Neither does he suggest that one should respond to the law-breaking rather than the personal affront.[101] Instead, we see here the familiar distinction between swift (*ὀξέως*) and delayed retaliation. In the reckless moments at the onset of anger, bad decisions can be made and revenge can be misdirected or disproportionate, whereas those who wait until they have caught (*λάβωσι*) those they know to have wronged them will make a decision they can be proud of in future.[102]

There was a line that separated right from wrong at Athens, the condonable from the punishable, but it was not drawn with laws. The laws were like a ruler, attempting with frequent success to guide where the line was drawn, but that ruler and the pencil itself were in the hands of the jurors and their fundamental concern was whether or not (and to what degree) they felt angry. In the right circumstances, under the influence of the right arguments, the ruler could be skewed and shifted or even abandoned altogether, and the line drawn freehand.

The public speeches, and a few of the private ones, are full of accusations of public offence, attempts to evoke anger in jurors. We saw that in Homer, the anger of the community could be roused against its own members when one of them was seen clearly to have harmed their interests and caused them dishonour. But this, if Homer is any guide, was far less common in early Archaic communities than it became in classical Athens. What we do see more of in Homer is *νέμεσις*, a sense of indignation at those who break social norms. This emotion places some burden of action on the sufferer but, without the sense of personal dishonour, it lacks anger's compulsive drive to avenge. Why, then, this emotional shift from indignation towards anger at those who broke with the community's norms? The answer may be that these norms came to be written down. Before written laws, the decision to break a norm risked harming one's reputation within the community but, so long as there was no victim, it was not especially likely to result in sanctions. But a written law changed the rules of the game because now there was always going to be a victim – the law itself.

And these laws carried an explicit threat, a promise on the part of the community to inflict the punishment that the breaking of that law warranted. Oral law could achieve this to an extent because not all threatened consequences need to be written down in order for those who break the norm to know what to expect. Taking part in a raid on an ally, for example, is obviously a sign of contempt for the community. But the breaking of other norms, such as holding back from battle, might be in a greyer area in that the offender could expect indignation but perhaps not force.[103] However, a law stating that certain punishments will follow such an act means that regardless of how offensive that act appears in itself, it will at least show contempt for the power of those responsible for upholding that law. The breaking of the law now not only invited personal shame and the community's indignation, but also constituted a direct challenge to the community's power and authority and displayed a belief that the *δῆμος* either would not or could not follow through on its threats.

Conclusion

The development of justice administration from the world of Homer's audiences to that of classical Athens is a story of both continuity and change. Continuity can be seen in the nature of punishment, which stayed an act of anger at a personal slight. Anger's problematic tendency to undermine judgement remained a challenge for its subjects and just as Achilles bemoans the folly to which his anger led him, so the Athenians sometimes regretted the punishments they had rashly imposed in their wrath. In trials where public offence was alleged, the emotional discipline of the jurors was put to the test in a way not unlike that of Homer's heroes. The question was: would they lash out like Achilles, perhaps even before the accused were allowed a chance to make their case, or wait for the right moment like Odysseus, making sure that they punished only the guilty and acquitted the innocent? But there was no suggestion that they should punish without having felt anger, only that their anger should be subject to reason.

It is in what constituted a slight that change can be observed. In essence the paradigm remained, as ever, the perception that someone thought too little of one. Individuals still had an idea of what they were worth and they still took it to heart when others appeared to value them beneath that measure. It is in the actions and behaviours that communicated such an appraisal that we see a difference. In Homer, the community values its norms and disapproves of those who break them, rebuking and perhaps limiting such behaviour, but it does not tend to take personal offence. In classical Athens, though, the honour of the individual was considerably more bound up with the community and its institutions. Where once *hybris* had provoked indignation, it now could provoke anger. Even private and relatively innocuous physical altercations could, in the hands of the right orator, be massaged into displays of contempt for the entire community that betrayed a view of oneself as being of comparable or greater worth. There was no guarantee that jurors would take an alleged public offence personally, and often they would turn against prosecutors who attempted to have public punishments inflicted on purely private enemies, but there was almost no wrongdoing that could not plausibly be presented as a slight against the jurors or the community they represented.

This change was part of a process of increasing centralisation and growing identification of citizen with city. One factor contributing to this change was the introduction of written law. Laws typically existed because the behaviour they legislated against had been understood, at least at the time the law was passed, to be against the community's interests and therefore offensive.[104] This did not mean that all citizens would always take similar behaviour as a slight in all future political contexts, but when law-breaking had occurred that did not necessarily matter. The breaking of customary norms had once promised popular indignation; now it also came with the formal and unambiguous threat of force. With every written law, the *δῆμος* made clear what place it saw itself to occupy in the honorific hierarchy: it was at the top and ready to defend its position. And its laws were not simply guidelines for those who wished to have a good reputation, but they constituted an ally of all who counted themselves members of the community so that an offence against them was liable to evoke third-party anger among citizens. Despite this, law-breaking was like any other apparent wrongdoing: it only led to punishment if jurors perceived a slight. For the most part, and depending on the persuasive work of the orators, the law and the jurors' anger tended to work hand-in-hand, but there was always the potential for illegal acts to be perceived as inoffensive and for seemingly legal acts to provoke the wrath of the jurors.

5

Moral Authority and the Appeal to Anger

Introduction

If the emotion of anger motivated the jurors' punishments, then why do some of our public prosecutions fail to appeal to it explicitly? First, it is important to remember that emotions can be called for or otherwise evoked without naming them. Indeed, even when *ὀργή* is not invoked, we can see clear attempts to convince the jurors that they have been slighted and I would suggest that whenever a (partly) public punishment was available, public anger was being sought, at least implicitly but usually explicitly. That said, any speech would have its own flavour depending on what tone the writer considered the occasion to demand. One prosecutor might be unambiguous and demanding in his appeals to dicastic anger, while another might be understated and reliant on the accusations to evoke the anger required. The rate at which appeals are made is not therefore a reliable indicator of which prosecutors most desired dicastic anger. Yet the five public prosecutions that *do* happen to lack anger appeals offer us an insight into some of the pressures that could advise against plainly calling for dicastic anger.

The speeches

Just five of the twenty-nine surviving public prosecution speeches include no explicit appeals to anger, and in each case their absence is explainable. They are those brought against Agoratus (Lys. 13), the grain dealers (Lys. 22), Nicostratus (Dem. 53), Theocrines (Dem. 58) and Philippides (Hyp. 2). Of these we can dismiss the last on the grounds that it is too fragmentary for us to know whether it contained any anger appeals, but, judging from the rest of the public prosecutions, its four appeals to *τιμωρία* /*τιμωρεῖσθαι* suggest that anger is being sought and that there probably were explicit appeals in the missing chapters.

Regardless, the attempt to rouse anger through exposing the defendant's slights against the community can be seen in the repeated accusations of traitorous activity and sentiment (2.2–9). Demosthenes' *Against Nicostratus* is an *ἀπογραφή* (deposition) which carried no known possibility of a public punishment beyond enforcing the handing over of the denounced property.[1] Dicastic *ὀργή* was, it seems, so tied to punishment that prosecutors hardly mentioned it when no punitive response was available.

Our other three cases are more complicated. All ought to be seeking anger in that they accuse the defendants of acts that are surely publicly offensive. The failure of three speeches in twenty-nine to employ explicit anger appeals in no way undermines the principle that punishment ought to be a product of anger. In departing from the norm in this way, these speeches remind us that although making the jurors angry was an important consideration for a public prosecutor, it was not the only one. Another, I think, was whether or not they had the moral authority on which to base anger and punishment appeals.

For different reasons, these three speakers lack the moral authority necessary to carry off appeals to anger. Such appeals required not only the ability to persuade the jurors of the truth, but also the significant moral authority necessary to support assertions about what was or was not offensive and to tell jurors how they should feel. If a prosecutor felt they possessed such authority, they could proceed in a more aggressive manner and appeal openly to anger. But if they were aware that their perceived character lacked such authority, the vocabulary of *ὀργή* might be best avoided or at least only carefully employed.[2] The remaining speeches point to two such issues of character: the prosecutors of Agoratus (Lys. 13) and the grain dealers (Lys. 22) invite, in different ways, suspicions of sycophancy, while the prosecutor of Theocrines (Dem. 58) is younger than deemed appropriate for a public prosecutor.

Tolerable sycophancy

The absence of anger appeals in Lysias' *Against Agoratus* is surprising for a number of reasons. First, *τιμωρία* is called for with the middle voice verb on six occasions in this speech – the second most of any speech – despite the fact that *τιμωρεῖσθαι* is almost never called for in speeches which do not also call for *ὀργή*.[3] Second, this speech makes accusations that closely resemble offences presented by Lysias as reasons for anger in the similar and contemporaneous *Against Eratosthenes*.[4] The destruction of the city is supposed to cause anger towards Eratosthenes (Lys.

12.88–90), but not Agoratus, who has harmed the whole city by depriving it of men of character (13.2), has destroyed the democracy (4), is the 'author of all the city's troubles' (33) and has caused the misfortunes suffered not only privately by each individual but publicly by the city (48). Unspecified association with the traitor Theramenes is a cause for anger towards Eratosthenes (12.80; cf. 62–4) but not Agoratus who supported Theramenes as a sycophant (13.18).[5] The similarities between these two speeches – also including their length, subject matter and desire for the death penalty – only accentuate the peculiarity of the fact that one of them makes five appeals to anger while the other makes none. Third, Agoratus has also shown contempt (*κατεφρόνει*) for the jurors by falsely living as a citizen (73), an offence expected to motivate anger elsewhere.[6]

Lysias' *Against the Grain dealers*, which accuses certain grain dealers of illegally stock-piling grain in order to raise prices, refers to *ὀργή* once.[7]

> *ἐπειδὴ γὰρ οἱ πρυτάνεις ἀπέδοσαν εἰς τὴν βουλὴν περὶ αὐτῶν, οὕτως ὠργίσθησαν αὐτοῖς, ὥστε ἔλεγόν τινες τῶν ῥητόρων ὡς ἀκρίτους αὐτοὺς χρὴ τοῖς ἕνδεκα παραδοῦναι θανάτῳ ζημιῶσαι.*
>
> (Lys. 22.2)

> When the Committee of the time brought their case before the Council, they were so angered at [the grain dealers] that some of the speakers said that we ought to hand them over untried to the eleven, for the penalty of death.

Though the speaker makes no explicit claim that the jurors ought to feel anger now, he does lead them in that direction, mentioning that these allegations have already made citizens angry enough to call for the death penalty. The speaker's desire for the jurors' anger is implied by his numerous calls for punishment and confirmed by his accusations. He dismisses the notion that the dealers are aiming to keep prices low, asserting instead that they would be the last men to act out of goodwill towards the people (13) and that they profit from (sometimes fabricated) bad news (14). He goes on to call them enemies (*ἔχθρας*) in that they, like *πολέμιοι*, strike at the moment of greatest weakness (14–15). Anger, though not called for, is certainly being sought in both these very different speeches, but not explicitly. These speeches have different strategies but appear to share an awareness that they display sycophantic traits.

The strategy of manipulating dicastic anger to hide the weakness of one's argument is a trait strongly associated with sycophancy. Isocrates makes this clear in his *Antidosis*, a speech written in defence of himself for a fictional trial. A major concern running throughout it is the danger that sycophants, such as his opponent Lysimachus (Isoc. 15.8), can deceive jurors (18) and bring about judgements through *ὀργή* and without proof (*ἐλέγχου*) – something which, when discovered, has led before to the desire to punish the deceivers (19). Reflecting the familiar concern that *ὀργή* can undermine jurors' perception of the facts and willingness to give the defence a fair hearing, he tells the jurors not to 'trust too hastily the assertions of the accuser nor hear the defendant in uproar and difficulty (*θορύβου καὶ χαλεπότητος*)' (20). Sycophants, he says, have an advantage because

> *τοσοῦτον δὲ τὸ μεταξὺ ποιεῖν, ὥστε τῶν μὲν αἰτιωμένων ὅ τι ἂν λέγωσιν ἀποδέχεσθαι, τῶν δὲ τούτους ἐξελέγχειν πειρωμένων ἐνίοτε μηδὲ τὴν φωνὴν ἀκούοντας ἀνέχεσθαι.*
>
> (Isoc. 15.21–2)

> we so depart from [the jurors' oath] that when it comes to the accuser we accept whatever he may say, and yet when it comes to the accused's attempt to refute them we sometimes do not even deign to hear their voice.

Appealing to anger is apparently a tactic of this particular sycophant who, by accusing him of corrupting the young, has sought to stir up the jurors' *ὀργή* and *μῖσος* (30–1).[8]

Theocrines, characterised in 330 by Demosthenes as a sycophant (18.313), brought a *γραφὴ παρανόμων* against a man for proposing a decree that would supposedly alienate an orphan from his inheritance (58.30–1). According to the man's son, this was a sycophantic prosecution that successfully evoked the jurors' anger because Theocrines 'had been believed as one who is not altogether depraved' (32). Theocrines apparently won the jurors' anger not only because they believed his story, but also because they trusted his motives. The implication, however, is that as a sycophant he really is depraved and if only the jurors had realised this he would not have been able to stir them to anger. Some sycophantic prosecutions would have plenty of anger appeals, emphasising offensiveness in the hopes of obscuring the lack of substance behind the relevant charge. But this would succeed only if the jurors accepted the prosecutor as truthful and genuine.

Against Agoratus (Lys. 13) and *Against the Grain Dealers* (Lys. 22) both, for different reasons, appear sycophantic.[9] *Against Agoratus* prosecutes for crimes committed under the Thirty, a category of prosecution so renowned for sycophancy that it inspired the creation of a special procedure, the *παραγραφή*, to be brought in bar of litigation (Isoc. 18.2–3).[10] More specifically, two traits often labelled as sycophantic are also in evidence. First, the speaker relies heavily on 'sophistical quibbling' to evade legal constraints.[11] One of these is the interpretation of the clause requiring that the accused be caught 'in the act' (*ἐπ' αὐτοφώρῳ*) to be arrested through *ἀπαγωγή*.[12] Absurdly, the speaker claims that to cite this in defence would be to admit guilt because 'this is like agreeing that he has killed but was not caught in the act, and to rely on that is to say that if he was not caught in the act but did kill he ought to be saved' (Lys. 13.85). Stretching credulity further, he then interprets this phrase as referring not only to killers found with a club or dagger in hand but also to those found to have deposed someone who was then sentenced to death, otherwise how could the killer ever be caught 'in the act' when the mode of death was self-administered hemlock? (86–7). Even if it is reasonable to claim that a deposition is equivalent to a dagger, it is surely against the spirit of the clause given that the alleged crime is years old and simply proving that an accusation is true (which is all this interpretation amounts to) is a basic requirement of any procedure. Moreover, the framing of this argument points to the amnesty's stipulation that all are to be exempt from prosecution for involvement in homicide under the Thirty unless they have killed with their 'own hands (*αὐτοχειρία*)' (*Ath. Const.* 39.5); surely the *αὐτόφωρος* clause required that Agoratus be caught in the act to be deemed the *αὐτόχειρος*.[13] More suspect still is the next argument, again attempting to remove the protection of the amnesty, in which he summarises the deal as having been struck between the Town and Peiraeus parties; thus, since Agoratus was in the Peiraeus at the time of the oath, he is prosecutable by others of the Peiraeus party (Lys. 13.88–90). Arguments such as these which exploit loopholes but flout the spirit of the laws are strongly associated with sycophancy and would likely, under normal circumstances, cause jurors to question the case's validity.

Second, there has been a delay in the bringing of this case as the speaker himself admits in urging the jurors not to listen to the argument 'that we are exacting the penalty a long time after the offence. For I do not think there is any statute of limitations for such crimes as his' (Lys. 13.83).[14] We should not assume from this that the speaker anticipated a procedural challenge (even if he implies as much) since the *ἀπαγωγή* does not appear to have been subject to a statute of limitations anyway (Dem. 23.80). Rather, he probably expects the delay to be highlighted as an indication of sycophancy.

In *Against the Grain Dealers* the concern over appearing sycophantic is spelled out:

> *πολλοί μοι προσεληλύθασιν, ὦ ἄνδρες δικασταί, θαυμάζοντες ὅτι ἐγὼ τῶν σιτοπωλῶν ἐν τῇ βουλῇ κατηγόρουν, καὶ λέγοντες ὅτι ὑμεῖς, εἰ ὡς μάλιστα αὐτοὺς ἀδικεῖν ἡγεῖσθε, οὐδὲν ἧττον καὶ τοὺς περὶ τούτων λόγους ποιουμένους συκοφαντεῖν νομίζετε.*
>
> (Lys. 22.1)

> Many people have come to me, gentlemen of the jury, surprised that I accused the grain dealers in the council, and saying that you, however much you believe them to have done wrong, nonetheless consider those who deliver speeches about them to be dealing in sycophancy.[15]

Grain dealers are so despised that they make easy targets for prosecution, but this vulnerability means that the motives of those who prosecute them are suspected.[16] This prosecutor's situation is worsened by the fact that the defendants were going to be put to death anyway had he not argued for a proper trial and then volunteered himself as prosecutor. Why has he interfered, the jurors might wonder, if not for profit?[17] On top of this, he apparently has no personal enmity towards the defendants which could serve as a compelling sign of sincere motive.[18] Here we see the avoidance of anger appeals alongside an acknowledged anxiety about appearing sycophantic.

It seems to me that there are at least two reasons, one negative and one positive for the failure of these prosecutors to appeal to anger. In negative terms, they are concerned that the jurors may respond badly to a show of moral authority from someone displaying the sycophantic traits of legal chicanery and prosecuting easy (and perhaps innocent) targets for monetary reward. In positive terms, they have no need to appeal to anger because the jurors already feel it.

This explanation brings up a new problem though: if the jurors believed the prosecutor a sycophant, would they not simply vote to acquit? Here we meet the debate started by Robin Osborne and David Harvey as to whether sycophants were fundamentally always 'bad'.[19] Osborne's reappraisal helpfully broadened our understanding of sycophancy to include not only money-grubbing exploitations of the role of volunteer prosecutor but any prosecutorial abuse of the legal system for personal (but not necessarily pecuniary) benefit.[20] However, while Osborne may be technically correct in saying that the term implied simply that the prosecutor's case was weak not necessarily that his motives were corrupt, I suspect that the bringing of a weak case was generally taken as a sign of corrupt motives because the attempt to have a jury uphold 'improbable assumptions, empty assertions or over-meticulous quibbling', as Osborne puts it, was in itself offensive.[21] It seems to me clear that the term sycophant was a pejorative and that to label behaviour as sycophantic was to identify it as undesirable to all.[22] That does not mean, however, that a juror would always vote against someone they perceived to be presenting a sycophantic case. Not everyone targeted by a sycophantic prosecutor was innocent (as charged or otherwise) and sometimes the desire to punish the defendant was greater than that to deny and perhaps punish the sycophant.[23] Indeed, occasionally punishment could only be achieved by tolerating sycophancy.

The other *ἀπαγωγή* homicide prosecution – Antiphon's *On the Murder of Herodes* – shows how certain political contexts could create a socially tolerable niche for the sycophant's methods. Euxitheus was a Mytilenean accused of murdering the Athenian citizen Herodes about a decade after the Mytilenean revolt. He points to a previous rash conviction and execution, that of the Hellenotamiai on the grounds of embezzlement, and reminds the jurors that on that occasion it was a reliance on 'anger rather than reason' that brought about the error (Antiph. 5.69–72). The implication that anger might unduly influence the present trial is intriguing since homicide accusations stand out among our sources for their lack of anger appeals.[24] But this trial, like Agoratus', has been brought before a dicastic court via the public procedure of *ἀπαγωγή* rather than before the Areopagus meaning that the rules of engagement are different. There may be several reasons for this decision, and the prevention of the defendant from leaving the city was probably among those the prosecutors espoused, but so perhaps was the opportunity to escape some of the rhetorical restrictions that the Areopagus placed on litigants. As Christine Plastow has shown, the obligation to speak only about what was relevant to the charge was more strictly adhered to by orators and enforced by jurors at the Areopagus than at the dicastic courts.[25] This defendant objects strongly on procedural grounds (8–19) and refers to an oath that apparently would have been taken by the litigants and their witnesses had the case appeared as a *δίκη φόνου* at the Areopagus, requiring them to confine their arguments only to the accused's involvement in the alleged murder (11–12). The fact that the jurors' anger, whether the prosecutors have openly called for it or not, is thought likely to influence this decision suggests that the accusations, like those against Agoratus, go beyond homicide. Indeed, Euxitheus' Mytilenean identity may well be relevant. In the first of two references to sycophancy, he excuses his father for choosing, on the grounds that he shares the jurors' hatred of sycophants, to reside in Thrace (Ant. 5.78); he then applies the label to the current prosecutors too, urging the jurors to help him rather than allow sycophants to become greater than them (80).[26] Post-revolt Mytileneans were seemingly targeted by prosecutors who thought they stood to win easy convictions by exploiting the lasting popular resentment. Often, no doubt, the accused were guilty of little more than being Mytilenean at a time when Athenian citizens were keen to avenge themselves but were not especially discriminating as to on whom.

The sycophantic facilitating of the expression of popular anger against demonised groups is also a feature of *Against Agoratus*. The trial probably occurred in or around 399,[27] a year renowned for its political trials when there appears to have been a particularly strong appetite for settling scores against the Thirty and their accomplices.[28] The amnesty had not removed that anger; it was an attempt to enforce restraint but anger remained dormant for years to come and, in the context of this kind of political sentiment, sycophancy could flourish. Part of what was normally so offensive about sycophancy was the disrespect it showed for the much valued legal system, yet the degree to which Athenians valued that system was fluid, capable of changing according to the current political climate. The sycophancy-associated ability to twist and reinterpret laws to suit an argument could invite public anger for it represented an undermining of the laws' true purpose in the service of purely private ends. But when the vengeful desires of the angry community were in conflict with the laws, those skills could be precisely what the people needed. The case against Agoratus was largely specious, but that does not mean it failed. Perhaps the case did not need to be strong to win a conviction, merely plausible. By presenting a case, however flimsy, that satisfied the legal stipulations preventing the condemnation of Agoratus – the requirements that the killer be caught in the act and have killed with his own hands, and the amnesty's bar on the prosecution of those who had been members of the opposing party – this speaker offers the jurors the chance to vote for vengeance.

In a sense, the prosecutor of the grain dealers does the opposite: the Council would have omitted procedure and moved straight to execution but our speaker intervened to ensure a trial occurred in the interests, so he says, of the integrity of the system. But, however this case started, the appetite for revenge is now high. There is (according to the speaker) already anger at the defendants sufficient to execute without trial, and the more general allegations towards grain dealers as a group – that they profit from the city's hardships and even invent bad news to increase demand (Lys. 22.13–15) – suggest that they were objects of popular resentment even in the absence of specific accusations. The jurors do not need cajoling into a punitive frame of mind, they need the procedural box ticked so that they can give vent to the anger they have brought with them to court.

Youth

Concern over their lack of moral authority could also affect the rhetorical strategies of young men.[29] As we shall see, youth was a significant handicap for public prosecutors, yet in some ways it could also be a strength.[30] Epichares' inexperience means he lacks the knowledge and skill of orators like Demosthenes, but, as he asserts, that also means he lacks their capacity to deceive (Dem. 58.41). The young could play their greenness to their advantage by acknowledging their weakness just as early-career Demosthenes admits to his lack of experience in court (27.2) and Ariston faces up to his ignorance of the laws (54.17).[31] This trustworthiness would lend credence to Epichares' version of events while his plight, combined with his unassuming youth, strengthened his command of the jurors' pity.[32] And yet these qualities will not on their own have persuaded the jurors to punish the accused man, Theocrines; for that, they needed to be angry with him.

Epichares avoids explicit anger appeals but he does have a discernable strategy for leading the jurors into anger. He recounts Theocrines' earlier prosecution of his father:

> *ὀργισθέντων δὲ τῶν δικαστῶν ἐπὶ τοῖς λεγομένοις, καὶ νομισάντων αὐτὸ μὲν τὸ ψήφισμα καὶ τὴν δωρεὰν κατὰ τοὺς νόμους εἶναι, τῷ δὲ ὄντι τὸν παῖδα μέλλειν ἀποστερεῖσθαι τῶν χρημάτων, τῷ μὲν πατρὶ δέκα ταλάντων ἐτίμησαν ὡς μετὰ Πολυεύκτου ταῦτα πράττοντι, τούτῳ δ' ἐπίστευσαν ὡς δὴ βοηθήσαντι τῷ παιδί.*
>
> (Dem. 58.31)
>
> The jurymen were angered at his statements, considering that while both the decree itself and the grant were legal, the boy would be robbed of his estate; and they fined my father ten talents as doing these things with Polyeuctus, and trusted Theocrines as having assisted the boy.[33]

His father had drawn up a decree that an orphan, Charidemus, should enjoy maintenance in the Prytaneum in honour of his father, but Theocrines subsequently brought a *γραφὴ παρανόμων* against him asserting that this was a plot designed to alienate Charidemus from his adoptive inheritance. The jurors, believing this, became angry. Through this past case involving his father, Epichares is able to raise the theme of dicastic anger and present the jurors with reasons for feeling it.

The main provocation here is the maltreatment of an orphan, an offence covered by a specific public procedure (*Ath. Const.* 56.6).[34] Lysias' *Against Diogeiton* is a prosecution of a guardian brought on behalf of an orphan who is of age but lacking experience. It contains a single anger appeal based on the claim that 'Diogeiton is reducing all people to a state of such suspicion towards others that neither the living nor the dead can place any more trust in their closest family members than in their bitterest enemies' (Lys. 32.19). The jurors are expected to feel especially angry at this guardian's treatment of his orphan wards because he ought to have been trustworthy. On the other hand, Demosthenes, despite stating that he was victimised as an orphan (Dem. 31.14), manages to deliver five prosecutorial speeches (27–31) devoted to the recovery of his estate from allegedly fraudulent guardians without ever appealing to anger. It seems that the maltreatment of orphans could evoke public anger (especially when the culprit was a close relation) but certain factors, including age, could prevent one from openly appealing to it.

Epichares is not an orphan like Charidemus, but he presents himself as similarly (if not more) disadvantaged because, like an orphan, he lacks a citizen-father who can defend the family's interests in public and teach his son to do the same in time, but, unlike an orphan, he carries the added burden of a father whose interests he must now represent.

> *πολλῶν δ' ἡμῖν, ὦ ἄνδρες δικασταί, διὰ τουτονὶ Θεοκρίνην ἀτυχημάτων ἐν οὐκ ὀλίγῳ χρόνῳ συμβεβηκότων, οὐδενὸς ἔλαττόν ἐστιν τὸ νῦν συμβαῖνον, ὅτι τὰ δεινὰ καὶ τὰ παρὰ τοὺς νόμους πεπραγμένα Θεοκρίνῃ τῷ μὲν πατρὶ τῷ πεπονθότι καὶ δυναμένῳ ἂν δηλῶσαι πρὸς ὑμᾶς ἐξ ἀνάγκης ἡσυχίαν ἑκτέον ἐστίν (οἱ γὰρ νόμοι ταῦτα κελεύουσιν), ἐμοὶ δὲ τῷ πάντων τούτων ὑστερίζοντι λεκτέον, καὶ τοῖς μὲν ἄλλοις τοῖς τηλικούτοις οἱ πατέρες βοηθοῦσιν, οὗτος δ' ἐν ἐμοὶ νῦν ἔχει τὰς ἐλπίδας. τοιοῦτον οὖν ἀγωνιζόμενοι ἀγῶνα δεόμεθ' ὑμῶν ἐπικουρεῖν ἡμῖν, καὶ δεῖξαι πᾶσιν ὅτι, κἂν παῖς κἂν γέρων κἂν ἡντινοῦν ἡλικίαν ἔχων ἥκῃ πρὸς ὑμᾶς κατὰ τοὺς νόμους, οὗτος τεύξεται πάντων τῶν δικαίων.*
>
> (Dem. 58.60–1)

> Although, jurymen, we have endured many misfortunes in no short period of time because of this Theocrines, what we are now enduring is by no means the least of them: that though my father suffered the terrible and illegal acts of Theocrines and would be able to illuminate them for you, he is compelled to remain silent (for the laws demand it). I then, being unequal to all these tasks, must speak; and while others of my age are assisted by their fathers, my father now rests his hopes in me. Being in such a trial, we need you to help us and demonstrate to all that whether a boy or an old man or one of any age comes before you in accordance with the laws, he gets all he deserves.

An indication that Epichares is intentionally likening himself to Charidemus can be seen in his use of the word *παῖς*. Epichares was at least eighteen and yet implies that he, like Charidemus, is a child.[35] He appears to be pursuing in this current case an outcome like that which occurred in the prior one.

Just as Epichares is a new Charidemus, so is Theocrines a new iteration of Charidemus' exploiter. Epichares' father apparently provoked anger not only by exploiting an orphan but by abusing state institutions to do so. Epichares repeatedly accuses Theocrines of lying to the jurors (Dem. 58.27, 31, 36), a common cause of dicastic anger.[36] Manipulation of jurors or citizens and their authority for unjust private gain is fundamental to both Theocrines' prosecution of Epichares' father and Epichares' prosecution of Theocrines. The father incurred dicastic anger in part because he was believed to have persuaded the Athenians to pass a decree that would ostensibly honour a dead hero, but which would also result in the ruining of that hero's orphan son. Theocrines' actions are portrayed similarly. *Against Theocrines* is not a prosecution for sycophancy but the accusation runs throughout and is the most prominent feature of the defendant's character.[37] He has apparently made a habit of bringing false accusations and using the courts as leverage for extortion. Thus, by enforcing the crippling fine on Epichares' father, the jurors enabled Theocrines to scare Polyeuctus into paying the bribe to avoid a similar fate. Epichares even asserts that it was upon seeing how angry the jurors were in the first trial that Theocrines felt encouraged to bring the second suit and seek Polyeuctus' pay-off (32). Epichares' hope is that, just as the jurors were angry at having been manipulated into error by his father, so will they feel angry in light of the new revelation that the true manipulation has in fact been carried out by Theocrines.

Epichares' youth advises that he adopt this subtle strategy. Any citizen over the age of eighteen could bring a public suit but in practice prosecutors tended to be significantly older. Another young prosecutor, Ariston, forwent his right to bring a *γραφή* because of how he might be perceived, opting instead to bring an alternative private suit.[38] This pressure to appear to be concerned purely with private matters is reflected by Mantitheus who answers the accusation that he has been speaking before the people at too young an age with the assertion that he has been forced to do so in order to protect his own interests (Lys. 16.20–1). Hyperides tells Demosthenes he ought to be ashamed to be prosecuted for bribery by mere boys (*μειρακίων*) who should be avoiding risky actions but are instead doing the opposite and prosecuting men over the age of sixty (Hyp. 5.21–2). Though these young men, along with older co-prosecutors, achieved Demosthenes' conviction in this case, Hyperides evidently considers the age gap to be an obstacle under normal circumstances. A young prosecutor, more so than an older one, needed to have sincere private interests in a case and would ideally avoid ambitious public charges.[39]

The norm of age-based deference affected decisions over not only whom to prosecute and what procedure to use but also how to address jurors in court.[40] All jurors were at least thirty years old, many considerably older, meaning that any litigant under thirty was talking exclusively to his elders and from ignorance of their role.[41] We can imagine, then, a resistance among jurors to receiving direction from their inexperienced juniors and a reticence among young prosecutors to risk telling their experienced seniors when they ought to be angry and punish. Young prosecutors, especially those under thirty, lacked the moral authority necessary to deliver such instruction.

An illustration of the impact of youth on anger appeals can be seen in our two prosecution speeches for assault. *Against Conon*'s forty-four chapters contain only one explicit call for *ὀργή*, whereas the twenty-two chapters of *Against Lochites* contain four over what was almost certainly a less serious assault.[42] These different approaches may simply reflect the stylistic differences of the logographers and the speakers they tailored their speeches for, but there may be other factors too. Given that Ariston apparently almost died and was then crowed over in a display of great *hybris*, whereas Lochites' victim seems to have suffered no more than a punch, the frequency of anger appeals does not reflect the severity of the offence. Indeed, *Against Conon* is littered with accusations of *hybris*,[43] more than any speech except *Against Meidias* which also contains by far the most appeals to *ὀργή*. One reason is probably the political climate that allowed Lochites' prosecutor to link the behaviour of his assailant to the attitude that drove the recent overthrowers of democracy. But Ariston's youth may also have been an obstacle for him, preventing him from making grand assertions about the threat that men like Conon posed to democracy and claiming authoritatively that his actions constituted offences to the jurors.[44]

While Ariston's youth leads him to settle for a private suit, Epichares' desperate situation compels him, despite his tender years, to bring a public one (Dem. 58.1–4).[45] His father is now *ἄτιμος* ('deprived of civic rights') and will pass this debt-bound status on to his son upon death. Epichares' avenging of his father requires a public suit (in this instance an *ἔνδειξις* for prosecuting cases as a citizen despite being a public-debtor) to allow him to seek Theocrines' disenfranchisement in return and even his punishment for false-citizenship on top of that.[46] This puts Epichares at risk of appearing overly ambitious and presumptuous for his age. Avoiding anger appeals is one of a number of means employed by Epichares in his attempt to combat this impression.

Epichares attempts to mitigate the damaging impact of his youth on his perceived character as a public prosecutor by framing it as an act of obedience to his father (Dem. 58.2) and is as hesitant in arguing the suit as he claims to have been in bringing it. The substance of the case rests on proving that Theocrines, as a state-debtor, is *ἄτιμος* and should not therefore have been prosecuting cases. The debt is due to a fine which Theocrines allegedly incurred for bringing a case but abandoning it before trial on receipt of payment from the defendant (6). To this are added a fine for theft from his tribe's funds and another inherited from his grandfather from the undisclosed sale of a slave (17–21).[47] These amount to accusations of unpaid public debt, sycophancy and false-citizenship – all offences on the basis of which jurors can become angry – yet Epichares makes no appeals to anger and only two carefully hidden appeals to punishment.[48] In the first instance, the jurors are told that the law stipulates extra *τιμωρίαι* for public debtors who have failed to have their names removed from the register (52), while in the second the instruction to punish is given indirectly by anticipating critically the advice of Theocrines' *synegoros*, Moerocles, that they 'should not punish (*τιμωρήσασθαι*) but acquit' (54). This tactic of adding legitimacy to important statements by attributing them to more authoritative sources is also seen when knowledge and wisdom are twice ascribed to 'older men' whom he claims have advised him.[49] The tentative approach continues into the concluding lines with the extraordinarily timid line: 'so that, if nothing else, we might have the consolation of seeing this man too brought to silence, help us' (69).[50] The vocabulary of anger and punishment is abandoned in favour of an allusion to *ἀτιμία* which is not demanded or even requested, but merely hoped-for and framed in terms of private help.

This leads us to an even more striking abnormality: the great emphasis placed on private rather than public motive.[51] Acknowledgement of private motive is a commonly used means of dispelling suspicions of sycophancy, but it is the jurors' motive for punishment which elsewhere soon becomes the prominent theme. In the opening to this speech however, the jurors are asked to help the speaker take vengeance for a wrong against his father (Dem. 58.1–2).[52] They are given reasons to listen to him which include that he is doing the will of his father, is young and inexperienced and has been betrayed by his anticipated co-pleaders (4). And, despite many of the accusations having public implications, the closing remarks stick to his private interest (68–70). This apparently blatant use of a public procedure in pursuit of an exclusively private enmity is roundly condemned elsewhere and is highly unusual. In the jurors' eyes, a private trial was where a young litigant belonged and Epichares is largely speaking as if that is precisely where he is; he has chosen to invite the accusation that he is using a public procedure to prosecute a purely private enemy, rather than potentially alienate the jurors by instructing them on what they ought to be offended by and how they should respond.

Conclusion

The few public prosecutors who do not openly call for dicastic *ὀργή* present no problem for the claims that the Athenian courts were supposed to punish because of anger and that public prosecutors usually sought to evoke this emotion. However, strategic considerations, particularly pertaining to the speaker's character, meant that anger could not always be explicitly invoked. An instruction for someone to be angry implies a presumption of moral authority, a quality that the act of public prosecution generally demanded but that some could manage without.

Among the qualities that could undermine a prosecutor's moral authority were the traits associated with sycophancy. Specious arguments, feeble evidence and an over-reliance on accusations outside the actual charge were all potential red flags indicating a conscious attempt to persuade the jurors of a weak case. The sort of person who would knowingly seek to manipulate the jurors and the legal system in this way was not the sort of person who had the right to instruct the jurors as to when, why and at whom they ought to be angry. Typically, this was a deal-breaker because, regardless of whether one explicitly appealed to anger, the bringing of a public prosecution was itself a statement to the effect that the accused has offended the jurors and should be punished. But what we see in two of our speeches is that sometimes the political context could create an opportunity and even a demand for the skills of the sycophant so long as he knew his place. When the law stood in the way of anger, orators like the prosecutor of Agoratus could be tolerated so long as they were able plausibly to meet the legal stipulations. And when the procedural box needed ticking, prosecutors like that of the grain dealers could be permitted to make some money out of the system if it afforded the jurors the opportunity to punish.

The young had also to account for a deficiency of moral authority or avoid public procedure. Epichares' youth means he cannot presume to offer moral instruction to the older, more experienced men who made up the jury, and so he opts to observe what has made them angry in the past, seeking to demonstrate that the same offence is again in play. A lack of years, perhaps like other character weaknesses, was a problem for public prosecutors whose job it was to persuade jurors that they had something to be angry about. But as *Against Theocrines* shows, where direct appeals were inadvisable, other strategies for leading the jurors into anger were available.

6

Public Offence and Private Procedure

Introduction

If the punishments of the Athenian courts were supposed to be motivated by anger at a personal slight, we should expect cases where the charge is of a primarily private nature to contain only very few calls for anger and punishment, if any. However, not all private speeches conform to this expectation. Many are limited to requests for the jurors to judge fairly, vote for them, believe them and so on, but some openly call for dicastic anger and punishment. These cases challenge the idea that the jurors punished only when they felt personally slighted. Why would a juror feel dishonoured by a slanderous insult of one man against another or by a private debt?

Underpinning the appeals to anger and punishment in the private corpus are four main themes: failing the state, *hybristic* violence, putting the *polis* at risk and undermining justice. Those whose conduct amounts to one of these are at risk of provoking dicastic anger and inviting public punishment because their behaviour not only was illegal but presented a slight to Athenian jurors whose honour was bound up in their city.

The evidence of these cases also presents challenges to our tendency to distinguish private from public according to procedure. But, if the distribution of anger and punishment appeals is any indication, the boundary did not reliably match the distinction between *δίκη* and *γραφή*.

Private disputes and public punishments: the model

Our expectation, based on the fact that private trials are supposed to deal with private offences, might be that the private prosecutions tend not to call for anger or punishment and the private defences tend not to urge against them. The majority of speeches – eighteen of thirty-one prosecutions, seven of ten defences and all nine *διαδικασίαι* – conform to this. In most private cases it is the plaintiff alone who has been offended, has become angry and is in search of recompense, and there is no expectation that the jurors will take umbrage alongside him. Furthermore, the correlation with anger remains: most speeches that call for punishment call also for anger and vice versa, and both occur in greater quantity when together. This indicates that the punishments prosecutors sought were understood to be expressions of that emotion, responses to slighted honour. And, apart from one prosecution speech and one defence (addressed below), calls *for* anger and punishment occur in prosecutions while appeals *against* them occur in defences. The data from the private speeches support the conclusion that dicastic anger was much more useful to prosecutors than defendants and that it was closely related to punishment.

But there are also those speeches that depart from our expectation, and they are too many and too emphatic for us to dismiss as orators taking liberties. Ten private prosecutions call for punishment, ten call for anger and seven call for both. Conversely, one appeal against anger and three against punishment appear across two private defences. Evidently it was not out of the question for jurors to become angry at and punish private defendants. We shall see that this does not mean the classical Athenian state could also serve as a dispassionate agent, punishing on behalf of its citizens for the wrongdoings they had suffered.[1] Rather, the evidence confirms what we have seen elsewhere – that when jurors felt angry and punished it was conceived of as a response to their own perception of personal offence, even if that happened to take place in a private trial.

Rubinstein observed in her study of anger and punishment appeals that the exceptional speeches share a sense of public interest.[2] One indication of this is the fact that four of them were delivered in trials where there was potential for not only the enforcement of restitution to the victim, but also public punishment.[3] The strength of this apparent link is weakened not only by the three significant exceptions (Isoc. 20, Dem. [50], 54) and their large share of the appeals, but also by the numerous speeches from trials with potential for public penalties yet with no punishment or anger appeals. All *παραγραφαί* carried a potential *ἐπωβελία* fine but only one, *Against Callimachus* (Isoc. 18), contains any appeals.[4] And the *δίκη ψευδομαρτυριῶν* (Dem. [44], 45, [46] and [47]) could, after three convictions, result in the loss of civic rights (*ἀτιμία*) but again not all such cases call for anger or punishment.[5] On its own, the potential for public penalties is not predictive of appeals to dicastic anger or punishment, but the implication that public interest is important is surely there.[6]

Some private suits carried public implications and others did not. An explanation for this distinction is offered by Apollodorus in his prosecution of Polycles – one of our exceptional speeches. The significance of Apollodorus' argument is best brought out through comparison with another suit for damages, Callistratus's prosecution of Olympiodorus.[7]

> *ἀναγκαῖον ἴσως ἐστίν, ὦ ἄνδρες δικασταί, καὶ τοὺς μὴ εἰωθότας μηδὲ δυναμένους εἰπεῖν εἰσιέναι εἰς δικαστήριον, ἐπειδὰν ὑπό τινος ἀδικῶνται, ἄλλως τε καὶ ὑφ' ὧν ἥκιστα προσῆκεν ἀδικεῖσθαι, οἷον καὶ ἐμοὶ νυνὶ συμβαίνει. οὐ βουλόμενος γάρ, ὦ ἄνδρες δικασταί, ἀγωνίζεσθαι πρὸς Ὀλυμπιόδωρον οἰκεῖον ὄντα καὶ ἀδελφὴν τούτου ἔχων, ἠνάγκασμαι διὰ τὸ μεγάλ' ἀδικεῖσθαι ὑπὸ τούτου. εἰ μὲν οὖν μὴ ἀδικούμενος, ὦ ἄνδρες δικασταί, ἀλλὰ ψεῦδός τι ἐγκαλῶν Ὀλυμπιοδώρῳ τούτων τι ἐποίουν, ἢ τοῖς ἐπιτηδείοις τοῖς ἐμοῖς καὶ Ὀλυμπιοδώρου μὴ ἐθέλων ἐπιτρέπειν, ἢ ἄλλου τινὸς τῶν δικαίων ἀφιστάμενος, εὖ ἴστε ὅτι πάνυ ἂν ᾐσχυνόμην καὶ ἐνόμιζον ἂν ἐμαυτὸν φαῦλον εἶναι ἄνθρωπον· νῦν δ' οὔτε μικρὰ ἐλαττούμενος ὑπὸ Ὀλυμπιοδώρου, οὔτε διαλλακτὴν οὐδένα φεύγων, οὔτ' αὖ μὰ τὸν Δία τὸν μέγιστον ἑκών, ἀλλ' ὡς οἷόν τε μάλιστα ἄκων, ἠνάγκασμαι ὑπὸ τούτου ἀγωνίζεσθαι ταύτην τὴν δίκην.*
>
> (Dem. 48.1–2)

> It is perhaps necessary, jurymen, even for those unaccustomed and unskilled in speaking to go to court when they have been wronged by someone, especially when it is by those who ought to be the last to wrong them as has come now to pass for me. For I do not want, jurymen, to go to trial with Olympiodorus, him being a relative and his sister my wife, but I have been forced to through the greatness of his wrongdoing. If I had not been wronged, jurymen, but were bringing false charges against Olympiodorus, or if I were not willing to refer the matters to friends of myself and Olympiodorus, or if I were refusing any other just option, know for certain that I would be altogether ashamed and would consider myself a worthless man. But as it is I have suffered no small loss by Olympiodorus, I have not refused any mediator, nor by Zeus the greatest have I voluntarily done this, but with the most profound unwillingness I have been forced by this man to bring this dispute to trial.

Callistratus adopts an apologetic tone, desiring to persuade the jurors that he does not want to be there, has tried every other option available and has been forced (by the defendant) to bring the suit.[8] The jurors in this trial are asked to reconcile (*διαλλάξαντας*) the litigants if possible or simply vote for the party whose cause is just (3, 48), to persuade the defendant not to wrong the plaintiff (58) and to form a fair judgement which is to the advantage of all, including the defendant (58). Appeals like these are found throughout the forensic corpus because jurors are always supposed to aim for what is 'just' or 'fair', but, unlike the public prosecutors, private plaintiffs generally do not define 'justice' as an act of anger on the jurors' part.[9]

Apollodorus opens his speech in contrasting fashion:

> *τοῖς τοιούτοις τῶν ἀγώνων, ὦ ἄνδρες δικασταί, καὶ τοὺς διαγνωσομένους προσήκει μάλιστα προσέχειν τὸν νοῦν. οὐ γὰρ ἐμὸς καὶ Πολυκλέους ἴδιός ἐστιν ὁ ἀγὼν μόνον, ἀλλὰ καὶ τῆς πόλεως κοινός. ὧν γὰρ τὰ μὲν ἐγκλήματα ἴδιά ἐστιν, αἱ δὲ βλάβαι κοιναί, πῶς οὐχ ὑπὲρ τούτων εἰκός ἐστιν ἀκούσαντας ὑμᾶς ὀρθῶς διαγνῶναι; εἰ μὲν γὰρ περὶ ἄλλου τινὸς συμβολαίου ἐγὼ διαφερόμενος πρὸς Πολυκλέα εἰσῄειν εἰς ὑμᾶς, ἐμὸς ἂν ἦν καὶ Πολυκλέους ὁ ἀγών· νῦν δὲ περί τε διαδοχῆς νεώς ἐστιν ὁ λόγος καὶ ἐπιτριηραρχήματος πέντε μηνῶν καὶ ἓξ ἡμερῶν ἀνηλωμένου, καὶ περὶ τῶν νόμων, πότερα κύριοί εἰσιν ἢ οὔ.*
>
> ([Dem.] 50.1)

> In trials of this sort, jurymen, those who are going to make the decision should pay closest attention. For the trial belongs not only to myself and Polycles, but to the polis as well. For when the accusations are private but the damages are communal, surely it is fitting that you listen and make the correct decision. If I had come before you quarrelling with Polycles over some other sort of contract, the trial would have concerned only Polycles and myself. But as it is the argument is over succession to a ship and trierarchal expenses extended by five months and six days, and it concerns the laws, whether they are to be in power or not.

Apollodorus' statements suggest that the jurors recognised different kinds of dispute that warranted different kinds of approach and placed different kinds of burden on the jurors. Apollodorus sets out his stall by identifying not only what kind of procedure this is but also whose interests are at stake. There are, he asserts, different kinds of private dispute: those that concern only the plaintiff and the defendant, and those that concern the *polis* also and demand greater attention. His explanation for including this trial among the latter appears to work from the assumption that in most cases the nature of the procedure – public or private – would help the jurors identify which sort of dispute they are dealing with. In this case however, though the charge is private, the interest is public because, crucially, the damages are public.

This reasoning cuts to the heart of what justified a prosecutor calling for dicastic anger and punishment. This trial carried no potential for a public penalty and yet Apollodorus can make his appeals and generally characterise the trial as being of public interest because Polycles' actions slighted the city and its citizens.[10] The presence of anger and punishment appeals in some of the private speeches highlights how blurred the line could sometimes be between public and private procedure. The citizen jurors were always, as we shall see, open to the possibility that they themselves had been slighted as well.

Failing the state

The basis of Apollodorus' call for punishment comes down to an accusation that Polycles has failed to meet the state's expectations. Polycles allegedly failed to succeed him promptly as trierarch, meaning that he had to remain in post accruing more expenses than he ought to. Apollodorus says that Polycles' behaviour has 'shown contempt (*κατεφρόνησεν*) not only for me, but also for you and the laws' ([Dem.] 50.57), repeating twice more the allegation of *καταφρόνησις* alongside appeals for them to be angry and punish (65, 66). He tells them to avenge themselves (64) and says he considers it his duty to convict and take vengeance, along with the jurors, on wrongdoers (65). In reassuring them that 'you will not be taking revenge on Polycles for my own sake more than for your own' (66), Apollodorus highlights the tension at play for private prosecutors who used such terminology – jurors did not want to punish on behalf of victims but *as* victims. And as this speech shows, one way of showing them to be victims is to reveal the defendant as one who has failed to serve them as promised and treated them, their demands and their laws with contempt.

In another speech (probably written by Demosthenes), Apollodorus tells the jurors 'now then, men of Athens, though [Stephanus] would justly give satisfaction (*δοὺς δίκην*) for all these things, there is much more reason for him to be punished by you for the rest of his actions' (Dem. 45.63; cf. 67). 'The wrongs' include the theft of an important document and false testimony whereas 'the rest of his actions' refers to his ongoing practice of attaching himself to wealthy men and deserting them when they fall into difficulty (63–5).[11] Demosthenes seeks to present this as reprehensible to all, not simply the direct victims, when he suggests that the jurors should 'hate (*μισεῖν*) this man as by nature the common enemy of all humanity' (65), on the basis that Stephanus does not mind mistreating relatives or gaining a bad reputation so long as he enriches himself. Significantly, the emotion Demosthenes seeks to incite over this behaviour – which does not personally slight anyone besides those he is betraying – is *μῖσος* rather than *ὀργή*. This conforms to Aristotle's distinction whereby the object of *ὀργή* is always an individual whereas the object of *μῖσος* may be a particular kind of person such as a thief or sycophant (*Rh*. 2.4.31). While *μῖσος* will certainly prejudice the jurors (cf. 1.1.7), Demosthenes knows that *ὀργή* is needed to provoke legitimate punishment and for that they must be personally offended. The substance of this offence, and the basis of Apollodorus' final anger appeal (Dem. 45.67), is the allegation that Stephanus has been hiding his wealth in order to withhold it from the state and evade his liturgical obligations (66). Apollodorus then concludes this argument as he began it, with a call for the jurors to chastise (*κολάζητε*) the defendant (67). Demosthenes needed to make the jurors feel not simply resentful but personally offended if they were to exact punishment, and the rich withholding the wealth and service they owed the city was likely to achieve that goal.

Lysias' *Against Theomnestus* demonstrates the impact that public accusations could have on the kinds of response one could ask of jurors. This speech employs vengeful rhetoric from the start but, being primarily to do with a private accusation of slander, the hoped-for revenge is also primarily of a private nature. The speaker, having been accused by Theomnestus of patricide, says 'it would be disgraceful... not to take revenge (*τιμωρήσασθαι*)' and wants to know from the jurors whether Theomnestus 'will give satisfaction (*δώσει δίκην*)' (Lys. 10.3; cf. 13, 22), presumably to him. From the beginning, however, an undertone of public offence is maintained through references to the previous trial (during which this slander occurred) at which Theomnestus was being prosecuted for speaking in the assembly despite having lost the right to do so through cowardice (1, 9, 12, 21). Once he has made his case regarding the slander charge, the speaker turns to the cowardice theme in earnest and speaks no longer of his own vengeance but of the jurors'. Having asserted that the defendant's prior acquittal was unjust (22–5) and having praised the military service of his own father (26–7), he links the present case to the former by comparing the trophies of his father's battles, dedicated in Athenian temples, with those of Athens' enemies, namely the armour which Theomnestus discarded in flight. On this evocative note, he makes his two appeals for the jurors' anger (28–9) and finally calls for revenge (*τιμωρεῖσθε*) over Theomnestus' cowardice (30).[12]

A cowardice allegation also supports Hyperides' client's isolated call for punishment. The plaintiff highlights

> *πραχθέντα καὶ ὃν τρόπον ἐπιβεβούλευκέν μοι Ἀθηνογένης, καὶ ὡς ὑμῖν προσενήνεκται. τὸν δὴ καὶ ἰδίᾳ πονηρὸν καὶ τῆς πόλεως τὴν σωτηρίαν ἀπελπίσαντα καὶ ὑμᾶς ἐγκαταλιπόντα, καὶ παρ' οὓς ἐξῴκησεν ἀναστάτους ποιήσαντα, τοῦτον ὑμεῖς συνειληφότες οὐ κολάσετε;*
>
> (Hyp. 3.35)

> the way in which Athenogenes has plotted against me and how he has behaved towards you (the jurors). He is wicked in private and, despairing of the city's safety, has abandoned you and expelled those with whom he had made a home. Will you, having laid hands on this man, not discipline him?

Athenogenes' desertion (cf. 29, 32) shows contempt (*καταφρονήσας*) for his obligations to the jurors (31). This echoing of the argument used against the young Alcibiades indicates that anger is being sought, even if no appeals are preserved, and explains the call for *κόλασις*.[13] The jurors considered their community to deserve certain sacrifices – including those of time, wealth and personal safety – from its citizens. To fail to meet those expectations, such as by fleeing the city at times of war, was to disregard the community's right to make such claims and its power to back them up.[14]

Violence

The two prosecutions for assault (*δίκαι αἰκείας*; Isoc. 20 and Dem. 54) have already been dealt with in some detail (pp. 129–34), but it is worth highlighting how offences of this sort could cause public anger even when brought to court via a private procedure. Not all violent assaults were sure to incur punishment. No Athenian would question whether the violent assault of one man by others constituted an act of *hybris* – Ariston has clearly been intentionally insulted – but that would not necessarily trigger the jurors' anger. Ariston says, 'terrible as was the *hybris* that came to pass, no less so was the subsequent insolence (*ἀσέλγεια*) of this man' (Dem. 54.2). Here Ariston distinguishes between two displays of *hybris*: the violent assault and Conon's triumphant celebration afterwards in which he crowed like a victorious fighting cock, flapping his elbows like wings (9). Ariston fears that this *hybristic* assault alone will not draw punishment. Conon is expected to present the violent episode as an alcohol-fuelled altercation over a courtesan (13–16), thereby quelling the anger of the jurors through laughter. This 'boys-will-be-boys' defence ought never, in Ariston's opinion, to be accepted because all assault and *hybris* needs to be punished to deter escalation (17–19), but he recognises that it might.[15] His antidotes to humour are twofold. He highlights the severity of his injuries through the image of the women of his household shrieking and crying at the sight of him, believing him to be dying (20). And he points to Conon as one who should know better, being over fifty years old (21–2). Evidently, allowance was sometimes made for violence in the young.

In theory, all violence was the concern of the state; in practice, only violence that demonstrated contempt for the state's power was likely to be punished. Ariston appears to recognise this, saying that even if Conon had done nothing wrong himself but merely stood by while his son committed assault he would still deserve the jurors' hatred (Dem. 54.22).

> *εἰ γὰρ οὕτω τοὺς αὑτοῦ προῆκται παῖδας ὥστ' ἐναντίον ἐξαμαρτάνοντας ἑαυτοῦ, καὶ ταῦτ' ἐφ' ὧν ἐνίοις θάνατος ἡ ζημία κεῖται, μήτε φοβεῖσθαι μήτ' αἰσχύνεσθαι, τί τοῦτον οὐκ ἂν εἰκότως παθεῖν οἴεσθε;*
>
> (Dem. 54.23)
>
> for if he has raised his sons in such a way that they commit crimes in front of him, for some of which the penalty of death is ordained, with neither fear nor shame, what punishment do you think would be inappropriate for him to suffer?

This character attack paints Conon as a poor father, but it also introduces the implication that Conon does not respect the laws, even those threatening death. It is in the jurors' interests to protect the laws because they rely on them for their own protection, and accordingly Ariston urges the jurors to be angry with all assailants as if they themselves had been the victim (42). Again, he reasons that it is to their advantage if they punish (*κολάζητε*) Conon because their decision will give either warning or licence to those considering such behaviour in future (43).[16]

The prosecutor of Lochites uses *hybris* words eight times in the short speech while the word which describes the actual charge, *αἰκία*, appears only twice.[17] Again, the speaker goes beyond describing how the *hybris* represents a personal insult to emphasise the threat that such *hybris* poses to the city as a whole, particularly in the context of the recent oligarchic regimes. The actions of men like Lochites, he says, signify contempt (*καταφρονεῖν*) for the citizenry (Isoc. 20.21). As in *Against Conon*, we see that if one wants the jurors to inflict a (harsh) penalty it is crucial to prove not only violence but *hybris*, and not only *hybris* but *hybris* that represents contempt for the jurors and their city.[18]

The threat of *stasis*

Against Lochites shows that, particularly in the period following the restoration of democracy, political fears provided a fertile seam for prosecutors to exploit. These years saw two opposing narratives competing for dicastic anger: the one employed in *Against Lochites* and elsewhere that emphasised the crimes associated with the oligarchs and played on the desire for revenge, and a reactionary second kind that sought anger at alleged sycophants who unjustly exploited the first kind. As a *παραγραφή* from this period, *Against Callimachus* is a hybrid of a speech. Whereas typically a prosecutor aims to ignite anger while the defendant aims to extinguish it, the speaker in this case is aiming to do both. He wants to quell anger towards himself based on Callimachus' charges and to inspire anger towards Callimachus for attempting to prosecute him illegally. Thus, we have appeals both for and against anger and punishment, allowing insight into both these narratives, each of which is rooted in the jurors' protectiveness over their city.

In the speaker's defensive mode, we see again the tension that is sometimes exposed between slight and law, particularly at times of heightened political anxiety. He points out that under the amnesty the jurors do not even punish wrongdoers, so an innocent man like him certainly ought not to be punished (Isoc. 18.22; cf. 68). He considers himself to stand on firm ground legally, the *παραγραφή* procedure having been brought in for precisely this sort of case, and if he happens to lose this suit he will still have the chance to defend his actions at the actual trial.[19] Yet he also feels the need to address the charges against him and demonstrate that the jurors have no reason to be angry with him. He does this by distancing himself from the Thirty and their crimes and by characterising Callimachus' strategy as that of the sycophant (an allegation found throughout this speech) who, having a weak case against the individual, plays on the prejudicial anger felt at the individual's supposed group (36, 42).[20]

On the other hand he also appeals *for* anger and punishment, pointing to the chaos that would ensue should the amnesty be violated (Isoc. 18.4).[21] He grounds his appeals in the defendant's alleged request that the jurors break their oath and points to the *ὀργή* they felt at others who called for the amnesty's repeal – an act they ought not to leave unpunished (*ἀζήμιον*) now (26) – and the anger they would feel (*ἀγανακτήσειεν*) were the Lacedaemonians to break their covenant with the Athenians (29). Whether or not simply being asked to break their oath would have been enough to offend and anger the jurors is not clear – indeed Callimachus' desire was no doubt to inspire even greater anger at the injustices which the amnesty forgave – but the speaker clearly feels the need to spell out why it should provoke them. He states that this case is different from other private suits because this one represents a danger to the whole city (34; cf. 24). And he goes on to call for Callimachus to be 'punished with extreme penalties' (*ζημίαις κολάζειν. . . ταῖς ἐσχάταις*) for daring to 'transgress the covenant' (47). The hope is that the jurors will perceive Callimachus as risking a return to the awful political environment that had preceded the amnesty. The speaker has already done the groundwork by speaking of a regression from the current state of concord (*ὁμόνοια*) to one of civil war (*στάσις*; 42–4), and this impacts not only on the city's security but also on its honour because, while in its former state 'we were viewed as the most foolish and unfortunate of all', in its current state 'we seem to be the happiest and most sound of mind' (46). The jurors in this trial were more or less sure to become angry with someone or other, whether at the prosecutor over his association with the offences of the oligarchy, or at the defendant over his sycophantic undermining of the city's renewed status as a reconciled and thriving *polis*.

Undermining justice

Aristotle says that acts of wrongdoing are worse when committed 'in the place where wrongdoers are disciplined, as false witnesses do, for where might a man not do wrong if he does it in court?' (*Rh.* 1.14.6). The slights considered so far have been such as might offend any citizen. The following cases reveal a category of slights that offended jurors specifically because they were jurors and where the courtroom itself was the scene of the crime.

Most significant among these is the offence to which Aristotle refers: false testimony (*δίκη ψευδομαρτυριῶν*). The procedure for prosecuting false testimony has puzzled many on account of it not being a *γραφή*, even though the court has been lied to. Todd has dismissed Bonner and Smith's suggestion that it was a 'criminal rather than civil suit' and countered with the equally categorical assertion that '*pseudomarturion* was an offence against the opposing litigant and not against the court; and it was a matter in which the state took no interest'.[22] This need not be a dichotomy. Athenian procedures and laws often confound rigid categorisation and the *δίκη ψευδομαρτυριῶν* is a good example. It is surely private, both in name and in that conviction would result primarily in compensation paid by defendant to plaintiff. Furthermore, extant speeches never attempt, like so many public prosecutions, to evade accusations that the suit has been brought for purely private reasons and without public interest at stake. But this procedure is not a typical *δίκη*. It was heard by 501 jurors (Is. 5.20) rather than the 201 or 401 typical for private cases (*Ath. Const.* 53.3, 68.1) and it could result in the additional public sanction of *ἀτιμία* (e.g. Lys. 10.12; Is. 5.19; Dem. 29.50).[23] Mogens Herman Hansen therefore places the procedure between private and public actions while Rubinstein has posited that litigants may, as in public procedures, have had more time available and have used strategies more like those of litigants in public actions.[24] The appeals made by prosecutors suggest, and a closer analysis will confirm, both that Rubinstein is correct with regard to strategy and that the state, through its jurors, took a great deal of interest in accusations of false testimony.

Three prosecutions, two from the same trial, include appeals for dicastic anger and vengeance specifically over accusations of false testimony.[25] Apollodorus tells the jurors they ought to feel anger at those who not only caused them to make a wrong conviction in the previous *παραγραφή* but even persuaded them not to hear the defence (Dem. 45.7).[26] Later, his use of the comparative in saying that false testimony against kin 'deserves greater anger' (*πλείονος ὀργῆς ἄξιον*) implies that all false testimony warrants at least some anger, but more should be felt when the victim is a relation since the act destroys 'the natural ties of kinship' (53).[27] In *Against Euergus and Mnesibulus*, the speaker tells the jurors that the laws stipulate a lesser penalty (*ἐπιτίμια*) for one who fails to win a conviction for false testimony but a heavy vengeance (*τιμωρία*) for the one who is convicted of it ([Dem.] 47.2). Even if this use of *τιμωρία* is a product of paraphrasing rather than quoting the inscribed law, it was at least reasonable for a speaker to present the giving of false testimony as deserving of public revenge.[28]

We have seen that *Against Stephanus I* attacks the defendant's character before appealing for punishment on the basis of an offence more personal to the jurors (Dem. 45.63–7). That tactic is repeated immediately but while the offence in the first instance is the withholding of wealth from the state, the offence in the second is that of false testimony. Apollodorus characterises Stephanus as one who carefully avoids helping others and does terrible things to his own kin (68–70). Again, these are traits over which the jurors may feel *μῖσος* rather than *ὀργή*, but Apollodorus goes on to say, 'so one whom you see to be so savage (*ἄγριον*) and repulsive (*μιαρόν*) in all things, will you, having taken him in the act of wrongdoing, not take revenge (*τιμωρήσεσθε*) on him?' (70). For all that the jurors may have been persuaded to feel *μῖσος* towards Stephanus, they need a specific slight in order to feel *ὀργή* and desire vengeance. Here that slight is false testimony.

In apparent objection to this argument stand our three other prosecutions for false testimony (Is. 3, 6, [Dem.] 44) and two defences (Is. 2, Dem. 29), which contain only a single appeal for or against anger among them. Critically, all these suits are brought for the undoing of *διαμαρτυρίαι* (affidavits of objection) and, as such, the false testimony they are intended to expose was made not to the jurors in court but to a single magistrate who decided that the case need not go to court.[29] In part, then, perhaps these speeches lack anger appeals because, as Aristotle implies, falsehood would have been less offensive if uttered away from court. However, it matters not only where the individual lied but also to whom. In *Against Phormio*, claiming to have been a victim of false testimony before an arbitrator, Chrysippus tells the jurors:

> *οὐ γὰρ ὅμοιόν ἐστιν, ὦ ἄνδρες Ἀθηναῖοι, εἰς τὰ ὑμέτερα πρόσωπα ἐμβλέποντα τὰ ψευδῆ μαρτυρεῖν καὶ πρὸς διαιτητῇ· παρ' ὑμῖν μὲν γὰρ ὀργὴ μεγάλη καὶ τιμωρία ὑπόκειται τοῖς τὰ ψευδῆ μαρτυροῦσιν, πρὸς δὲ τῷ διαιτητῇ ἀκινδύνως καὶ ἀναισχύντως μαρτυροῦσιν ὅ τι ἂν βούλωνται.*
>
> (Dem. 34.19)

> it is not the same, men of Athens, to give false testimony face-to-face with you and to do so before an arbitrator. For great anger and vengeance await those who give false testimony before you, but people can give whatever testimony they want before an arbitrator and face no danger or shame.

There were categories of false testimony because it was only those to whom one lied and whose decision one influenced that were likely to perceive a slight. Jurors became angry with those who had lied to their faces in court, misleading the judgements they passed, but not with those who had lied to an individual magistrate outside of court.

The one exceptional appeal to anger among these five cases demonstrates an option available to those attacking the use of a special plea (*διαμαρτυρία* or *παραγραφή*): to accuse their opponent of obstructing justice. The speaker asserts that '*διαμαρτυρίαι* are the most unjust of all legal actions and those who use them are most deserving of your anger' ([Dem.] 44.57).[30] He reasons: 'if those who used *διαμαρτυρίαι* had it their way there would be neither courts nor trials, for by nature *διαμαρτυρίαι* hinder all these things (legal actions) and block each case from entering the court' (59). It is for the use of this procedure, which apparently alienates the jurors from their judicial role, and not for the false testimony that the jurors are asked to consider the defendant and those like him as 'the common enemies of all people' (59). The plaintiff anticipates the counter-accusation – that he is attacking a public institution and even the lawgiver himself – by arguing that the purpose of the procedure is simply to reveal the bad character and desperation of those who use it. This is certainly wrong, and the accusation that the jurors have been robbed of their judicial power is undermined by the very trial it is made in, but this speaker is not alone in perceiving jurors as possessing a certain touchiness about challenges to their role as dispensers of justice.[31] Whatever the weaknesses of the argument, it assumes that jurors can be offended and angered by attempts to evade or undermine their judicial authority.

In the only instance of an appeal for anger or punishment among the private defences, the apparently personal matter of an unpaid loan is at issue.[32]

> *ταῦτα ἡγούμεθα δίκαια εἶναι, καὶ ὑμῶν δεόμεθα, ὦ ἄνδρες δικασταί, βοηθεῖν ἡμῖν τοῖς ἀδικουμένοις, καὶ κολάζειν τοὺς κακοτεχνοῦντας καὶ σοφιζομένους, ὥσπερ οὗτοι σοφίζονται. καὶ ἐὰν ταῦτα ποιῆτε, ὑμῖν τε αὐτοῖς τὰ συμφέροντα ἔσεσθε ἐψηφισμένοι, καὶ περιαιρήσεσθε τῶν πονηρῶν ἀνθρώπων τὰς πανουργίας ἁπάσας, ἃς ἔνιοι πανουργοῦσι περὶ τὰ συμβόλαια τὰ ναυτικά.*
>
> (Dem. 35.56)

> We consider this to be just, and we need you, jurymen, to help us who are being wronged and to discipline (κολάζειν) those who deal in fraud and sophisms as these men do. And if you do this, you will have voted for what benefits you and do away with all the villainies of wicked men, which some of them are committing with regard to maritime contracts.

Appeals to anger and punishment may have been relatively common in *παραγραφαί* defences, which aimed to defend the right to prosecute. Presumably, this often meant highlighting the offences on which the proposed trial would be based, but anger could also be sought, as in this case, on the basis of the prosecutor's use of procedure.[33] The key to understanding *κολάζειν* here is in the accusation that the defendant (in the proposed trial) is using 'sophistries' to get away with his fraud. On one level the speaker, Androcles, is appealing to the same attitude as those who bring charges of false testimony – the jurors' indignation at being deceived. However, it is not only Lacritus' speech that he is attacking here but his use of procedure to gain an advantage. A *παραγραφή* allowed a defendant to reclaim some initiative in court by granting him the first speech, but jurors would be wary of what a guilty man might do with that opportunity. Androcles, therefore, associates Lacritus' bringing of a *παραγραφή* with his use of sophistic arguments saying that Phaselites (such as Lacritus), instead of paying their debts, 'invent sophisms (*σοφίσματα*), special pleas (*παραγραφὰς*) and excuses (*προφάσεις*)' (2).[34] It was common for defendants to oppose the use of the *παραγραφή* on the grounds that it was unfair, but Androcles considers not only himself a victim of this procedural evasion but the jurors too.[35] Both special pleas then, the *διαμαρτυρία* and the *παραγραφή*, were vulnerable to accusations of evading justice. The sense of ownership and protectiveness jurors felt towards their role meant an opponent's procedural choices could sometimes be portrayed as slights. Through these abuses of procedure, the argument goes, the jurors are being taken for fools.

Finally, Mantitheus calls for the jurors to show anger against Boeotus and his brother:

> *ὥστ' ἐμοὶ μὲν δικαίως ἂν ἀδικουμένῳ διὰ πολλὰ βοηθήσαιτε, τούτοις δὲ εἰκότως ἂν ὀργίζοισθε· οἵτινες, ὦ γῆ καὶ θεοί, ἐξὸν αὐτοῖς τὰ δίκαια ποιήσασι μὴ εἰσιέναι εἰς δικαστήριον, οὐκ αἰσχύνονται μὲν ἀναμιμνῄσκοντες ὑμᾶς εἴ τι ἢ ὁ πατὴρ ἡμῶν μὴ ὀρθῶς διεπράξατο ἢ οὗτοι εἰς ἐκεῖνον ἥμαρτον, ἀναγκάζουσι δ' ἐμὲ δικάζεσθαι αὐτοῖς. ἵνα δὲ ἀκριβῶς εἰδῆτε, ὡς οὐκ ἐγὼ τούτου αἴτιός εἰμι ἀλλ' οὗτοι, ἐξ ἀρχῆς ὑμῖν, ὡς ἂν ἐν βραχυτάτοις δύνωμαι, διηγήσομαι τὰ πραχθέντα.*
>
> (Dem. 40.5)

> therefore it is just for many reasons for you to help me who am being wronged, and that you should be angry (ὀργίζοισθε) with these men who, O Earth and Gods, though had they done what was just need not have gone to court, feel no shame in reminding you of anything my father did improperly or of the wrongs they committed against him, and force me to sue them. In order that you might know with clarity that it is not I who am responsible for this but them, I will describe what has been done from the beginning as briefly as I am able.

Plaintiffs often excuse themselves for bringing their cases to court, typically blaming their opponent for forcing their hand.[36] Evidently, jurors could be irascible about the frivolous use of the courts to settle quarrels that mutual friends or arbitrators might have resolved. This plaintiff is simply going one step further by urging the jurors to be angry with the defendant for leaving him no choice but to involve the courts. This appeal to *ὀργή* points again to the jurors' self-regard in the context of the court. They felt their job was important and perceived slights in the careless wasting of their time.

Conclusion

The private speeches present no objection to the claim that the punishments of the classical Athenian state were acts of vengeance. Purely private matters were not punished; they were adjudicated in a way intended to ensure the fair settling of debts between individuals. But sometimes the jurors perceived implications for their own honour and became emotionally involved. Slights against the jurors as representatives of the city manifested in the failure to meet the state's expectations, in *hybristic* violence that expressed contempt for the state's power to protect its citizens and enforce its laws, and in acts that jeopardised *polis* security for personal gain. But jurors could also take particular offence at apparent slights to them in their judicial role such as through testifying falsely to them in court, evading or manipulating their power through the abuse of procedure, and wasting their time on matters that ought to have been settled out of court. In private cases, as in public ones, jurors punished out of anger at perceived slights.

Private prosecutors who pursued a strategy of attempting to demonstrate a slight against the jurors in order to win a harsher verdict were not necessarily abusing the system. Though we refer to *δίκαι* as 'private' suits, that does not mean that they precluded any sense of public interest. No juror wanted to be duped into giving an angry and vindictive judgement when the only person who stood to benefit was the plaintiff. But the Athenian system was flexible and potentially cooperative so that, as the split fines in some cases imply, a court judgement could mean in part a demand that the plaintiff be compensated and in part a vengeful settling of a personal score between the jurors and the defendant.

7

Homicide, Impiety and the Myth of Angerless Punishment

Introduction

Up to this point, the link between anger and punishment has held. Whether the agent was an individual acting in a private capacity or a juror acting in a public one, the punishments they inflicted were motivated by anger. Indeed, only the angry could justly punish because only the angry had perceived any offence. Homicide presents a final and quite different challenge for this picture of Athenian punishment.

Society's response to homicide tends to be at the heart of scholars' attempts to explain the supposed transition from private revenge to public punishment. It was when the nobility 'renounced blood-vengeance and self-help' that the state could attain 'legal supremacy', says Victor Ehrenberg.[1] 'When blood-feud was still customary', reasons Wolff, 'homicide was a common way of settling disputes and the principal cause of controversy among the aristocracy. This was the one of which the community would first feel compelled to take care by repressing the unrestrained use of private force and establishing trial.'[2] There was certainly a trend towards increasing state involvement, particularly in the volatile area of homicide, but did the state's intervention in private blood-vengeance constitute a replacement of 'revenge' with 'punishment'?

The complete absence of anger appeals over the act of homicide suggests as much. Whether the numbers reflect reality or rhetoric, the pattern of personal slight, anger and reclaimed honour that characterises punishment in the rest of the corpus is not present in the same way. Whether or not we conclude that punishments for homicide were vengeful, the homicide speeches certainly reveal deeper complexities in the emotions involved in punishment. And here, in studying the oldest of Athens' laws and procedures, it is perhaps unsurprising that answers continue to be found in Homer.

Homicide and dicastic anger

Rich as the Athenian forensic corpus is in general, the extant material on homicide is sorely limited. Six speeches relate substantially to an accusation of homicide, three of these are prosecution speeches from three different kinds of procedure, and only one comes from a standard homicide trial, a *δίκη φόνου*. There are also problems of chronological and authorial spread with Antiphon and Lysias contributing three speeches each, the latest of which is generally thought to have been delivered in 399, leaving us with no homicide speeches from almost the entire fourth century. We must, therefore, temper our confidence in any conclusions taken from the speeches available. That said, I think there are some striking patterns with regard to anger and punishment appeals that demand explanation.

Antiphon's *Against the Stepmother for Poisoning* was delivered at a *δίκη φόνου*, and contains no appeals for anger despite calling five times for *τιμωρία*. Furthermore, unlike almost all other speeches that call for *τιμωρία*, this one renders the verb only in the active voice, *τιμωρεῖν*, rather than the middle, *τιμωρεῖσθαι*, meaning that the honour being reclaimed and the anger satisfied is that of a third party (the deceased here) and not the avenger(s). The jurors must avenge (*τιμωρῆσαι*) the laws and the dead (Ant. 1.3, 22) and 'become avengers' (*τιμωροὺς γενέσθαι*) for the wrongly killed man who deserves 'pity, help and *τιμωρίας*' from them (21). He says it would be most just if *τιμωρία* should happen (27) in order that the killer might suffer what she inflicted. Furthermore, though there are five demands that the accused 'give satisfaction' (*δίκην διδόναι*), there is no mention of 'taking satisfaction' (*δίκην λαμβάνειν*) because the would-be 'taker' is dead.[3] This speech's vocabulary does not allow us to conceive of the punishment as a self-interested act – the jurors' honour appears to have nothing to do with it.

Yet there are reasons to expect that homicide might evoke public anger.[4] For one, homicide endangers everyone by placing the victim's loved ones under pressure to avenge, leading potentially to ongoing escalation. The very existence of the homicide law and procedure demonstrates the community's belief that simply allowing homicides is against its interests. We have also seen that violence could provoke anger in jurors because it often communicated the belief that one was above the community and its laws. It would be odd if the offences said to escalate towards homicide – slander, assault and wounding – should all have the potential to arouse dicastic anger, but the final dreadful climax should not.[5] Even in this speech, it is not only the deceased but also the laws that have been slighted (Antiph. 1.3, 24) and are owed vengeance, but unlike elsewhere this is not used to support anger appeals. Not all violence caused public offence. Deeds done in anger or under the influence of alcohol, for instance, may not be taken to signify disregard for the supremacy of the *δῆμος*. But this cannot apply to a poisoning plot, or indeed to any cases heard by the Areopagus, since they would necessarily be intentional.

In fact, we can be sure that jurors might feel anger at homicide because defendants appeal against it. Euphiletus defends his supposedly legal killing of his wife's lover Eratosthenes by accusing his accusers of lying about the circumstances in order to evoke anger (Lys. 1.28). They have apparently claimed that he had not caught his victim in the act but dragged him into the house to make it appear that he had been found there and/or that Eratosthenes had not received mercy despite taking refuge at the hearth (27). The jurors, Euphiletus fears, might be angry if they believe he has killed in cold blood one whose offence he has not witnessed. We have already seen that Euxitheus, defending himself in an *ἀπαγωγή* procedure for homicide, urges against anger because it destroys reason (Antiph. 5.71–2). There is every possibility that the remembered Mytilenean revolt contributes to the alleged offensiveness but I suspect the homicide goes with it: the killing of an Athenian cleruch by the son of a Mytilenean rebel.[6]

The willingness of defendants to appeal against anger alongside the refusal of prosecutors to appeal for it suggests that jurors could feel anger towards killers but that their anger did not have a legitimate role in the decision to punish. The need to avoid appealing to anger certainly appears to be on Lysias' mind in *Against Eratosthenes*. This is not a prosecution for homicide but a special accounting for a member of the Thirty, yet the speech does make a prolonged accusation of one homicide while alluding to others.[7] The speech appears to separate the homicide narrative, where anger is not called for, from the rest of the speech where it is called for five times and *τιμωρεῖσθαι* is sought once. Lysias states at the outset that his accusations are going to demonstrate enmity between Eratosthenes and the city, so his audience knows to expect a cause for them to be angry and vengeful over (Lys. 12.2). He then informs them of his intention to tell them first of his own interests in prosecuting Eratosthenes before outlining theirs (5). The following narrative, describing the threat to his own life and the arrest and execution of his brother Polemarchus (6–36), contains no anger appeals. Then Lysias turns, as promised, to matters concerning the jurors (37–100) and the anger appeals return (all in relation to the crimes of the Thirty) along with a call for those from both the town and Peiraeus to take revenge (*τιμωρεῖσθαι*) for their exploitation (94).[8] One instance that might be considered an appeal proves the point:

> *ὑμεῖς δὲ πᾶσιν ὀργίζεσθε, ὅσοι εἰς τὰς οἰκίας ἦλθον τὰς ὑμετέρας ζήτησιν ποιούμενοι ἢ ὑμῶν ἢ τῶν ὑμετέρων τινός.*
>
> (Lys. 12.30)
>
> And you feel anger towards all who come into your homes conducting a search for either you or one of your own.

Lysias does not call the jurors to anger at what he or his brother have suffered but seeks only their understanding on the basis of the anger they would feel if they experienced what he has. He might hope that their pity will benefit him, but it is telling that he never invites them to be angry about his brother's killing.

The final homicide prosecution displays a similar pattern but this time there are no anger appeals, only a series of calls for *τιμωρία* through verbs that are neatly separated according to voice.[9] Having opened by stating that all should avenge (*τιμωρεῖν*) the dead (Lys. 13.1), the speaker begins his account of Agoratus' crimes with a call to take revenge (3) and follows later in the narrative with three more appeals (48, 76, 76), all for offences against the jurors and their city and all in the middle voice. Towards the end of the speech the speaker returns to the active, making a flurry of calls for the jurors to avenge (*τιμωρεῖν*) the dead.[10] In this section, the tone of the speech changes from one of personal umbrage to one of debt and obligation. He refers to the victims as men who, having done good to the jurors, their city and their democracy, ought to be considered the jurors' friends (92). And he warns that to acquit Agoratus would be to condemn his victims (93–4). It would apparently be a terrible fate for the victims to suffer if they asked their friends (including the jurors) to avenge them only to be condemned by them as they had been by the Thirty (94). Given the appeals to *τιμωρεῖσθαι* and the theme of public offence, it is clear this speaker wants the jurors to be angry and that the absence of anger appeals requires another explanation (see chapter five), but the switch from *τιμωρεῖσθαι* to *τιμωρεῖν* in the section focused on homicide fits the emerging pattern: dicastic anger did not have the legitimate role in punishing homicide that it had in punishing other offences.[11]

Other emotional pressures take over from anger in these speeches. In the passages above, guilt over siding with the killers of one's friends or allies is emphasised.[12] The jurors, usually presented as those to whom honour is owed, are now presented as the debtors, owing respect and assistance to the dead. The prosecutor in *Against the Stepmother* takes this further, moving beyond moral obligation to introduce fear at the religious consequences of failing to avenge. In closing, he says that he has done his part and it remains for the jurors to decide what justice demands, finishing with 'and I think the gods below are mindful of the victims of wrongdoing' (Antiph. 1.31). This hints at what Antiphon states more explicitly in the tetralogies:[13] that victims, with supernatural aid, are a threat to those who fail to avenge them.[14] The unavenged victim is said to 'weigh on the minds' (*ἐνθύμιος γενήσεται*) of those who acquit, an experience associated with pollution (2.3.10–11).[15] What precisely pollution was remains contested, but it appears to have been open to various associations including, in the tetralogies, anger.[16] This comes across most strongly in the third tetralogy where we are reunited with the theme of *μῆνις* (specifically *μήνιμα*, 'cause of anger'). Whoever fails in his role as avenger – the prosecutor who makes a weak case or the jurors who acquit despite proven guilt – will be a *μήνιμα* for the 'avenging spirits' (*τῶν ἀλιτηρίων*);[17] the same awaits jurors who condemn an innocent man to death (4.2.8). It is the job of the jurors, on behalf of the dead man, to 'heal the cause of the avenging spirits' anger and cleanse the whole city of pollution' (4.3.7).[18] As in Homer, *μῆνις* refers here to the jurors not as direct offenders but as those who, in failing to condemn norm-breaking behaviour, place themselves within the victim's sphere of anger.[19] The unavenged dead are like Achilles towards Agamemnon: at first their anger pursues the killer, but its prospect hangs over those responsible for vengeance, eventually threatening any in the community who fail to play their part in shunning and condemning the offender.[20]

Τιμωρεῖν and impiety

Τιμωρεῖν is also used in relation to impiety, the only other offence said to cause pollution. One prosecutorial call for punishment and one defensive call against it occur in the same trial. The *synegoros* assisting in the prosecution of Andocides in 399–400 accuses him of 'showing contempt (*καταπεφρόνηκε*) for the gods and those responsible for avenging (*τιμωρεῖν*) them' ([Lys.] 6.11; cf. Andoc. 1.31). Later in the speech the sense of danger associated with pollution is emphasised.

> *ποῖον φίλον, ποῖον συγγενῆ, ποῖον δημότην χρὴ τούτῳ χαρισάμενον κρύβδην φανερῶς τοῖς θεοῖς ἀπεχθέσθαι; νῦν οὖν χρὴ νομίζειν τιμωρουμένους καὶ ἀπαλλαττομένους Ἀνδοκίδου τὴν πόλιν καθαίρειν καὶ ἀποδιοπομπεῖσθαι καὶ φαρμακὸν ἀποπέμπειν καὶ ἀλιτηρίου ἀπαλλάττεσθαι.*
>
> (Lys. 6.53)

What friend, what relative, what demesman needs secretly to show favour for [Andocides] and openly become the enemy of the gods? Now, you need to

> consider that by taking revenge on and getting rid of Andocides you cleanse the city and free it from pollution, drive away a scapegoat and get rid of something offensive.

For all the reasons the jurors have to take offence and avenge themselves, there is also the very different concern to do, not with their own anger, but with the gods' anger, which would turn on them should they fail to punish Andocides. Elsewhere, Aeschines refers to an oath requiring revenge (*τιμωρήσειν*) against any who should violate a shrine or plot against the city's holy places (2.115). Evidently, the victim's honour remains the focus, but again, as with homicide, it is not the victim who is reclaiming it.[21]

The punishments of both homicide and impiety are describable as *τιμωρεῖν* and without reference to dicastic anger. But while homicide prosecutors used this language exclusively, those alleging impiety referred to *τιμωρεῖσθαι* too, often explicitly as a product of anger, including in the prosecution of Andocides ([Lys.] 6.15, 17, 18, 53).[22] Evidently these two kinds of prosecutor operated under different rhetorical restrictions. Those alleging impiety had the strategic option of appealing either to anger (at the slight that impious acts implied towards the community) or to a different set of emotions (based on the jurors' obligation to the gods). For those alleging homicide, the former was not available. Regardless of procedure or court setting, speakers were obliged not to refer to the punishment for homicide as an act of dicastic anger and honour reclamation. Why it is that the avenging of the dead was treated as being strictly about the dead's own honour while the avenging of the gods was openly acknowledged to be an issue of the community's honour too is a bigger subject than can fully be covered here, but the effect that death (particularly by homicide) had on the dynamics of the relationship between the victim and the avenger will be explored below.

Non-vengeful punishment?

A variety of emotions might underlie an act of *τιμωρεῖν*. Personal anger was not precluded as Apollodorus makes clear when he says that in bringing the case against Neaera he is 'avenging (*τιμωρῶν*) the gods… and myself', and that the jurors must 'avenge (*τιμωρεῖν*) the gods… and your own selves' ([Dem.] 59.126). This is atypical and may occur here only because the phrasing – the pairing of self with another avenged object – requires it, but it does demonstrate the compatibility of personal anger with this type of vengeance. According to the *Athenaion*

Constitution, Solon's second most democratic reform was 'the allowance for any who wished to take revenge on behalf of the wronged' (*τὸ ἐξεῖναι τῷ βουλομένῳ τιμωρεῖν ὑπὲρ τῶν ἀδικουμένων*; *Ath. Const.* 9.1). This reveals *τιμωρεῖν*'s potential to gain (rather than 'regain') honour for its subject – an acquisitive aspect that jurors were not generally supposed to explore. Prosecutors could, with ostensible generosity, volunteer to prosecute on behalf of others – perhaps those unequipped to avenge themselves in court – and thereby win payment, recognition, the indebtedness of those they helped, or the destruction of enemies. Jurors worked within a more reactive and defensive emotional register. Typically, they chose to *τιμωρεῖν* out of guilt, shame or fear; an interest in preserving either one's honour, by fulfilling obligations, or even one's physical security from vengeful deities.

Compared to *τιμωρεῖσθαι*, *τιμωρεῖν* had a broad emotional scope; its agent could be feeling almost anything and not necessarily anger. Yet, in terms of the victim, anger remained essential. Like all vengeance, *τιμωρεῖν* assumes anger at a perceived slight. The goal of this action is honour reclamation and, as such, 'revenge' remains an appropriate concept. But it is also driven, as always, by the punisher's own sense of honour. To refer to one's vengeance as *τιμωρεῖν* is to state both that one's honour is tied to the victim, and that it is the victim's honour that one is reclaiming. Plato's Socrates refers to Achilles' avenging of Patroclus using this term (*Apol.* 28c) and by returning to this quintessential act of Greek vengeance, we can see why prioritising the victim's honour when punishing was so important, and why it does not take away from the vengeance paradigm.

Patroclus' ghost appears, unhappy, (*Il.* 23.65) to Achilles in a dream and says 'you sleep, yet I escape your attention, Achilles. You were not careless of me when I was alive, but now when I am dead' (69–70).[23] He urges Achilles to bury him so the shades will allow him to enter Hades' house (71–4). Patroclus has challenged Achilles' behaviour before, sorrowfully expressing his exasperation at his friend's refusal to join the fight and rescue the Achaeans (16.20–45). On that occasion though, he had spoken through tears (2–11), apprehensive of Achilles' indignation (22). Now he speaks with what seems to be indignation of his own, not pleading with his master but accusing and instructing his debtor.[24]

The change in the dynamic of their relationship becomes clear later when Achilles, having ransomed Hector, betrays concern over whether Patroclus will be satisfied with the payment received from Priam or angry that Achilles has released his killer's body (*Il.* 24.592–5). Previously, it had invariably been Achilles' anger that inspired fear in others, including Patroclus; now Achilles fears the anger of one who was always unquestionably his inferior. Achilles has accepted ransoms for living captives before and presumably would not object to doing so for the dead, but now it is not only his honour at stake. It takes threats from the gods to force him to part with the body of his friend's killer and, when he does, it is in dread of Patroclus' reaction. Achilles demonstrates that even someone with supreme self-regard must do what he can to prove to the dead and to the community that his act of vengeance has satisfactorily restored the victim's honour. Achilles' own honour is also at stake, as we have seen, but it takes second place far behind the honour of the dead man. Whatever Athenian jurors actually felt, by treating homicide punishment as an act that recognised only the victim's anger and restored only the victim's honour, they respectfully fulfilled their roles as third-party avengers.

Conclusion

Prosecutors approach punishment appeals differently in homicide trials. They call on jurors to avenge others (*τιμωρεῖν*) rather than themselves (*τιμωρεῖσθαι*); they talk in terms of obligation towards third-party victims rather than umbrage at personal slights; and these obligations are motivated by guilt, shame and fear rather than anger. Prosecutors of impiety could embrace these themes too, but for them it was a choice. Over impiety, dicastic anger was not inappropriate; over homicide it was thoroughly suppressed.

This reveals a tension between the honour of the living and that of the gods and the unjustly killed that resonates with Homer. Like Achilles, Athenian citizens thought of themselves, in the identity of *δῆμος*, as the uncontested champions of the mortal community in terms of honour, most to be feared and respected. But gods and homicide victims were different. The honour reclaimed by revenge went, in cases of impiety, to both the community and the gods. Speakers, through the language of *τιμωρεῖν*, could remind jurors that it was not only their own honour that called for punishment but also that of the gods. With victims of homicide, this dynamic was more dominant. The honour demanded by the dead placed a claim on the living with which their own honour ought not to compete. To call for anger and the avenging of the self over a homicide was to muddy the waters, implying that the punishment would restore honour to the jurors when the present concern was supposed to be the honour of the victim alone. The deceased themselves, the gods and the rest of the community expected nothing else. The punishment of homicide was not a dispassionate application of the law by a disinterested third party; it was the reclaiming of a respected victim's honour. The language of anger (if not necessarily the emotion itself) is absent and the language of punishment has changed, but the act remains one of revenge.

Conclusion

This has been a tale of two communities, centuries apart, presenting such different faces that it can be hard to appreciate how similar they are at heart. Homer gives the impression of a world where judicial institutions matter little, occurring in the shadow of the transcendent lives of the mighty heroes. The honour of these men is all that matters, the slightest of slights cause bitter quarrels and all is solved at the point of a sword. But beneath the surface lies a different picture, one where anger's sharpest edges are blunted by the presence of a community, and where institutions cannot be hidden even by plots that obsess over individuals and revolve around societal breakdown. Classical Athens on the other hand displays and boasts of its sophisticated system of courts, procedures and laws that exert control over private anger, tempting today's reader to see a world turning its back on revenge and embracing a more enlightened and rational mode of punishment. But the emotional heart of Athenian justice is visible, and it is as unapologetically angry and vengeful as ever.

Homer

Anger has a clear place in Aristotle's understanding of honour. People have a sense of their own worth, their own 'honour' or *τιμή*; they feel pain when that honour is depleted; if someone else is perceived to be responsible, then we are in the realm of anger and its intrinsic desire to reclaim that lost honour through revenge. Aristotle considered this to be as true of the Homeric emotion as it was of the fourth-century Athenian one, and he was right. Surely the most important emotion in Homer, the one that pulls the most weight in the lives and motivations of his characters, is anger. The pattern of perceiving a slight, feeling pain and desiring revenge is clearly present and essential to several of Homer's many emotion terms. This emotional state drives disputes of all kinds, including the great plotlines: Achilles and Agamemnon, Achilles and Hector, and Odysseus and the suitors. Anger of this kind will remain, in principle, the same until the late fourth century, and we can already see in Homer how that emotional mechanism in the individual can interact with the wider community.

Homer shows us how, in two main ways, anger can reach beyond the original parties – offender and offended – to draw others into the quarrel. Individuals are interested in their own honour and they feel angry when that honour is slighted, but Aristotle also allows for anger to be felt at slights against 'one's own'. Homer reveals precisely why this is the case. In harming or killing someone, the culprit communicates the belief that they are more powerful than not only the direct victim but also any potential avengers. Thus, by killing Patroclus, Hector displays contempt for Achilles' strength. But honour ties reach beyond this: one need only be a fellow Achaean to feel pain at a comrade's killing and seek revenge. In this way, offences against one individual can rouse anger throughout the community.

Anger also has a way of expanding its circle of blame. In the emotion of *μῆνις* we see anger at slights that break group norms, obliging the rest of the community to choose sides. Will the Achaeans simply accept Agamemnon's outrageous appropriation of the woman they had gifted to Achilles, or will they take a stand and condemn his actions? The Achaeans are brought together in negative fashion through their silent communal endorsement of Agamemnon's norm-breaking offence. Anger might be provoked by one person in the heart of another, but it has the potential to be felt both *by* and *towards* others, even the entire community.

If we could isolate the emotion of anger from its community context we may find aggressive revenge to be close to inevitable, deterred only by the fear of the offender. But the angry have always to consider their relationship with the wider community as they calculate how best to respond to a slight. Even so, revenge is frequently a sound option because it can restore one's standing through retribution, deter the culprit and others from future (re)offence and win the glory available to successful avengers.

But the idea that angry victims must either take revenge or suffer dishonour is too simplistic both for Homer's heroes and for the concept of honour in general. The option of compensation is often available and its acceptance is an outcome over which the community sometimes wields influence. When a dispute is causing harm to all, both sides can come under significant pressure to find an amicable resolution. For the offended party the pain of anger might not be assuaged without revenge, but compensatory gifts and the appreciation of the community bring an honour of their own.

And whether for compensation or not, restraint has value, protecting the angry from the consequences of rash decisions and winning them broad respect.

Anger must compete with other emotions for influence over victims' decisions. The angry can be swayed by feelings of pity for loved ones who might suffer the consequences of revenge, the prospect of shame over pursuing petty or taboo acts of vengeance, and fear of the strength of the culprit and perhaps the wider community who might resist them. Even anger at a newer and more pressing grievance can cause the abandonment of an older unsatisfied anger. In these ways, the community exerts informal pressure on its members to keep their anger under some control.

But Homer also depicts formal, institutionalised means of anger control in a centralised system for administrating justice. This is not a toothless system of arbitration, but an authoritative system of judgement with the power of enforcement. At its head is a ruler with ultimate responsibility for ensuring justice and, in so doing, ensuring for the land supernatural blessing rather than destruction. The system for reaching a judgement is loosely comparable to that of Draco's Athens, and the two alike possess authority even over how the kin of homicide victims may pursue justice.

Even in these elite-focused poems and in a society that affords no formal role to the vast majority, it is clear that the *δῆμος* has a part to play alongside the elders in the judicial process. Common people influence the judgements of their superiors through their greater numbers and vocal engagement at trial. But they also supply the ultimate means of coercion, motivated in part by indignation at the breaking of the community's norms and sometimes by anger at acts that slighted them or their community. This sense of popular anger at public offence would later become a major cog in the Athenian state machine, but already we see the emotional mechanism at work in Homer. This early state reflects the humans that comprise it: it has its own sense of honour, it feels anger when that honour is slighted and it takes revenge on the objects of that anger.

Athens

Comparisons of the administration of justice in Homer and in classical Athens have tended to overstate difference and understate similarity. Quantitative analysis of anger and punishment appeals in the forensic corpus suggests, and qualitative analysis confirms, that the fundamental principles of justice went unchanged: the act of punishment, even when carried out by the state, was motivated by anger at a perceived slight to the punisher. This emotional dynamic had always been problematic for anger's tendency towards misjudgement and haste, but the solution to this was not to abandon anger as the legitimate motive for punishment, not in Homer and not in Athens. Athenian jurors were supposed merely to delay gratifying their anger until the facts were clear. Punishment without anger was not punishment at all, it was unprovoked, unjust; legitimacy demanded a perceived personal slight.

In their need for a slight, the apparent underestimation of one's worth, the punishments of Homer and Athens were alike. But while similar in essence, they differed in manifestation. Public jurors, like private Athenian citizens and Homeric heroes, possessed a sense of their own honour and an awareness of when that honour had been undervalued. Community harm can hurt and anger individuals in Homer, but the scope for this in classical Athens is far greater. As the state and its institutions grew, they became increasingly relevant to individuals' calculations of their own worth. The honour of the individual was more tightly bound up with that of the city. Norm-breaking had always invited community disapproval, even rebuke or active resistance, but anger came only from direct victims and those close to them. In Athens, by the late fifth century, this had changed so that norm-breaking could personally offend more than the victim alone. Acts of *hybris*, physical assaults, even slander might be perceived as slights against all.

One major reason for this was the codification of customs as written laws through which the state claimed authority over particular behaviours and promised a forceful response against transgressors. Thus, while the breaking of a norm had always represented a rejection of the community's standards, the breaking of a law represented contempt for the state's power to follow through on its threats. The *δῆμος* was ruler of Athens: it had the most honour, it told the rest of the community where the boundaries of acceptable behaviour lay, and it punished those who crossed them.

The distribution of anger and punishment appeals emphatically supports this model but there are exceptions that, without undermining the model, offer interesting insights into the workings of Athenian justice. Since the charge he brought identified a slight against the jurors, a public prosecutor typically called for anger. Some prosecutors, however, lacked the moral authority necessary for such an instruction. Sycophantic tactics might be tolerated by jurors whose desire for revenge needed a way through the apparent confines of the laws, but the employer of such tactics was not the sort from whom emotional instruction would be well received. And the young public prosecutor, possessing neither the standing nor the jury experience of his older audience, lacked the social position for explicit anger appeals and needed to rouse dicastic anger by other means.

The appeals to anger and punishment within the private prosecutions demonstrate the Athenian system's flexibility. There was nothing stopping a private prosecutor from making public allegations on top of the private one, or from presenting the private allegation in public terms – as a slight on the jurors as well as the plaintiff. The split fines attached to particular offences demonstrate recognition of the public-private nature of some offences. Certain public-dishonouring themes include the failure to meet one's obligations to the city, *hybristic* violence or slander, and endangering the city. But jurors could perceive slights not only as 'citizens' but also specifically as 'jurors'. These men thought highly of their role as upholders of justice and defenders of the city's honour and so, when false testimony was presented to them, procedures were sycophantically abused, or litigants wasted their time on petty quarrels, they took it personally.

Finally, there is the striking absence of anger appeals in relation to accusations of homicide, and the preference for homicide (and occasionally impiety) prosecutors to call for *τιμωρεῖν* and not *τιμωρεῖσθαι*. In this, we do at last see the Athenian state punishing on the victim's behalf, but not as a dispassionate agent with no personal interest in the matter. In other cases the *δῆμος* was presented as supremely honoured, beyond the pretentions of all others in the community. But, relative to the gods and homicide victims, the *δῆμος* was the inferior. Punishments reclaimed the honour not of the jurors or their city, but of the gods or the dead. Murdered loved ones exerted a special influence over those they left behind. Through shame, guilt and fear the dead drove the living to avenge them. Murder, like assault, often did evoke dicastic anger, but that was not relevant to the honorific transaction taking place. A conviction would satisfy anger, but not, formally speaking, the anger of the living. It was the honour of the dead that was at stake in a homicide trial, the anger of the dead that hung over the proceedings and the avenging of the dead that punishment would achieve; to talk of avenging the jurors would only have diluted the satisfaction owed to the dead.

Anger and the state

As I wrote in the Introduction, this study has something to say about what state formation can look like, particularly regarding the place of anger among its causes and consequences.

In terms of causes, anger is traditionally viewed as among the aggressive impulses that state institutions are supposed to control, a problem for the state to solve. This is clearly correct. Anger presents a threat to the whole community:

it can be felt *by* not only victims but also those who care for them; it can be felt *towards* not only initial offenders but also any who fail to condemn them; and it tends towards escalation because dishonour typically appears greater to the offended than the offender. To some extent, laws and law courts represented an intentional effort to minimise the damage anger could inflict on the community.

However, anger is also part of the solution. The community offered legitimacy to those it deemed justified in avenging themselves, but its authority to do so was rooted in the belief of its members that it could and would react angrily towards those who ignored or resisted its judgements. The anger felt by the Ithacans towards Eupeithes is an early reference to what would become commonplace in classical Athens: the community perceiving slights, feeling anger and taking revenge. The state monopolised legitimate force because people feared its anger.

As for the consequences of state formation, the rise of institutions has generally been associated with a fall in the opportunity for and acceptability of anger expression, especially through violence. Elias's 'civilising process' accurately describes how private aggression diminishes as the state grows, including in the ancient Greek world, but this study reveals an important complicating factor: the expanding role of anger *within* the state. Anger and aggression, violently expressed, gradually diminish in the private sphere between the seventh and fourth centuries, but not because they have been cast aside. Rather, they migrate into a public sphere that offers greater scope as an outlet for anger, and at a safer distance too. A fourth-century Athenian citizen could not hunt down and butcher the man he suspected of being his wife's lover, but he could vote in court to execute a man accused of embezzling public money. Was the average Athenian from 700, when institutions were in their infancy and violent self-help was still the main route to justice, really any more angry, aggressive, or violent than his fourth-century counterpart who had a whole catalogue of new offences at which he might become angry, and who had frequent opportunities to take part in killing or otherwise harming those he felt had wronged him? The growth of the state, in the Athenian case at least, did not simply bring about a contraction in anger. Rather, it was a product, in part, of the appropriation and organisation of anger.

I began this book with reference to twelve fictional American jurors, eleven of whom are characterised by prejudice, hatred, sadism, callousness and all the other characteristics that we today abhor for their tendency towards injustice. These men, many bitter and vengeful about some remembered slight from their own lives, are a poor advert for the value of anger as a tool for achieving justice. Thank goodness, we in the audience think, that there is a cool head in the room capable of applying reason to this madness. But the film is not called *Eleven*

Angry Men. Juror Eight is thoughtful, sceptical, empathetic, possessed of all the admirable and necessary qualities that his co-jurors appear in one respect or another to lack. But he is also, at times, angry. He stops mid-sentence, evidently bridling, and walks over to screw up a piece of paper on which two others are playing tic-tac-toe: 'this isn't a game,' he says, with feeling.[1] Later he berates Juror Two for the pleasure he evidently hopes to take in sending the defendant to the electric chair: 'you're a sadist!', he says, voice raised.[2] Americans, like the citizens of most Western nations, celebrate a judicial system that is designed to avoid or at least minimise prejudice and emotion, but none would want a system so devoid of feeling that no one cares when it fails or is treated lightly by those to whom it is entrusted. We approve of the anger that Juror Eight exhibits in defence of justice and we hope we would be courageous enough to act like him if justice and life were so threatened. *Twelve Angry Men* may have little or no bearing on the reality of the modern jury room, but it does speak to modern values, and it seems to me that human anger, on which the Athenian state was so clearly reliant, might still be playing a role even in the nation states of the modern world.

Appendix

Anger and Punishment Appeals in the Athenian Law-court Speeches

This catalogue is much like that found in Rubinstein's 2004 chapter, 'Stirring up Dicastic Anger'. Like Rubinstein, I have counted every instance where certain terms for anger and punishment are used in attempts to direct the jurors to feel that emotion or perform that action. But there are important differences. Rubinstein tallied appeals for *μῖσος*, *ὀργή*, *τιμωρία*, *κόλασις* and *ζημία* and their cognates; I have recounted these (excluding *μῖσος*), added the phrases *δίκην λαμβάνειν* and *δίκην διδόναι* and incorporated negative appeals. Also, whereas Rubinstein counted the chapters containing appeals, the tally below allows for multiple instances of the same term within each chapter. Mostly this recognises discrete appeals that happen to lie in the same chapter. Occasionally, however, a single appeal may use the same term more than once or combine two terms in one phrase meaning that the table does not strictly count appeals so much as occurrences of words within appeals.[1] This method has no impact on overall implications, it only makes the findings a little more emphatic.

More significantly, the reader must judge when a speaker is making an appeal – attempting to evoke the relevant emotion or response from his audience – and my judgement occasionally differs from Rubinstein's. The vast majority of cases are uncontentious. Sometimes, however, appeals are implicit (e.g. Lys. 14.10) or based on *a fortiori* reasoning (e.g. Dem. 21.181) and the modern reader (like the ancient hearer) is left to determine the meaning. As a rule, I have aimed to include only instances where the speaker is not attempting to obfuscate but appears happy for the jurors to perceive him as recommending anger or punishment.

The phrase *δίκην διδόναι* presents an interpretative challenge because it, unlike *δίκην λαμβάνειν*, does not identify the punisher. This is a problem since in many trials the prosecutor is seeking redress while also recommending that the jurors do so too.[2] This means that the reader must infer (if they are not explicitly told, e.g. Lys. 30.8) to whom the satisfaction is to be given. In determining whether or not instances of *δίκην διδόναι* relate to the jurors (and so belong in my catalogue) I have had to rely on context. Demosthenes begins one prosecution by stating that Onetor is more deserving of giving satisfaction than Aphobus was (30.1); given the absence of public interest or other appeals to dicastic punishment, it is clear that Demosthenes is to receive satisfaction here. Whereas, when Lysias uses the phrase with reference to the need to deter people from attempting to become tyrants (12.35), the city is evidently among the putative punishers.

One need not use the word 'anger' to make people feel it, and surely plenty of attempts to evoke it have been overlooked here. This then is not an exhaustive list of the forensic corpus's rhetorical attempts at anger arousal, and nor can it replace a close reading of the text, but it can indicate trends.

Public prosecutions

Speech	*ὀργή*		*τιμωρία*		*κόλασις*		*δίκην λαμβάνειν*		*δίκην διδόναι*		*ζημία*	
	For	Ag.	For	Ag.	For	Ag.	For	Ag.	For	Ag.	For	Ag.
[Lys.] 6	17	–	11, 15, 18, 53	–	13, 42, 43, 44	–	–	–	10, 34, 19, 20, 34, 41	–	15	–
Lys. 12	2, 58, 80, 90, 96	–	94, 100	–	36	–	29, 36, 37, 60, 79, 82, 83, 100	–	26, 35, 37, 82	–	36, 36	–
Lys. 13	–	–	1, 1, 3, 48, 76, 76, 92, 93, 94, 95, 97	–	–	–	–	–	–	–	69, 91	–
Lys. 14	8, 13, 20, 39	–	2, 10, 12, 19, 30	–	12	–	10, 21	–	–	–	9	–
Lys. 15	9	–	9	–	–	–	6	–	–	–	9	–
Lys. 22	–	–	–	–	20	–	16, 18	–	10	–	5, 13, 17, 19	–
Lys. 27	11, 15	–	13, 15, 16	–	5	–	5, 6, 7, 16	–	8, 9	–	16, 16	–
Lys. 28	3, 13	–	9, 11, 15	–	3	–	9, 15, 17, 17	–	1	–	–	–
Lys. 29	5, 9, 11	–	8, 9, 11, 13	–	–	–	–	–	–	–	–	–
Lys. 30	23	–	6, 16, 23, 33, 33, 35	–	6, 24	–	6, 23, 24, 30, 32, 33	–	8, 24	–	–	–

Public prosecutions

Speech	*ὀργή*		*τιμωρία*		*κόλασις*		*δίκην λαμβάνειν*		*δίκην διδόναι*		*ζημία*	
	For	Ag.	For	Ag.	For	Ag.	For	Ag.	For	Ag.	For	Ag.
Dem. 19	7, 45, 91, 133, 302	–	3, 86, 87, 276, 282, 289, 343	–	71, 177, 258, 267, 267, 272, 299, 301	–	8, 183, 284, 313	–	77, 82, 134, 215, 255, 276, 299, 328	–	126, 131, 276, 286, 287	–
Dem. 20	119	–	–	–	–	–	–	–	–	–	–	–
Dem. 21	34, 36, 42, 43, 46, 57, 70, 100, 108, 123, 127, 147, 175, 183, 183, 186, 196, 215, 222	–	28, 30, 34, 40, 127, 142, 227	–	27, 30, 37, 37, 70, 218, 218	–	12, 37, 92, 127	–	12, 27, 35, 37, 50, 57, 99, 123, 125, 128, 131, 151, 166, 169, 202, 207, 225	–	42, 49, 181, 182	–
Dem. 22	39	–	29	–	4	–	68	–	7, 28, 29, 29, 29, 43	–	–	–
Dem. 23	184	–	–	–	144	–	204	–	144	–	–	–
Dem. 24	138, 143, 152, 200, 211, 215, 218	–	110, 119, 120, 130, 131, 143, 175, 205, 215	–	65, 101, 175, 204, 210, 211, 213, 218	–	125	–	107, 154, 199	–	104, 208	–

Public prosecutions

Speech	*ὀργή*		*τιμωρία*		*κόλασις*		*δίκην λαμβάνειν*		*δίκην διδόναι*		*ζημία*	
	For	Ag.	For	Ag.	For	Ag.	For	Ag.	For	Ag.	For	Ag.
Dem. 25	6, 27, 94	–	6, 17, 53, 53, 59, 96	–	17, 21, 48, 97	–	–	–	2, 101	–	–	–
[Dem.] 26	24	–	23, 24	–	21	–	–	–	–	–	24	–
[Dem.] 53	–	–	–	–	–	–	–	–	–	–	–	–
[Dem.] 58	–	–	52, 54, 63	–	–	–	–	–	–	–	47	–
[Dem.] 59	5	–	74, 74, 77, 86, 107, 117	–	74, 109, 109, 116, 117	–	–	–	44, 77, 117, 126	–	–	–
Aesch. 1	166, 176	–	34, 112, 122	–	6, 36, 118, 177	–	179	–	192	–	87, 88, 184	–
Aesch. 3	16, 66, 144, 198	–	121, 144, 244, 253	–	8	–	–	–	53, 230, 246	–	131	–
Hyp. 2	–	–	5, 9, 10, 12	–	–	–	–	–	–	–	–	–
Hyp. 5	22	–	26, 34, 39	–	5, 25, 38	–	–	–	–	–	–	–
Din. 1	2, 77	–	3, 15, 22, 23, 29, 41, 47, 64, 85, 98, 105, 109, 113	–	27, 62	–	103, 112	–	47, 65, 103, 112	–	6, 8, 60, 61, 61, 108	–
Din. 2	4	–	3, 5, 11, 12, 20, 21, 21, 22	–	3	–	–	–	22	–	20	–

Public prosecutions

Speech	*ὀργή*		*τιμωρία*		*κόλασις*		*δίκην λαμβάνειν*		*δίκην διδόναι*		*ζημία*	
	For	Ag.	For	Ag.	For	Ag.	For	Ag.	For	Ag.	For	Ag.
Din. 3	8	–	5, 8, 8, 14, 14, 14, 15, 16	–	11	–	–	–	–	–	5	–
Lyc. 1	16, 27, 58, 78, 111, 138	–	8, 8, 9, 10, 15, 27, 34, 51, 53, 53, 53, 54, 56, 67, 71, 76, 78, 91, 91, 93, 111, 115, 116, 116, 123, 123, 126, 126, 127, 130, 134, 134, 134, 137, 140, 141, 141, 146	–	4, 9, 10, 51, 65, 67, 71, 74, 82, 93, 97, 111, 121, 123, 146	–	126	–	91	–	45, 65, 65, 71, 130, 130	–
TOTAL	75	0	161	0	73	0	42	0	67	0	44	0
Speeches (of 29)	24	0	25	0	22	0	15	0	18	0	18	0

Public defences

Speech	ὀργή		τιμωρία		κόλασις		δίκην λαμβάνειν		δίκην διδόναι		ζημία	
	For	Ag.	For	Ag.	For	Ag.	For	Ag.	For	Ag.	For	Ag.
Ant. 5	–	71, 72, 72	–	–	–	94	–	–	–	–	–	–
And. 1	24	8, 30	–	31, 32, 140	–	–	–	–	–	113	–	72
Lys. 3	–	–	–	42, 43	–	–	–	–	–	–	–	–
Lys. 4	–	–	–	–	–	–	–	–	–	–	–	–
Lys. 5	–	–	–	–	–	–	–	–	–	–	–	–
Lys. 7	–	–	–	–	–	–	–	7	–	6	–	5, 8, 13, 15, 15
Lys. 9	–	–	–	–	–	–	–	–	–	–	–	–
Lys. 18	–	19	–	19	–	–	–	–	–	–	–	–
Lys. 19	–	2	–	–	–	–	–	–	–	–	–	–
[Lys.] 20	–	1	–	–	–	–	–	–	–	6, 10	–	–
Lys. 21	–	–	–	–	–	–	–	–	–	–	–	–
Lys. 25	–	1, 5, 16, 18	–	35	–	–	–	–	–	11, 32	–	–
Isa. 11	–	–	–	–	–	–	–	–	–	–	–	–
Dem. 18	138	274	–	274, 274	–	–	–	12	–	–	–	–
Aesch. 2	–	3	–	–	–	–	–	–	–	–	–	–
Hyp. 1	–	–	–	–	–	–	–	–	–	–	–	–
Hyp. 4	–	19, 31	–	–	–	–	–	–	–	–	–	–
TOTAL	2	16	0	9	0	1	0	2	0	6	0	6
Speeches (of 17)	2	9	0	5	0	1	0	2	0	4	0	2

Private prosecutions

Speech	*ὀργή*		*τιμωρία*		*κόλασις*		*δίκην λαμβάνειν*		*δίκην διδόναι*		*ζημία*	
	For	Ag.	For	Ag.	For	Ag.	For	Ag.	For	Ag.	For	Ag.
Lys. 10	28, 29	–	30	–	–	–	–	–	–	–	30	–
Lys. 32	19	–	–	–	–	–	–	–	–	–	–	–
Isoc. 17	–	–	–	–	–	–	–	–	–	–	–	–
Isoc. 18	4, 26	36, 42	3	68	47	36	35	22	–	–	3, 26, 37, 47	–
Isoc. 20	3, 6, 9, 22	–	1, 3, 4, 6, 12, 13, 15, 19	–	1, 6, 14, 15	–	7, 12	–	–	–	1, 4, 6, 17	–
Isoc. 21	–	–	–	–	–	–	–	–	–	–	–	–
Isa. 3	–	–	–	–	–	–	–	–	–	–	–	–
Isa. 5	–	–	–	–	–	–	–	–	–	–	–	–
Isa. 6	–	–	–	–	–	–	–	–	–	–	–	–
Dem. 27	–	–	–	–	–	–	–	–	–	–	–	–
Dem. 28	–	–	–	–	–	–	–	–	–	–	–	–
Dem. 30	–	–	–	–	–	–	–	–	–	–	–	–
Dem. 31	–	–	–	–	–	–	–	–	–	–	–	–
Dem. 32	–	–	–	–	–	–	–	–	–	–	–	–
Dem. 33	–	–	–	–	–	–	–	–	–	–	–	–
Dem. 36	–	–	–	–	–	–	–	–	–	–	–	–
Dem. 37	–	–	–	–	–	–	–	–	–	–	–	–

Private prosecutions

Speech	ὀργή		τιμωρία		κόλασις		δίκην λαμβάνειν		δίκην διδόναι		ζημία	
	For	Ag.	For	Ag.	For	Ag.	For	Ag.	For	Ag.	For	Ag.
Dem. 38	–	–	–	–	–	–	–	–	–	–	–	–
Dem. 39	–	–	–	–	–	–	–	–	–	–	–	–
Dem. 40	5	–	–	–	–	–	–	–	–	–	–	–
Dem. 41	–	–	–	–	–	–	–	–	–	–	–	–
[Dem.] 44	57	–	–	–	–	–	–	–	–	–	–	–
Dem. 45	7, 53, 67	–	70, 87	–	63, 67	–	39	–	63, 88	–	80	–
[Dem.] 46	–	–	28	–	–	–	–	–	–	–	–	–
[Dem.] 47	79, 79	–	2	–	–	–	–	–	48	–	–	–
Dem. 48	–	–	–	–	–	–	–	–	–	–	–	–
Dem. 49	–	–	–	–	–	–	–	–	–	–	–	–
[Dem.] 50	67, 67	–	64, 64, 65, 66	–	–	–	–	–	–	–	–	–
Dem. 54	42	–	–	–	43	–	–	–	–	–	23	–
Dem. 56	–	–	–	–	–	–	–	–	–	–	27, 44, 44	–
Hyp. 3	–	–	–	–	35	–	–	–	–	–	–	–
TOTAL	19	2	18	1	9	1	4	1	3	0	14	0
Speeches (of 31)	10	1	7	1	5	1	3	1	2	0	6	0

Private defences

Speech	*ὀργή*		*τιμωρία*		*κόλασις*		*δίκην λαμβάνειν*		*δίκην διδόναι*		*ζημία*	
	For	Ag.	For	Ag.	For	Ag.	For	Ag.	For	Ag.	For	Ag.
Lys. 23	–	–	–	–	–	–	–	–	–	–	–	–
Isoc. 16	–	–	–	–	–	–	–	–	–	–	–	11, 47
Isa. 2	–	–	–	–	–	–	–	–	–	–	–	–
Isa. 12	–	–	–	–	–	–	–	–	–	–	–	–
Dem. 29	–	–	–	–	–	–	–	–	–	–	–	–
Dem. 34	–	–	–	–	–	–	–	–	–	–	–	–
Dem. 35	–	–	–	–	56	–	–	–	–	–	–	–
Dem. 52	–	–	–	–	–	–	–	–	–	–	–	–
Dem. 55	–	–	–	–	–	–	–	–	–	–	–	–
[Dem.] 57	–	3	–	–	–	–	–	–	–	3	–	–
TOTAL	0	1	0	0	1	0	0	0	0	1	0	2
Speeches (of 10)	0	1	0	0	1	0	0	0	0	1	0	1

Διαδικασίαι

Speech	*ὀργή*		*τιμωρία*		*κόλασις*		*δίκην λαμβάνειν*		*δίκην διδόναι*		*ζημία*	
	For	Ag.	For	Ag.	For	Ag.	For	Ag.	For	Ag.	For	Ag.
Lys. 17	–	–	–	–	–	–	–	–	–	–	–	–
Isa. 1	–	–	–	–	–	–	–	–	–	–	–	–
Isa. 4	–	–	–	–	–	–	–	–	–	–	–	–
Isa. 7	–	–	–	–	–	–	–	–	–	–	–	–
Isa. 8	–	–	–	–	–	–	–	–	–	–	–	–
Isa. 9	–	–	–	–	–	–	–	–	–	–	–	–
Isa. 10	–	–	–	–	–	–	–	–	–	–	–	–
Dem. 42	–	–	–	–	–	–	–	–	–	–	–	–
[Dem.] 43	–	–	–	–	–	–	–	–	–	–	–	–
TOTAL	0	0	0	0	0	0	0	0	0	0	0	0
Speeches (of 9)	0	0	0	0	0	0	0	0	0	0	0	0

Homicides (δίκη φόνου)

Speech	*ὀργή*		*τιμωρία*		*κόλασις*		*δίκην λαμβάνειν*		*δίκην διδόναι*		*ζημία*	
	For	Ag.	For	Ag.	For	Ag.	For	Ag.	For	Ag.	For	Ag.
Ant. 1 (pros.)	–	–	3, 21, 21, 22, 27	–	–	–	–	–	–	–	–	–
Ant. 6 (def.)	–	–	–	6	–	–	–	10	–	–	–	–
Lys. 1 (def.)	–	28	–	–	–	–	–	44	–	–	–	–
TOTAL	0	1	5	1	0	0	0	2	0	0	0	0
Speeches (of 3)	0	1	1	1	0	0	0	2	0	0	0	0

Totals

Speech type	ὀργή		punishment	
	For	Ag.	For	Ag.
Public prosecutions	75	0	387	0
Public defences	2	16	0	24
Private prosecutions	19	2	48	3
Private defences	0	1	1	3
Διαδικασίαι	0	0	0	0
Homicide prosecutions	0	0	5	0
Homicide defences	0	1	0	3
TOTAL	96	20	441	33

Notes

Introduction

1 Lumet (1957: 0:58:54).
2 'A Film locks itself up in the Jury Room' (1957).
3 Kerry (2011).
4 W. Harris (2001: 150).
5 Kalimtzis (2012: 18)
6 Van Wees (1998).
7 Elias (2000: 372).
8 Herman (2006: 266).
9 Herman (2006: 267).
10 Hobbes (1998: 84).
11 E.g. Pinker (2011: 56).
12 Van Wees (1992: 69); cf. (2011a).
13 Black-Michaud (1975).
14 Black-Michaud (1975: 122).
15 See Feinberg (1970), Nozick (1981: 366–7), Elster (1990: 862), Cragg (1992), Barton (1999: 25–6), Uniacke (2000: 62); Zaibert (2006) is a notable exception.
16 On *τιμωρία*, see pp. 109–11.
17 Allen (2000: 23); cf. Cairns (2015: 659): 'the very fact that *timōria* spans the entire range of such contexts, legal and extra-legal, is one of several signs that it will not do reductively to identify it either with punishment or with revenge.'
18 As Adkins (1960a: 24) said of translating Homer: 'if we translate *tinesthai*, *tinusthai* by "punish", our use of "punish" depends in part on the existence of a centralized organization for settling disputes and exacting penalties, and must have different implications; while if we translate these words by "revenge oneself upon", "requite" and so on, we meet another difficulty: these words in English are so far from common usage, and when used are so much used simply as emotionally loaded words for any type of punishment of which the speaker disapproves, that their implications are as unclear as those of *tinesthai*, *tinusthai*.'
19 Foucault (1991: 48).
20 E.g. Psalm 91, Isaiah 47.3, Jeremiah 46.10, 50.28, Ezekiel 25.17, Micah 5.15, Second Thessalonians 1.5–9.
21 Pitt-Rivers (1965: 21).

22 This assumption tends to go hand in hand with a value on female sexual purity.

23 Pitt-Rivers (1965: 26).

24 Pinker (2011: 72); cf. Black-Michaud (1975: 179–80), Boehm (1986: 10), Elster (1990: 867), Miller (1990: 30–1).

25 Bourdieu (1965: 200) recognised that one can invite still more dishonour by 'sullying oneself in an unworthy revenge'.

26 Cairns (2011a: 23).

27 Lendon (1997: 90); cf. Kalimtzis (2012: 138–41).

28 Lendon (1997: 93).

29 *ἔστω δὴ ὀργὴ ὄρεξις μετὰ λύπης τιμωρίας φαινομένης διὰ φαινομένην ὀλιγωρίαν εἰς αὐτὸν ἤ τι τῶν αὐτοῦ, τοῦ ὀλιγωρεῖν μὴ προσήκοντος* (*Rh.* 2.2.1). Chapter 1 will present a defence of this definition's suitability for Homer. All Greek translations are my own unless otherwise stated.

30 Stearns and Stearns (1985).

31 Reddy (1997); cf. Boddice (2016) who employs the more rigid, hierarchical metaphor of 'moral economies' that sit within one another like nesting dolls, constantly adjusting to accommodate the 'economies' within and without.

32 Rosenwein (2006).

33 Rosenwein (2006: 1).

34 Ekman (1999).

35 Boddice (2016: 5).

36 Feldman Barrett (2006a).

37 Feldman Barrett (2006b).

38 Boddice (2017: 12).

39 Feldman Barrett (2017: xi).

40 For Cummins (2003) and McCoy (1977), anger is a response to invalidation.

41 Daly and Wilson (1988), McCullogh (2008: 72–8).

42 Weber (1976).

43 Xydopoulos and Vlassopoulos (2017: 6).

44 Lintott (1982: 26), Osborne (1985a: 7), Hunter (1994: 120), Manville (1994), Berent (2000: 261), Osiander (2007: 53–4).

45 Hansen (2002), Herman (2006: 216–57), E. Harris (2013b: 21–59).

46 For more detailed arguments in defence of the state in Greece, see van der Vliet (2005) and Grinin (2004).

47 Osiander (2007: 5).

48 Mackenzie (1981: 86, 88); cf. Herman (2006: 261–9).

49 Seaford (1994: 205).

50 E. Harris (2013b: 98).

51 Muellner (1996), Konstan (2006: 48–55), Cairns (2003).

52 Cf. Gouldner (1967: 49–51), M. Edwards (1987: 150), Tandy (1997: 137); Adkins (1960a: 30–1) predates the phrase but clearly accepts the principle.

53 W. Harris (2001: 134).
54 Adkins (1972: 15).
55 Steinwenter (1925: 29–30), Calhoun (1927: 18), Bonner and Smith (1930: 31), Hommel (1969).
56 Adkins (1972: 16).
57 Wolff (1946: 40–3); cf. Gagarin (1986: 22), Papakonstantinou (2008: 34–5), Elmer (2013: 182–7).
58 Wolff (1946: 45); Gagarin (1986: 28) dismisses this, favouring the purely voluntary model.
59 Carlier (1984: 172–7); cf. Grote (1851, Vol. 2: 99), Luce (1978: 10), van Wees (1992: 34–5), Westbrook (1992: 67–76).
60 Herman (2006: 192).
61 Todd (1993: 169); cf. Gehrke (1987: 129).
62 D. Cohen (1995). The term 'feud' has met resistance for the reason that Athenian enmity was more regulated than the feuds of traditional Mediterranean societies: Herman (1996, 2006), E. Harris (2013b: 60–98); cf. Alwine (2015: 24–7).
63 Those who emphasise civic values include: Herman (2006), Kurihara (2003), E. Harris (2013b: 60–98); acceptance of Cohen's argument can be found in Christ (1998: 162–3), Allen (2000: 127–8); Alwine (2015: 94–116) agrees that private enmity could be a legitimate prosecutorial motive but emphasises that it was only one strategic option.
64 Todd, (1993: 79), Hunter (1994), Allen (2000: 20–1).
65 Allen (2000: 21).
66 Allen (2000: 35).
67 Allen (2000: 61).
68 Rubinstein (2004).
69 Foucault (1991: 47).
70 Foucault (1991: 48).
71 E. Harris (2006: 4; cf. 2013b; 2018); cf. Ostwald (1986), Herman (2006), Meyer-Laurin (2007), Sickinger (2008).
72 Christ (1998: 195); cf. Ober (1989), Todd (1993), D. Cohen (1995), Sundahl (2003), Lanni (2006; 2016), Forsdyke (2018: 208).
73 Thonissen (1875: 70). My translation.
74 Karabélias (1991: 81). My translation.
75 McHardy (2008: 2).
76 Rubinstein (2016).
77 On the methodologies best suited to extracting historical reality from Homer, see: Morris (1986), van Wees (1992: 5–23), Raaflaub (1998), Grethlein (2009); in defence of the society depicted being of an early archaic date, see: van Wees (1992: 10–16; 1994), Crielaard (1995, 2002), West (1995).
78 Markle (1985), Todd (1990a), Hansen (1991: 183–6); contra Jones (1957: 35–7, 50, 124).

79 Cf. Todd (1990a: 148).
80 Rubinstein (2004).
81 See Allen (2005: 391), who says 'tragedy becomes useful for studying Athenian law only after scholars have already taken the time to work out not merely the procedures of Athenian law but also its conceptual foundation and implications'.
82 Blundell (1989).
83 Burnett (1998).
84 Allen (2000).
85 McHardy (2008: 119).
86 E.g. Herman (2006: 261–9).
87 Lendon (2010: 6–7; cf. 2000).
88 McHardy (2008).

1 Anger and the Community in Homeric Society

1 *ἔστω δὴ ὀργὴ ὄρεξις μετὰ λύπης τιμωρίας φαινομένης διὰ φαινομένην ὀλιγωρίαν εἰς αὐτὸν ἤ τι τῶν αὐτοῦ, τοῦ ὀλιγωρεῖν μὴ προσήκοντος* (*Rh.* 2.2.1).
2 Arist. *Rh.* 2.2.1–7: *χόλος* (*Il.* 18.109–10, 9.648, 2.196), *κότος* (1.82), none (1.356); 2.196 refers directly to *θυμός*, which is more like the seat of anger and other emotions, but the preceding line demonstrates that Odysseus is referring to *χόλος*.
3 Cf. Arist. *Rh.* 2.2.2
4 Lossau's (1979) article, which approaches the theme of anger without interrogating the individual Homeric terms, marks a notable exception in which Aristotle is found to be one 'der schon bezüglich der Phänomene des Zornes und der Rache sich mit Homer in Einklang zeigte' (126).
5 Cairns (2003: 26), Konstan (2006: 48–55).
6 Muellner (1996: 27–8).
7 In order of frequency: *χόλος*, *χώομαι*, *κότος*, *μῆνις*, *ὑπόδρα ἰδών*, *σκύζομαι* and *ὀδύσσομαι*. While *χαλεπός* can describe experiences with no relation to anger, such as the difficulty of identifying corpses (*Il.* 7.424), it can also modify anger (5.178) or an expression of anger such as words (23.489), telling us that someone is particularly hard in their anger, and as such can reveal anger metonymically. The verb, *χαλεπαίνω*, indicates the hardening of those who feel anger rather than the emotion's first onset as Achilles suggests when he refers to '*χόλος* which sets a great-minded man to *χαλεπῆναι*' (18.108). Thus, when Agamemnon admits that, out of himself and Achilles, *ἐγὼ δ' ἦρχον χαλεπαίνων* (2.378), he is really saying that he was the first to become 'hard' or 'intransigent' in his anger, rather than that he was the first to become angry at all. Another term often translated with anger words is *ὀχθέω*, but if this is

anger at all it is of a different kind. It is the sense of frustration at the thwarting of one's desires, such as a spear throw not hitting its mark (20.343), or apparently certain destruction at sea (*Od.* 5.298), but implies that the obstacle of this feeling, even if someone intended it, is not perceived as dishonouring. Thus, Achilles is not 'angry' (in the Aristotelian sense) with Apollo so much as frustrated in his endeavours (*Il.* 22.14; contra W. Harris, 2001: 151). This bears similarity (as we shall see below) to some instances of *χώομαι*, but Adkins (1969: 17) rightly notes that while *ὀχθέω* comes with a sense or 'distress and bafflement', and I would say hopelessness, *χώομαι* implies determination in the face of a setback.

8 Hobbes (1998: 84); cf. Elias (2000).

9 Van Wees (1992: 69).

10 Cairns (2003: 26).

11 Cairns (2003: 27).

12 It may be that Achilles is avoiding a fraught situation such as this when he prevents Meriones and Agamemnon competing with the javelin, protecting the greater man's honour by acknowledging that he would have won (*Il.* 23.884–94); cf. van Wees (1992: 94–5), Scodel (2008: 153–7).

13 Cf. Hesk (2017: 118–19).

14 Cf. *Il.* 1.356, 507, 2.239–40, 9.110–11.

15 Adkins (1969: 13) also includes the *χωόμενοι* of some of the gods (*Il.* 21.519) at the city's peril. However, as Cairns (2003: 30n84) points out, it is not problematic that the losing side has been left angry at the end of a series of acrimonious and insult-ridden exchanges.

16 Adkins (1969: 17), Cairns (2003: 30).

17 Adkins (1969: 17) sees *χώομαι* as felt 'when a project is frustrated', whereas Cairns (2003: 30) sees it as suffered at the 'loss of face'. Both may be true, but only the latter may account for all instances of this term and even in the above examples I would say it is the personal failing that causes anger rather than the missed acquisition of greater honour.

18 Some translate *φαινομένην* emphatically as 'manifest' (Cope 1877) or 'conspicuous' (Remer 2013: 433n97); Cairns (2003: 27n24) concludes that it refers to the perspective of the angry rather than observers, cf. Konstan (2006: 41), Dow (2015: 189–90, 202–3).

19 Cf. W. Harris (2001: 60–1) who sees Plato's Leontius (*Rep.* 439e–40a) as being angry not with himself but with 'the appetitive element in his soul'.

20 Apollo has dashed the whip from his hand but there is no suggestion that Diomedes perceives this.

21 See also the withdrawal of Aeneas (*Il.* 13.459–61).

22 On the theme of restraint, see the next chapter.

23 Walsh (2005).

24 On the one instance of battlefield *κότος* (*Il.* 13.517), see Walsh (2005: 28–9).

25 Contra Walsh (2005: 29, 42).

26 Cairns (2003: 31).

27 ἔμπεσε θυμῷ: *Il.* 9.436, 14.207, 306, 16.206; δύω: *Il.* 9.553, 19.16, 22.94; λαμβάνω: *Il.* 1.387, 6.166; cf. Cairns (2003: 24–5).

28 *Il.* 4.513, 9.260, 565.

29 *Il.* 1.188–92, 15.208–12, 16.581. The presence of pain is a feature that, for Aristotle, distinguishes anger from hatred (*μῖσος*), and another is that only the former fades with time (*Rh.* 2.4.31). In these respects *κότος* is arguably closer to *μῖσος* than to *ὀργή*. We have already seen, however, that an instance of *κότος* is among the examples of Homeric anger Aristotle cites (2.2.7). Here Aristotle's point that anger is one of the three causes of enmity and hatred becomes relevant. In some cases *κότος* is felt by those who have previously been said to feel *χόλος* (e.g. *Il.* 9.501, cf. 480) and in all but one ambiguous instance it results from perceived offence. Thus, if to feel *κότος* is to feel hatred, and I think that a reasonable conclusion, then it is a hatred born of anger.

30 *ἔχω*: *Il.* 1.82, 13.517; *τίθημι*: 8.449; *ἐντίθημι*: *Od.* 11.102, 13.342.

31 On the link between *χόλος* and bodily bile, see Smith (1966: 555–6), Langholf (1992: 37–40), M. Clarke (1999: 92–7), Cairns (2003: 25n59), de Jong (2012: 81, 82).

32 See Horn (2018: 282–5) on the refusal of the angry to show mercy in battle.

33 Van der Mije's (2011: 359–82) argument – that this passage indicates Hector's irrationality at this moment in that the correct decision is to return within the walls – assumes that his fear of shame is irrational, and requires the rather stretched likening of the snake's evil herbs to Hector's 'considerations' (*Il.* 22.377, 379), both of which lead them foolishly to stay outside their place of safety.

34 On anger as incompatible with fear, see Konstan (2006: 51).

35 Holoka (1983).

36 Walsh (2005: 238).

37 Hesk (2017: 126–7).

38 This phrase marks the first outward manifestation of anger for Achilles at *Il.* 1.148 as it does for every other case of anger to which it refers; the prior comment that Agamemnon is 'greedy for gain' (*φιλοκτεανώτατε*; 122) is surely a criticism but is not, as Daude (2007: 42) has supposed, an expression of anger.

39 And perhaps Achilles' hope that the Achaeans would *ἐπισκύζωνται* at Agamemnon (*Il.* 9.370) is fulfilled by the *χόλον* they are later said to feel (14.50). Penelope fears that Odysseus will *σκύζευ* at (23.209) and *χώεο* her (213).

40 Cairns (2003: 29).

41 Hera's anger is doubly identified here too but while Athena manages to limit her anger's manifestation to her face, Hera's *χόλος* compels her to rail against Zeus in speech (*Il.* 8.461) and he claims not to care for her *σκυζομένης* (483).

42 Konstan (2006: 50).

43 The former anger is termed 'first-party' by some (van Doorn et al.: 2018) and 'second-party' (FeldmanHall et al. 2014, Nelissen and Zeelenberg 2009, Fehr and Fischbacher 2004) by others; to avoid confusion I will refer to it as 'victim anger'. Within modern psychology 'personal anger' and 'empathic anger' are often preferred, which is unproblematic only if we assume that angry third parties have not themselves also been personally offended. However, as I will demonstrate, this is rarely, if ever, the case in Homer.

44 Van Doorn et al. (2018: 586–8); cf. FeldmanHall et al. (2014).

45 Konstan (2006: 51); cf. Graziosi and Haubold (2003).

46 Konstan (2006: 52) sees Achilles anger towards Hector as unfocused.

47 Konstan (2006: 52).

48 *χόλος*: *Il.* 4.494, 501, 13.203, 206, 660, 15.138, 16.320, 546, 585, 21.146, 24.584, *Od.* 1.69, 78, 14.282, 22.26; *χώομαι*: *Il.* 13.662, 16.553, *Od.* 5.284, 11.103, 13.343; *κότος*: *Il.* 13.517, *Od.* 11.102, 13.342; *ὀδύσσομαι*: *Od.* 5.340, 423.

49 Other instances of anger and vengeance following pain at the death of a relative or friend include: *Il.* 8.316–28, 13.581–95, 14.458–507, 16.581–5.

50 Lendon (2000: 8).

51 Zanker (1994: 101).

52 Konstan (2006: 50); cf. Cairns (2003: 26–7).

53 E.g. *Il.* 18.121, 20.502, 21.543, 570, 596, 22.18, 57–8, 207, 217, 393.

54 See also the shame that will be Achilles' if he fails to prevent Patroclus' body from being taken back to Troy, his head impaled and his body left for the dogs (*Il.* 18.174–80).

55 See Chapter 3 on the relationship between anger and the state.

56 The traditional view: Montada and Schneider (1989), Haidt (2003); studies that show the role of personal care for victims: Batson et al. (2007), Batson, Chao and Givens (2009), O'Mara et al. (2011).

57 That 'moral outrage' is a construct: Batson et al. (2007).

58 E.g. Schwyzer (1931: 214), Frisk (1946: 29), Irmscher (1950: 7), Chantraine (1968: 696–7), Watkins (1977: 190), Clay (1983: 67).

59 Of the less common noun forms, *μηνιθμός* denotes Achilles' anger three times (*Il.* 16.62, 202, 282), *μήνιμα* relates to the gods' anger twice (22.358, *Od.* 11.73).

60 Irmscher (1950: 7).

61 Considine (1966: 19–20); cf. Latacz (2009: 13).

62 Cf. Kalimtzis (2012: 7).

63 Clay (1983: 65).

64 Zeus denies that he *ὠδύσατο* Odysseus (*Od.* 1.62–7) but notes that Poseidon *κεχόλωται* for Polyphemus (69, cf. 78). Poseidon's anger, which is later also described as *κότος* (11.102, 13.342) and *χώομαι* (5.284, 11.103, 13.343), is confirmed to be

ὀδύσσομαι by Ino (5.340, 423). Similarly, Helios feels *χώομαι* (12.376) and *ὀδύσσομαι* (19.275) and is expected to feel *χόλος* (12.348) over the killing of his cattle.

65 Watkins (1977: 194); Cairns (2003: 32n93) and Kalimtzis (2012: 7) disagree. Redfield (1979: 97n5); cf. Muellner (1996: 189–94).

66 On the differences between the noun and verb forms, see: Watkins (1977), Redfield (1979: 97–8).

67 (*Ἀπο/ἐπι)μηνίω*, is used for the angers of Agamemnon towards Achilles (*Il.* 1.247), Aeneas towards Priam for failing to honour him (13.460), Telemachus towards the suitors for attempting to kill him (*Od.* 16.378) and the disguised Odysseus towards Telemachus for sending him away to beg in the city (17.14).

68 For Cairns (2003: 32), the idea is refuted by *Il.* 5.177–8 where Aeneas suspects that Diomedes may be a god who is 'angry (*μηνίσας*) with the Trojans over an offering; hard to deal with is the anger (*μῆνις*) of the gods', but the co-occurrence of *μηνίω* and *μῆνις* does not prove that they always denote the same experience any more than *Od.* 5.146–7 does of *κοτέω* and *μῆνις*. However, Aeneas' clarification that it is the anger of the gods that is particularly hard to deal with may imply that, though it can be less harsh, mortals feel *μῆνις* too. Cf. Muellner (1996: 9).

69 Muellner (1996: 8); this has already been said in a more restricted form by Clay (1983: 65–6). For Cairns (2003: 39), the focus is on the victim's honour rather than the community's norms.

70 Muellner (1996: 8) provides a similar, but not identical, list.

71 Disobeying authority: *Il.* 1.247, 5.34, 444, 15.122, 16.711, 22.358, *Od.* 5.146; taking already distributed prizes: *Il.* 1.1, 422, 488, 2.769, 772, 7.230, 9.426, 517, 12.10, 16.62, 202, 282, 18.257, 19.35, 62, 75; failing to honour subordinates appropriately: 13.460; breaking a vow: 1.93; desecrating a sacrifice: 1.93, 5.178; dishonouring a priest: 1.75; mistreating a host or guest: 13.624, *Od.*14.283, 17.14; failing to provide burial rites for one's own: 11.73; the 'evil deeds' of the suitors: 2.66; attempted murder: 16.378; the reasons for anger are not always given such as that which leads the gods to destroy a city (*Il.* 21.523), and that of Athena (*Od.* 3.135) which Dawe (1993: 134) speculates may be to do with Ajax's rape of Cassandra.

72 Definitions that emphasise intensity or severity are common: Considine (1966: 21) sees *μῆνις* as a '*solemn epic* term' whereas Poseidon's anger lacks the 'note of sustained resolve'; Cairns (2003: 32) suggests that it is the 'gravity and intensity of *mēnis* that makes it suitable as a term both for divine wrath and for human anger which exceeds the norm'; Scodel (2008: 52) defines *μῆνις* as 'anger that is a powerful force'; for Latacz (2009: 13) *μῆνις* 'bezeichnet einen chronischen Erzürntheitszustand'. Latacz (13) also argues that *μῆνις* ought to be translated 'Groll' rather than 'Zorn' for the former term's greater persistence, but Kuhn (2005) has dismissed this convincingly, demonstrating that *μῆνις* is not inherently persistent.

73 The *μῆνις* Zeus is expected to feel towards Calypso if she maintains her romantic pursuit of Odysseus (*Od.* 5.146) is probably another case of anger at disobedience.

74 Muellner (1996: 26) sees *μῆνις* as 'a sanction meant to guarantee and maintain the sanctity of the world order', a definition that Kalimtzis (2012: 7–10) dismisses in favour of a view of Homeric anger in general as hinging on honour and slight. I would point out that the 'world order' is built on hierarchies of honour so that displays of obedience such as these both maintain that order and avoid dishonour.

75 Clay's (1983: 65–6) argument that gods can feel *μῆνις* towards those whose behaviour 'tends to erase the distinctions between gods and men' seems to me to be symptomatic of the broader (and not exclusively divine) tendency to be angry at disobedience, the erasure of distinctions between superior and inferior. Cf. Muellner (1996: 129).

76 The mortal supplicant himself can also feel *μῆνις* as a consequence of being denied help as Telemachus understands when he anticipates it from Odysseus for sending him away to beg elsewhere (*Od.* 17.14). Frisk (1946: 35) has said that this word is unexpected here and reasons that, in order not to betray his father's identity, he speaks with deliberate coldness and condescension.

77 E.g. Segal (1971), Garlan (1975: 61), Lendon (2000: 5).

78 Kucewicz (2016: 430n25) counts thirty-six references to the devouring of people by animals. Examples of bringing back enemy corpses include: *Il.* 13.374–84, 17.580–90.

79 Even so, the gods do not immediately become angry over Hector because, as Kucewicz (2016: 434) has shown, the gods 'do not take offence at the mutilation until the day of Patroclus' funeral – the point, it seems, at which the act becomes excessive; cf. van Wees (2004: 288n22).

80 Cf. Yamagata (1994: 16).

81 Yamagata (1994: 15).

82 Apollo also covers the body with the golden aegis so that it is not damaged by the dragging (*Il.* 24.18–21).

83 Muellner (1996: 37).

84 Holmes' (2007: 51–2) view that the honour Achilles takes from Agamemnon is 'traded in Achaean corpses' tells one side of the story – Agamemnon's worth, measured in the number of men he commands, diminishes with their destruction – however this line indicates that the Achaeans are not merely currency but are themselves agents of offence, albeit to a much lesser degree than their leader.

85 The superlative here (*φίλτατοί*) implies that he sees other Achaeans as 'friends' too.

86 Muellner (1996: 141–2) makes the rather stretched claim that 'this exchange is a distribution to Achilles by the group, not a gift from Agamemnon to Achilles'.

87 See also *Il.* 1.506–10 where Thetis tells Zeus that Agamemnon has dishonoured her son and yet, without explanation, that the Achaeans must repay him.

88 But *μῆνις* is not, as Loney (2019: 50) puts it, 'an unstable hatred whose reasons and objects can readily slip'. The primary object of *μῆνις* is subject not so much to change as to expansion so that Achilles' *μῆνις*, though it lands on all the Achaeans as well, can never be thought to deviate from its focus on Agamemnon and his original slight.

89 Achilles perceives not only that he has been 'dishonoured', but that he has been treated as a 'wanderer' (*Il.* 9.648) and as such the theme of exclusion from the community is clearly implied; cf. Ready (2011: 34–9).

90 Cf. Muellner (1996: 39).

2 Revenge and the Community in Homeric Society

1 Contra Loney (2019: 29), who states that 'the idealized logic of [archaic] retribution is that it ought to occur instantaneously and come in the form of an identical harm' and even claims that 'avengers feel retribution is at its purest when a wrongdoer simultaneously harms himself by his own attack' (28). The most fundamental problem with this idea is that the act of intending someone harm is itself a slight to be avenged.

2 Consider also Hera, for whom the destruction of Troy is an appropriate expression of her anger at Paris' choice of Aphrodite over her not because the two harms are in any way equivalent, but because she is the oldest of the goddesses and the wife of Zeus (*Il.* 18.361–7). On the analogousness of the gods to mortal elites, see Griffin (1978).

3 Adkins (1960b: 46–7).

4 *Il.* 1.73, 253, 2.78, 283, 7.326, 367, 9.95, 15.285, 18.253, *Od.* 2.160, 228, 7.158, 16.399, 24.53, 453, cf. 7.74. For Leaf (1886: 6), this phrase could mean 'good sense', referring to wisdom rather than intent. However, in view of the risk that Calchas is about to take in criticising Agamemnon, it is more fitting to suppose that *ἐὺ φρονέων* is meant to tell us that he is putting public interest ahead of his own, that his intentions are good. Likewise, Cheiron did not simply give medicines to Asclepius, but he did so with 'friendly (*φίλα*) intentions' (*Il.* 4.219; cf. 5.116), and Hermes, though he 'intended good (*ἀγαθὰ*)', failed to persuade Aegisthus against his evil plan (*Od.* 1.43; cf. *Il.* 6.162).

5 As Carawan (1998: 47–8) outlines, this term also modifies impressions of blame at *Il.* 6.522–3, *Od.* 2.133, 3.214–15.

6 Long (1970: 124n9) also asserts that one can find in Homer an appreciation of intentions in terms of 'trying one's best to succeed'.

7 On the potential for *αἴτιος* to be dependent on intent, see Pepe (2015: 45–8).

8 Van Wees (1992: 112) has also pointed out Zeus and Poseidon's lack of interest in whether the Phaeacians intended to thwart, or even knew of, Poseidon's plans (*Od.* 13.128–48).

9 Spencer (1897: 362). Hobbes (1998: 101) placed the deterrent quality of revenge among his laws of nature.

10 Boehm (1984: 65), Daly and Wilson (1988: 229–31), Miller (2006: 23).

11 As noted by McHardy (2008: 52–3); cf. Cairns (2003: 15–21).

12 Consider also Odysseus' advice to Arnaeus that he should not look to be lord of strangers and beggars 'lest somehow you incur a greater evil' (*Od.* 18.106–7).

13 See van Wees (1992: 109–15) on the touchiness of Homeric men.

14 Bourdieu (1977: 6). Cf. Widzisz (2012), Loney (2019: 27–30).

15 Bourdieu (1977: 7). Loney (2019: 28) presents his view – that in its ideal form archaic vengeance occurred simultaneously with the offence – as the reasoned conclusion of Bourdieu's principle that the offended are under pressure to perform revenge sooner rather than later.

16 1. Melanthius kicks and insults him (*Od.* 17.212–54); 2. Antinous insults and throws a stool at him (17.375–465); 3. Arnaeus insults him and demands that he leave the doorway (18.8–31) to which Odysseus responds by beating him but resists killing him (90–4); 4. Melantho and other maidservants disobey and insult him (18.320–36), so Odysseus insults and threatens them back and they obey but he watches them go and ponders 'things that would not be unfulfilled' (343–5); 5. Eurymachus mocks his baldness, insults his work ethic (350–64), threatens him and throws a stool at him (389–97); 6. Melantho insults him again (19.65–9) and Odysseus retorts (70–88); 7. Melanthius insults him again (20.177–82); 8. Ctesippus throws an ox foot at him (292–300); 9. The suitors laugh at Telemachus and his guests (347–83), specifically at Odysseus for being a worthless vagrant (376–9); 10. Antinous rebukes and threatens him for asking to string the bow (21.285–310).

17 In three instances he 'looks from beneath his brows' (*ὑπόδρα ἰδών*), but on each occasion it is at someone of similarly lowly status – once at the beggar Arnaeus (*Od.* 18.14) and twice at the slave-girl Melantho (337, 19.70) – so his anger, appropriate to his character, will not compromise his disguise.

18 Note that Odysseus, when lying down unnoticed awaiting sleep, is *ἀγαιομένου* towards the maidservants whom he contemplates killing (*Od.* 20.16). On this occasion and in Hesiod (*WD* 333) when it appears in this form, 'anger' (e.g. I. Johnston 2006) or 'wrath' (e.g. Murray 1995) may seem appropriate translations. However, if this is indeed an epic form of *ἄγαμαι* then a sense of jealousy is presumably implied which, in view of the metaphor of a dog guarding her puppies from a strange man, would suggest that it is towards the suitors that he feels this emotion, wondering if he ought to kill the women now rather than allow the suitors another night with them. It seems then that this is not so much anger at what has been done, as a begrudging of what his enemies are about to enjoy. Either way, restraint is again on display as he pounds on his chest and instructs his heart to endure (*Od.* 20.13–21).

19 The only death Odysseus desires without achieving having returned home is that of Arnaeus the beggar, but his fate, which is to be sent away to the terrible ruler Echetus (*Od.* 18.79–87, 90–4), is presumably a satisfying alternative, albeit one that is ultimately left uncertain with Arnaeus last seen sitting by the door.

20 Wilson (2002: 60–1).

21 Cook (1995: 47). The *Odyssey* clearly contrasts brute or thoughtless force with guile but the focus appears to rest more on *δόλος* than *μῆτις*.

22 Horn (2018: 286n40) understates Achilles' agency here, saying that 'Achilles' impulsivity and aggression is not checked from the inside, but requires restraint from an outside influence.' It is true that but for Athena violence would have ensued, but it is Achilles who decides that it is better to restrain his anger in obedience to the gods because they will then listen to him in turn.

23 Achilles anger as *μῆνις*: *Il.* 1.1, 1.422, 488, 2.769, 772, 9.517, 12.10, 16.62, 202, 283, 257, 19.35, 75; *χόλος*: 1.192, 217, 224, 2.241, 4.513, 9.158, 260, 261, 299, 436, 523, 646, 675, 678, 10.107, 14.50, 367, 16.30, 61, 203, 206, 18.111, 19.67, 24.395; *χώομαι*: 1.429, 2.689, 9.107; *κότος*: 1.181; *ὑπόδρα ἰδών*: 1.148.

24 Example of Trojan awareness: *Il.* 16.283. Achilles even explicitly tells Odysseus that 'as hateful to him as the gates of Hades, is the one who conceals one thing in his heart and speaks another' (9.312–13).

25 On the contrast between Achilles' 'quickness to anger' and Odysseus' embracing of disguise, see Murnaghan (2011: 4–5).

26 Van Wees (1992: 132).

27 *Il.* 6.46, 9.261, 11.131.

28 Nestor deems them gifts 'none could scorn' (*Il.* 9.164).

29 Cf. Scodel (2008: 85).

30 Leaf's (1892: 170; cf. Wilson, 1999: 132–3) suggestion that this represents a rejection of the satisfaction of honour in favour of 'unreasoning vengeance', overlooks the fact that Achilles' pursuit of revenge is aiming at honour as well.

31 Zanker (1994: 50).

32 In another instance Tros makes no offer of gifts, having only his pitiable state as a youth to rely on, and the narrator confirms that mercy in such situations is the product of a gentle and not an angry heart but there is no suggestion that Achilles' honour is at stake (*Il.* 20.463–8).

33 For Zanker (1994: 103), as for many, these and other such refusals represent the flouting of a vital institution, whereas for Cairns (1993: 113–19), a desire for justified vengeance 'may legitimately override both the sense of *aidōs* and consideration for the rules of supplication'. However, while the acceptance of supplication is far more likely when the suppliant does not stand in the way of revenge, it is not clear what these 'rules of supplication' are in the context of battle or why a revenge motive would justify ignoring them. I see no reason to view the killing of suppliants in battle as in any way illegitimate, merely a missed opportunity for leveraging compensation from relatives or selling the captive into slavery. As Horn (2018: 282) has shown, battlefield supplications seem only to work when 'detached from emotions of anger and personal hatred'. But there does appear to be a blurrier line when the context is one of hospitality; respect for this institution and the god who defends it saves

Odysseus from the Egyptians when they are angry and vengeful (*Od.* 14.283), but it does nothing for Leodas when Odysseus is the one being supplicated (22.310–29).

34 The insurmountable obstacles facing Wilson's (2002) argument – that Agamemnon's offer is unacceptable based on its presentation as an *ἄποινα* rather than *ποινή* ('ransom' and 'revenge' respectively, according to Wilson) and is therefore a gift that fails to recognise his own responsibility for causing offence – have been outlined in detail by Cairns (2011b) and require no further attention here. This offering clearly represents an acceptance of culpability and an attempt to make good.

35 We need not conclude, as is commonly done (e.g. Whitman 1958: 191–4; Taplin 1992: 69–71; Donlan 1993; Cairns 2011b: 106–7), that Agamemnon has erred in imposing this condition. Odysseus' omission of this clause is a rhetorical strategy, a decision to leave unsaid that which speaks for itself. Achilles understands the implication anyway not because he is exceptionally intuitive, but because it can be no other way – a return to Agamemnon's army necessarily entails a return to Agamemnon's social order.

36 Van Wees (1992: 132).

37 Van Wees (1992: 132–3).

38 The only candidate for this is Odysseus' assertion that if Achilles does not act to rescue the Achaeans, he will suffer pain as a result (*Il.* 9.249), but the cause of that pain is surely thought to be the evil that will result from his decision (249–50) rather than the insult he has already suffered.

39 Eurymachus hopes to offer Odysseus gifts sufficient to 'melt' his heart (*ἰανθῇ*; *Od.* 22.58–9), which may suggest some potential for passive response in the angry but may equally be a rhetorical exaggeration of the effect that such generous gifts might have.

40 On the community's negativity towards Achilles' decision, see pp. 71–2.

41 There is no contradiction in Achilles despising the negative aspects of anger (or even anger altogether) and then immediately pursuing vengeance (contra Taplin 1992: 199–200); Achilles may long for a world without anger, but he lives in a world with it and must dance to its rhythm.

42 Even Aristotle (*Rh.* 2.2.2) uses this line to illustrate that point.

43 As representing pain: Moulton (1979: 285); destruction: Walsh (2005: 223–4), Stocking (2017: 38). As Cairns (2003: 25n57) points out, it is likely that *χόλος* itself, given that Odysseus speaks of it as something that might be quenched (*Il.* 9.678), is directly associated with fire. Ready (2011: 42–8), taking the smoke metaphor in isolation, sees an indication of slow growth, but this does not ring true given that Achilles' anger begins as homicidal (*Il.* 1.188–95) and then manifests itself consistently in his remaining by the ships (even the threats to leave for good are ever-present and never fulfilled; 1.169–71, 9.356–65).

44 This, we can assume, is due to the same cultural expectations that lead him to chide Phoenix for associating with Agamemnon and to instruct him to stay instead in his, Achilles', tent (*Il.* 9.613–19).

45 Van Wees (1992: 113–14).

46 W. Harris (2001: 134). Harris claims to have reached such a conclusion on the basis of Achilles' statement that he has no desire to go on living so long as Patroclus remains unavenged (*Il.* 18.90–3), but does not explain why Achilles reaction in this instance ought to be considered paradigmatic. Harris (2001: 152–3) refers to the *Iliad* as 'a lesson against uncontrolled and unassuaged wrath', but does not explore the implications this appraisal has for what exactly the teacher of this lesson (let alone the students) thought about restraint. See (2001: 81) on emotion restraint first emerging as a desirable quality in the fifth century.

47 Herman (2006: 265).

48 As van Wees (1998: 11–16) has shown, the restraint of tears is far less common than the free expression of them.

49 See also Odysseus' restraining of afraid and fleeing leaders (*Il.* 2.188–91).

50 *Il.* 4.350, 14.83, *Od.* 1.64, 3.230, 5.22, 19.492, 21.168, 23.70. Note Achilles' point that what has crossed one's teeth cannot be recaptured (ἑλετή; *Il.* 9.409). Consider also Circe's reference to the ἕρκος ὀδόντων as a barrier that protects one from harmful drugs (*Od.* 10.328); it seems that the teeth can be conceived of as a barrier to harm from without and from within.

51 Adkins (1982: 305).

52 Odysseus talks of the need for 'having a pitiless spirit' (*νηλέα θυμὸν ἔχοντας*) to bury a man who has died (*Il.* 19.229).

53 Cf. W. Harris (2001: 149–51).

54 On *ἔται* as 'citizens' rather than 'kin', see van Wees (1992: 272–3). Cf. Finley (1981: 295n74).

55 Blaming people for excessive anger is common enough for this phrase to be formulaic with Odysseus receiving the same veiled warning from the less reliable Eurymachus (*Od.* 22.59).

56 Donlan's (1993: 164) influential characterisation of Agamemnon's offering as a 'gift-attack' that, were it accepted, would put Achilles into his debt and make him a vassal (examples of the same sort of argument include: Wilson 2002: 79–81; Cairns 2011b: 106–7; Lentini 2016: 17–18) is undermined by these criticisms aimed at Achilles and by the absence of any criticism aimed at Agamemnon himself from those around him who are desperate to see the embassy succeed (save only the implied critique in Odysseus' omittance of Agamemnon's demand at *Il.* 9.164–5; see p. 213n35). The gifts are excessively generous because Achilles holds all the cards; and he would be subordinated (as he was before) to the ruler, Agamemnon, because all Homeric societies are organised thus – one man above all others. To propose that Achilles should return to the army without Agamemnon as his superior would be altogether revolutionary.

57 Cf. Roguin (2008: 226–7).

58 It is referred to as 'wearisome' (ἀργαλέος; *Il.* 10.107), and even Achilles begins to see it as unusually long-lasting when he calls it 'ceaseless' (ἀσπερχὲς; 16.61).

59 None of the criticism Achilles faces, however, justifies the claim of some scholars that his refusal breaks a 'heroic code' (e.g. Finley 1977: 117–18; Mueller 1984: 52). Van Wees (1992: 133–4), noting that for all the criticism of Achilles' anger, it is Agamemnon who is clearly held responsible in the end, has argued for a more fluid treatment of behavioural standards that allows for pressure to be exerted on the angry to accept the offer even as their right to reject is respected. At the other extreme, Daude (2007: 61) reasonably states that Achilles was right to become angry but goes too far in saying that 'le reste – la guerre, l'issue des batailles, le nombre des morts, et même la mort de Patrocle, malgré les éléments parfaitement explicite de la responsibilité humaine, - relève de la responsibilité des dieux'; the appeals made to him and his own guilt and regret demonstrate otherwise.

60 As van Wees (1992: 154) has said, 'anger is needed to overcome hesitation and fear'.

61 These two emotions seem to be fundamentally incompatible in Homer, as they are deemed by Aristotle (*Rh.* 2.3.10), so it is perhaps inappropriate to describe the abatement of anger as 'restraint' in cases such as that of the suitors where the onset of fear drives out anger apparently without any cognition.

62 This anticipates a new slight from Priam, not, as Roguin (2008: 240–1) has claimed, a rekindling of the anger he felt at the death of Patroclus. It may be that Achilles is in a more sensitive disposition following his friend's death, but it is equally possible (and, to me, more likely) that he has learned what precautions his prickly nature requires him to take.

63 Odysseus certainly carries anger for a great number of different people.

64 Odysseus' insistence on what is evidently the more appropriate path as he (and surely Homer's audience) sees it demonstrates that there is nothing wrong with Agamemnon's timing here (contra Widzisz 2012: 171); it is Achilles who would, in haste, forego custom. This procedure will be examined more closely in the next chapter.

3 Punishment and the State in Homeric Society

1 On the debate surrounding the reasons for which laws were first written down, see Gagarin (2008: 67–92), Papakonstantinou (2008: 47–70), Wallace (2017).

2 For discussion of the date for Homeric composition, taken here to be *c.* 670–650, see p. 203n77. Draco's law is taken, with greater consensus, to have been written around 620.

3 Stroud's (1968: 6–7) translation with alterations. The opening words of this document – *καί ἐάμ* – are problematic for the suggestion that they follow on from something for which there was no space beneath the preceding decree. Stroud's

(1968: 37–8) proposed 'even if' translation removes the need for a preceding clause (in English at least) and has found supporters – Gagarin (1981: 96–110), Carawan (1998: 33–45, 70), Phillips (2008: 50–2) – and detractors – Sealey (1983: 292), Robertson (1990: 55), Rhodes (1991: 91). Todd (1993: 55n6) has noted that the law on homicide is the only survivor of many with which Draco was credited, so the words 'and if' may merely be an artefact of the since superseded law it once followed. Encouragingly, the *καί ἐάμ* opening supports the claim (apparently believed by fifth- and fourth-century Athenians) that the law had remained unchanged because presumably, had those responsible felt free to edit, they would have omitted this opening.

4 Finley (1977: 110); cf. Mackenzie (1981: 86).

5 E.g. Steinwenter (1925: 29–30), Calhoun (1927: 18), Bonner and Smith (1930: 31), Havelock (1978: 130–8), Biscardi (1982: 275–8), Gagarin (1986: 30, 42–3), Papakonstantinou (2008: 22, 34), Hawke (2011: 53–4), Erler (2019: 16–17).

6 Westbrook (1992: 67–76); Luce (1978: 10) says that the king's 'word is law', though in his model it is the elders who 'act as judges' (3); Elmer (2013: 92–7) recognises the need for some coercion in the Homeric community but only in order to facilitate debate.

7 Finley (1977: 110) dismissed this problem by reasoning that 'although there are a few fragmentary phrases in the poems about royal judgements, they are contemporary notes, and therefore anachronistic, which slipped by the poet'.

8 Maschke (1926: 28–63, esp. 50–63), Stroud (1968: 70–4), Humphreys (1991), Cantarella (2001: 474), Phillips (2008: 14), Pepe (2015: 53); but Humphreys (1988: 467) has previously said that Draco was appointed 'to clarify disputed points of law'. Carawan (1998: 80) reasons that some sort of central restraint on private action probably preceded Draco; Hawke (2011: 58–9) views the law as a reinforcement of custom, but where that custom was for the family, not the state, to determine the killer's liability and proceed accordingly.

9 Heralds: *Il.* 2.50–2, 18.503–5 *Od.* 2.6–8 (heralds are even called 'community workers', *δημιοεργοὶ*; 19.135); Phaeacian umpires: *Od.* 8.258.

10 Sceptres: *Il.* 2.268, 9.97–9, 18.505; Polished stones: *Il.* 18.504.

11 On institutions in Homer, see Scully (1990: 100–12), van Wees (1992: 25–58), Raaflaub (1997), Hölkeskamp (2002), Crielaard (2009: 239–47).

12 In support of this view, see Carlier (1984: 176–7), van Wees (1992: 34–5), Gagarin (2008: 19–23); contra: Geddes (1984: 33), Posner (1979: 31); Runciman (1982: 360) states that despite the role the 'elders and chiefs' have in arbitration, they 'cannot yet be called the incumbents of judicial roles'.

13 The precise meaning of *θέμιστας* is debated with translations ranging across custom, laws, judgements, trials and more. Whichever it may be, it is at least clear that it refers to a feature of justice for which Agamemnon is responsible. Faraguna (2006: 66) translates it as 'complesso di regole'. Cf. Hammer (2002: 115–34).

14 See Gagarin (1973: 94) on *δίκη* as meaning 'law' or 'legal process'; Dickie (1978) prefers 'justice'.

15 Cf. Gagarin (1986: 33), van Wees (1992: 277, and on Homeric sceptres in general: 274–80).

16 Cf. Lloyd-Jones (1971).

17 As Tsagarakis (2000: 107) says, 'the "physical" dead retain their corporeal characteristics and mental faculties, and are described as carrying on the activities of their former lives'. Tsagarakis (116) and Gonzalez Merino (2013: 74) have noted the corelation between Minos the judge and the *ἵστωρ* of the *Iliad* (18.501; on *ἵστωρ*, see pp. 84–5). Minos is not judging the dead for what they did when alive, as H. Clarke (1967: 64) has supposed, but for their actions within the community of the dead (cf. Sourvinou-Inwood 1995: 84–9; Farenga 2006: 223–6).

18 Farenga (2006: 225) sees in Minos the depiction of a 'judicial *basileus* whose cognitive virtuosity benefited the community'.

19 Cf. Gagarin (2008: 19). It is important to note that Sarpedon is not only a 'leader' (*ἀγός*), but a *basileus* and elder too and as such takes part in the administration of justice; indeed he is 'first' (*ἦρχεν*; *Il.* 2.876) among the Lycians, meaning their ruler and judge.

20 Cf. Morris (1986: 124), van Wees (2002: 102).

21 This term is often taken to mean 'bribe-devouring', implying that the judgement has been bought: Bonner and Smith (1930: 56), Lloyd-Jones (1971: 32), Osborne (1996: 138), Ober (2009: 72), Malamis (2012: 26), Hall (2013: 121), Erler (2019: 16), but we need not assume that the 'gifts' they have 'eaten' are illegitimate; they may simply be the kind of gifts people are expected to give to their lords, perhaps analogous to those on offer to the elder whose judgement is preferred at the trial on Achilles' shield (*Il.* 18.507; see below).

22 For a more detailed analysis of the contrast between the ideal and the reality of early archaic *basileis*, see van Wees (1999: 2–10). Gagarin (2008: 20–3) extrapolates from this that the authority of a king whose judgements are not 'fair and acceptable' will diminish, 'people will lose confidence in his judgements and they will take their disputes to someone else'; and this is supposedly like the system that, according to Herodotus (1.96–100), allowed Deioces to become the first king of the Medes. Unlike Herodotus, though, Hesiod gives no indication that one might choose between judges. The point here is that just rulers are good for the community and therefore respected. Perhaps a corrupt ruler risks inviting unrest, but we cannot infer that there is market competition for his services.

23 Those who perceive a 'big man' or 'chief' include Donlan (1989: 28) and Hall (2013: 11–12); Carlier (1984: 155, 177) and van Wees (1992: 281–94) argue for 'king'.

24 Raaflaub (2013: 82) claims that *basileis* 'lead' but do not 'rule'.

25 Raaflaub (1991: 235–6); Luraghi (2013b: 15) asks 'what monarchy can exist that does not have a different name for the king and its nobles?'

26 Luraghi (2013b: 15) does not offer any specific reasons for this conclusion.

27 Van Wees (1992: 274–80).

28 Cf. Luraghi (2013a: 132–3).

29 The view that this is not one scene but two – a marketplace quarrel and a trial (Leaf 1887: 123; M. Edwards 1991: 217) – is unnecessary; the *agora* is the trial venue.

30 That the *ἵστωρ* is the elder with the straightest judgement: cf. Wolff (1946: 40), Havelock (1978: 136), Humphreys (1983: 231), M. Edwards (1991: 218), Nagy (1997: 197), Lentini (2016: 18); that the *ἵστωρ* decides which of the elders has presented the straightest judgement: Andersen (1976: 11), van Wees (1992: 34). Much has been made of the etymological link between this term and *εἶδον* (to see) and *οἶδα* (to know): e.g. Snell (1924: 59–71), Nagy (1990: 250–5), Lentini (2016: 18–25; 2009: 50), Avramovic (2017: 737–40). It seems to me that such links support neither position better than the other: the ability to 'see' and 'know', whether metaphorically or literally, is sure to have been desirable either way. This study will therefore avoid adding to the already detailed scholarship on this.

31 Gagarin (2008: 17); cf. Wolff (1946: 41), M. Edwards (1991: 218), Nagy (1997: 197), Elmer (2013: 269–70n24). Pflüger (1942: 148) has argued that the disputants will choose the judgement they can both accept.

32 Cf. Carlier (1984: 176).

33 According to Wolff (1946: 40), the text does not 'admit of any interpretation to the effect that a third man – whether a king or other official or a trusted man called upon by the parties – acted as a judge'; this is of course true only if we assume from the outset that this individual cannot be the *ἵστωρ*.

34 Contra Lentini (2016: 18). Basile (2018: 23) sees the correlation as lying between the cauldron in Book Twenty-three and the *ποινή*, rather than the talents, in Book Eighteen, but these are very different matters, one being a wager that may go to either party, the other a payment allegedly owed by the defendant (if, that is, we accept the view that the issue is one of fact). This also relies on the assumption that the *ποινή* is a 'material object', a blood-price; as I explain below (p. 93), this is mistaken. It is occasionally argued that the *ποινή* and the talents are the same thing: Leaf (1887: 128), M. Edwards (1991: 218), Cantarella (2001: 478); but see Andersen (1976: 11).

35 Elmer (2013: 188) sees the two instances as analogous in that just as the winner of the chariot race will determine the winner of the wager, so will the winner among the elders determine the winner of the dispute but this misunderstands the nature of Ajax and Idomeneus' competition. They are not arguing about who will win, but who happens to be in front at that moment. Unlike the trial on the shield, Idomeneus' wager is a discrete contest dependent on but separate from the race. The arguments of Thür (1996: 68), Carawan (1998: 63) and Kyriaco (2019: 369) are based on a similar misunderstanding (cf. Lentini 2009: 51–2).

36 Havelock (1978: 352n19); cf. M. Edwards (1991: 217), Becker (1995: 112).

37 As discussed above, this verb does describe what Menelaus is proposing to do himself in his dispute with Antilochus, but in that instance it is initially presumed that the 'leaders' will take that role and it is only because Menelaus believes himself to have a solution that none will deem unfair that he claims the task for himself (*Il.* 23.573–80).

38 The competitive element also bears similarity with Hesiod who, as Zanker (1994: 151–2) has argued, sees the cooperative results of the judicial process as a product of competition for honour.

39 For Geddes (1984: 35), Homer's rulers have no role in the making of decisions and judgements and instead we see that 'Agamemnon asks for advice (*Il.* 10. 17–20)' and Nestor tells him that kings ought to do so (2.360, 9.100; cf. Kõiv 2016: 12–13n48–9). But this proves the opposite, for it is only to decision-makers that advice is relevant.

40 Cf. *Il.* 7.403–4, 9.710–11.

41 Elsewhere Nestor refers to his reputation for giving good advice in the past as a reason to listen to him now (*Il.* 7.324–5, cf. 9.93–4).

42 In this instance, we cannot speak of a 'loser'; Nestor saves Diomedes' blushes by commending him for his speech and goes on not to disagree with it but merely to delay the decision. Perhaps in such an instance one man simply wins more respect than the other.

43 Seaford (1994: 25) has rightly distinguished between 'the world of the shield [that] seems to represent the everyday life of the audience, including a city at peace' and 'the heroic world', but the difference does not lie in the latter's absence of a 'judicial mechanism to resolve the crisis of reciprocity' so much as in the inability of the Homeric judicial mechanism to resolve such a crisis as this.

44 Loney (2019: 48); cf. Finley (1977: 110).

45 That a community could last twenty years without ever formally settling disputes or making other decisions is an unrealistic conceit that serves the plot.

46 This is clearly not a trial, but Farenga (2006: 206–7) goes only a little too far in suggesting that 'we identify Odysseus, Telemachus, and Penelope as potential "plaintiffs" in a dispute-settlement (like the one on Achilles' shield) with their enemies, particularly the suitors'.

47 Halitherses and Mentor are both referred to as γέρων by the narrator (*Od.* 2.157), Eurymachus (178) and Odysseus (227).

48 Cf. Yamagata (1994: 242).

49 Humphreys (1983: 230–1).

50 Rhetorically at least, as Haubold (2000: 111) has said, 'Telemachus has won the day' because only he unites the people in their emotional response.

51 Cf. Lentini (2016: 18–19).

52 On the people as only informally influential in decisions, see: Finley (1977: 80–1), Luce (1978: 10), van Wees (1992: 32–3), Hammer (1998: 337; 2002: 130), Raaflaub and Wallace (2007: 28); Elmer (2013: 4) argues that Agamemnon's 'often arbitrary

exercise of power' contrasts with 'the narrator's normative point of view' that is more consensus-based (3–6).

53 Donlan (1989: 17n40) uses this last example to support the claim that 'the will of the assembled *demos*. . . was ultimately supreme; the basileis had very limited means of coercion'; but it proves the opposite given that the mob's attempt at violence is stymied by Odysseus.

54 Cf. Runciman (1982: 360), van Wees (1992: 33), Hammer (2002: 150–2), Elmer (2013).

55 *Od.* 2.272 suggests inconclusively that *λαοὶ* could include *basileis*, but LSJ (1996: 1029) demonstrates that it 'almost always means *men* or *people*; as *subjects* of a prince' in the Odyssey.

56 On the *λαοὶ* as the common people who need to be led, see Hammer (2002: 233n14), Haubold (2014). Odysseus' different treatment of the *basileis* and the *δῆμος* (*Il.* 2.188–206) has led some to conclude that *δῆμος* is inherently exclusive of the *basileis* (Elmer 2013: 92–4; cf. Cammack 2019: 45); but see Westbrook (1992: 74–5) who argues that it refers, particularly in this instance, 'not to the population but to the community as a legal entity represented by a body of notables'. Cf. Donlan (1989: 13–16), van Wees (1992: 31–6), Raaflaub (1997: 633–6), Crielaard (2020: 231). *Δῆμος* also frequently refers to the land in which the community lives.

57 Elmer's (2013: 185, 188) claim that the straightest judgement 'will be confirmed by the *epainos* of the *dēmos* and that this *epainos* will determine the recipient of the prize' unnecessarily formalises the crowd's function. They surely have an impact on the decision of the *ἵστωρ* when, as here, they are present and partisan, but the decision is his nonetheless. As Agamemnon has already shown, even unanimous disapproval could not always sway him.

58 Whether Hesiod also disapproves of Perses' watching of trials in a moral sense depends on whether we take '*νείκε̕ ὀπιπεύοντ᾽ ἀγορῆς ἐπακουὸν ἐόντα*' (*WD* 29) to be a scornful or simply realistic characterisation of one who watches and listens to disputes.

59 Malamis (2012: 25, cf. 27) has rightly highlighted the threat of 'divine retribution' as a deterrent against corrupt judgements, but this is not the only such threat and it is not correct to say that such wrongs 'cannot be addressed by the community itself' because 'they fall beyond its regulatory scope'. The anger of the common people (and other elites) was a meaningful threat.

60 Arguing that the system was entirely voluntary and non-coercive: Steinwenter (1925: 29–30), Calhoun (1927: 18), Bonner and Smith (1930: 31), Biscardi (1982: 275–8), Gagarin (1986: 30, 42–3), Malamis (2012: 18), Erler (2019: 16–17); that the court's decision is authoritative: Westbrook (1992: 75); Gagarin's (2008: 17) view appears to have developed so that he now sees the disputants as effectively forced to accept the decision (chosen by the crowd) because one could not remain in the community with those whose decision he had rejected.

61 Favouring the legal view: Andersen (1976), van Wees (1992: 134), Westbrook (1992), Wilson (2002: 159–61), Lentini (2016); favouring the factual view: Lipsius (1890: 225–31), Sidgwick (1894), Wolff (1946), Cantarella (2001, 2002), Papakonstantinou (2008: 32–3), Avramovic (2017).

62 Cf. Lentini (2016: 15–16).

63 Gagarin (1981: 14); cf. Lipsius (1890), Sidgwick (1894), Kyriaco (2019: 368). Examples of aorist infinitive: *Il.* 8.254, 21.501, *Od.* 11.261; examples of future: *Il.* 4.119–20, *Od.* 17.59–60.

64 Muellner (1976: 306); see also Westbrook (1992), Nagy (1997).

65 Cantarella (2001: 476); cf. Frisch (1976: 40), Gagarin (1986: 26–7), Sealey (1994: 102), Basile (2018: 20).

66 Muellner (1976: 102).

67 Elmer (2013: 184) links all four occurrences of this verb in Book Nine to the characterising of Achilles' and Agamemnon's quarrel; however, in the first instance (*Il.* 9.116) Agamemnon says to Nestor 'I was foolish, I do not deny it' (*ἀασάμην, οὐδ' αὐτὸς ἀναίνομαι*), and while this does relate to the quarrel, it does not indicate a refusal of reconciliation but demonstrates the possible validity of the 'deny' translation (cf. *Il.* 14.149).

68 Gagarin (1981: 15–16, 1989: 31–3), having argued that the killer is claiming to have paid the full price already, then seeks to accommodate *ἀναίνετο* by proposing that while one of the deceased's family members has accepted the payment another is now rejecting it. Despite the text offering no support for such a theory beyond failing to preclude it, this idea has found several supporters: e.g. Sealey (1994: 103–4), Carawan (1998: 65–7) and Farenga (2006: 36–7). This explanation is necessary only if the more natural meaning – that the family want revenge but the killer believes he should be allowed to pay a blood-price – is deemed unacceptable for other reasons.

69 Gagarin (1981: 14); cf. Kyriaco (2019: 368).

70 Loney (2019: 47). *Πάντα* also describes the vengeance taken by Orestes' on Aegisthus (*Od.* 1.43) and, as Carawan (1998: 55–6) has pointed out, the payment promised by Poseidon to Hephaestus on Ares' behalf (*Od.* 8.347–8).

71 Roebuck (2001: 60).

72 Cantarella's (2001: 478) recognition of this fact appears to conflict with her translation of line 499 (*ὁ δ' ἀναίνετο μηδὲν ἑλέσθαι*) as 'the one claimed that he had received nothing' (476). Scodel (2008: 87) and Elmer (2013: 183) have also noted the public nature of such compensation and the resulting problem for the factual interpretation.

73 Cf. Becker (1995: 112), Lentini (2016: 17); Andersen's (1976: 7) view, that the shield is 'a kind of mirror for the *Iliad*', is held by many in one form or another: e.g. Nagy (1997: 203).

74 Elmer's (2013: 185–7) claim that an agreement in the trial scene remains 'elusive' is based on the mistaken idea that the avenger's refusal to accept anything applies to the

verdict of the court. In fact, he refuses to accept the offer of compensation, which is why the case has come to court; he actually is willing to accept the verdict (*Il.* 18.501).

75 E.g. Westbrook (1992: 55), Cantarella (2001: 477), Avramović (2017: 750), Basile (2019: 23).

76 Wilson (2002: 9). Cf. Gagarin (1989: 26), Loney (2019: 46). Examples of *ποινή* as material repayment: *Il.* 5.266, 9.633, 636, 13.659; as blood vengeance: *Il.* 14.483, 16.398, 21.28, *Od.* 23.312.

77 Exile: Tlepolemus (*Il.* 2.661–70), Medon (13.694–7), Lycophron (15.430–9), Epeigus (16.570–6), Patroclus (23.83–90), Odysseus (invented; *Od.* 13.256–86), Aetolian (14.379–85), Theoclymenus (15.223–5, 272–8), Polypheides (252–5); blood-vengeance: Aegisthus (3.305–10), attempted on Odysseus (22.27–30), attempted on Odysseus and his household (24.429–37, 463–71); blood-price references: Ajax's statement (*Il.* 9.632–4), Achilles' shield (18.498–9). Unanswered homicides include Orestes (*Od.* 3.309–10) and Oedipus (11.273–80) who would themselves be the natural avengers and occupy less vulnerable positions, Heracles (21.24–30) and Telemachus for executing the twelve maidservants and Melanthius whose fates are Odysseus' to determine (22.465–77).

78 Steinwenter (1925: 34–6) suggested that the apparently different kinds of system reflect different chronological layers in the *Iliad*; Andersen (1976: 12) supposes this to be 'a transitional phase of jurisdiction and the rule of law'; but see Westbrook (1992: 68–9).

79 Gagarin (1981: 10; cf. 2008: 27) has claimed that 'it is clear that the most common result of homicide in the epics is that the killer flees and goes into exile' but also acknowledges that exile may simply be the 'most likely [consequence] to occasion comment' (16n22). Beye (1964: 358) has cited 'migration to avoid blood vengeance' as an important theme in the identifying information attached to *Iliadic* characters. Perry's (2010) thesis offers a literary explanation for the 'exile motif'.

80 Homer conveys a sense of how familiar exile felt to his audience when he likens the arrival of Priam in Achilles' tent to the sight of an imagined killer arriving in supplication before a wealthy man in a foreign town (*Il.* 24.480–4). Evidently exiles were rare enough to cause profound amazement to those who saw them, but common enough for the idea of their arrival to serve as a meaningful simile.

81 E.g. Schlunk (1976: 201), Gagarin (1981: 10–11), Pepe (2015: 50); often the role of blood-price is ignored (Adkins, 1960b: 52–3).

82 Adkins (1960b: 53); cf. Mackenzie (1981: 94).

83 The *prima facie* acceptance of the notion that all Homeric exiles have not been tried is widespread: e.g. Carawan (1998: 70), Hawke (2011: 58). Bowie (2007) has also considered the possibility that exiles may not all be of one sort but concludes that all homicide exiles are to be considered unwilling.

84 Draco's law does not mention compensation (contra Cantarella 2001: 477), but whether or not payment was permitted, it shares the principle of pardon with Homer.

85 Gagarin (2008: 101; cf. Faraguna, 2006: 67–9) refers to this as 'the rule that a killer must go into exile' and (31) considers it incompatible with another 'rule', Ajax's statement that a man will accept a *ποινή* for the killing of his son or brother, but these statements are neither incompatible nor rules. Both instances observe a familiar behaviour, not a required one. Possible explanations for their coherent coexistence as normal behaviours include: that killers would choose exile until they or their family could agree a material settlement, and that killers would flee in haste when they expected retaliation (because they had killed intentionally), but would risk trial when they expected the judgement to permit material compensation rather than blood (because they had killed unintentionally).

86 Not all exiles are in such a hurry. Tlepolemus, having killed his uncle, had time and means to build ships and gather many people before going into exile (*Il.* 2.661–70).

87 Stroud (1968: 37–8). The law as we have it sits beneath the heading 'First Axon' (which appears to preclude the law on intentional homicide having come first), while the fifty-sixth line appears to contain the heading 'Second Axon'; on this line, see Stroud (58–60).

88 Stroud (1968: 40) also points out that Plato organises homicide categories according to increasing intentionality in the *Laws* (865a–74b). For the counter-arguments, see Gagarin (1981: 72–9). I would also note that this is not the only sense in which the order here confounds our expectations: the rules pertaining to pardon precede those on punishment.

89 Gagarin (1981: 111–21); refuted by Sealey (1983: 292) and Pepe (2015: 54–5).

90 Adkins (1960b: 52–3), Gagarin (1981: 11); but see Westbrook (1992), Carawan (1998: 45–8), Cantarella (2011: 49).

91 On intent in Homer, see pp. 50–1.

92 Contra Gagarin (1981: 11). Note, on the other hand, that each of the (attempted) killers who expect a violent response – Odysseus' Cretan persona, Odysseus and Telemachus, the suitors – have acted with clear intent.

93 The suitors do jump up and look for shields and spears (*Od.* 22.21–5) but their confidence and assertiveness show that they fear not his intentions but only that he may repeat the apparently drunken error.

94 See also Carawan (1998: 46) who highlights the beggar's status 'as a known felon… and one without aristocratic ties or citizen rights [who] could expect none of the customary protections that the suitors themselves would claim'.

95 Note that here the stringing of the bow, not its fatal use (which they do not yet fear), is the act which the proud suitors are prohibiting.

96 Westbrook (1992: 72) sees this scene as evidence that 'inebriation… serves to negate mitigation', but I think it comes closer to demonstrating the opposite.

97 In classical Athens drunkenness could help or hinder a defendant's case, being cited both as a mitigating factor that disproves intent (Dem. 21.180, cf. 74, Arist. *Pol.* 1274b) and as evidence against an assailant's character (Dem. 54.3, 7, 33).

98 Odysseus not only admits to premeditation, but even invents a story in which he plans and executes an ambush (*Od.* 13.259–75).

99 Bonner and Smith (1930: 21), Adkins (1960b: 52–3), Cantarella (1976: 33–4), Gagarin (1981: 11–13), Pepe (2015: 50).

100 See also Euaeon (Dem. 21.71–5) who, since his murder of Boeotus was done in anger, was condemned by a margin of only one vote; cf. Plat. *Laws* 867b; Riess (2012: 118), E. Harris (2013b: 290).

101 Westbrook (1992: 71) sees two points of mitigation: that the act was done in anger and was therefore provoked, and that the death was an unintended consequence of the blow. But anger is presented, by classical sources at least, as a factor that could render 'unintentional' even a killing that was, in the moment of anger, precisely what the killer meant to achieve. As well as anger, youth might be taken into account according to Ariston whose alleged abuser is older and therefore deserving of no special treatment (Dem. 54.1), so perhaps Patroclus, as implied by his reference to his youthful folly (*νήπιος*), is emphasising another mitigating factor.

102 I would also note that the Trojan expedition reunites exiled killers and the men of the *poleis* from which they fled. Medon fled Locris for Phylake after killing his step-uncle (*Il.* 13.694–7) and yet stands alongside his old compatriots in the fight against Hector (685–7) – a dramatically different approach to that of Theoclymenus. This rests of course on the sizeable assumption that the poet has considered such implications, but perhaps he simply conceives of Medon (and Patroclus) as the sort of exile who need not watch his back so long as he keeps away from his hometown.

103 Konstan (2006: 116); cf. Kirk (1985: 285), Yamagata (1994: 149), Cairns (2003: 33–4); Mackenzie's (1981: 86) claim that the injuries inflicted in Homer are offensive towards 'the individual victim alone' and are 'undesirable to a wider section of society only when their consequences are unpleasant to others', appears to conflict with this term.

104 Cairns (2003: 33n99): *Il.* 6.335–6, 8.407, 421, 10.115, 129, 145, 15.103, 115–16, 211, 227, 16.21–2. Cf. Redfield (1975: 117).

105 The *οὐδὲ* here is often translated 'and', implying a stronger link between the emotions than the more natural 'nor'.

106 It is also plausible that Paris' hypothetical *χόλος* and *νέμεσις* are understood to relate to the Trojans' disliking of him and blaming of Helen for their troubles (*Il.* 3.156–60, 410–12) respectively.

107 Redfield (1975: 117–18) presents two other instances supposedly rooted in personal offence towards Achilles who has 'made of his own will a moral law'. In both instances, Patroclus imagines Achilles to feel *νέμεσις* towards him for his interactions with the rest of the Achaeans: his lingering among them while on an errand (*Il.* 11.649) and his tears of pity for them in their suffering (16.22). These cases do indeed stand out for the fact that it is the supposed victim who feels

indignation but it seems to me that they are symptomatic of Achilles' ambiguous relationship with the rest of the army. They are no longer his allies but neither are they (excepting Agamemnon) truly his enemies. Patroclus' care for his injured friends might be considered blameworthy by Achilles (in that it is technically a betrayal) and yet not insulting. Cf. Cairns (2003: 35n108).

108 The *νέμεσις* Ares anticipates from the other gods when he intends to go and avenge his son (*Il.* 15.115–16) would be caused by his disobeying of Zeus' authority, an act which would endanger them all (cf. *Il.* 15.128–41).

109 Cairns (2003: 38); cf. *Il.* 10.129, 17.93, 100; and Hera *νεμέσησε* and rebukes Poseidon whom she blames for failing to help the Achaeans against Hector (8.198–207).

110 Redfield (1975: 117) sees this as felt simply at foolishness but it seems to me that Odysseus would presume Nestor to understand the implications of his actions.

111 Given that it causes *νέμεσις* elsewhere, the suitors' abuse of courtship and hospitality customs here is presumably the trigger. But see Fisher (1992: 162–3) for the suggestion that Mentes is observing how these men 'behave, in another's house, as if they owned it and controlled it, and yet even so they do not stop to welcome a stranger who arrives at the door'.

112 Redfield (1975: 116–17) is right to contrast *νέμεσις*, 'an invasive passion that drives one to intervene in the affairs of others', with *αἰδώς*, which 'shrinks away and draws back'.

113 Other examples of *νέμεσις* towards oneself include the feeling that leads Telemachus to open his door quickly so that the visitor will not have to wait long (*Od.* 1.119), and the emotion that Helen wishes Paris knew (*Il.* 6.351); cf. Redfield (1975: 116), Cairns (2003: 35–6).

114 Cf. Fisher (1992: 166). Farenga's (2006: 213) suggestion that the inaction is 'motivated by the traditionally passive role of the *λαοὶ* in epic' understates how animated they are on Achilles' shield and at some other assemblies. Hawke (2011: 110) has rightly noted that the people are sometimes supposed to act, but is wrong to suppose that the reason for their inaction here is that the dispute is private not public; Leocritus makes no such defence, and if so then why are private matters ever brought to assembly as Aegyptius' opening implies?

115 This, I think, disproves Perry's (2010: 10) claim that 'there is no evidence in Homeric epic for a public, legally sanctioned means to compel another to go into exile'.

116 Bonner and Smith (1930: vii); Carey (2013: 47) says Solon 'extended the scope of public action dramatically, but there was legislation already in place to deal with political offences'.

117 Posner (1979: 31) has said that the only 'governmental function' in the Homeric world is 'defense... against foreign invaders' (which rather overlooks the mutually necessary function of 'invading'), while 'other violations of internal public order are not public offenses.' Malamis (2012: 21–7) has recognised that corrupt political

and judicial decisions were wrongs against the community as a whole but sees no recourse to justice for the victimised community beyond the indiscriminate retribution of the gods.

118 According to Cantarella (1976: 74), there is no set of rules whose violation results in a penalty inflicted by the state, but only judicial bodies that assess disputes and authorise injured parties to take revenge as a 'delegato della comunità.' Although, as Stahl and Walter (2009: 142) have pointed out, the broad range of family and phratry members that could become involved in decisions pertaining to pardon show that homicide 'was far more than a "private affair"'.

119 Raiding as heroic behaviour: *Il.* 9.328–33, *Od.* 14.229–34. Cf. van Wees (2004: 203–6).

120 Even Donlan (1989: 18) has recognised how this distinction implies the beginnings of the state.

121 Eupeithes' reference to 'friends' here does not limit the crowd to personal friends, elders or any other category within the community as a whole; Agamemnon uses the same phrase before all the Achaeans on the Trojan beach (*Il.* 19.78). It may be, though, that the words are being spoken directly to the elders in the presence of a larger crowd.

122 For Bonner and Smith (1930: 25), Eupeithes opens 'not by asking for aid in avenging the deaths of the suitors, but asking for the punishment of Odysseus as a public offender'.

4 Punishment and Anger in the Athenian Courts

1 Herman (2006: 191–4).

2 These are the most common terms but there are others (including *ἐπιτίμιον* and *τίμημα*) as well as numerous references to punishment through metaphor, metonymy and so on; cf. Kucharski (2016). One term for anger is used almost exclusively: *ὀργή*. On Aristotle's definition, see Chapter 1. One other term, *ἀγανάκτησις/ἀγανακτέω*, is occasionally used synonymously.

3 Cf. Beekes (2010: 1486).

4 E.g. Antiph. 1.2, Lys. 3.39, Dem. 21.75.

5 Herman (2006: 196); on this point Herman and D. Cohen (2005b: 179n18) appear to share some common ground.

6 Herman (2006: 197, cf. 1998: 614). Herman does recognise that 'Athenian litigants' – specifically the prosecutors in *Against Agoratus* who assert that they have been charged with executing *τιμωρία* for their condemned relative (Lys. 13.39–42) – 'were seeking 'vengeance' for their wrongs in conformity with the laws of their state', but fails to explain why the term means vengeance in this case but not in others. Cf. Cairns (2015: 656n41).

7 Allen (2000) argues that *τιμωρία* cannot be translated exclusively as either 'revenge' or 'punishment' but proceeds with the latter; it is often taken to mean revenge in private instances and punishment in public: e.g. W. Harris (2001: 167), Reiss (2012: 380); cf. Cairns (2015: 659).

8 Aristotle's definition of *ὀργή* is preferred to that found in the *Rhetoric to Alexander* (34.14) for the reason expressed in Chapter 1 (pp. 24–5): it better explains the way the term is used in the forensic corpus. By this I mean that it indicates the perception of a slight and that it is felt only by those who feel personally victimised. This and the following chapters are in large part intended to make this case.

9 Herman (2006: 129–33) has dismissed Aristotle's definitions on the grounds that Aristotle's subject was human nature and does not allow for the impact of the Athenian political context on Athenian men in particular. This seems a careless and unlikely oversight by Aristotle whose intention was to advise litigants on how to persuade; cf. Nichols (2013: 17n26).

10 Nichols' thesis (2013), offering a systematic appraisal of the term in Athenian oratory and elsewhere, reaches the same conclusion. See Nichols (2013: 17–37) for a survey of the implications for this term in Aristotle and the playwrights. Scholarship on the forensic corpus tends to agree that the term means revenge: e.g. Blundell (1989: 48–9), Fisher (1992: 10), Burnett (1998: 7–8), Rubinstein (2004: 192; 2016). W. Harris (2001: 134n12; cf. Blundell, 1998: 2–3) has reasonably objected that 'English "revenge" normally follows a delay', and Cairns (2015: 659–65) has contended that while 'revenge' recognises the importance of 'interpersonal forms of dignity and respect', it fails to account for the individual's 'legal status as a member of the community' (665).

11 Allen (2000: 70); W. Harris (2001: 167) associates *κόλασις* with a mid-fifth-century turn away from revenge in favour of 'non-retributive' punishment; McHardy (2008: 122n24) refers to *ζημία* and *κόλασις* as terms that refer 'exclusively to punishment' rather than revenge; Kucharski (2016: 109) claims that while other punishment terms blur 'the fundamental distinctions between penalties, damages and revenge', *κόλαζειν* 'remains clear of such ambiguities'; Cairns (2015: 657–8) rightly points out that orators could distinguish between the act of punishment and the satisfaction taken from it but his example (Dem. 23.69) pertains to homicide and is symptomatic of the peculiar nature of punishment in that context (see Chapter 7). It happens to be *κόλασις* that is the concept attributed to the punishers and withheld from the victim in this example, but another example (Andoc. 1.136) demonstrates that *κόλασις* can also be performed by the plaintiff.

12 Nichols (2013: 44).

13 Cf. *NE*. 1103a–1104b, 1109a; *Rh*. 1.9.9, 2.14.3

14 The *προ* prefix here cannot mean that this is something which happens before *κόλασις* since it is followed by '*ἀγανακτοῦσιν γὰρ ἧττον κολαζόμενοι καὶ οἱ δοῦλοι*' (Arist. *Rh*. 2.3.15), which confirms *prokolazein* to be a kind of *κόλασις* in itself.

15 E.g. Dem. 21.27, 45.67, 54.43. On *κόλασις* teaching the wrongdoer 'his or her place in the social order', see Allen (2000: 69–71).

16 Other instances where *κόλασις* means the disciplining of a child include: Ar. *Cl.* 1107, 1399–1435; Xen. *Cy.* 1.6.33; *Lac. Const.* 2.2, 2.10.

17 E.g. Freese (1926), Allen (2000: 70); Fisher (1992: 10n16) goes further, translating *ἕνεκα* as 'for the benefit of'.

18 E.g. Isoc. 20.6, Dem. 19.259; the act of *κόλασις* is directly associated with killing in the phrase '*θανάτῳ κολάσαι*' (Dem. 21.176, Lys. 28.4).

19 One possible distinction is the uncertain implication at Dem. 18.279 that a prosecutor might *δίκην λαμβάνῃ* on behalf of the court; *τιμωρέομαι* is never used in this way.

20 'To give/take justice' is perhaps most popular (e.g. Allen, 2000: 70; McHardy, 2008: 4) but typically translators switch between the available English terms depending on context.

21 A point noted by McHardy (2008: 4); cf. Miller (2006: 17–20) has outlined the theoretical problems with ideas of 'getting even'.

22 Herman (2006: 213–14); Cf. Saunders (1991: 99).

23 E. Harris (2017: 226–7).

24 The following numbers are based on my own collation, which is similar but not identical to Rubinstein's (2004); see the Appendix for a fuller explanation.

25 A given speech does not necessarily account for the entire case it represents. Often a main prosecutor or defendant would be supported by others and it is reasonable to suppose that such tasks as making the factual case and appealing directly to certain emotions may have been distributed across the team. Thus, the absence of anger or punishment appeals in certain speeches does not indicate the absence of such appeals in that case altogether. The one prosecution speech that appeals against anger and punishment (Isoc. 18) proves the rule in that it is from a *παραγραφή*, a procedure in which the prosecutor is defending his right not to be prosecuted.

26 The private numbers include those from homicide trials.

27 On these cases, see pp. 168–9.

28 Rubinstein (2013: 136). Cf. Saunders (1991: 99), W. Harris (2001: 185), Riess (2012: 120).

29 Warning: Lyc. 1.116; anger appeals: 27, 58, 78, 111, 138.

30 Aeschin. 3.4; anger appeals: 16, 144, 198.

31 Dem. 19.228; anger appeals: 7, 91, 302.

32 Cf. Konstan (2006: 69).

33 E.g. Dem. 45.6; cf. Andoc. 2.15. On the dicastic *thorubos* see Bers (1985); cf. Allen (2000: 170).

34 Dem. 18. 1–2; Aesch. 2.1–3; cf. Lys. 19.2–6; Hyp. 1.1. fr.1, 4.11.

35 Cf. Dem. 24.171, 175.

36 E.g. Lys. 20.1, 25.1, 5, 16, 18, Dem. 18.138.

37 Cf. E. Harris (2013b: 131–2). It is worth noting that jurors did not always have the freedom to consider what kind of punishment they thought a particular offence deserved, because some procedures carried fixed penalties. In such cases the jurors were required, as ever, to consider whether they thought the offence had occurred and, if they were the victims, whether they felt angry. But they had no opportunity to allow their perception of the gravity of the wrongdoing or the honour of the two parties to influence the kind of punishment they would impose. In this, we can see a degree of limitation imposed by the state on the anger and vengefulness of its law enforcers. It also suggests, in some respects, a principle of equal honour shared by all citizens so that whether one was wealthy or poor, elite or common, certain rules applied without prejudice.

38 This was the ideal – anger was the emotion of justice – but I have no doubt that jurors who perceived no insult and felt no anger might nevertheless often have ‘punished’ those they envied, hated, feared and so on, even if such an action was not truly punishment.

39 See Rubinstein (2004) for a catalogue of appeals to *μῖσος*.

40 Demosthenes, aware of the potential for jurors to listen with prejudiced ears to the defendants, says he is praying ‘that the gods inspire you not to accept my opponent’s advice on how you should listen to me, for that would be cruel, and instead to heed the laws and your oath, for beyond all your other obligations, you have specifically sworn to listen to both sides equally’ (18.1–2).

41 Note Aristophanes’ jurors coming to court ready with three days’ worth of anger (*Wasps* 243); cf. Allen (2003: 83–4).

42 Allen’s (2000) argument that the universal goal of litigants was to evoke pity towards themselves and anger towards their enemies cannot, as Rubinstein (2004) has clearly demonstrated, explain (at least not sufficiently) the distribution of anger appeals across the forensic corpus. Instead, I think the tug-of-war between these emotions ought to be viewed as relevant to the punishment decision: when a defendant is found guilty, then feelings of pity towards the condemned may mitigate the punishment. Of course, as Rubinstein has also shown (2013; cf. Whitchurch 2020), pity could, like all emotions, be put to persuasive use throughout any speech.

43 Albeit not always the anger of the jurors; it was the anger of victims that was relevant and sometimes that meant the jurors but sometimes it meant a private individual.

44 E.g. Carey (1994), Johnstone (1999), Allen (2000, 2003), Kurihara (2003), Rubinstein (2004, 2005, 2013, 2016), Sanders (2012), Cairns (2015), Kucharski (2016), Fisher (2017).

45 Allen (2000: 59–62).

46 Allen (2000: 61; cf. 110).

47 Rubinstein (2004).

48 Rubinstein (2016: 68, 70–2) finds that appeals occur most frequently on the basis of ‘religious offences, treason and katapolitical bribery, but more rarely in connection

with other types of offence that concerned the purely internal workings of the Athenian community and its democratic institutions'. See Harvey (1985) on katapolitical bribery.

49 Examples of anger and punishment appeals for treason: Lys. 12.58, Dem. 19.302, Din. 1.77, 2.4, 3.8, Lyc. 1.27, 78, 111; desertion: Lys. 14.9; embezzlement and theft: Lys. 27.11, 28.13, *Din.* 1.77; bribery: Dem. 19.7, Din. 2.4, 3.8.

50 Most (but not all: E. Harris, 1989: 118–36; 2008: 84–6) agree that the speech was probably not actually delivered (cf. Aeschin. 3.52).

51 E. Harris (1989, 2008: 79–81, 2019). Harrison (1971: 62–3) argues that the *προβολή* was confined to the assembly but that the speech relates to a *γραφή ἀσεβείας* procedure.

52 Rhodes (1981: 659–60), Osborne (1985b: 51), MacDowell (1990: 16–17), Fisher (1992: 38), Rowe (1994).

53 Rhodes (1981: 660), Osborne (1985b: 51), MacDowell (1990: 16).

54 E. Harris (1989: 130) links this to Chapter 28, where Demosthenes admits that the law afforded him a choice between a *δίκας ἰδίας* and a *γραφὴν ὕβρεως*, but while Harris assumes these to denote the options he refused and chose respectively, they could equally both be alternatives to the procedure he chose. Even then, Rowe (1994: 56) is over-confident in stating that this 'decisively proves that the action is not a γραφή'; perhaps, as in Chapter 25, he is acknowledging that though he has brought a *γραφή* where the people are the victim, he might have brought one where he was the victim.

55 Fisher (1992: 36–68).

56 E. Harris (2013a: 224–31; cf. 1992: 77–8, 2008: 103n95–9) listed six reasons and has since added four more (Canevaro and Harris, 2019: 97–100). Among those who consider the text (mostly) genuine are MacDowell (1990: 263–8), Fisher (1992: 36; 2001: 139) and van Wees (2011b).

57 E. Harris (2013a: 228; cf. 2008: 104n97). MacDowell (1990: 267–8) has concluded that *γραφὰς ἰδίας κατὰ τὸν νόμον* is a later insertion.

58 E. Harris (1989: 130n32) treats *δημοσίᾳ κρίνειν* as 'equivalent to "bring a *graphe*"' but does not appear to recognise the implied *δίκη ὕβρεως* in such an interpretation. MacDowell (1990: 247) suggests that the difference was that the *γραφή ὕβρεως* 'involved less publicity than a *probole*, because it was not heard in the Ekklesia'. This is problematic because it assumes some 'legal inaccuracy', as MacDowell puts it, in Demosthenes' categorising of *hybris* under *δίκαι ἰδίαι*. But more importantly it does not account for the final line, which implies that the *γραφή ὕβρεως* he has in mind would prevent him proposing the penalty. The general absence of references to *γραφαί* as *ἰδίαι* simply reflects the rarity of *γραφαί* in which a private victim prosecutes on his own behalf.

59 E.g. Ar. *Wasps* 1417–41; cf. van Wees (2011b: 139n20).

60 Cf. Lipsius (1905: 429n39). MacDowell (1990: 267–8) has questioned why the penalty for failing to obtain one-fifth of the votes should stand only for those who

had prosecuted on their own behalf, but as van Wees (2011b: 131) has suggested, the law appears to have deterred victims from resorting too freely to public procedures but not 'the third-party prosecutor, for whom the burden of taking on another person's case was presumably deemed deterrent enough in itself'.

61 I fail to see how the 'private' (rather than the later Hellenistic 'one's own') meaning of *ἴδιος* is relevant (cf. E. Harris 2008: 104n97, 2013a: 228; Canevaro and Harris, 2019: 96). A trial of this sort is simply one where the prosecutor is acting in a 'private' capacity, which is to say they are acting on their own behalf, rather than as 'one who wishes' (*ὁ βουλόμενος*) on behalf of another individual or the community as a whole.

62 That this phrase also appears in Aeschines' summary (1.15) strongly suggests its veracity; but see the plausible explanation of E. Harris (1992: 77).

63 E. Harris (2013a: 225).

64 E. Harris (1992: 77).

65 For a full defence of this view, see van Wees (2011b). Fisher (2001: 140) has suggested that the term is supposed to emphasise the illegality of *hybris*, but it seems to me unlikely that the lawgiver chose wording that, read literally, allowed for such a different interpretation.

66 Gernet (1917: 187, cf. 183–97).

67 Fisher (1992: 61).

68 Cf. Isoc. 20.8, Dem. 54.18–19.

69 There are nineteen explicit anger appeals and thirty-five punishment appeals in *Against Meidias*, while *Against Timocrates* has the second most of any Demosthenic public prosecution in both categories with seven and twenty respectively. These also occur at Demosthenes' highest frequency of one every 11.95 and 6.49 chapters respectively.

70 Fisher (1992: 65).

71 Here it is the jurors' *ἀγανάκτησις* that is invoked, but he appears to be treating this as a synonym for *ὀργή* to vary from the term he has just used to refer to his own anger.

72 It is not clear whether Euthynus was the killer or the killed; cf. MacDowell (1990: 288).

73 Demosthenes pre-empts such a defence (Dem. 21.29–30); his acknowledged desire to avenge himself by handing his enemy over to the city in this way (26, 45, 226) does not to his mind present any contradiction.

74 Cf. Fisher (1992: 65).

75 There are many possible reasons for this difference (such as stylistic preference), but given the references to recent attacks on democracy, it may be that invoking citizenship could more effectively tie one's honour to that of the jurors when democracy was under threat. In one speech Demosthenes attempts such a warning, but acknowledges that some may object to this in view of the different political conditions (19.154).

76 *Hybris* does not need to be violent; cf. Fisher (1992: 11).

77 Ariston refers to escalation that moves from abusive words to assault to wounding to homicide (Dem. 54.18–19). MacDowell (2009: 240–1) sees this list as incomplete without *hybris*, but Chapter 17 shows that all these acts can be characterised by *hybris*.

78 Cf. Fisher (1992: 62–8).

79 Fisher (1992: 36–85), Todd (1993: 270), Ober (2007: 123), Lanni (2016: 86–91).

80 We cannot be sure that this did not include one's own slaves. E. Harris (2008:103n92) has claimed as much on the basis that masters seemingly had the right to kill their slaves (Antiph. 6.4) but killing is not the same as committing *hybris*; a master may kill a slave in the act of punishment, acting in anger rather than *hybris*, and they may harm their slave unprovoked with the intention to shame and so commit *hybris* without necessarily killing. Others who hold Harris's view include Todd (1993: 189), Harrison (1968: 172); contra: Morrow (1937: 222–3), Fisher (1995), E. Cohen (2000: 166), Lanni (2016: 88–91). Murray (1990: 140) has highlighted the apparent inconsistency in the law's protection of slaves, saying that 'such a law would have had to envisage a situation involving the treatment of free men as if they were slaves… [and] slaves… as if they were – what?' But this is paradoxical only if we treat *hybris* in absolute terms – treating slaves as slaves is surely not *hybristic*. But *hybris*, like all honour-related matters, was relative and to treat a slave with *hybris* was, implicitly, to treat them as less than a slave.

81 Mactoux (1988: 336–8), Murray (1990: 140), Canevaro (2019: 50–1), E. Harris (2019: 159), Fisher (1992); this law clearly did allow for *hybris* against slaves, whether or not the law text is genuine (cf. Aeschin. 1.17, Dem. 21.46, Dem. 22.54).

82 Canevaro (2019); Cairns (1996); for a similar view, see: MacDowell (1976: 23), Mackenzie (1981: 91), Allen (2000: 70).

83 Canevaro (2019: 72–3).

84 Lanni (2016: 88–91) does take Aeschines' summary to be an accurate reflection of what the law on *hybris* meant.

85 Demosthenes does say that the lawgiver thought that 'it was necessary to consider not who the victim was but the nature of the act that had occurred' (21.46), but this refers only to who has the right to prosecute (or have a prosecution brought on their behalf) for *hybris*; it does not imply that acts of *hybris* are the same regardless of who the victim is.

86 Fisher (1995) has shown that there is substantial evidence that slaves were afforded some degree of honour that *hybris* might harm.

87 This is precisely the opposite of Mackenzie's (1981: 108–10) argument that in Homer the standard response to wrongdoing was one of anger but by the classical period 'individual resentment becomes generalised into indignation' (109).

88 Claiming that Athens knew and upheld the rule of law: Ostwald (1986), Herman (2006), E. Harris (2006; 2013b; 2018), Meyer-Laurin (2007), Sickinger (2008). Arguing it did not: Ober (1989), Todd (1993), D. Cohen (1995), Christ (1998), Sundahl (2003), Lanni (2006; 2016). Recently, Forsdyke (2018: 208) has found the Athenians to have 'achieved a high degree of the [rule of law], yet also wisely recognised necessary trade-offs'.
89 Kurihara (2003). Cf. Phillips (2008: 20n14), Alwine (2015: 95–6).
90 D. Cohen (1995: 102), Johnstone (1999: 54–60), Fisher (2001: 119), Alwine (2015: 78).
91 In particular, see E. Harris (2013b: 60–98).
92 E.g. Lys. 6.15, 15.9, 22.17, 30.35, Dem. 21.225, 58.41, Isoc. 20.7, Lyc. 1.4, 9.
93 E.g. Dem. 21.34, 177, 58.25, 36.
94 As Todd (2000: 161–2) points out, the prosecution uses the law against failing to appear for the land army (*τῇ πεζῇ στρατιᾷ*) and attempts to take this as referring to the foot soldiers when it surely is meant to refer to the 'non-sea' army.
95 Lys. 14 was a supplementary speech and we do not know what approach the main prosecutor took, but for our purposes it is enough to note that the surviving speech made a close connection between anger, punishment and public offence.
96 *Καταφρονέω*: Isoc. 16.2, 20.10, 22, Dem. 26.2, 30.8, 42.2, 43.78, 50.57, 65, 66, 56.10, 57.65, Aeschin. 3.203, Hyp. 5.3, Din. 1.85; Isaeus 4.11 recommends higher fines as the way of ensuring the laws are not disdained. *Καταφρόνησίς* is among the three (*ἐπηρεασμός* and *ὕβρις*) kinds of slight that Aristotle (*Rh.* 2.2.3) lists as causes of anger. *Ὑπεροράω*: Aeschin. 1.67. *Hybris:* Dem. 21.7, 32, 43.71; Demosthenes 47.41 speaks of the *hybris* as directed at the assembly (*δῆμον*) who had first passed the law.
97 Cf. Lys. 6.52, Dem. 21.57, 25.27, 44.36, 59.28.
98 *Φύλακες*: Dem. 21.34, 177, 22.57, 24.36, 37, 25.6, 45, Aeschin. 1.7, Din.3.16; avenge: Antiph. 1.3, 24, Dem. 21.40.
99 See Chapter 7.
100 Dem. 24.138, 143, 152, 200, 211, 215, 218.
101 Konstan (2006: 69) has supposed that the anger referred to here belongs to an individual who ought to appeal 'to the courts' rather than seek 'individual vengeance', but in context that is clearly mistaken.
102 The irony here is that Demosthenes does not apparently want these jurors to render a fair conviction of the sort he refers to. He repeats (cf. Dem. 24.171) here a recommendation that the jurors ought not to listen to the defence and his supporters. This is a warning then, not against judging too quickly in anger but against *appearing* to have done so in the past. The important thing now is to guard their reputations with consistency, and that means punishing these men regardless of whether the jurors are convinced they have done wrong.
103 Failing to pull one's weight in battle tends to evoke *νέμεσις* in Homer (see p. 99), but could rouse Athenian jurors to anger (cf. Lys. 14 and 15).

104 It is worth distinguishing between the motives at work in legislators and punishers. Though some laws were enacted in a spirit of anger at some new offence that the community has discovered it needs to sanction, anger is not essential and some laws will have been enacted pre-emptively in anticipation of potentially harmful behaviour. But while the legislator need not feel anger, the punisher is expected to, and it is on the basis of that presumed anger that the threat of the law rests.

5 Moral Authority and the Appeal to Anger

1 Rubinstein (2004: 192) has made this point. Note also that only one anger appeal and no punishment appeals occur in *Against Leptines* (Dem. 20), an action brought beyond the one-year limit within which prosecution of the individual was permitted. Even this single appeal is probably not related to formal punishment. Apsephion, the speaker, urges the jurors to 'be angry' should anyone deny that their ancestors agreed with the principles that people should honour their benefactors and keep what has been given to them (Dem. 20.119). The jurors ought, he implies, to object vocally in their anger should they hear this sentiment from the defence.

2 According to Aristotle, *ἦθος* (character) is the most potent of the three kinds of proof which contribute to the art of rhetoric (*Rh.* 1.2.3–4).

3 Middle: Lys. 13.3, 48, 76, 76, 84, 84; there is also one use of the passive: 1. The other instances include a tentatively implied appeal, 'he will have the audacity to advise you that you ought not to take revenge' (Dem. 58.54), two appeals in a fragmentary speech (Hyp. 2.5, 10) and an appeal (Dem. 46.28) in the second speech from a trial in which the first speech (Dem. 45) has already called for *ὀργή* three times. The use of the middle voice also signifies that this prosecution is about more than simply homicide; cf. p. 176.

4 Note, however, that these are different procedures in that Agoratus has been arrested under *ἀπαγωγή* whereas Eratosthenes is probably facing an accounting (*εὔθυναι*), if the case occurred at all.

5 Cf. Lys. 25.5.

6 Examples of anger at false citizens: Dem. 57.3, 49; *καταφρόνησις* is sometimes explicitly given as a reason for *ὀργή*: Isoc. 20.22, Dem. 50.65–7; cf. Arist. *Rh.* 2.2.3–6.

7 On the debate over the meaning of *συνωνεῖσθαι*, see Seager (1966: 172–84) claiming that the law forbade stockpiling, and Figueira (1986: 149–71) claiming that the law forbade cartels; cf. Todd (2000: 238).

8 Having written this speech for posterity rather than the court, Isocrates may feel some licence to exaggerate these negative character traits but probably not to invent them altogether.

9 According to the traditional understanding of sycophancy – that it was motivated by money (the payment received by the successful volunteer prosecutor or that extorted from the defendant in order to drop the case) and not by revenge (for this view see MacDowell 1978: 62–3; Hansen 1991: 194–5, 405; E. Harris 2013b: 62; Alwine 2015: 70; Gagarin 2020: 3n6) – *Against Agoratus* cannot have been seen as sycophantic since the suit was brought by the alleged victim's brother and the speech delivered by his cousin and brother-in-law. However, this definition is clearly too narrow: sycophants could be personal enemies (See Kucharski 2009: 43–6, 2012: 191–2); cf. Phillips (2013: 33). More fundamental were the perceptions that the case was weak and that an individual was abusing the system for his own ends.

10 Cf. And. 1.86. Note also that the other prosecutions brought in apparent conflict with the amnesty (Lys. 6 and 30) both contain only a single anger appeal, and the defences make frequent accusations of sycophancy (Andoc. 1. 86, 93, 99, 104, 105, Lys. 25.3, 24, 27, 29). *Against Callimachus* (Isoc. 18), a *παραγραφή* delivered shortly after the restoration of the democracy, makes ten accusations of sycophancy (3, 7, 10, 14, 22, 24, 37, 43, 55, 64) and twice calls for anger (4, 26), but it is also unique among prosecution speeches for appealing against anger (36, 42), reflecting the fundamentally defensive nature of this procedure.

11 This is Harvey's (1990: 112–14) term and one of the few points of agreement with Osborne (1990: 93), who refers to 'improbable assumptions, empty assertions, and over-meticulous quibbling'; cf. Christ (1998: 50).

12 E. Harris (2006:384) translates the phrase as '"manifest," "clear," or "obvious"'.

13 On the debate surrounding *αὐτόφωρος*, see Carawan (2013: 125–7); Phillips (2008: 186–90); E. Harris (1994).

14 This is not a necessary quality of a sycophantic prosecution but it is a red flag (Dem. 41.23; cf. Harvey, 1990: 113–14) because, it was supposed, if a prosecutor genuinely felt wronged by the defendant he would retaliate as soon as possible; cf. Dem. 36.53, 41.23, 57.49.

15 Though, as I have explained, *Against Nicostratus* should not be expected to contain anger appeals since no punishment was available, the speaker could yet have called for anger as in *Against Leptines* (119). Note, then, that Apollodorus also feels the need to deny sycophancy ([Dem.] 53.1), perhaps for similar reasons to the prosecutor of the grain dealers.

16 Todd's (2000: 239) reference to the 'strident use of anti-metic rhetoric' is not supported by the text which mentions the metic status of one of the defendants, perhaps prejudicially, only once (Lys. 22.5). There is also an implication that non-citizens such as these ought to suffer worse punishment than citizens (16). But the criticisms found throughout the speech are directed towards grain dealers, not metics, while other presumed foreigners, grain-importers, are portrayed favourably by comparison (17, 21). That said, Seager (1966: 172–3) may be correct to suppose

that the inferior status of grain dealers as metics increased their vulnerability to sycophantic prosecutions.

17 Given that this is most likely an *εἰσαγγελία* or *ἔνδειξις* (cf. Todd, 2000: 237n3), procedures which offered no reward to prosecutors, the association of this kind of prosecution with sycophancy suggests that it was common for prosecutors to bring charges against grain dealers in the hope that the defendants would bribe them to drop the case.

18 On personal enmity as evidence against sycophancy, see Fisher (2001: 119–20), Alwine (2015: 70).

19 Harvey (1990), Osborne (1990); cf. Lofberg (1917), Harrison (1971: 60–2), MacDowell (1978: 62–6), Christ (1998: 48–71), Rubinstein (2000: 198–212).

20 Osborne (1990). The narrow 'money-grubbing' definition remains commonplace nonetheless: Hansen (1991: 194–5, 405), E. Harris (2013b: 62), Alwine (2015: 70), Gagarin (2020: 3n6).

21 Osborne (1990: 93).

22 The black-and-white view of prosecutors as motivated by either selfless civic-interest or by corrupt self-interest (E. Harris 2013b: 62–3) describes two stereotypes, neither of which actually existed as anything more substantial than a rhetorical construct.

23 Cf. Osborne (1990: 87).

24 See Chapter 7.

25 Plastow (2020: 89–118) also observes a more lax attitude to relevance in *Against Agoratus* in particular (93), indicating that it was the kind of court (and presumably the kind of audience) that determined how strictly one needed to stay on track, not the fact that the case was for a charge of homicide. Cf. Arist. *Rh.* 1.1.5.

26 These accusations appear during the defence of his father's involvement in the Mytilenean revolt (Ant. 5.74–80).

27 Cf. Todd (2000: 138–9).

28 Todd (1996: 120; 2000: 139–40). Jurors were often expected to be angry at crimes associated with the oligarchic regime: Lys. 23.2, 58, 80, 90, 96, 25.1, 5, 16, 18, 30.13, 23, Isoc. 18.36.

29 This section is an adapted version of a published paper: Whitchurch (2020). Libanius calls him Epichares but in the text only the speaker's grandfather receives the name.

30 Cf. Roisman (2005: 21–3).

31 See also Dem. 34.1, 53.13, 55.7, 59.14. Orators of all ages might claim inexperience (e.g. Dem. 48.1) or ignorance of the laws (e.g. Dem. 44.4) but the young especially, never having been jurors and bringing perhaps their first case, had the stronger claim.

32 Cf. Roisman (2005: 22).

33 For Rubinstein (2013: 141–2) the claim here is 'that the wrong verdict had been reached because the successful litigant had played the "orphan card", and that the emotion that had swayed the judges had been one of anger'; however, the reverse may just as easily be correct: that the jurors felt anger upon believing Theocrines'

allegation, meaning their anger was an appropriate product of their (allegedly misguided) conviction.

34 On this procedure, see Avotins (2004).

35 The contrast with *γέρων* 'old man' makes it clear that *παῖς* means 'boy' rather than 'son'. Charidemus is also referred to as a *παῖς* (Dem. 58.30–1).

36 On anger at false testimony, see pp. 167–9.

37 Dem. 58. 2, 6, 10–13, 23, 27, 37, 63–5.

38 Ariston says he might have brought public charges for cloak-theft or *hybris* but wanted neither to take on more than he was 'able to carry' nor 'to appear' (*φαίνομαι*) to be bringing such a prosecution at his age (Dem. 54.1); cf. Christ (1998: 59–60, 131); Dem. 58.57–9.

39 Youth was also a weakness for the defendant Callicles, whose father dammed a watercourse, causing seasonal flooding in his neighbours' land, but it was fifteen years later when the father had died that a suit was brought. Those bringing the suit are said to 'despise one so young as I am and so inexperienced in affairs' (Dem. 55.3–7).

40 On respect for elders, see Plat. *Rep.* 465a, Dem. 25.24, Aeschin. 1.23, 3.2, Plut. *An. Seni* 784c–d; Dover (1974: 102–8), Hansen (1991: 223–4).

41 Cf. *Ath. Const.* 63.3. On the make-up of juries see Hansen (1991: 181–6). Roisman (2005: 23) supposes that jurors would suspect that suits brought by young men were 'motivated by a typically excessive agonistic drive, attendant on youth, or by an improper search for notoriety at the expense of an elder and better'.

42 Dem. 54. 42; Isoc. 20. 3, 6, 9, 22; the beginning of *Against Lochites* is lost.

43 Dem. 54.1, 2, 8, 9, 10, 11, 13, 17, 20, 21, 24, 28, 32, 33, 37, 43.

44 Sanders (2012: 365–6) suggests that, compared to Demosthenes, whose accusation was obviously publicly offensive, Ariston has to wait until 'the idea of *hybris* will have lodged firmly enough in the jury's mind' before appealing to anger.

45 Dem. 58.1–4.

46 The precise nature of the *ἔνδειξις* procedure is debated but it is generally agreed that it involved a denunciation before the magistrates and perhaps a subsequent arrest by the prosecutor. See Hansen (1976: esp. 9–24).

47 Epichares labels this an act of *ἀποστέρησις* (fraud; Dem. 58.20).

48 For example: Lys. 29.11–13 (public debt), Isoc. 15.19, 139 (sycophancy), Dem. 57.3 (false-citizenship).

49 'Older men' (*πρεσβυτέρων*) have told him that pardon should never be shown to law-breakers (58.24) and that it is a mistake to believe that men like Theocrines are important for the running of the state (62).

50 Epichares' pitiful description of himself receiving no mercy from Theocrines, even as he clasped the man's knees and begged for a lenient penalty (Dem. 58.70), is an evocative attempt to win similar mercilessness from the jurors towards Theocrines now and exemplifies how a speaker can seek to manipulate emotions without naming them.

51 According to Libanius' hypothesis, this speech was often thought to be private even in antiquity.

52 The phrase *ἡγησάμην δεῖν ἐπὶ τῷ τιμωρεῖσθαι μεθ' ὑμῶν* (Dem. 58.1) means that he thinks it necessary to take vengeance either 'with the help of' the jurors or 'along with' them and may even be intentionally ambiguous, but given that it is preceded by a description purely of how Theocrines has wronged Epichares' father, it seems that private vengeance is all that is meant.

6 Public Offence and Private Procedure

1 Herman (2006: 191–4) adduces only public cases as evidence of this but, as we have seen, the success of public prosecutions hinged on being able to persuade the jurors that they, not the prosecutor, had been offended. It seems to me that if there were any evidence for this model, it would have to be found in cases where the offence is clearly private.

2 Rubinstein (2004: 191–2).

3 Cf. Rubinstein (2004: 192; 2005: 139–40); Isoc. 18, Lys. 10, Dem. 45, [47]. As noted by Rubinstein (201–2 n15) *δίκαι αἰκίας* may have carried the possibility of an *epōbelia* but [Dem.] 47.64 probably means that the speaker in this case is referring to his having paid court fees.

4 Other *παραγραφαί*: Dem. 32, 33, 36, 37, 38. The only other instance in a *παραγραφή* (Dem. 35.56) occurs in a defence (cf. p. 170).

5 *Δίκαι ψευδομαρτυριῶν*: Is. 3, 6.

6 Rubinstein (2016: 59) also convincingly suggests that the personalities of authors and their clients influenced whether they would make these appeals; this need not conflict with the more general standards explored here.

7 *Against Polycles* is certainly concerned with claiming damages but we cannot be sure that it was a *δίκη βλάβης*. I suspect, like Ballin (1978: 43–4), that it was, but see Gernet (1955: 177). Cf. E. Cohen (1973: 14n31).

8 For similar, see Dem. 27, 30, 39, 41.

9 Appeals for the jurors to vote a certain way: Isoc. 17.56, 58, Dem. 28.23, 39.40; to be fair or just: Dem. 38.28, 39.40–1. Other appeals include: to help the speaker (Dem. 27.3, 28.24, 40.3, 18, 61, 49.69, 56.4, 46) or to hear him (Isoc. 17.35; Dem. 37.3).

10 The extra charge for intentional damage in the *δίκη βλάβης* is most likely to have been payable to the plaintiff, not the state, cf. Dem. 21.43, MacDowell (1978: 151), E. Harris (2013b: 122); but Saunders (1991: 102) suggests the state receives it.

11 On false testimony, see pp. 167–9.

12 For Rubinstein (2016: 58; cf. 2004: 198), the speaker 'stops short of exhorting the judges themselves to take revenge (*timōreisthai* or *dikēn lambanein*)'. But I have

taken the sarcastic remark at Lys. 10.30 (*οὐ γὰρ πω ἤδη ὅτι ὑμεῖς τοὺς μὲν ἰδόντας τιμωρεῖσθε, τοῖς δὲ ἀποβαλοῦσι συγγνώμην ἔχετε*) as an implicit appeal since this observation that the previous trial's jurors had taken vengeance on the wrong man is surely a recommendation that they now remedy that error.

13 On the young Alcibiades case, see pp. 137–8, cf. Lys. 14.9. The speech is fragmentary, increasingly so towards the end where appeals tend to occur more frequently.

14 The jurors may well have taken offence not only at his cowardice in fleeing the city but also at his role in the destruction of Troezen, a city that retained a special relationship with Athens as a result of the help it had given the city by harbouring its women and children during the battle of Salamis in 480 (Hyp. 3.32). Hyperides attempts to portray Athenogenes' act against Troezen as almost treasonous by contrasting it with the Athenians' decision to honour their historic helpers by offering them sanctuary.

15 Ariston's escalatory chain of offences begins not with violence but with slander because it may provoke violence (Dem. 54.17–18) and the inherent public interest in the crime of slander is implied by the fact that the penalty it incurred went partly to the treasury. So, although the appeals to *ὀργή* and *τιμωρία* in *Against Theomnestus* all appear related to the accusation of cowardice (see above), it may on occasion have been possible to evoke anger over slander simply on the grounds that it was an inherently *hybristic* act that could precipitate escalatory violence.

16 Note the use of *κόλασις* to indicate concern about the future, but in the context of anger about the past at an act of *hybris* against what might easily have been one of them.

17 *Hybris* terms: Isoc. 20.2, 4, 5, 7, 9, 11, 15, 16; αἰκία terms: 5, 15. Mirhady's (and Too 2000: 123) suggestion that this prosecutor 'attempts to obscure whether the speech arose from a *γραφὴ ὕβρεως* or a *δίκη αἰκείας*' is impractical – the charge was posted in public and the jurors would surely recognise the short length of the speech and be (made) aware of what penalties were available at the end.

18 On *hybris,* see pp. 126–36.

19 It is now widely accepted that the original suit would proceed in the event that the *παραγραφή* should fail: Harrison (1971: 107), MacDowell (1978: 215), Hansen (2001: 196), Phillips (2013: 14).

20 See Chapter 5 on sycophancy.

21 Cf. Carawan (2013: 91–100).

22 Bonner and Smith (1938: 262–3); Todd (1990b: 37).

23 On numbers of jurors, see Hansen (1991: 186–8).

24 Hansen (1982: 114–15); Rubinstein (2000: 69).

25 Referring to both lying under oath (*ἐπιορκία*) and false testimony (*ψευδομαρτυρία*) as 'perjury' is common practice (e.g. Plescia 1970: 88; D. Cohen 1995: 107; Allen 2000: 239; E. Harris 2013b: 364), but note that witnesses were not always under oath (though, like Stephanus, they could choose to be; Dem. 45.58) and so anger felt at

ψευδομαρτυρία was over an offence against the jurors themselves rather than the gods (cf. Todd 1990b: 36).

26 There is just one formulaic appeal for τιμωρία in the second prosecution speech from this trial (Dem. 46.28) made without apparent justification, the jurors' motivation for punishment having already been established in the first speech. The second speech must answer the challenges thrown up by the defendant's response. It seems that Stephanus has focused on refuting Apollodorus' factual claims – namely that the deposition on which the case rests is inaccurate (1) – rather than the implications of those facts for the jurors' verdict.

27 Rubinstein's (2004: 194; cf. 2005: 144) proposition that 'a speaker who appealed too strongly and too openly to negative dicastic emotions against his relatives, and who was too vehement in expressing his desire for personal revenge, would very likely have met with precisely the type of resentment that he wanted to stir up against his opponent' is certainly supported (e.g. Dem. 48.8), but this demonstrates that it could also work the other way; Christ (1998: 169). The idea that jurors should be angrier when false testimony victimises kin echoes the sentiment of Lysias' *Against Diogeiton*, a prosecution of a dishonest guardian, which bases its solitary call for anger on the claim that 'Diogeiton is establishing in all men such suspicion towards others that neither the living nor the dead can trust any more in their nearest relations than in their most hated enemies' (Lys. 32.19). Jurors did not, I think, feel slighted by people mistreating their kin, but they did rely on certain assumptions about family when making judgements and thus felt angrier when false witnesses exploited their trust in the norm of familial loyalty.

28 Rubinstein (2016: 57–8) has found that τιμωρ- words are almost (perhaps completely) absent from inscribed laws.

29 The διαμαρτυρία was likely an old procedure, gradually superseded in the fourth century by the παραγραφή (cf. Gernet, 1955: 83). It probably retained a role in inheritance disputes because they tended to result in διαδικασίαι which involved no defendant or prosecutor and therefore no one to initiate or face a παραγραφή (Isager and Hansen, 1975: 135–7); cf. Harrison (1971: 127–9), MacDowell (1978: 211–13), Todd (1993: 137n18).

30 Cf. Johnstone (1999: 27–8), Bonner (1969: 190).

31 Another prosecutor in a similar case makes a similar complaint (Is. 6.3–4) and a litigant in a διαδικασία asserts that he forwent the option of a διαμαρτυρία to prevent accusations of avoiding justice (7.3); cf. Christ (1998: 213–16).

32 Our other παραγραφή defendant also attempts to portray the trial as being of personal interest to the jurors when he says that his opponent and his associates not only do wrong to those with whom they do business, but also do public injury to the Athenian market (Dem. 34.51–2). That only these two of the defence speeches make such appeals reflects the role reversal that occurred in παραγραφαί.

33 Christ (1998: 186–7) has pointed to Androcles' attempts to play on 'Athenian prejudice towards outsiders', Lacritus being a metic.

34 Cf. Bonner (1969: 189–90). Christ (1998: 217) understands Apollodorus (Dem. 45.5–6) to be attacking the use of a *παραγραφή* as 'devious' and not just the 'suborning of witnesses'.

35 E.g. Dem. 34.4, 45.6; Christ (1998: 216–18).

36 Speeches which excuse the bringing of the suit or deflect blame onto the defendant include Dem. 27, 30, 39, 41.

7 Homicide, Impiety and the Myth of Angerless Punishment

1 Ehrenberg (1969: 21).

2 Wolff (1946: 81); cf. Smith (1924: 7–10).

3 Antiph. 1.23, 23, 24, 24, 25.

4 Scholars once took for granted that homicide in Greece was treated as a criminal offence (e.g. Thonissen 1875: 80n2; cf. Leist 1884: 379). Calhoun's (1927: 9–11; cf. Bonner and Smith, 1930: 63) framing of homicide as a private matter subject to a *δίκη* is now widely accepted (cf. Evjen 1970: 414–15, Gagarin 1979: 322–3; but MacDowell 1963: 133–5 and Hansen 1981 argue for the existence of a *γραφή* too). Procedure aside, D. Cohen (2005a: 227–8) has argued that the threat of pollution and political instability would have made homicide a matter of public concern; but Carawan (1998: 377) maintains that 'the *dike* remains quintessentially a matter of private liability: it does not allow much scope for the judges to determine the deeper wrong to the greater community'.

5 Cf. Dem. 54.18–19.

6 On the supposition that Herodes was a cleruch, see Gagarin (2011: 52).

7 On the procedure, see Carawan (2013: 150–3).

8 Lys. 12.58, 80, 90, 96.

9 This speech is from an *ἀπαγωγή* and so is not under the same rhetorical restrictions as those made before the Areopagus. The homicide accusation explains the absence of anger appeals in part, but the appeals to *τιμωρεῖσθαι* reveal a clear interest in the jurors' anger and demand another explanation (pp. 145–9).

10 Lys. 13.92, 93, 94, 95, 97.

11 Cf. Cairns (2015: 662–3).

12 See Burkert (1984: 77) on pollution and guilt.

13 That Antiphon authored the tetralogies is uncertain; cf. Plastow (2020: 10–11).

14 Since they were not (designed to be) heard in court, the usefulness of the tetralogies as sources is questionable. Parker's (1983: 130, cf. 108; Williams, 1993: 189n28;

Carawan, 1998: 192–8; S. Johnston 1999: 128; contra E. Harris, 2015: 15n20) claim – that 'the author of the *Tetralogies* has taken the doctrine of pollution to a theoretical extreme some way beyond the level of unease that it in practice created' – seems fair. Relatives and jurors clearly were motivated by emotions associated with the thought of the unavenged dead, even if not everyone felt the threat to the extent that the tetralogies suggest.

15 On *ἐνθύμιος*, see Hatch (1908: 172–5), Parker (1983: 253–4).

16 Parker (1983: 106); cf. S. Johnston (1999: 129), Plastow (2020: 53).

17 On *ἀλιτήριος,* see Hatch (1908: 157–62), Phillips (2008: 209).

18 See Mossman (1999: 172–3) on victims' anger being a threat to the whole city.

19 MacDowell (1963) attributes three goals to homicide punishment: deterrence, vengeance and the cleansing of pollution. It seems to me that the act of vengeance is precisely the cleansing that pollution demands; any other purification such as ritual cleansing occurs outside the context of punishment.

20 This evidence presents a challenge to Parker's (1983: 126) argument that the place we should expect to see 'a belief in murder-pollution is in a society without courts' and that it was beginning to 'wither away' in fifth-century Athens. 'If Orestes had been taken in charge by a policeman', Parker hypothesises (125), 'there would have been no need for the Erinyes.' But why would this 'policeman' make the arrest? Why would a prosecutor bring charges and the jurors convict? Normally, such acts were motivated primarily by anger. But this motivation had no (legitimate) place in homicide trials. Instead, we see pollution and the associated feelings of guilt, shame and fear. The distribution of evidence for pollution (none in Homer; plenty in the classical sources) resists Parker's thesis. (Though the evidence in the orators is thinner than we might expect, recent studies have shown it to be substantial nonetheless; E. Harris 2015: 18–19; Plastow 2020: 62–80; cf. Arnaoutoglou 1993: 122–3.) Perhaps then, pollution actually became *more* important as the state increased its control over blood-vengeance: in a society where justice relies on the family, anger will motivate revenge; but in a society where justice must pass through people with little or no personal attachment to the deceased, anger will need to be supplemented with the guilt, shame and fear associated with pollution.

21 Plastow (2020: 52–3) has taken the fact that both homicide and impiety caused pollution as an indication that the cause of pollution was the offending of divinities.

22 Other examples of appeals for dicastic anger over impiety: Dem. 21.34, 147, 175, Lyc. 1.27; for self-interested vengeance (*τιμωρεῖσθαι*): Dem. 19.87, 21.227, [59.]77, 117, Lyc. 1.76, 146.

23 See S. Johnston (1999: 127–60) on those who have died a violent death, and especially pp. 148–55 on the link between the dead's dishonour and the threat they consequently pose.

24 D. Cohen (2005a: 228) distinguishes between private blood-vengeance and the non-vengeful punishment of the courts in homicide cases.

Conclusion

1 Lumet (1957:0:55:45).
2 Lumet (1957:0:59:03).

Appendix

1 Rubinstein does count each different term used in a given chapter e.g. *ταῖς ἐσχάταις ζημίαις κολάζεσθαι* (Lys. 12.36).
2 Cf. Kucharski (2012: 106–7).

Bibliography

Adkins, A. W. H. (1960a), '"Honour" and "Punishment" in the Homeric Poems', *Bulletin of the Institute of Classical Studies* 7: 23–32.
Adkins, A. W. H. (1960b), *Merit and Responsibility: A Study in Greek Values*, Oxford.
Adkins, A. W. H. (1969), 'Threatening, Abusing and Feeling Angry in the Homeric Poems', *The Journal of Hellenic Studies* 89: 7–21.
Adkins, A. W. H. (1972), *Moral Values and Political Behaviour in Ancient Greece: From Homer to the End of the Fifth Century*, London.
Adkins, A. W. H. (1982), 'Values, Goals, and Emotions in the *Iliad*', *Classical Philology* 77(4): 292–326.
Allen, D. S. (2000), *The World of Prometheus: The Politics of Punishing in Democratic Athens*, Princeton.
Allen, D. S. (2003), 'Angry Bees, Wasps, and Jurors: The Symbolic Politics of *Ὀργή* in Athens', in *Ancient Anger Perspectives from Homer to Galen*, edited by S. M. Braund and G. W. Most, New York, 76–98.
Allen, D. S. (2005), 'Greek Tragedy and Law', in *The Cambridge Companion to Ancient Greek Law*, edited by M. Gagarin and D. Cohen, Cambridge, 374–93.
Alwine, A. (2015), *Enmity and Feuding in Classical Athens*, Austin.
Andersen, Ø. (1976), 'Some Thoughts on the Shield of Achilles', *Symbolae Osloenses* 51: 5–18.
'A Film Locks Itself up in the Jury Room', (1957, April 22), *The Times*, 10.
Arnaoutoglou, I. (1993), 'Pollution in the Athenian Homicide Law', *Revue Internationale des Droits de l'Antiquité* 40: 109–37.
Avotins, I. (2004), 'Athenaion Politeia 56.6 and the Protection of the Weak', *The Classical Quarterly* 54(2): 461–9.
Avramovic, S. (2017), 'Blood-Money in Homer – Role of *Istor* in the Trial Scene on the Shield of Achilles (*Il.* 18, 497–508)', *Zbornik Pravnog Fakulteta u Zagrebu* 67(5): 723–56.
Ballin, T. (1978), 'A Commentary on [Demosthenes] 50, Against Polykles', University of Washington.
Barton, C. K. B. (1999), *Getting Even: Revenge as a Form of Justice*, Chicago.
Basile, G. (2018), 'Homeric *Ἴστωρ* and Oath-Taking', *Cuadernos de Filología Clásica, Estudios Griegos e Indoeuropeos* 28: 17–39.
Batson, C., M. Chao and J. Givens (2009), 'Pursuing Moral Outrage: Anger at Torture', *Journal of Experimental Social Psychology* 45: 155–60.
Batson, C., et al. (2007), 'Anger at Unfairness: Is It Moral Outrage?' *European Journal of Social Psychology* 37: 1272–85.
Becker, A. (1995), *The Shield of Achilles and the Poetics of Ekphrasis*, Lanham.

Beekes, R. S. P. (2010), *Etymological Dictionary of Greek*, Leiden.
Berent, M. (2000), 'Anthropology and the Classics: War, Violence and the Stateless *Polis*', *The Classical Quarterly* 50(1): 257–89.
Bers, V. (1985), 'Dikastic "Thorubos"', *History of Political Thought* 6(1): 1–15.
Beye, C. (1964), 'Homeric Battle Narrative and Catalogues', *Harvard Studies in Classical Philology* 68: 345–73.
Biscardi, A. (1982), *Diritto Greco Antico*, Milan.
Black-Michaud, J. (1975), *Cohesive Force: Feud in the Mediterranean and the Middle East*, New York.
Blundell, M. (1989), *Helping Friends and Harming Enemies: A Study in Sophocles and Greek Ethics*, Cambridge.
Boddice, R. (2016), *The Science of Sympathy: Morality, Evolution, and Victorian Civilization*, Champaign.
Boddice, R. (2017), 'The History of Emotions: Past, Present, Future', *Revista de Estudios Sociales* 62: 10–15.
Boehm, C. (1984), *Blood Revenge: The Enactment and Management of Conflict in Montenegro and Other Tribal Societies*, Philadelphia.
Bonner, R. J., and G. Smith (1930), *The Administration of Justice from Homer to Aristotle*, Vol. 1. Chicago.
Bonner, R. J., and G. Smith (1938), *The Administration of Justice from Homer to Aristotle*, Vol. 2. Chicago.
Bonner, R. J. (1969), *Lawyers and Litigants in Ancient Athens: The Genesis of the Legal Profession*, New York.
Bourdieu, P. (1965), 'The Sentiment of Honour in Kabyle Society', in *Honour and Shame: The Values of Mediterranean Society*, edited by J. G. Peristiany, London, 191–241.
Bourdieu, P. ([1972] 1977), *Outline of a Theory of Practice*, Cambridge.
Bowie, E. (2007), '"Early Expatriates: Displacement and Exile in Archaic Poetry', in *Writing Exile: The Discourse of Displacement in Greco-Roman Antiquity and Beyond*, edited by J. Gaertner, Leiden, 21–49.
Burkert, W. (1984), *Greek Religion*, Oxford.
Burnett, A. P. (1998), *Revenge in Attic and Later Tragedy*, Berkeley.
Cairns, D. L. (1993), Aidōs*: The Psychology and Ethics of Honour and Shame in Ancient Greek Literature*, Oxford.
Cairns, D. L. (1996), '*Hybris*, Dishonour, and Thinking Big', *The Journal of Hellenic Studies* 116: 1–32.
Cairns, D. L. (2003), 'Ethics, Ethology, Terminology: Iliadic Anger and the Cross-Cultural Study of Emotion', in *Ancient Anger: Perspectives from Homer to Galen*, edited by S. M. Braund and G. W. Most, Cambridge, 11–49.
Cairns, D. L. (2011a), 'Honour and Shame: Modern Controversies and Ancient Values', *The Classical Quarterly* 53(1): 23–41.
Cairns, D. L. (2011b), 'Ransom and Revenge in the *Iliad*', in *Sociable Man*, edited by S. D. Lambert. Swansea, 87–116.

Cairns, D. L. (2015), 'Revenge, Punishment, and Justice in Athenian Homicide Law', *Journal of Value Inquiry* 49(4): 645–65.
Calhoun, G. M. (1927), *The Growth of Criminal Law in Ancient Greece*, Berkeley.
Cammack, D. (2019), 'The *Dēmos* in *Dēmokratia*', *The Classical Quarterly* 69(1): 42–61.
Canevaro, M. (2013), *Documents in the Attic Orators: Laws and Decrees in the Public Speeches of the Demosthenic Corpus*, Oxford.
Canevaro, M. (2019), 'L'Accusa Pubblica di *Hybris* Contro gli Schiavi: L'Onore della Vittima e l'Onore dell'Hybristes', in ΥΒΡΙΣ, Vol. 9, *Rivista di Diritto Ellenico*, edited by C. Pelloso and P. C. Ghiggia. 43–90.
Canevaro, M., and E. Harris (2019), 'The Authenticity of the Document at Demosth., in Mid. XXI.47', in ΥΒΡΙΣ, Vol. 9, *Rivista di Diritto Ellenico*, edited by C. Pelloso and P. C. Ghiggia, 91–108.
Cantarella, E. (1976), *Studi Sull'omicidio in Diritto Greco e Romano*, Milan.
Cantarella, E. (2001), 'Private Revenge and Public Justice: The Settling of Disputes in Homer's *Iliad*', *Punishment & Society* 3(4): 473–83.
Cantarella, E. (2002), 'Dispute Settlement in Homer: Once Again on the Shield of Achilles', in *Mélanges en l'honneur Panayotis D. Dimakis*, Athens, 147–65.
Cantarella, E. (2011), '*ΑΙΤΙΟΣ*. Archeologia di un Concetto', in *I diritti degli altri in Grecia e a Roma*, Sankt Augustin, 45–74.
Carawan, E. (1998), *Rhetoric and the Law of Draco*, Oxford.
Carawan, E. (2013), *The Athenian Amnesty and Reconstructing the Law*, Oxford.
Carey, C. (1994), 'Rhetorical Means of Persuasion', in *Persuasion: Greek Rhetoric in Action*, edited by I. Worthington, London, 26–45.
Carey, C. (2013), 'In Search of Drakon', *The Cambridge Classical Journal* 59: 29–51.
Carlier, P. (1984), *La Rouyauté En Grèce Avant Alexandre*, Strasbourg.
Chantraine, P. (1968), *Dictionnaire Étymologique de la Langue Grecque Histoire des Mots*, Paris.
Christ, M. (1998), *The Litigious Athenian*, Baltimore.
Clarke, H. W. (1967), *The Art of the* Odyssey, Englewood Cliffs.
Clarke, M. (1999), *Flesh and Spirit in the Songs of Homer: A Study of Words and Myths*, Oxford.
Clay, J. (1983), *The Wrath of Athena: Gods and Men in the Odyssey*, Princeton.
Cohen, D. (1995), *Law, Violence, and Community in Classical Greece*, Cambridge.
Cohen, D. (2005a), 'Crime, Punishment, and the Rule of Law in Classical Athens', in *The Cambridge Companion to Ancient Greek Law*, edited by M. Gagarin and D. Cohen, Cambridge, 211–35.
Cohen, D. (2005b), 'Theories of Punishment', in *The Cambridge Companion to Ancient Greek Law*, edited by M. Gagarin and D. Cohen, Cambridge, 170–90.
Cohen, E. E. (1973), *Ancient Athenian Maritime Courts*, Princeton.
Cohen, E. E. (2000), *The Athenian Nation*, Princeton.
Considine, P. (1966), 'Some Homeric Terms for Anger', *Acta Classica* 9: 15–25.
Cook, E. F. (1995), *The* Odyssey *in Athens: Myths of Cultural Origins*, Ithaca.
Cope, E. (1877), *Commentary on the Rhetoric of Aristotle*, Cambridge.

Cragg, W. (1992), *The Practice of Punishment*, London.

Crielaard, J. P. (1995), 'Homer, History and Archaeology: Some Remarks on the Date of the Homeric World', in *Homeric Questions*, edited by J. P. Crielaard, Amsterdam, 201–88.

Crielaard, J. P. (2002), 'Past or Present? Epic Poetry, Aristocratic Self-Representation and the Concept of Time in the Eighth and Seventh Centuries BC', in *Omero tremila anni dopo*, edited by F. Montanari and P. Ascheri, Rome, 239–95.

Crielaard, J. P. (2009), 'Cities', in *A Companion to Archaic Greece*, edited by K. Raaflaub and H. van Wees, Chichester, 349–72.

Crielaard, J. P. (2020), 'Homeric Communities', in *The Cambridge Guide to Homer*, edited by C. O. Pache, Cambridge, 225–44.

Cummins, P. (2003), 'Working with Anger', in *International Handbook of Personal Construct Psychology*, Chichester, 83–91.

Daly, M., and M. Wilson (1988), *Homicide*, New York.

Daude, C. (2007), 'Pourquoi Je Crois Que, Tout Compte Fait, Homère ne Désapprouve pas la Colère d'Achille', in *Troika: Parcours Antiques: Mélanges Offerts à Michel Woronoff*, edited by S. David and E. Geny, Besançon, 39–62.

Dawe, R. (1993), *The* 'Odyssey'*: Translation and Analysis*, Lewes.

Dickie, M. W. (1978), '*Dike* as a Moral Term in Homer and Hesiod', *Classical Philology* 73(2): 91–101.

Donlan, W. (1989), 'The Pre-State Community in Greece', *Symbolae Osloenses* 64(1): 5–29.

Donlan, W. (1993), 'Duelling with Gifts in the *Iliad*: As the Audience Saw It', *Colby Quarterly* 29(3): 155–72.

Dover, K. (1974), *Greek Popular Morality in the Time of Plato and Aristotle*, Cambridge.

Dow, J. (2015), *Passions and Persuasion in Aristotle's* Rhetoric, Oxford.

Edwards, M. W. (1987), *Homer: Poet of the Iliad*, London.

Edwards, M. W. (1991), *The* Iliad*: A Commentary, Books 17–20*, Vol. 5, Cambridge.

Ehrenberg, V. (1969), *The Greek State*, 2nd edn, London.

Ekman, P. (1999), 'Basic Emotions', in *Handbook of Cognition and Emotion*, edited by T. Dalgleish and M. Power, Chichester, 45–60.

Elias, N. ([1939] 2000), *The Civilizing Process: Sociogenetic and Psychogenetic Investigations*, Oxford.

Elmer, D. F. (2013), *The Poetics of Consent: Collective Decision Making in the* Iliad, Baltimore.

Elster, J. (1990), 'Norms of Revenge', *Ethics* 100(4): 862–85.

Erler, M. (2019), 'Role as Norm, Role and Norm: Homer's Hero, Hesiod's Just City, and Plato's *Kallipolis*', *Frontiers of Philosophy in China* 1: 14–28.

Evjen, H. D. (1970), '*ΑΠΟΓΩΓΗ* and Athenian Homicide Procedures', *Revue d'Histoire du Droit* 38: 403–15.

Faraguna, M. (2006), 'Tra Oralità e Scrittura: Dritto e Forme della Comunicazione dai Poemi Omerici a Teofrasto', Dike – *Rivista di Storia del Diritto Greco ed Ellenistico* 9: 63–91.

Farenga, V. (2006), *Citizen and Self in Ancient Greece: Individuals Performing Justice and the Law*, Cambridge.

Fehr, E., and U. Fischbacher (2004), 'Third-party punishment and social norms', *Evolution and Human Behaviour*, 25: 63–87.

Feinberg, J. (1970), *Doing and Deserving*, Princeton.

Feldman Barrett, L. (2006a), 'Are Emotions Natural Kinds?', *Perspectives on Psychological Science* 1(1): 28–58.

Feldman Barrett, L. (2006b), 'Solving the Emotion Paradox: Categorization and the Experience of Emotion', *Personality and Social Psychology Review* 10(1): 20–46.

Feldman Barrett, L. (2017), *How Emotions Are Made: The Secret Life of the Brain*, Boston.

FeldmanHall, O., et al. (2014), 'Fairness Violations Elicit Greater Punishment on Behalf of Another than for Oneself', *Nature Communications* 5: 5306.

Figueira, T. (1986), '*Sitopōlai* and *Sitophulakes* in Lysias' Against the Graindealers: Governmental Intervention in the Athenian Economy', *Phoenix* 40: 149–71.

Finley, M. I. ([1954] 1977), *The World of Odysseus*, 2nd edn, Harmondsworth.

Finley, M. I. ([1953] 1981), *Economy and Society in Ancient Greece*, London.

Fisher, N. R. E. (1992), Hybris*: A Study in the Values of Honour and Shame in Ancient Greece*, Warminster.

Fisher, N. R. E. (1995), '*Hybris*, Status and Slavery', in *The Greek World*, edited by A. Powell, London, 44–84.

Fisher, N. R. E. (2001), *Aeschines Against Timarchos*, Oxford.

Fisher, N. R. E. (2017), 'Demosthenes and the Use of Disgust', in *Disgust: An Ancient Emotion*, edited by D. Lateiner and D. Spatharas, Oxford, 103–24.

Forsdyke, S. (2018), 'Ancient and Modern Conceptions of the Rule of Law', in *Ancient Greek History and Contemporary Social Science*, edited by M. Canevaro, A. Erskine, B. Gray, and J. Ober, Edinburgh, 184–212.

Foucault, M. ([1977] 1991), *Discipline and Punish: The Birth of the Prison*, London.

Freese, J. H. (1926), *Aristotle in 23 Volumes*, Vol. 22, Cambridge.

Frisch, H. (1976), *Might and Right in Antiquity*, New York.

Frisk, H. (1946), '*ΜΗΝΙΣ*: Zur Geschichte eines Begriffes', *Eranos* 44: 28–40.

Gagarin, M. (1973), '*Dikē* in the Works and Days', *Classical Philology* 68(2): 81–94.

Gagarin, M. (1979), 'The Prosecution of Homicide in Athens', *Greek, Roman and Byzantine Studies* 20(4): 301–23.

Gagarin, M. (1981), *Drakon and Early Athenian Homicide Law*, London.

Gagarin, M. (1986), *Early Greek Law*, Berkeley.

Gagarin, M. (2008), *Writing Greek Law*, Cambridge.

Gagarin, M. (2011), *Speeches from Athenian Law*, Austin.

Gagarin, M. (2020), *Democratic Law in Classical Athens*, Austin.

Garlan, Y. (1975), *War in the Ancient World*, London.

Geddes, A. (1984), 'Who's Who in Homeric Society', *The Classical Quarterly* 34(1): 17–36.

Gehrke, H. J. (1987), 'Die Griechen und die Rache, Ein Versuch in Historischer Psychologie', *Saeculum* 38: 121–49.

Gernet, L. (1917), *Recherches sur le Développement de la Pensée Juridique et Morale en Grèce*, Paris.
Gernet, L. (1955), *Droit et Société dans la Grèce Ancienne*, Paris.
Gonzalez Merino, J. I. (2013), 'El Final de la Nekuia (Od. 568–640)', *Cuadernos de Filología Clásica, Estudios Griegos e Indoeuropeos* 23: 71–81.
Gouldner, A. (1967), *Enter Plato: Classical Greece and the Origins of Social Theory*, London.
Graziosi, B., and J. Haubold (2003), 'Homeric Masculinity: *Ἠνορέη* and *Ἀγηνορίη*', *The Journal of Hellenic Studies* 123: 60–76.
Grethlein, J. (2009), 'From "Imperishable Glory" to History: The *Iliad* and the Trojan War', in *Epic and History*, edited by D. Konstan and K. Raaflaub, Chichester, 122–44.
Griffin, J. (1978), 'The Divine Audience and the Religion of the *Iliad*', *The Classical Quarterly* 28: 1–22.
Grinin, L. E. (2004), 'Democracy and Early State', *Social Evolution & History* 3(2): 93–149.
Grote, G. (1851), *A History of Greece; From the Earliest Period to the Close of the Generation Contemporary with Alexander the Great*, Vol. 5, 2nd edn, London.
Haidt, J. (2003), 'The Moral Emotions', in *Handbook of Affective Sciences*, edited by R. Davidson, K. Scherer, and H. Goldsmith, Oxford, 852–70.
Hall, J. (2013), 'The Rise of State Action in the Archaic Age', in *A Companion to Ancient Greek Government*, edited by H. A. Beck, Oxford, 7–21.
Hammer, D. (1998), 'Homer, Tyranny, and Democracy', *Greek, Roman and Byzantine Studies* 39(4): 331–60.
Hammer, D. (2002), *The* Iliad *as Politics: The Performance of Political Thought*, Norman.
Hansen, M. H. (1976), Apagoge, Endeixis *and* Ephegesis *Against* Kakagourgoi, Atimoi, *and* Pheugontes, Odense.
Hansen, M. H. (1981), 'The Prosecution of Homicide in Athens: A Reply', *Greek, Roman and Byzantine Studies* 22(1): 11–30.
Hansen, M. H. (1982), '*Atimia* a Consequence of Private Debts', in *Symposion 1977: Vorträge zur Griechischen und Hellenistischen Rechtsgeschichte*, edited by J. Modrzejewski and D. Liebs, Cologne, 113–20.
Hansen, M. H. (1991), *The Athenian Democracy in the Age of Demosthenes: Structure, Principles, and Ideology*, Oxford.
Hansen, M. H. (2002), 'Was the *Polis* a State or Stateless Society?', in *Even More Studies in the Ancient Greek* Polis, edited by T. H. Nielsen, Stuttgart, 17–48.
Harris, E. (1989), 'Demosthenes' Speech Against Meidias', *Harvard Studies in Classical Philology* 92: 117–36.
Harris, E. (1992), 'Review: Demosthenes: Against Meidias (Oration 21) by Douglas M. MacDowell', *Classical Philology* 87(1): 71–80.
Harris, E. (2006), *Democracy and the Rule of Law in Classical Athens*, Cambridge.
Harris, E. (2008), *Demosthenes, Speeches 20–22*, Austin.
Harris, E. (2013a), 'The Against Meidias (Dem. 21)', in *The Documents in the Attic Orators: Laws and Decrees in the Public Speeches of the Demosthenic Corpus*, edited by M. Canevaro, Oxford, 209–36.

Harris, E. (2013b), *The Rule of Law in Action in Democratic Athens*, Oxford.

Harris, E. (2015), 'The Family, the Community and Murder: The Role of Pollution in Athenian Homicide Law', in *Public and Private in Ancient Mediterranean Law and Religion*, edited by C. Ando and J. Rüpke, Berlin, 11–36.

Harris, E. (2017), 'How to "Act" in an Athenian Court: Emotions and Forensic Performance', in *The Theatre of Justice: Aspects of Performance in Greco-Roman Oratory and Rhetoric*, Vol. 403, *Mnemosyne, Supplements*, edited by S. Papaioannou, A. Serafim, and B. da Vela, Leiden, 223–42.

Harris, E. (2018), 'The Athenian View of an Athenian Trial', in *Use and Abuse of Law in the Athenian Courts*, edited by C. Carey, I. Giannadaki, and B. Griffith-Williams, Leiden, 42–74.

Harris, E. (2019), '*Hybris* nelle Corti Giudiziarie Ateniesi: Il Profilo Legale dell'Accusa nella Contro Midia di Demostene', in *ΥΒΡΙΣ*, Vol. 9, *Rivista di Diritto Ellenico*, edited by C. Pelloso and P. C. Ghiggia, 143–70.

Harris, W. (2001), *Restraining Rage: The Ideology of Anger Control in Classical Antiquity*, Harvard.

Harrison, A. R. W. (1968), *The Law of Athens, Volume 1: Family and Property*, Oxford.

Harrison, A. R. W. (1971), *The Law of Athens, Volume 2: Procedure*, Oxford.

Harvey, D. (1985), 'Dona Ferentes: Some Aspects of Bribery in Greek Politics', in *Crux: Essays in Greek History Presented to G. E. M. de Ste Croix*, London, 76–117.

Harvey, D. (1990), 'The *Sykophant* and *Sykophancy*: Vexatious Redefinition?' In *Nomos: Essays in Athenian Law, Politics and Society*, edited by P. Cartledge, P. Millet, and S. Todd, Cambridge, 103–22.

Hatch, W. H. P. (1908), 'The Use of *Αλιτηριος*, *Αλιτρος*, *Αραιος*, *Εναγης*, *Ενθυμιος*, *Παλαμναιος*, and *Προστροπαιος*: A Study in Greek Lexicography', *Harvard Studies in Classical Philology* 19: 157–86.

Haubold, J. (2000), *Homer's People: Epic Poetry and Social Formation*, Cambridge.

Haubold, J. (2014), '"Shepherds of the People" Greek and Mesopotamian Perspectives', in *Mesopotamia in the Ancient World: Impact, Continuities, Parallels*, edited by R. Rollinger and E. van Dongen, Münster, 245–54.

Havelock, E. A. (1978), *The Greek Concept of Justice: From Its Shadow in Homer to Its Substance in Plato*, Cambridge, MA.

Hawke, J. (2011), *Writing Authority: Elite Competition and Written Law in Early Greece*, DeKalb.

Herman, G. (1996), 'Ancient Athens and the Values of Mediterranean Society', *Mediterranean Historical Review* 11(1): 5–36.

Herman, G. (2006), *Morality and Behaviour in Democratic Athens*, Cambridge.

Hesk, J. (2017), 'Uncertainty and the Possibility of Violence', in *Conflict and Consensus in Early Greek Hexameter Poetry*, edited by P. Bassino, L. Canevaro, and B. Graziosi, Cambridge, 109–31.

Hobbes, T. ([1651] 1998), *Leviathan*, edited by J. C. A. Gaskin, Oxford.

Hölkeskamp, K. J. (2002), '*Ptolis* and *Agore*: Homer and the Archaeology of the City-State', in *Omero tremila anni dopo*, edited by F. Montinari, Rome, 297–342.

Holmes, B. (2007), 'The *Iliad*'s Economy of Pain', *Transactions of the American Philological Association* 137: 45–84.

Holoka, J. (1983), '"Looking Darkly" (*ΥΠΟΔΡΑ ΙΔΩΝ*): Reflections on Status and Decorum in Homer', *Transactions and the Proceedings of the American Philological Association* 113: 1–16.

Hommel, H. (1969), 'Die Gerichtsszene auf dem Schild des Achilleus: Zur Pflege des Rechts in Homerischer Zeit', in *Politeia und Res Publica: Beiträge zum Verständis von Politik, Recht und Stadt in der Antike den Andenken*, Vol. 4, edited by P. Steinmetz, Wiesbaden, 11–38.

Horn, F. (2018), 'The Psychology of Aggression: Achilles' Wrath and Hector's Flight in *Iliad* 22.131–7', *Hermes* 146(3): 277–89.

Humphreys, S. (1983), 'The Evolution of Legal Process in Ancient Attica', in *Tria Corda: Scritti in onore di Arnaldo Momigliano*, edited by E. Gabba, Como, 229–56.

Humphreys, S. (1988), 'The Discourse of Law in Archaic and Classical Greece', *Law and History Review* 6(2): 465–93.

Humphreys, S. (1991), 'A Historical Approach to Drakon's Law on Homicide', in *Symposion 1990*, edited by M. Gagarin, Cologne, 17–45.

Hunter, V. J. (1994), *Policing Athens: Social Control in the Attic Lawsuits, 420–320* BC, Princeton.

Irmscher, J. (1950), *Götterzorn bei Homer*, Leipzig.

Isager, S., and M. H. Hansen (1975), *Aspects of Athenian Society in the Fourth Century* BC*: A Historical Introduction and Commentary on the Paragraphē Speeches and the Speech Against Dionysiodorus in the Corpus Demosthenicum*, Odense.

Johnston, I. (2006), *Homer: The* Odyssey, Arlington.

Johnston, S. I. (1999), *Restless Dead: Encounters between the Living and the Dead in Ancient Greece*, Berkeley.

Johnstone, S. (1999), *Disputes and Democracy: The Consequences of Litigation in Ancient Athens,* Austin.

Jones, A. H. M. (1957), *Athenian Democracy*, Oxford.

De Jong, I. (2012), *Homer:* Iliad *Book XXII*, Cambridge.

Kalimtzis, K. (2012), *Taming Anger: The Hellenic Approach to the Limitations of Reason*, London.

Karabélias, E. (1991), 'La Peine dans Athènes Classique', *Recueils de la Société Jean Bodin* 55(1): 77–132.

Kerry, J. (2 May 2011), 'Chairman Kerry on the Death of Osama Bin Laden', retrieved 1 September 2021 (https://www.foreign.senate.gov/press/chair/release/chairman-kerry-on-the-death-of-osama-bin-laden).

Kirk, G. S. (1985), *The* Iliad*: A Commentary*, Vols 1, Books 1–4, Cambridge.

Kõiv, M. (2016), '*Basileus*, *Tyrannos* and *Polis*: The Dynamics of Monarchy in Early Greece', *Klio* 98(1): 1–89.

Konstan, D. (2006), *The Emotions of the Ancient Greeks: Studies in Aristotle and Classical Literature*, Toronto.

Kucewicz, C. (2016), 'Mutilation of the Dead and the Homeric Gods', *The Classical Quarterly* 66(2): 425–36.

Kucharski, J. (2009), 'The Rhetoric of Simon's Adversary (Lysias 3)', *Scripta Classica* 6: 35–50.

Kucharski, J. (2012), 'Vindictive Prosecution in Classical Athens: On Some Recent Theories', *Greek, Roman and Byzantine Studies* 52(2): 167–97.

Kucharski, J. (2016), 'How to Punish in Classical Greek Rhetoric', in *'They Called Me to Destroy the Wicked and the Evil': Selected Essays on Crime and Punishment in Antiquity*, edited by S. Nowicki, Münster, 93–112.

Kuhn, I. (2005), 'Der Zorn des Achilleus: Eine Kritische Bemerkung zu Joachim Latacz', *Hermes* 133(4): 496–500.

Kurihara, A. (2003), 'Personal Enmity as Motivation in Forensic Speeches', *The Classical Quarterly* 53(2): 464–77.

Kyriaco, N. (2019), 'The Voice of the People in Homer', *Polemos* 13(2): 349–77.

Langholf, V. (1992), *Medical Theories in Hippocrates: Early Texts and the 'Epidemics'*, New York.

Lanni, A. (2006), *Law and Justice in the Courts of Classical Athens*, Cambridge.

Lanni, A. (2016), *Law and Order in Ancient Athens*, Cambridge.

Latacz, J. (2009), *Homers* Ilias, *Gesamtkommentar, Band I: Erster Gesang (A), Faszikel 2: Kommentar*, 3rd Durchgesehene Auflage, edited by J. Latacz, M. Nünlist, and M. Stoevesandt, Berlin.

Leaf, W. (1886), *The* Iliad, Vol. 1, Books 1–12, London.

Leaf, W. (1887), 'The Trial Scene in *Iliad* XVIII', *The Journal of Hellenic Studies* 8: 122–32.

Leaf, W. (1892), *Companion to the* Iliad, London.

Leist, B. W. (1884), *Graeco-Italische Rechtsgeschichte*, Jena.

Lendon, J. E. (1997), *Empire of Honour: The Art of Government in the Roman World*, Oxford.

Lendon, J. E. (2000), 'Homeric Vengeance and the Outbreak of Greek Wars', in *War and Violence in Ancient Greece*, edited by H. van Wees, Swansea, 1–30.

Lendon, J. E. (2010), *The Song of Wrath: The Peloponnesian War Begins*, New York.

Lentini, G. (2009), 'Gioco e Diritto in Omero', *Gaia* 12: 45–68.

Lentini, G. (2016), 'La Scena Giudiziaria dello Scudo di Achille (Hom. Il. 18, 497–508) e l'Immaginario della Giustizia nella Grecia Arcaica', *Materiali e Discussioni per l'Analisi dei Testi Classici* 76: 15–31.

Liddell, H. G., R. Scott, and H. S. Jones (1996), *A Greek English Lexicon*, 9th edn, with a revised supplement, Oxford.

Lintott, A. (1982), *Violence, Civil Strife, and Revolution in the Classical City 750–330* BC, London.

Lipsius, J. H. (1890), *Leipziger Studien*, Vol. XII, Leipzig.

Lipsius, J. H. (1905), *Das Attische Recht und Rechtsverfahren*, Leipzig.

Lloyd-Jones, H. (1971), *The Justice of Zeus*, London.

Lofberg, J. O. (1917), Sycophancy *in Athens*, Menasha.

Loney, A. C. (2019), *The Ethics of Revenge and the Meanings of the* Odyssey, New York.

Long, A. A. (1970), 'Morals and Values in Homer', *The Journal of Hellenic Studies* 90: 121–39.

Lossau, M. (1979), 'Achills Rache und Aristotelische Ethik', *Antike und Abendland: Beiträge zum Verständnis der Griechen und Römer und Ihres Nachlebens* 25(2): 120–9.

Luce, J. (1978), 'The *Polis* in Homer and Hesiod', *Proceedings of the Royal Irish Academy* 78: 1–15.

Lumet, S. (1957), *Twelve Angry Men*, United Artists.

Luraghi, N. (2013a), 'One-Man Government: The Greeks and Monarchy', in *A Companion to Ancient Greek Government*, edited by H. A. Beck, Oxford, 131–45.

Luraghi, N. (2013b), 'Ruling Alone', in *The Splendors and Miseries of Ruling Alone*, edited by N. Luraghi, Stuttgart, 11–24.

MacDowell, D. M. (1963), *Athenian Homicide Law in the Age of the Orators*, Manchester.

MacDowell, D. M. (1976), '*Hybris* in Athens', *Greece and Rome* 23: 14–31.

MacDowell, D. M. (1978), *The Law in Classical Athens*, London.

MacDowell, D. M. (1990), *Demosthenes Against Meidias*, Oxford.

MacDowell, D. M. (2009), *Demosthenes the Orator*, Oxford.

Mackenzie, M. M. (1981), *Plato on Punishment*, Cambridge.

Mactoux, M. M. (1988), 'Lois de Solon sur les Esclaves et Formation d'une Société Esclavagiste', in *Forms of Control and Subordination in Antiquity*, edited by T. Yuge and M. Doi, Leiden, 331–54.

Malamis, D. (2012), 'Crimes of the Agora: Corruption in Homer and Hesiod', *Acta Classica* 4: 17–29.

Manville, P. (1994), 'Toward a New Paradigm of Athenian Citizenship', in *Athenian Identity and Civic Ideology*, edited by A. Boegehold and A. Scafuro, Baltimore, 21–33.

Markle, M. M. (1985), 'Jury Pay and Assembly Pay at Athens', in *Crux: Essays Presented to G. E. M. de Ste. Croix on his 75th Birthday*, Exeter, 165–97.

Maschke, R. (1926), *Die Willenslehre im Griechischen Recht*, Berlin.

McCoy, M. M. (1977), 'A Reconstruction of Emotion', in *New Perspectives in Personal Construct Theory*, edited by D. Bannister, London, 93–124.

McCullough, M. E. (2008), *Beyond Revenge: The Evolution of the Forgiveness Instinct*, San Fransisco.

McHardy, F. (2008), *Revenge in Athenian Culture*, London.

Meyer-Laurin, H. (2007), 'Law and Equity in the Attic Trial', in *Oxford Readings in the Attic Orators*, edited by E. Carawan, Oxford, 116–39.

Miller, W. I. (1990), *Bloodtaking and Peacemaking: Feud, Law, and Society in Saga Iceland*, London.

Miller, W. I. (2006), *Eye for an Eye*, Michigan.

Mirhady, D. C., and Y. L. Too (2000), *Isocrates I*, Austin.

Montada, L., and A. Schneider (1989), 'Justice and Emotional Reaction to the Disadvantaged', *Social Justice Research* 3: 313–44.

Morris, I. (1986), 'The Use and Abuse of Homer', *Classical Antiquity* 5(1): 81–138.
Morrow, G. R. (1937), 'The Murder of Slaves in Attic Law', *Classical Philology* 32(3): 210–26.
Mossman, J. (1999), *Wild Justice: A Study of Euripides'* Hecuba, London.
Moulton, C. (1979), 'Homeric Metaphor', *Classical Philology* 74(4): 279–93.
Mueller, M. (1984), *The* Iliad, London.
Muellner, L. (1976), *The Meaning of Homeric [*Euchomai*] through Its Formulas*, Innsbruck.
Muellner, L. (1996), *The Anger of Achilles:* Menis *in Greek Epic*, Ithaca.
Murnaghan, S. (2011), *Disguise and Recognition in the* Odyssey, 2nd edn, Plymouth.
Murray, A. T. (1995), *Homer: The* Odyssey, revised by George Dimock, London.
Murray, O. (1990), 'The Solonian Law of *Hubris*', in *Nomos: Essays in Athenian Law, Politics and Society*, edited by P. Cartledge, P. Millet, and S. Todd, Cambridge, 139–46.
Nagy, G. (1990), *Pindar's Homer: The Lyric Possession of an Epic Past*, Baltimore.
Nagy, G. (1997), 'The Shield of Achilles: Ends of the *Iliad* and Beginnings of the *Polis*', in *New Light on a Dark Age: Exploring the Culture of Geometric Greece*, edited by S. Langdon, Columbia, 194–207.
Nelissen, R. M. A., and M. Zeelenberg (2009), 'Moral emotions as determinants of third-party punishment: Anger, guilt, and the functions of altruistic sanctions', *Judgment and Decision Making* 4(7): 543–53.
Nichols, R. J. (2013), 'The Rhetoric of Vengeance (Timōria) in Athenian Forensic Oratory', Indiana University, Indiana.
Nozick, R. (1981), *Philosophical Explanations*, Cambridge.
Ober, J. (1989), *Mass and Elite in Democratic Athens: Rhetoric, Ideology, and the Power of the People*, Princeton.
Ober, J. (2007), *Athenian Legacies: Essays on the Politics of Going on Together*, Princeton.
Ober, J. (2009), 'Public Action and Rational Choice in Classical Greek Political Theory', in *A Companion to Greek and Roman Political Thought*, edited by R. K. Balot, Chichester, 70–84.
O'Mara, E., et al. (2011), 'Will Moral Outrage Stand up?: Distinguishing between Emotional Reactions to Moral Violation', *European Journal of Social Psychology* 41: 173–9.
Osborne, R. (1985a), Demos*: The Discovery of Classical Attika*, Cambridge.
Osborne, R. (1985b), 'Law in Action in Classical Athens', *The Journal of Hellenic Studies* 105: 40–58.
Osborne, R. (1990), 'Vexatious Litigation in Classical Athens: *Sycophancy* and the *Sycophant*', in *Nomos: Essays in Athenian Law, Politics and Society*, edited by P. Cartledge, P. Millet, and S. Todd, Cambridge, 83–102.
Osborne, R. (1996), *Greece in the Making, 1200–479* BC, London.
Osiander, A. (2007), *Before the State: Systemic Political Change in the West from the Greeks to the French Revolution*, Oxford.
Ostwald, M. (1986), *From Popular Sovereignty to Sovereignty of the Law*, Berkeley.

Papakonstantinou, Z. (2008), *Lawmaking and Adjudication in Archaic Greece*, Bristol.
Parker, R. (1983), *Miasma: Pollution and Purification in Early Greek Religion*, Oxford.
Pepe, L. (2015), 'Some Remarks on Homicide and Criminal Responsibility in Ancient Greece', *Mètis: Anthropologie des Mondes Grecs Anciens* 13: 45–67.
Perry, T. P. (2010), 'Exile in Homeric Epic', University of Toronto, Toronto.
Pflüger, H. H. (1942), 'Die Gerichtsszene auf dem Schilde des Achilleus', *Hermes* 77: 140–8.
Phillips, D. (2008), *Avengers of Blood: Homicide in Athenian Law and Custom from Draco to Demosthenes*, Stuttgart.
Phillips, D. (2013), *The Law of Ancient Athens*, Ann Arbor.
Pinker, S. (2011), *The Better Angels of Our Nature: Why Violence Has Declined*, London.
Pitt-Rivers, W. (1965), 'Honour and Social Status', in *Honour and Shame: The Values of Mediterranean Society*, edited by J. G. Peristiany, London, 19–77.
Plastow, C. (2020), *Homicide in the Attic Orators: Rhetoric, Ideology, and Context*, London.
Plescia, J. (1970), *The Oath and Perjury in Ancient Greece*, Tallahassee.
Posner, R. A. (1979), 'The Homeric Version of the Minimal State', *Ethics* 90(1): 27–46.
Raaflaub, K. (1991), 'Homer und die Geschichte des 8. Jh.s v. Chr.' In *Zweihundert Jahre Homer Forschung: Rückblick und Ausblick*, Stuttgart, 205–56.
Raaflaub, K. (1997), 'Homeric Society', in *A New Companion to Homer*, Leiden, 624–48.
Raaflaub, K. (1998), 'A Historian's Headache: How to Read "Homeric Society" ', in *Archaic Greece: New Approaches and New Evidence*, edited by H. van Wees and N. R. E. Fisher, London, 169–94.
Raaflaub, K. (2013), 'Archaic Greek Reflections on Politics and Government: From Description to Conceptualization, Analysis, and Theory', in *A Companion to Ancient Greek Government*, edited by H. A. Beck, Oxford, 71–92.
Raaflaub, K., and R. W. Wallace (2007), ' "People's Power" and Egalitarian Trends in Archaic Greece', in *Origins of Democracy in Ancient Greece*, edited by K. Raaflaub, J. Ober, and R. W. Wallace, Berkeley, 22–48.
Ready, J. L. (2011), *Character, Narrator, and Simile in the* Iliad, Cambridge.
Reddy, W. M. (1997), 'Against Constructionism: The Historical Ethnography of Emotions', *Current Anthropology* 38(3): 327–51.
Redfield, J. (1975), *Nature and Culture in the* Iliad*: The Tragedy of Hector*, Chicago.
Redfield, J. (1979), 'The Proem of the *Iliad*: Homer's Art', *Classical Philology* 74(2): 95–110.
Remer, G. (2013), 'Rhetoric, Emotional Manipulation, and Political Morality: The Modern Relevance of Cicero vis-à-vis Aristotle', *A Journal of the History of Rhetoric* 31(4): 402–43.
Rhodes, P. J. (1981), *A Commentary on the Aristotelian* Athenaion Politeia, London.
Rhodes, P. J. (1991), 'The Athenian Code of Laws, 410–399 BC', *Journal of Hellenic Studies* 111: 87–100.
Riess, W. (2012), *Performing Interpersonal Violence: Court, Curse, and Comedy in Fourth-Century* BCE *Athens*, Berlin.
Robertson, N. (1990), 'The Laws of Athens, 410–399 BC: The Evidence for Review and Publication', *The Journal of Hellenic Studies* 110: 43–75.

Roebuck, D. (2001), *Ancient Greek Arbitration*, Oxford.

Roguin, C. F. (2008), 'Quand le Divin Achille se Met à Penser: Colère, Désespoir et Pitié dans l'*Iliade*', *Revue de l'Histoire des Religions* 225(2): 223–41.

Roisman, J. (2005), *The Rhetoric of Manhood: Masculinity in the Attic Orators*, London.

Rosenwein, B. H. (2006), *Emotional Communities in the Early Middle Ages*, London.

Rowe, G. O. (1994), 'The Charge against Meidias', *Hermes* 122(1): 55–63.

Rubinstein, L. (2000), *Litigation and Cooperation: The Use of Supporting Speakers in the Courts of Classical Athens*, Vol. 147, Stuttgart.

Rubinstein, L. (2004), 'Stirring up Dicastic Anger', in *Law, Rhetoric and Comedy in Classical Athens: Essays in Honour of Douglas M. MacDowell*, edited by D. L. Cairns and R. A. Knox, Swansea, 187–203.

Rubinstein, L. (2005), 'Differentiated Rhetorical Strategies in the Athenian Courts', in *The Cambridge Companion to Ancient Greek Law*, edited by M. Gagarin and D. Cohen, Cambridge, 129–45.

Rubinstein, L. (2013), 'Evoking Anger through Pity: Portraits of the Vulnerable and Defenceless in Attic Oratory', in *Unveiling Emotions II: Emotions in Greece and Rome: Texts, Images, Material Culture*, edited by A. Chaniotis and P. Ducrey, Stuttgart, 136–65.

Rubinstein, L. (2016), 'Communal Revenge and Appeals to Dicastic Emotions', in *Die Athenische Demokratie im 4. Jahrhundert*, edited by C. Tiersch, Stuttgart, 56–73.

Runciman, W. G. (1982), 'Origins of States: The Case of Archaic Greece', *Comparative Studies in Society and History* 24(3): 351–77.

Sanders, E. (2012), ' "He's a Liar, a Bounder, and a Cad": The Arousal of Hostile Emotions in Attic Forensic Oratory', in *Unveiling Emotions: Sources and Methods for the Study of Emotions in the Greek World*, edited by A. Chaniotis, Stuttgart, 359–88.

Saunders, T. J. (1991), *Plato's Penal Code: Tradition, Controversy, and Reform in Greek Penology*, Oxford.

Schlunk, R. R. (1976), 'The Theme of the Suppliant-Exile in the *Iliad*', *The American Journal of Philology* 97(3): 199–209.

Schwyzer, E. (1931), 'Drei Griechische Wörter', *Rheinisches Museum für Philologie* 80(3): 209–17.

Scodel, R. (2008), *Epic Facework: Self-Presentation and Social Interaction in Homer*, Swansea.

Scully, S. (1990), *Homer and the Sacred City*, Ithaca.

Seaford, R. (1994), *Reciprocity and Ritual: Homer and Tragedy in the Developing City-State*, Oxford.

Seager, R. (1966), 'Lysias Against the Corndealers', *Historia* 15: 172–84.

Sealey, R. (1983), 'The Athenian Courts for Homicide', *Classical Philology* 78: 275–96.

Sealey, R. (1994), *The Justice of the Greeks*, Ann Arbor.

Segal, C. (1971), *The Theme of the Mutilation of the Corpse in the* Iliad, Leiden.

Sickinger, J. (2008), 'Indeterminacy in Greek Law: Statutory Gaps and Conflicts', in *Symposion 2007: Vorträge zur griechischen und hellenistischen Rechtsgeschichte*, edited by E. Harris and G. Thür, Vienna, 99–112.

Sidgwick, H. (1894), 'The Trial Scene in Homer', *The Classical Review* 8(1–2): 1–3.

Smith, G. (1924), 'The Administration of Justice from Hesiod to Solon', University of Chicago.
Smith, W. (1966), 'Physiology in the Homeric Poems', *Transactions and the Proceedings of the American Philological Association* 97: 547–56.
Snell, B. (1924), *Die Ausdriicke für den Begriff des Wissens in der Vorplatonische Philosophie*, Berlin.
Sourvinou-Inwood, C. (1995), *'Reading' Greek Death to the End of the Classical Period*, Oxford.
Spencer, H. (1897), *The Principles of Ethics, Vol. 1*, New York.
Stahl, M., and U. Walter (2009), 'Athens', in *A Companion to Archaic Greece*, edited by K. Raaflaub and H. van Wees, Chichester, 138–61.
Stearns, P. N., and C. Z. Stearns (1985), 'Emotionology: Clarifying the History of Emotions and Emotional Standards', *American Historical Review* 90: 813–36.
Steinwenter, A. (1925), *Die Streitbeendigung durch Urteil, Schiedsspruch und Vergleich nach Griechischen Rechte*, Munich.
Stocking, C. H. (2017), *The Politics of Sacrifice in Early Greek Myth and Poetry*, Cambridge.
Stroud, R. S. (1968), *Drakon's Law on Homicide*, Berkeley.
Sundahl, M. J. (2003), 'The Rule of Law and the Nature of the Fourth-Century Democracy', *Classica et Mediaevalia* 54: 127–56.
Tandy, D. W. (1997), *Warriors into Traders: The Power of the Market in Early Greece*, London.
Taplin, O. (1992), *Homeric Soundings: The Shaping of the* Iliad, Oxford.
Thonissen, J. J. (1875), *Le Droit Pénal de la République Athénienne*, Paris.
Thür, G. (1996), 'Oaths and Dispute Settlement in Ancient Greek Law', in *Greek Law and Its Political Setting*, edited by L. Foxhall and D. Lewis, Oxford, 57–72.
Todd, S. (1990a), 'Lady Chatterley's Lover and the Attic Orators: The Social Composition of the Athenian Jury', *The Journal of Hellenic Studies* 110: 146–73.
Todd, S. (1990b), 'The Purpose of Evidence in Athenian Courts', in Nomos*: Essays in Athenian Law, Politics and Society*, edited by P. Cartledge, P. Millet, and S. Todd, Cambridge.
Todd, S. (1993), *The Shape of Athenian Law*, Oxford, 19–40.
Todd, S. (1996), 'Lysias against Nikomachos: The Fate of the Expert in Athenian Law', in *Greek Law in Its Political Setting: Justification not Justice*, edited by L. Foxhall and A. D. E. Lewis, Oxford, 101–32.
Todd, S. (2000), *Lysias*, Austin.
Tsagarakis, O. (2000), *Studies in* Odyssey *11*, Stuttgart.
Uniacke, S. (2000), 'Why Is Revenge Wrong?', *The Journal of Value Inquiry* 34: 61–9.
Van der Mije, S. (2011), 'Bad Herbs – The Snake Simile in "*Iliad*" 22', *Mnemosyne* 64: 359–82.
Van der Vliet, E. C. L. (2005), 'The Problem of Statehood', *Social Evolution and History* 4(2): 120–50.
Van Doorn, J., et al. (2018), 'Prosocial Consequences of Third-Party Anger', *Theory and Decision* 84: 585–99.

Van Wees, H. (1992), *Status Warriors: War, Violence and Society in Homer and History*, Amsterdam.

Van Wees, H. (1994), 'The Homeric Way of War: The *Iliad* and the Hoplite Phalanx (I)', *Greece and Rome* 41: 1–18.

Van Wees, H. (1998), 'Greeks Bearing Arms: The State, the Leisure Class, and the Display of Weapons in Archaic Greece', in *Archaic Greece: New Approaches and New Evidence*, edited by N. R. E. Fisher and H. van Wees, Swansea, 333–78.

Van Wees, H. (1999), 'The Mafia of Early Greece: Violent Exploitation in the Seventh and Sixth Centuries BC', in *Organised Crime in Antiquity*, edited by K. Hopwood, Swansea, 1–51.

Van Wees, H. (2002), 'Homer and Early Greece', *Colby Quarterly* 38(1): 94–117.

Van Wees, H. (2004), *Greek Warfare: Myths and Realities*, London.

Van Wees, H. (2011a), 'Rivalry in History: A Comparative Perspective', in *Competition in the Ancient World*, edited by N. Fisher and H. van Wees, Swansea, 1–36.

Van Wees, H. (2011b), 'The "Law of *Hybris*" and Solon's Reform of Justice', in *Sociable Man: Essays on Ancient Greek Social Behaviour in Honour of Nick Fisher*, Swansea, 117–44.

Wallace, R. W. (2017), 'Equality, the *Dêmos*, and Law in Archaic Greece', in *Symposion 2015: Vorträge zur griechischen und hellenistischen Rechtsgeschichte*, edited by D. F. Leão and G. Thür, Verlag der österreichischen Akademie der Wissenschaften, 1–13.

Walsh, T. R. (2005), *Fighting Words and Feuding Words: Anger and the Homeric Poems*, Lanham.

Watkins, C. (1977), 'A Propos de *Μῆνις*', in *Bulletin de La Société Linguistique de Paris* 72: 187–209.

Weber, M. (1976), *Wirtschaft und Gesellschaft, Gundriss der Verstehenden Soziologie*, 5th edn, edited by J. Winckelmann, Tübingen.

West, M. L. (1995), 'The Date of the *Iliad*', *Museum Helveticum* 52: 203–19.

Westbrook, R. (1992), 'The Trial Scene in the *Iliad*', *Harvard Studies in Classical Philology* 94: 53–76.

Whitchurch, J. S. (2020), '"Show, Don't Tell": How to Make Jurors Angry as a Young Athenian Prosecutor', *Rhesis* 11(1): 281–9.

Whitman, C. H. (1958), *Homer and the Heroic Tradition*, Cambridge, MA.

Widzisz, M. (2012), 'Timing Reciprocity in the *Iliad*', *Arethusa* 45: 153–75.

Williams, B. (1993), *Shame and Necessity*, Berkeley.

Wilson, D. (1999), 'Symbolic Violence in "Iliad" Book 9', *The Classical World* 93(2): 131–47.

Wilson, D. (2002), *Ransom, Revenge, and Heroic Identity in the* Iliad, Cambridge.

Wolff, H. J. (1946), 'The Origin of Judicial Litigation among the Greeks', *Traditio* 4: 31–87.

Xydopoulos, I., and K. Vlassopoulos (2017), 'Introduction', in *Violence and Community: Law, Space and Identity in the Ancient Eastern Mediterranean World*, edited by I. Xydopoulos, K. Vlassopoulos, and E. Tounta, London, 1–27.

Yamagata, N. (1994), *Homeric Morality*, Leiden.

Zanker, G. (1994), *The Heart of Achilles: Characterization and Personal Ethics in the* Iliad, Ann Arbor.

Index of Passages Cited

General Index

www.ingramcontent.com/pod-product-compliance
Ingram Content Group UK Ltd.
Pitfield, Milton Keynes, MK11 3LW, UK
UKHW020248290926
15470UKWH00002B/811